ON LIMITED NUCLEAR WAR
IN THE 21ST CENTURY

ON LIMITED NUCLEAR WAR
IN THE 21ST CENTURY

Edited by Jeffrey A. Larsen and
Kerry M. Kartchner

Stanford Security Studies
An Imprint of Stanford University Press
Stanford, California

Stanford University Press
Stanford, California

Printed in the United States of America on acid-free, archival-quality paper

Library of Congress Cataloging-in-Publication Data

On limited nuclear war in the 21st century / edited by Jeffrey A. Larsen and Kerry
M. Kartchner.
pages cm — (Stanford security studies)
Includes bibliographical references and index.
ISBN 978-0-8047-8912-7 (cloth : alk. paper)
ISBN 978-0-8047-9089-5 (pbk. : alk.paper)
1. Nuclear warfare. 2. Limited war. 3. United States—Military policy. I. Larsen,
Jeffrey Arthur, 1954– editor of compilation. II. Kartchner, Kerry M., 1956– editor of
compilation. III. Series: Stanford security studies.
U263.O5   2014
355.02'17—dc23

2013033802

From Jeff to grandson Kai Weston Larsen, in the hope and belief that his generation will continue to find ways to avoid the scenarios discussed in this book.

From Kerry to Britt Weiler Kartchner and Reece Hansen; Michelle, Trevor, Brayden, and Max; Brittany and Chelsea, for their love and support, and in the hope that history need not repeat itself where nuclear weapons are involved.

The editors express special thanks to the Air Force Institute for National Security Studies (INSS), the Air Force National Security Division (A5XP), and Science Applications International Corporation for their early sponsorship of the study series that led to this volume.

Contents

List of Figures, Tables, and Map   ix

Foreword, Thomas C. Schelling   xi

Contributors   xv

Preface, Jeffrey A. Larsen and Kerry M. Kartchner   xix

PART I   Assessing the History of Limited Nuclear War

1   Limited War and the Advent of Nuclear Weapons   3
     Jeffrey A. Larsen

2   The Origins of Limited Nuclear War Theory   21
     Andrew L. Ross

3   The United States and Discriminate Nuclear Options
     in the Cold War   49
     Elbridge A. Colby

4   Post–Cold War US Nuclear Strategy   80
     Paul I. Bernstein

PART II Managing the Risk of Nuclear War
in the 21st Century

5   The Emerging Nuclear Landscape   101
    Paul I. Bernstein

6   Future Scenarios of Limited Nuclear Conflict   129
    Thomas G. Mahnken

7   Escalation to Limited Nuclear War in the 21st Century   144
    Kerry M. Kartchner and Michael S. Gerson

8   The End of the Nuclear Taboo?   172
    George H. Quester

9   Deterrence, Crisis Management, and Nuclear War Termination   191
    Schuyler Foerster

PART III   Confronting the Challenges of Nuclear War
in the 21st Century

10 On US Preparedness for Limited Nuclear War   211
    Bruce W. Bennett

11 Limited Nuclear Conflict and the American Way of War   244
    James M. Smith

12 Limited Nuclear War Reconsidered   263
    James J. Wirtz

    Index   273

Figures, Tables, and Map

Figures

1.1 Limited Nuclear War Thresholds   16
10.1 The Appropriateness of US Nuclear Responses
      to Adversary Actions   223
10.2 Geographic Areas Covered by Blast Effects
      at Varying Hardness   226

Tables

10.1 US Nuclear Forces, 2013 Vs. New START   213
10.2 Characteristics of US Strategic Forces   214
10.3 Matching US Nuclear Forces to Response Options   224
10.4 US ICBM Capability to Execute Limited Nuclear
      Attack Options Today   236
10.5 US SLBM Capability to Execute Limited Nuclear
      Attack Options Today   238
10.6 US Bomber Capability to Execute Limited Nuclear
      Attack Options Today   239

Map

10.1 Potential SSBN Patrol Areas to Minimize Overflight
      Concerns   231

Foreword

WHETHER A NUCLEAR WAR, IF ONE EVER OCCURS, can be kept limited may depend on who reads this book. That a nuclear war, if it were to occur, could be limited is not always judged a good thing. During the Cold War the possibility that the president of the United States might authorize nuclear weapons to be used selectively was opposed by hawks as "hold back SAC," a pusillanimous doctrine. It was also opposed by doves as possibly too much a temptation to a president facing a crisis or a troubled ground war. The judgment of the editors of this volume, and my judgment, is that both arguments have merit but that in the possible wars that we can imagine in the future, and not necessarily wars in which the United States is engaged, nuclear restraint ought to be encouraged and facilitated. And this book may help to encourage and facilitate, by calling attention to the important policy of mutual restraint, and increasing the likelihood that if nuclear use is ever contemplated the people making the decisions will have thought seriously about it before the moment of decision.

Depending on how you count, there have been, since 1945, eight or nine wars in which one side had nuclear weapons and chose not to use them (involving the USA, USSR, Britain, Israel, India, and Pakistan). That's one kind of limited nuclear war, limited "nuclear" because the weapons were available and undoubtedly influenced both sides in the war. Another kind of limited nuclear war would be one in which both sides—India and Pakistan perhaps, or Iran and Israel, or North Korea and the United States—had nuclear weapons and chose not to use them. That, too, I call "nuclear" because nuclear decisions have to be made almost continuously. The third kind would be one in which both sides have nuclear weapons and use them but do so discriminatingly, with restraint, each side presumably ready to escalate along some axis if the other side appears to change the rules.

That third kind is what most of the chapters in this book are primarily concerned with. It is also, if it actually happens that the two sides can successfully arrive at an understanding, a remarkably cooperative and intellectually impressive enterprise. The two sides must arrive, probably tacitly—no overt negotiation—at a common understanding of what the "limits" are to be. Limits could be placed on numbers of weapons, explosive yields, delivery means, targets selected, geographical areas, offensive or defensive use, advance warnings, height of bursts, and direct response to enemy action. But how to arrive at some number of weapons, or some yield limit, or some targets that are out of bounds without formal negotiation seems almost impossible. Perhaps somewhat "direct" negotiation, in the form of announcements or domestic discussion that the enemy can overhear, can help in arriving at a common understanding of what the proposed limits are.

Fifty years ago I published a couple of papers on this problem and reached a conclusion in one of them that it was hard to find any specific limit on nuclear weapons—numbers, yields, or targets—that was sufficiently conspicuous that both sides could confidently identify it as "obvious." I referred to such a limit as a "focal point." I conjectured that the only focal point for the number of weapons was zero. And I thought that both parties to the tacit agreement, or understanding, would recognize zero as the only compelling limit that could be arrived at without explicit negotiation. All that was assuming no prior communication between the parties, either before the war or before the introduction of nuclear weapons, not even "communication" that takes the form of public discussion intended to be overheard.

This thought brings me to the first sentence of this foreword: whether a nuclear war, if one ever occurs, can be kept limited may depend on who reads this book.

Exploring alternative possible limits, identifying plausibly agreeable limits, communicating suggestions or proposals, or just being seen and heard to discuss the idea of mutually recognized limits and how they may be arrived at is a likely prerequisite to arriving at understandings of how nuclear limitation—including the limit of no nuclear use—can be overtly or tacitly identified as common understanding. This book is the only one I know that can induce national leaders, or their advisers, to take seriously the prospect of minimizing mutual damage in a nuclear war.

I hope this book gets read by governments everywhere that possess or contemplate possessing nuclear weapons.

Thomas C. Schelling, College Park, MD

Contributors

Bruce W. Bennett is a Senior Defense Analyst at the RAND Corporation, where he started by working on strategic nuclear warfare in the 1970s. He specializes in strategy formulation, force requirements, and responding to asymmetric threats such as weapons of mass destruction (WMD). He is also an expert on Northeast Asian military issues, having visited the region over ninety times and written much about deterring North Korean WMD use. He received a PhD in policy analysis from the Pardee RAND Graduate School.

Paul I. Bernstein is a Senior Research Fellow at the Center for the Study of Weapons of Mass Destruction at National Defense University in Washington, DC, specializing in nuclear policy, deterrence, proliferation, arms control, missile defense, and regional security. He is engaged in a range of research, policy support, and professional military education activities, and is a regular guest instructor at National War College, Eisenhower School of National Security and Resource Strategy, Joint Forces Staff College, Army War College, and Defense Nuclear Weapons School. He holds a master's degree from Columbia University.

Elbridge A. Colby is a Fellow at the Center for a New American Century, where he focuses on deterrence, nuclear weapons, and related issues. Previously he served as a Principal Analyst at the Center for Naval Analyses, as a policy advisor on the Defense Department's New START negotiation and ratification team, and as an expert advisor to the Congressional Strategic Posture

Commission, and in other government positions focusing on intelligence reform. He writes and speaks frequently on strategic as well as on broader national security issues. He is a graduate of Yale Law School.

Schuyler Foerster is the Brent Scowcroft Professor of National Security Studies in the US Air Force Academy Department of Political Science. During his Air Force career he served as a senior advisor on security and arms control policy, and in his civilian career, led an award-winning educational nonprofit organization. He has coauthored two books and several articles on international politics and national security issues and regularly addresses academic, professional, and civic audiences on a broad range of global issues. He holds a DPhil from Oxford University.

Michael S. Gerson is a Senior Research Manager at the Gerson Lehrman Group, a consulting firm, in New York City. He was previously a Senior Analyst and Division Lead at the Center for Naval Analyses, where his work focused on nuclear and conventional deterrence. In 2011–12, he was on loan from CNA to the Office of the Secretary of Defense, and in 2009 he was a staff member on the Nuclear Posture Review. Mr. Gerson has presented his work on nuclear strategy and deterrence at numerous universities and think tanks, and has published articles in *International Security, Parameters*, and several edited volumes. He earned his MA in international relations from the University of Chicago.

Kerry M. Kartchner is a member of the Distinguished Faculty in Missouri State University's Graduate Department of Defense and Strategic Studies, Fairfax, VA. He was previously Acting Director of the Office of Strategic Planning and Outreach in the Bureau of International Security and Nonproliferation (ISN), US Department of State. He also served at the ISN Bureau Public Diplomacy Office as Senior Advisor for Strategic Planning. From 2004 to 2006 he served as Chief of the Division of Strategy and Policy Studies in the Advanced Systems and Concepts Office of the Defense Threat Reduction Agency. He is the coeditor, with Jeannie Johnson and Jeffrey Larsen, of *Strategic Culture and Weapons of Mass Destruction* (2009). His PhD in international relations is from the University of Southern California.

Jeffrey A. Larsen is Director of the Research Division at the NATO Defense College in Rome, Italy. Previously he served as a Senior Scientist with Science Applications International Corporation (SAIC) and as President of

Larsen Consulting Group. He has taught as an adjunct professor at Denver, Northwestern, and Texas A&M Universities, as well as the Defense Nuclear Weapons School. A retired Air Force Lieutenant Colonel and command pilot, he is widely published, including *Arms Control and Cooperative Security*, with James Wirtz (Lynne Rienner, 2009), and *Responding to Catastrophic Events: Consequence Management and Policies* (Palgrave Macmillan, 2013). He holds a PhD in politics from Princeton University.

Thomas G. Mahnken is Jerome E. Levy Chair of Economic Geography and National Security at the U.S. Naval War College and a senior research professor at the Philip Merrill Center for Strategic Studies at Johns Hopkins University's Paul H. Nitze School of Advanced International Studies (SAIS). Dr. Mahnken served as the Deputy Assistant Secretary of Defense for Policy Planning from 2006 to 2009. He is the author of *Competitive Strategies for the 21st Century: Theory, History, and Practice* (Stanford University Press, 2012) and *Technology and the American Way of War since 1945* (Columbia University Press, 2008). He is editor of the *Journal of Strategic Studies*. He earned his PhD in international affairs at SAIS.

George H. Quester is a Professor Emeritus of Government and Politics at the University of Maryland, and the Shapiro Visiting Professor at the Elliott School of International Affairs, George Washington University. His research focus throughout his career has been on the intersection of nuclear strategy and the likelihood of conventional war, and he is now working on a review of the years leading to the Manhattan Project. His latest book is *Nuclear First Strike: Consequences of a Broken Taboo* (Johns Hopkins University Press, 2006). Dr. Quester earned his PhD in political science from Harvard University.

Andrew L. Ross is Director, Center for Science, Technology and Policy, Director, Special Science, Engineering and Policy Initiatives in the Office of the Vice President for Research, and Professor of Political Science at the University of New Mexico. His work on nuclear policy, strategy and force structure, military innovation, and national security and defense planning has appeared in numerous journals and books. Professor Ross earned his PhD in political science from Cornell University.

Thomas C. Schelling is professor of foreign affairs, national security, nuclear strategy, and arms control at the School of Public Policy, University of Maryland. He was awarded the 2005 Nobel Memorial Prize in Economic

Sciences. He is the author of *Strategy of Conflict* (1960), *Strategy and Arms Control*, with Morton Halperin (1961), *Arms and Influence* (1966), and *Micromotives and Microbehavior* (1978). He earned his PhD in economics at Harvard University.

James M. Smith is Director, USAF Institute for National Security Studies and a professor at the USAF Academy. He teaches as an adjunct at the Korbel School, Denver University, and at the Bush School, Texas A&M. He is a retired USAF officer, and he has several publications on arms control and proliferation, including *Historical Dictionary of Arms Control and Disarmament*, with Jeffrey Larsen (Scarecrow, 2005; 2nd edition forthcoming 2014). Dr. Smith holds a doctorate in public policy from the University of Alabama.

James J. Wirtz is Dean of the School of International Graduate Studies at the US Naval Postgraduate School, and Director of the Global Center for Security Cooperation for the Defense Security Cooperation Agency. He has served as Visiting Professor at the Center for International Security and Cooperation, Stanford University, and as a John M. Olin Pre-Doctoral Fellow at the Center for International Affairs, Harvard University. Professor Wirtz earned his PhD from Columbia University.

Preface

WHILE THE THREAT OF ALL-OUT NUCLEAR WAR HAS diminished, the likelihood that nuclear weapons may be used in some way is increasing. This assessment is widely shared, and has become almost axiomatic among policymakers and within the strategic studies community. Yet little systematic thought has been given to what the future use of nuclear weapons might look like. This book addresses that shortfall. If nuclear weapons are used in a future conflict, that use is likely to be limited in ways that contrast sharply with the Cold War assumptions of a massive exchange of thousands of weapons. Given its international commitments and the possibility of future regional conflicts with small nuclear-armed powers, the United States needs to be prepared for the possibility that it may one day find itself in a limited nuclear war—one likely not of its choosing. Is the United States prepared for such a scenario?

This is not another book about nuclear proliferation. Rather, it considers the consequences of nuclear proliferation. That is to say, while this is not a book about the constraints that may shape the future pattern of nuclear proliferation, it does address arguments about the limited utility of nuclear weapons, either because they are considered by some to be unusable, or because systemic and technical limits on nuclear war may remain insurmountable even after the end of the Cold War. For example, the authors consider the possible use of nuclear weapons to compensate for manpower shortages and other conventional weaknesses. They are cognizant of the debate between "proliferation optimists" on the one hand and "proliferation pessimists" on the other hand. The optimists emphasize the constraints on further proliferation and anticipate a relatively benign proliferation future, due in large part to the success of initiatives to materially strengthen the nonproliferation regime, including the development of far-reaching norms and processes. Proliferation pessimists, on the other hand, are convinced that there are powerful incentives to acquire nuclear weapons, for purposes of political prestige, regional security, and getting more "bang for the buck" relative to the economics of building and sustaining large conventional forces.

While this book is not intended to contribute to this debate, the editors and authors, for the most part, find themselves squarely in the proliferation pessimists' camp. This set of essays represents one point of view. We believe this point of view is valid and timely given recent developments in the international security environment, including North Korea's ongoing nuclear tests.

Proliferation scholars from both sides of the optimist/pessimist divide have warned that among the many serious consequences of proliferation, the most ominous is the prospect of nuclear warfare. This book tackles the problematic yet urgent question of "what if nonproliferation fails, and nuclear weapons are actually used?" During the Cold War, this question was in the province of the "unthinkable." But given the unrelenting pursuit of nuclear weapon options by countries such as Iran and North Korea, as well as the ongoing adversarial dispute between nuclear powers India and Pakistan, this question can hardly be avoided—despite the putative successes of recent nonproliferation and counterproliferation initiatives.

Why a book on this subject more than twenty years after the end of the Cold War? Its publication is the result of three additional assumptions shared by the authors. First, the theory of limited nuclear war is one of the few major subfields of strategic thinking during the Cold War that has not been revisited in the generation since the fall of the Soviet Union. The reason this theory still matters brings us to the second assumption: there is a greater than zero possibility that a limited nuclear war may one day occur, and any nuclear war is likely to be limited, rather than apocalyptic, as was often the assumption in Cold War analyses. Analysts and political leaders regularly reiterate that while the possibility of a major nuclear war has decreased dramatically with the end of the superpower standoff, the chances of some type of nuclear use have actually increased.[1] The slow but steady increase in the number of nuclear-armed states, and the seemingly less constrained policy goals of some of the newer, so-called rogue states in the international system, mean that a time may come when one of them makes the conscious decision that using a nuclear weapon against the United States, its allies, or its forward deployed forces in the context of a crisis or a regional conventional conflict may be in that state's interests. In such a scenario, America's military and political leadership will find itself facing a limited nuclear scenario for which it is probably unprepared. Official documents also highlight the belief that the most dangerous potential threat facing the United States today is the intersection of the world's most dangerous weapons with its most dangerous organizations, leading to possible nuclear terrorism—another form of limited nuclear use.

The third assumption is the hope of the participants in this project that this book might encourage greater dialogue within the US strategic studies community over America's military and policy readiness to actually fight a conflict on a future nuclear battlefield, even if a limited one.

There are indications that we are on the cusp of a discussion within the strategic studies community over what the nature of nuclear use would be in the near future. This book is poised to make a substantial contribution to that emerging discussion. It specifically confronts the following critical questions, which will be at the heart of that dialogue:

- Do we need to reconsider the basic theory of limited nuclear war?
- Does the way we thought about and planned for limited nuclear war in the early part of the nuclear era hold any insights that could be applied to the current situation?
- Is the pursuit of nuclear disarmament jeopardizing America's ability to prevent or deter limited nuclear wars?
- Who are today's nuclear weapons states? And what are the prospects for those states to become involved in a limited nuclear war?
- Under what scenarios might a limited nuclear war be fought?
- Would traditional strategies of escalation control be enough to manage the risks of conflict leading to nuclear use?
- Can we count on newly nuclear states to adhere to the long-standing traditional presumption of nonuse to avoid a future limited nuclear war?
- How would a limited nuclear war end?

- Is the US military prepared to fight a limited nuclear war?
- What does the American "way of war" portend for America's ability to think through the implications of a future limited nuclear war?

These questions deserve thoughtful, scholarly attention before they become the province of policy deliberations so that those deliberations will be adequately informed and perspicacious. They also deserve explication to enhance US preparedness for the contingency of limited nuclear war, and to contribute to policies that may prevent, minimize, or end such a war.

Overview of the Book

This book reconsiders the theory and practice of limited nuclear war in the new century. This analysis considers a number of key concepts, among them the origins and early practice of limited war theory, and revisits the debate over whether nuclear war can be limited. In addition, it addresses factors leading to the prospect of limited nuclear war in the future, including the emergence of new nuclear powers, the operational strategies and command and control architectures contemplated by states with small nuclear arsenals, and the declining credibility and relevance of traditional approaches to nuclear deterrence. It examines the geopolitics of future limited nuclear war and conflict scenarios that might lead to small-scale nuclear use, and then assesses crisis management and escalation control, including distinctions between "escalation control" and "escalation dominance." Finally, the book considers some strategies and operational concepts for countering, controlling, or containing limited nuclear war.

Section I: Assessing the History of Limited Nuclear War

The book begins with a review of limited nuclear war theory, its historical development and metamorphosis through the Cold War, and the changing nature of nuclear conflict across nine presidential administrations.

Jeff Larsen's introductory chapter on "Limited War and the Advent of Nuclear Weapons" examines the development of the theory of limited nuclear war and how it came to be distinguished from limited war more generally. This evolution took place at the same time as the introduction of these new weapons and the theoretical design of new strategies, such as deterrence, containment, and crisis stability, beginning in the 1950s. The chapter lays out key questions that guide the discussion through the rest of the book.

In Chapter 2, "The Origins of Limited Nuclear War Theory," Andrew Ross provides an historical overview of limited nuclear war theory and operational considerations during the early years of the Cold War, particularly the intellectual origins of the concept of limited nuclear war as found in the work of Bernard Brodie, Robert Osgood, and Henry Kissinger in the 1950s.

Bridge Colby continues this historical review in Chapter 3, "The United States and Discriminate Nuclear Options in the Cold War," by addressing the rise of limited nuclear war as an operational concept from the early 1960s to the end of the Cold War, focusing especially on the Schlesinger era of the 1970s. These changes in thinking led to a more nuanced nuclear war plan (the Single Integrated Operational Plan, or SIOP) that contained multiple nuclear strike alternatives, including limited nuclear options.

Paul Bernstein continues the historical review of changing US perspectives on limited nuclear war theory by examining policy developments in the quarter century since the end of the Cold War in Chapter 4, "Post–Cold War US Nuclear Strategy." This final historical section brings the reader up to date on the policy changes of the Clinton, Bush, and Obama administrations, serving as an excellent overview of the origins and rationale behind current US nuclear strategy.

Section II: Managing the Risk of Nuclear War in the 21st Century
This section considers the manner in which a conventional conflict might escalate into a limited nuclear war, how it might be fought, and how it can be terminated with the restoration of deterrence to ensure strategic stability.

In Chapter 5, "The Emerging Nuclear Landscape," Paul Bernstein surveys the emerging global nuclear landscape and considers the prospects for limited nuclear war in light of trends in nuclear proliferation and emerging doctrine in states such as Russia, China, Pakistan, India, and North Korea.

In Chapter 6, "Future Scenarios of Limited Nuclear Conflict," Thomas Mahnken addresses scenarios that would potentially lead to the use of nuclear weapons. These build on a series of seminars sponsored by Johns Hopkins University on nuclear use scenarios held in late 2009.[2] In light of the adversarial behavior of Iran and North Korea toward the West, and particularly the United States, as well as their current political policies, it is not difficult to conceive of ways the United States or its allies might one day find themselves in a nuclear conflict with one or the other of these two states. But Mahnken's scenarios consider not only conflicts in which the United States might find itself on a nuclear battlefield. He also considers other instances of possible

nuclear use around the globe that would have political and economic reper-
cussions for the United States.

In Chapter 7, "Escalation to Limited Nuclear War in the 21st Century,"
Kerry Kartchner and Michael Gerson explain how the process of escalation
to nuclear use may be different now from what was anticipated during the
Cold War. They distinguish between "escalation control," "escalation management," "escalation dominance," and horizontal and vertical escalation.

Chapter 8, "The End of the Nuclear Taboo?," by George Quester, echoes
his book on the same subject by addressing the trends and factors that are
breaking down the long-standing taboo against nuclear use. This includes
a loss of confidence in US extended deterrence, incentives for asymmetric
responses to US conventional supremacy, the inability to resolve regional tensions, the proliferation of nuclear energy, and nuclear latency.

Sky Foerster's chapter, "Deterrence, Crisis Management, and Nuclear War
Termination," reviews strategies of deterrence and dissuasion and their applicability against smaller nuclear states and non-state actors in the 21st century.
It also considers the diplomatic, political, economic, and military options for
controlling, containing, and limiting a nuclear war; looks at how one termi-
nates such a conflict against the backdrop of pressures for horizontal escalation; and addresses the important question of how the world returns to stability and deterrence after a limited nuclear conflict ends.

Section III: Confronting the Challenges of
Nuclear War in the 21st Century
The final section covers existing US capabilities for fighting in a limited
nuclear conflict, and considers the American way of war and the implications
of US strategic culture for psychologically readying the country for such a
fight.

Bruce Bennett tackles one of the most challenging topics in Chapter 10,
"On US Preparedness for Limited Nuclear War." He considers the military
and policy implications of America's military finding itself on a nuclear
battlefield, and addresses US policies, capabilities, and psychological issues
associated with such a conflict, noting areas of strength and areas requiring
further attention if the United States is to adapt its nuclear force posture to
the requirements of confronting a limited nuclear war.

In Chapter 11, "Limited Nuclear Conflict and the American Way of War,"
Jim Smith explores the American way of war amid current concerns within
the US nuclear weapons enterprise about the loss of nuclear expertise and

the atrophying of nuclear priorities within the US government, both of which could impair or undermine American efforts to keep a future nuclear war limited.

Jim Wirtz's conclusion, "Limited Nuclear War Reconsidered," highlights the themes found in the book. The conclusion also considers implications for US nuclear policymakers and the nuclear weapons infrastructure, including research and development requirements, organizational change, and the role for tailored deterrence. It focuses on the changing international security environment that might lead to a limited nuclear conflict, with observations about how the theory of limited nuclear war might be revised for the security environment we find ourselves facing in the new century.

As the conclusion points out, US policymakers and combatant command commanders have not really thought through the implications of this situation. As a result, the United States has neither the right weapons nor the right doctrine to wage such a conflict if one were thrust upon it. Which brings the book full circle. War is inevitable. Limited nuclear war is possible. Yet neither the US government, its military, nor its allies appear fully prepared to deal with this eventuality. A full generation after the end of the Cold War, the strategic studies community has not addressed and updated limited nuclear war theory from that era. The authors hope this volume will serve to rekindle discussion on this terrifying but essential topic, and further steps to resolve that unpreparedness.

Jeffrey A. Larsen, Colorado Springs, CO
Kerry M. Kartchner, Stafford, VA
October 2013

Notes

1. For example, in a speech in Prague in April 2009, President Barack Obama said, "Today, the Cold War has disappeared but thousands of those weapons have not. In a strange turn of history, the threat of global nuclear war has gone down, but the risk of a nuclear attack has gone up." See www.whitehouse.gov/the_press_office/ Remarks-By-President-Barack-Obama-In-Prague-As-Delivered.

2. See Duncan Brown and Thomas Mahnken, "The Johns Hopkins Nuclear Futures Project," Strategic Assessments Project, Johns Hopkins University Applied Physics Laboratory, February 2011, at www.jhuapl.edu/ourwork/nsa/papers/Nuclear-Futures.pdf.

I ASSESSING THE HISTORY OF LIMITED NUCLEAR WAR

1   Limited War and the Advent of Nuclear Weapons

Jeffrey A. Larsen

THE CONCEPT OF LIMITED NUCLEAR WAR IS BUILT ON A much older idea: the notion that wars can be limited at all. The concept of limited war goes back millennia, and is typically associated with one of two approaches: limitations on one's objectives before the outbreak of war, or limitations on the conduct of war once hostilities have commenced. The former requires the combatants to believe they can achieve their goals without resort to unlimited conflict; the latter relates to the medieval concept of chivalry and some of its modern manifestations, such as efforts to limit the destructiveness of armed conflict, through such methods as arms control, international protocols, or tacit understandings. During the Cold War, the concept of limited war was adapted to the consideration of limited *nuclear* war, which represented a different approach to dealing with the nuclear threat from the Soviet Union.

The theory of limited nuclear war originated in connection with the development of the doctrine of flexible response as the United States and the Soviet Union reached rough parity in nuclear forces, thus rendering irrelevant the dangerous threats of massive retaliation. The search for ever more limited and discrete means of waging nuclear war contrasted with the debate over whether nuclear war could be limited through various means of controlling or containing escalation. Rather than simply trying to prevent the outbreak of conflict through a deterrence strategy that relied on deterrence by punishment, the latter approach focused on deterrence by denial—the ability to prevent an enemy from achieving his military and strategic objectives. This could be done, it was believed, by limiting either the scope of the conflict or the manner in which it was conducted. In short, the United States could decide whether it wanted to control the conflict, or to escalate the level of violence as necessary in order to win it. The problem, of course, was that, as Lawrence Freedman wrote, "It takes two to keep a war limited."[1] Just because one side wanted to keep things limited was no guarantee that the other side would agree. In addition, there has been a distinction between advocates of limited war who believe in the value of deterring an adversary by punitive threats and blows that impose unacceptable, but not ultimate, costs, and those who see the role of denying an adversary his goals by the use of limited military actions.[2]

Why is this subject still important more than two decades after the end of the Cold War? With the emergence of new nuclear powers and nuclear weapon aspirants, the possibility exists that the United States may, in the future, face regional adversaries armed with small nuclear arsenals. In such circumstances, it is equally possible that there will be little prospect that traditional deterrence will prevent such adversaries from employing those arsenals against the United States or its interests and allies. Such adversaries may believe that only the threat to employ nuclear weapons would dissuade the United States from engaging its superior conventional force. An opponent may also believe that it is facing the prospect of regime change, and thus has little to lose from employing limited nuclear strikes against either the United States, its forces deployed in the region, or regional US allies. In other words, even if the United States wants to avoid a limited nuclear war, it may nevertheless find itself in one not of its choosing. Each side gets a vote on how the conflict develops.

Reconsidering the Theory of Limited Nuclear War

The prospect of limited nuclear war has profound implications for US national security strategy, for regional crisis management, global nuclear nonproliferation regimes, and consequence management. While other basic concepts from the Cold War lexicon of strategic theories have been subjected to reexamination in light of the new international security landscape prevailing in the post–Cold War era, the theory of limited war has yet to be fully reconsidered. That is the principal purpose of this book. Most of the literature on limited nuclear war stems from the early days of the Cold War. Authors such as Henry Kissinger, William Kaufmann, Robert Osgood, Bernard Brodie, and others focused on the problem of how to deal with an adversary that had the ability to annihilate the United States in a conflict and with US and Soviet military doctrines that seemed to place all of the nation's eggs in the deterrence basket. If it failed, we were all dead. The lunacy of such an approach to dealing with issues of international security, and the certainty that we would have to fight limited conventional wars again one day, made the search for rational ways of conducting wars under the nuclear umbrella, perhaps even with the modest use of a few nuclear weapons (but not enough to trigger retaliatory Armageddon), a very real and important dimension of security studies from the 1950s through the 1970s.

The most recent literature on limited nuclear war was published in the mid-1980s. With the end of the Cold War and the demise of the Soviet empire in the early 1990s, the subject took a back seat to more pressing issues. Given the rise of rogue states and smaller nuclear powers, however, particularly in geographic regions where the United States is most likely to find itself in a limited conflict in the future, the issue is back.

Defining Limited Nuclear War

The concept of limited nuclear war is surprisingly difficult to nail down. After all, limited war encompasses a spectrum of possibilities, from limits on central war (where the antagonists may choose to limit their objectives in the conflict), to limits within regional conflicts (where the sides may limit the means used to achieve their objectives), to terrorist use of a weapon of mass destruction (where the initiating party will likely have no more than one, or at most a few, weapons, and the responding parties may choose to limit the level of their retaliation). A nuclear war may therefore be considered "limited" in one or more of multiple dimensions:

1. *Quantitative*, in terms of the numbers and types of nuclear weapons used (sometimes referred to as "intensity" of the conflict).
2. *Scope*, in terms of the geographic area covered, or the number of countries or other actors involved.
3. *Duration*, in terms of the time that passes between the first and last use of nuclear weapons in a conflict.
4. *Objectives*, in terms of the goals of the parties involved. A nuclear

war can be considered limited only if one or more of the parties seek limited objectives, or pursue an outcome that is something less than the complete annihilation of the other side's armed forces or its government.

5. *Targets*, in terms of constraints on the targets one or more parties choose for operational, ethical, legal, or cultural reasons.

Trying to capture all of these important and nuanced concepts on what limits a conflict is challenging. Nonetheless, the following definition serves as the basis for analysis in the chapters that follow: *Limited nuclear war is a conflict in which nuclear weapons are used in small numbers and in a constrained manner in pursuit of limited objectives (or are introduced by a country or non-state actor in the face of conventional defeat).*

On the Concept of Limited War

The concept of limited war has found expression in several forms. These have included conventions and international laws that proscribe certain actions and clarify the proper treatment of combatants, civilians, and prisoners; a body of just war theorizing that stretches back several centuries; and multiple efforts to mitigate the consequences of military action through protocols and arms control agreements.

Robert Osgood reminded us that limited wars are as old as mankind. "In the history of international conflict the wars that have been truly momentous and rare are those that were fought to annihilate, to completely defeat or completely dominate the adversary."[3] The rise of limited war thinking in modern times is a reaction, he wrote, to the increasing capacity and inclination of states to wage total war. A truly "limited" war requires both sides to pursue goals far short of complete subordination of the enemy's will, using far less than their total military capabilities. Limited war, he wrote, "is not only a matter of degree but also a matter of national perspective."[4]

Ian Clark pointed out that there are two basic issues associated with limits on war: what to limit in order to call a war limited, and the more challenging question, the extent to which a war can be limited while "still remaining the social institution that we recognize war to be." As he put it, "To some extent . . . the nature of war, and the form that it takes, is dependent upon our social conception of what is its point."[5]

There has never been an international consensus that placing limits on warfare is a universal good. Sometimes the end really does justify the means, at least to one of the combatants. This point is clear in the history of the debate over *jus ad bello* (war of just objectives) and *jus in bellum* (war fought with just means). Since at least the Middle Ages philosophers have argued over the realism of either concept, as well as which should take priority. Since the dawn of the nuclear age, and particularly during the Cold War, the nature of a war was often defined by the means employed to fight it. Hence the use of nuclear weapons made, to some minds, war unthinkable for any reason. This notion has carried over into the post–Cold War era, despite the increase in small wars fought around the world by the leading nuclear superpower and the possibility that one of these might involve a small nuclear power for whom such considerations on limits to conflict may not carry the same level of conviction.

There have always been arguments opposing the limitation of war or its conduct. Opponents worry that by making war less horrific one makes it more likely to occur, and that it may also protract the length and resultant agonies of the conflict. In other words, by trying to inject a little humanity into foreign policy decisions, one might actually increase the level of inhumanity.

The idea that one can place limitations on war arises from one or more underlying causal factors. Those can be based on religion or some other system of common values; they can rely on mutual self-interest; or they can grow out of unilateral restraint in hopes of a reciprocal response from one's enemy. Clausewitz pointed out that war is in fact a political condition, not one where indiscriminate (or "unlimited") violence has a place.[6] The purpose of war, according to this view, "could not be simply to apply maximum force toward the military defeat of the adversary; rather, it must be to employ force skillfully along a continuous spectrum—from diplomacy, to crises short of war, to an overt clash of arms—in order to exert the desired effect upon the adversary's will."[7] Others have argued that war is a legal condition and is, as such, subject to legal rules and restrictions, just as any other human activity. And a third argument points out that as abhorrent as war is, it is still a moral condition that should be subject to moral restraints. Others, of course, argue that the only aspect of war that needs to be considered is that of military efficiency; the attempt to introduce other rules or restrictions is self-contradictory.

There is also the question of whether seeking explicit limits on war may undermine other policy objectives. As Clark summarizes,

At core, there has been an ongoing and unresolved debate as to whether limitation is desirable, with the proponents of humane warfare consistently being opposed by a variety of philosophic arguments ranging from the superior rights of the just party, through the case for making war short by making it nasty and brutish, and to the argument for abolition that regards moderate war as tolerable war. At the same time, the argument about the desirability of limitation in war has been caught up in the diversity of opinions as to why, if at all, it should be considered a worthwhile goal and appeal, on this score, has been made to a broad spectrum of ideological and pragmatic principles.[8]

How to Limit War

Limitations on war may take the form of efforts to restrict the tempo, level of violence, or breadth of a conflict. For example, the parties can agree (tacitly or formally) to restrict the types of targets attacked or the weapons used; they can express their acceptance of less than total victory for either side as a result of the conflict; they can acknowledge special rights for noncombatants, or for wounded or imprisoned combatants; and so on. Traditionally, incorporating limits into an internationally recognized legal framework has been the most common form of seeking agreed restraints on war, yielding a set of laws of war. Richard Falk has listed four primary principles that underlie the laws of war: prohibitions on methods, tactics, and weapons calculated to inflict unnecessary suffering (the principle of necessity); a requirement that methods, tactics, and weapons generally discriminate between combatants and civilians (the principle of discrimination); a requirement that the military means used bear a proportional relationship to the military end pursued (the principle of proportionality); and an absolute prohibition on methods, tactics, and weapons that are inherently cruel in their effects or violate minimal notions of humanity (the principle of humanity).[9]

Most of the wars fought by the United States throughout its history have been limited. This includes the so-called expeditions in Latin America, the wars with Mexico, World War I, and the wars in Korea, Vietnam, Afghanistan, and Iraq. The only true total wars have arguably been the American Civil War and World War II—and even in those conflicts, despite localized deprivations, most American citizens lived normal lives little affected by the major battles being waged in distant lands.

In general, a war can be called "limited" if it meets one or more general rules. It may be limited in geographic scope, confined to one region. It may not utilize the full military might of one or both adversaries. In fact, as a general rule, in a limited war each side will use the minimum level of force necessary to achieve its objectives. It may remain conventional, not crossing the nuclear threshold. It may limit strikes to certain types of targets. But primarily a war is limited if the objectives for which it is fought remain limited. As Kissinger put it,

> A limited war . . . is fought for specific political objectives which, by their very existence, tend to establish a relationship between the force employed and the goal to be attained. It reflects an attempt to affect the opponent's will, not crush it, to make the conditions to be imposed seem more attractive than continued resistance, to strive for specific goals and not for complete annihilation. . . . The characteristic of a limited war . . . is the existence of ground rules which define the relationship of military to political objectives.[10]

A limited war can be the result of the disparity in power between the two antagonists; it may result from the inability of one or both sides to provide the logistical requirements of a major campaign; or it can reflect the self-restraint shown by the stronger power whose objectives are modest. This may be the result of tacit or implicit agreements between the parties that they both want to keep the war from escalating.[11] This was a common situation among the European great powers during the balance of power era of the 19th century. They realized that none of the issues over which they skirmished challenged their national survival, there was no revolutionary power trying to upset the international system, and the parties were equally matched in terms of size and technologies.[12] Basil Liddell Hart, one of the modern proponents of limited war theory, understood that one's enemy today might be needed as a friend or ally in the future. There was value in avoiding excessive damage, injury, or insult between adversaries even during unpleasant intervals such as wars. Bernard Brodie agreed with Liddell Hart's analysis. As Brodie put it, both sides were best served by exploring "ways of consciously limiting those conflicts we may be unable entirely to avoid."[13]

There is no a priori military solution to a limited war. It has a political aspect that determines how it is fought and when it is over. Total defeat of an enemy's military forces in the field, or total destruction of the society, or regime change need not be goals of the victor. Again quoting Kissinger, "the purpose of limited war is to inflict losses or to pose risks for the enemy out of proportion to the objectives under dispute."[14] The restraint in such a conflict is to a great extent a psychological one. The losing state must calculate the cost-benefit aspects of continuing to fight, or escalating the conflict, to simply giving in on the issue that led to the fighting in the first place. The consequences of total war must seem worse than defeat in a limited war. As Freedman put it, "Much of limited war theory is a plea for moderation in political rhetoric, a warning against a diplomacy based on belligerence and the rigid adherence to war aims that permit nothing but the enemy's unconditional surrender."[15] As George Kennan stated in his famous series of Cold War lectures, "There is no more dangerous illusion, none that has done us a greater disservice in the past or that threatens to do us greater disservice in the future, than the concept of total victory."[16] Both sides have to surrender the prospect of total victory if a conflict is going to remain limited.

Limited Nuclear War Theory in the Cold War

In the early days of the Cold War the United States, and presumably its chief adversary, the Soviet Union, considered the role of nuclear weapons solely as a deterrent. The US strategic perspective from the earliest days of the nuclear era held that the best way to ensure deterrence was to threaten an overwhelmingly destructive retaliatory strike against the adversary in the event he crossed some well-defined red line that triggered the response. This response would lead to an all-out thermonuclear war and the assured destruction of the enemy's homeland. Eventually, as Soviet capabilities caught up with America's, it meant *mutual* assured destruction. There was little thought about limiting the damage to either side, since, it was assumed, such a horrific scenario would prevent the one thing both sides wanted to avoid: a nuclear war. Indeed, as Bernard Brodie wrote in 1959, "all of us assume almost without question that peace is better than war, but it is curious and interesting that we do not have the same consensus that limited war is preferable to total war."[17]

Moreover, there was a school of thought which held that once an exchange of nuclear weapons began, it could not be kept limited.[18] It was, therefore, impossible to place any kind of limits on nuclear war. Nuclear war was, by definition, unlimited war. Societies needed to remain vulnerable to enemy retaliation for mutual assured destruction to work, hence systems like missile defenses had to be proscribed. This conclusion must also be reconsidered under those conditions of limited nuclear use that are likely to prevail in a future nuclear war.

By the early 1960s the Cold War environment had changed enough that analysts began considering how to deter the Soviet Union in ways other than simply threatening massive retaliation. The question thus became more nuanced: do we simply want to deter wars, or do we want to have a way of fighting them in a more logical way if they actually occur? And would the latter actually enhance deterrence against an adversary that considered nuclear war a reasonable possibility in his planning? Much of the creative work that went into limited war thinking grew out of opposition to the Eisenhower-Dulles emphasis on massive retaliation. As a result, two camps developed that did not see eye to eye on these questions—the assured destruction camp and the damage limitation camp. As one observer highlighted the different approaches at the time, "assured destruction may be regarded as an insane policy for fighting a war, but its supporters denounce the damage-limitation-ists for making the war more likely."[19]

Kissinger pointed out that the primary reason wars might remain limited in the nuclear age was that "our traditional insistence on reserving our military effort for an unambiguous threat and then going all out to defeat the enemy may lead to paralysis when total war augurs social disintegration even for the victor."[20] It would be wrong to assume that any war is going to be an all-out war, he wrote. Similarly, today we cannot assume that any war will remain conventional, particularly when facing a rogue state for whom the stakes are much higher than they are for the United States. Deterrence does not rely simply on numbers of weapons; the fact that the United States has thousands of nuclear warheads may not prevent an adversary, even in a small, limited conventional conflict, from crossing the threshold and using one or more of its weapons of mass destruction against the United States, its forces, or its allies. Kissinger recognized this in the 1950s, and it remains true today. In addition, one cannot assume that the adversary thinks the same way we do: as Kissinger wrote, "any strategy must count on a somewhat rational enemy; nothing can deter an opponent bent on self-destruction."[21] During the Cold War, the United States and NATO began to change their focus from one of deterring war by fear of overwhelming retaliation to one of how to fight a nuclear war should deterrence fail. In this view, limited nuclear war became just one stop on the gradual escalation of hostilities along the conflict spectrum as the United States attempted to force the aggressor to back down. As Osgood wrote, "The 'escalation' of war—that is, the graduated increase of its scope and intensity—although originally feared as an uncontrollable danger, came to be regarded as a controllable and reversible process by which adversaries would test each other's will and nerve in order to resolve their conflict at a cost reasonably related to the issues at stake."[22]

Kissinger listed four types of likely limited wars under the specter of Soviet-American confrontation. These included wars between secondary powers (such as Israel versus its neighbors); wars by one of the superpowers against a clearly outmatched opponent (such as the United States against Panama); conflicts between a major and minor power which had the potential to spread (such as the French in Indochina); and finally a limited war between two major powers, with its obvious and explosive potential to escalate.[23] The key to the last scenario remaining limited, of course, is that both sides must want to keep their conflict limited, for whatever self-interested reason.

The Nuclear Dilemma

William Kaufmann's seminal work on the central importance of credibility during the 1950s emphasized the concern about facing a Hobson's choice: relying on massive retaliation meant that "holocaust or humiliation," "suicide or surrender," or "sudden destruction or slow defeat" were the only options available to the United States, even in scenarios that clearly called for the limited use of force.[24] These concerns resonated in the John F. Kennedy administration, leading to a serious effort to find an alternative to mutual assured destruction. One result was the heightened credence given Robert Osgood's 1957 work on a theory of limited nuclear war. Osgood's main point was that "if there was to be a strategy of deterrence it had to credible, and credibility, in turn, requires that the means of deterrence be proportional to the objectives at stake."[25] All the leading proponents of limited nuclear war in the early Cold War agreed that America had to scale back its political and military aspirations and recognize the reality of its confrontation with the USSR, and to accept the novel idea that in the new, nuclear world, perhaps not all wars could be won at acceptable cost.[26] While it was impossible to dial down the political rhetoric and irreconcilable differences between the West and the Communist bloc, both sides had a vested interest in trying to restrain their military options for the self-serving purpose of national survival.

The Kennedy and Johnson administrations introduced the concept of flexible and controlled responses to US and NATO policy in order to enhance the credibility of Western deterrence strategy and to attempt to minimize the damage should war occur.[27] These efforts reached their zenith when the Schlesinger doctrine of limited and controlled nuclear strikes was operationalized in the Single Integrated Operational Plan (SIOP) of the late 1970s.

A whole new type of weapon category was developed during the Cold War in an attempt to keep the size and damage caused by a nuclear conflict to lower levels. These smaller atomic weapons, designed for battlefield or tactical use, became particularly important during the Army's pentomic era of the 1960s and to the US Air Force in Europe since the 1950s.[28] Freedman called these "apparently a tolerable species of an unpleasant genus," but pointed out that the West never really understood how to use these weapons: as larger conventional weapons in a warfighting manner, or as a deterrent, "a smaller punishment for a smaller crime," albeit with the implied threat of escalation to larger retaliatory strikes if the Soviet aggression did not stop.[29]

Today the United States still maintains a small arsenal of so-called tactical or nonstrategic nuclear weapons, primarily dedicated to extended deterrence over its allies in NATO, Europe and Northeast Asia. These weapons could conceivably also be forward deployed to other hot spots around the globe if necessary. In its 2010 Nuclear Posture Review the Obama administration made a commitment to its allies to maintain these capabilities for the indefinite future, and called for the development of a new generation of dual-capable aircraft to carry the remaining bombs, which will also be updated through a life-extension program. But the future for this category of weaponry appears uncertain, given European allied concerns over the continued necessity of this mission, American political and fiscal pressures, and the general diminishment of the nuclear enterprise.[30]

The Possibility of Limited Nuclear War in the Post–Cold War Environment

Writing over fifty years ago, Henry Kissinger predicted the rise of smaller nuclear powers and the consequent possibility of limited nuclear war: "As nuclear technology becomes more widely diffused, other and perhaps more irresponsible powers will enter the nuclear race. The fear of mutual destruction, today the chief deterrent to all-out war for the major powers, may prove less effective with nations who have less to lose and whose negotiating position might even be improved by a threat to commit suicide."[31]

Today's global security environment may once again force the United States to consider the possibility of fighting a war with limited use of nuclear weapons, and to try to convince certain modern states to agree to limit a conflict. A state bent on self-destruction, perhaps in a final paroxysm in the face of losing a conflict encompassing what it considers to be more than limited objectives, may not be deterred even by the threat of total devastation. In the 21st century this may involve the introduction of weapons of mass destruction to what had theretofore been a conventional war. In other words, what appears to be a war of limited objectives to a great power may look like total war to a smaller state. In such circumstances, the smaller state (or non-state actor) may feel it has little or nothing to lose by escalating the conflict. Indeed, the threat of such escalation, even at the risk to oneself, may be seen as the only way to deter the larger power from continuing its conventional campaign, or to deny the larger state access to the region. As Clark put it, "Whether it be because a war worth fighting at all is considered worth fighting hard to win or because cooperation, in any form, with an armed adversary is deemed inappropriate, many people believe that warfare is one area of social activity in which a principle of moderation is not to be applied unthinkingly."[32] Kissinger had already identified this future dilemma:

> Success in limited war requires . . . that the opponent be persuaded that national survival is not at stake and that a settlement is possible on reasonable terms. . . . A policy of limited war therefore presupposed three conditions: the ability to generate pressures other than the threat of all-out war; the ability to create a climate in which survival is not thought to be at stake in each issue; and the ability to keep control of public opinion in case disagreement arises over whether national survival is at stake.[33]

It also requires agile diplomacy by parties intent on keeping the war limited to ensure that the adversary understands that one's objectives are limited. While that may not necessarily restrain an adversary, it may prevent a war escalating due to miscalculation or misunderstanding of the other parties' goals.

Since the end of World War II, according to Osgood, there have been two strands of limited war thinking. His books reflect the times, focusing on the Soviet threat; accordingly, he identified one strand as the search for ways to make force an effective source of containment against global Communism.

The other strand reflected the view of the revolutionary states in the international system, those that use guerilla wars and low-level insurgencies to push their political agenda without incurring the overwhelming retaliation of the major Western nuclear powers. In general, theories of limited war, and limited nuclear war, were an attempt to figure out how to use military force against those lower-level threats, and contain the larger threat, without either leading to a third world war.[34]

During the Cold War analysts wrestled with the question of the utility of limited nuclear war as well as its value. Clark pointed out that

> we have to face the issue of whether limiting war is, in principle, desirable and if so, whether it is a goal that is capable of achievement; we are compelled to face the vexing question as to whether, by limiting the horrors of war, we make its onset more likely, or by alternative reasoning, whether a limited war is a more credible deterrent and hence an inhibition on resort to it.[35]

Limited War Threshold

As the nuclear superpowers continue to reduce the size of their nuclear arsenals, goes one intriguing argument, they will eventually reach a point below which they will be physically incapable of fighting anything but a limited nuclear exchange. At that point there simply will not be enough weapons or delivery systems remaining in their arsenal to carry out the kind of unlimited, civilization-threatening strategic nuclear war that was the stuff of planning and fear during the Cold War. Just as the United States and the Soviet Union passed through some threshold above which they could plan for and conduct unlimited war (probably in the realm of hundreds of deliverable weapons, reached in the early 1950s), so too will the United States and Russia pass back through a parallel threshold at some point in the future, should arms control and disarmament efforts continue to reduce overall numbers (as shown in Figure 1.1). The enhanced capabilities of nuclear weapons, delivery systems, and targeting processes available today imply that the threshold at which a state is limited to fighting only limited wars may be at lower overall numbers than was the threshold the two states climbed through during the arms race of the 1950s and 1960s, but such a threshold certainly exists.

Attempts to find ways to limit nuclear wars that were put in place in the 1970s were thought necessary at the time to signal the adversary and limit the

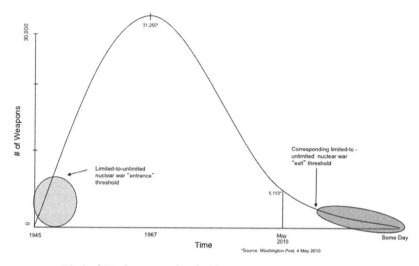

FIGURE 1.1. Limited Nuclear War Thresholds
SOURCE: Designed by Timothy D. Miller for an early authors' workshop. Used with permission.

potential for cataclysmic destruction. In the future, such contrived policy and targeting limits may prove unnecessary as they will be intrinsic to the force levels available. This will require rethinking nuclear warfighting by military planners and political leaders. No longer will US strategy be able to consider massive retaliation or major attack options; by default, the only available deterrent or retaliatory options will be of a limited nature. This may even require a return to considerations of countervalue targeting—threatening cities and things of value to the adversary, rather than focusing on counterforce targets, which was the focus of limited war conjecture in the 1970s and 1980s.

Theories of escalation control, or escalation dominance, are closely related to the theory and practice of limited war. According to a RAND study published early in the post–Cold War era:

> Unless the United States and its allies can develop and deploy capabilities that can prevent regional adversaries from employing nuclear weapons (as opposed to trying to deter them from doing so), future power-projection operations will likely revert from the post–Cold War model of "decisive defeat" back toward concepts incorporating elements that were prevalent in military planning during the Cold War: limited war and escalation management.[36]

The Likelihood of Limited War

A recent study for the US Air Force posed five categories of potential actors for whom the United States must consider the value of nuclear weapons for purposes of assuring, deterring, or prevailing in a conflict: allies, peers, near-peers, regional powers, and armed non-state actors.[37] As many potential actors as there are, there is a similarly broad range of likelihood regarding the prospects of limited nuclear war. For example, the likelihood of a nuclear conflict between peer or near-peer states is low today. Russia is a strategic partner of NATO and the United States. China is the second largest trading partner of the United States, and despite the drumbeat of some who see Beijing as the next generation's arch-rival, there is little possibility of military conflict between the two countries in the near term. But there are a total of nine nuclear nations in the world today, some of them potentially radical outlier states, and there are at least one or two other states seeking nuclear capabilities. In addition, some violent non-state actors have declared their desire to acquire nuclear weapons to use against the West. At the same time, the United States has been uncharacteristically active in military engagements around the world in the twenty-plus years since the end of the Cold War, leading coalition efforts involved in major conflicts in several regions of the Middle East and Southwest Asia. Accordingly, prudent military planning would consider the possibility that the United States or one of its allies could one day find itself engaged in a regional conflict with a nuclear-armed adversary—one which could escalate into a nuclear war not of America's choosing. As Kissinger put it in 1957,

> What about nuclear weapons in the hands of what are now secondary powers? . . . To the extent that nuclear weapons are thought to offer an advantage, they may be used regardless of what strategy we propose to follow. We, therefore, have no choice but to base our strategy on the assumption that a war between nuclear powers, even of the second rank, *may* involve the use of nuclear weapons.[38]

One of the more likely scenarios involves the West disarming or fighting a nuclear-armed Iran. Such a conflict would almost certainly be a limited nuclear engagement, at least from the US perspective. In a 2010 article in the *Atlantic,* for example, Robert Kaplan emphasized the need to reconsider early theories of limited nuclear war as the West faces an obstinate Iran bent on developing its own nuclear capability. In particular, he suggested that analysts and policymakers reread Kissinger's 1957 epic on limited war, since his analysis from half a century ago could prove valuable in developing countermoves and the psychological preparation necessary to deal with Tehran.[39]

Limited wars have always proven difficult for Americans; Kissinger recognized that in his book, and Kaplan makes it clear that will soon be the case regarding Iran. As he put it, Kissinger recognized that "limited war is something that the United States must be prepared to wage" while also acknowledging "the domestic upheavals that such wars inevitably trigger. To refuse as a matter of principle to fight limited wars is to leave America powerless, with only an inflexible and reactive policy against the subtle maneuvers of adversaries."[40] Kaplan summarizes that "we must be willing . . . to accept the prospect of a limited nuclear war between states."[41]

Donald Snow has described the rise of asymmetrical warfare in the post–Cold War era as a response to the paradox of US military power. The interest in nuclear weapons by regional powers and non-state actors may be a part of this response: nuclear weapons might be seen as another asymmetrical way to match the unbeatable conventional strength of American military force. Snow explains this paradox in the following terms: "The end of the Cold War started the process by which the United States' traditional power has become so great that it has made itself virtually obsolete, a kind of self-fulfilling prophecy in which American prowess has eliminated the problem for which it was devised."[42] In such a world, is it unreasonable to consider the possibility of one day facing a new type of asymmetric opponent that is prepared to use nuclear weapons?

Of particular concern to the authors in this book is the possibility that a conflict may "go nuclear" as the result of an adversary's decisionmaking calculus, at a time and manner that would be particularly bad for US forces. This is not a new concern, but it may be one that the US military has forgotten, or is not currently prepared to deal with in a serious manner. It is our contention that it is better to consider how we might react to such a situation now rather than later, for, as Kissinger put it, "a limited nuclear war which had to be improvised in the midst of military operations would be undertaken under the worst possible conditions, both psychological and military."[43] The advent of nuclear weapons has complicated the calculations and expectations of limited war, but has not rendered obsolete the theory of limited war. As the prospects for a cataclysmic and spasmodic all-out nuclear war with a rival superpower fade into the past, new dangers have arisen that require revisiting our thinking about limited war and its relevance to future nuclear conflicts.

Notes

1. Lawrence Freedman, *The Evolution of Nuclear Strategy*, 2nd ed. (New York: St. Martin's Press, 1989), p. 110.

2. Robert E. Osgood, *Limited War Revisited* (Boulder, CO: Westview Press, 1979), p. 9.

3. Ibid., p. 1.

4. Ibid., p. 3.

5. Ian Clark, *Limited Nuclear War* (Oxford: Martin Robertson, 1982), pp. 9–10.

6. See Carl von Clausewitz, *On War,* translated by J. J. Graham (Radford, VA: Wilder Publishers, 2008, orig. pub. 1832).

7. Osgood, *Limited War Revisited*, p. 10.

8. Clark, *Limited Nuclear War*, p. 24.

9. Richard Falk, "Methods and Means of Warfare," in P. Trooboff, ed., *Law and Responsibility in Warfare* (Chapel Hill: University of North Carolina Press, 1975), p. 40.

10. Henry Kissinger, *Nuclear Weapons and Foreign Policy*, abridged ed. (New York: W.W. Norton, 1969; orig. published 1957), pp. 120–121.

11. Ibid., p. 118.

12. Ibid., p. 122.

13. Bernard Brodie, "Unlimited Weapons and Limited War," *Reporter*, 1 November 1954, in Freedman, *The Evolution of Nuclear Strategy*, pp. 97–100.

14. Kissinger, *Nuclear Weapons and Foreign Policy*, p. 123.

15. Freedman, *The Evolution of Nuclear Strategy*, p. 96.

16. George F. Kennan, *American Diplomacy: Expanded Edition* (Chicago: University of Chicago Press, 1984).

17. Bernard Brodie, *Strategy in the Missile Age* (Princeton, NJ: Princeton University Press, 1959), p. 314.

18. Desmond Ball, *Can Nuclear War be Controlled?* Adelphi Paper No. #169 (London: IISS, 1981).

19. Clark, *Limited Nuclear War*, p. 17.

20. Kissinger, *Nuclear Weapons and Foreign Policy*, p. 11.

21. Ibid., p. 109.

22. Osgood, *Limited War Revisited,* p. 11. For more on escalation dynamics, see Herman Kahn, *On Escalation: Metaphors and Scenarios* (New York: Praeger, 1965), and Thomas Schelling, *The Strategy of Conflict* (Cambridge, MA: Harvard University Press, 1960) and *Arms and Influence* (New Haven, CT: Yale University Press, 1965).

23. Kissinger, *Nuclear Weapons and Foreign Policy*, p. 118.

24. See William Kaufmann, *Military Policy and National Security* (Princeton, NJ: Princeton University Press, 1956).

25. Robert Osgood, *Limited War: The Challenge to American Strategy* (Chicago: University of Chicago Press, 1957), pp. 26, 242.

26. Kaufmann, *Military Policy and National Security*, p. 103.

27. Osgood, *Limited War Revisited*, p. 31.

28. Air-delivered tactical nuclear bombs are the only remaining US nuclear weapon still stationed in Europe. See Jeffrey A. Larsen, "The Future of U.S. Non-Strategic Nuclear Weapons and Implications for NATO: Drifting toward the Foreseeable Future," Manfred Wörner Fellow paper prepared for the NATO Public Diplomacy Division, November 2006; Jeffrey A. Larsen and Kurt J. Klingenberger, eds., *Controlling Non-Strategic Nuclear Weapons: Obstacles and Opportunities* (Colorado Springs, CO: USAF Institute for National Security Studies, 2001); Brian Alexander and Alistair Millar, *Tactical Nuclear Weapons: Emergent Threats in an Evolving Security Environment* (Dulles, VA: Brassey's, 2003); and Hans Kristensen, *Non-Strategic Nuclear Weapons,* Special Report No. 3, Federation of American Scientists, May 2012, at www.fas.org/_docs/Non_Strategic_Nuclear_Weapons.pdf.

29. Freedman, *The Evolution of Nuclear Strategy*, p. 96.

30. Jeffrey A. Larsen, "Non-Strategic Nuclear Weapons: An American Perspective," in Tom Nichols, Douglas Stuart, and Jeffrey McCausland, eds., *Tactical Nuclear Weapons and NATO* (Carlisle, PA: Strategic Studies Institute, US Army War College, 2012); and Jeffrey A. Larsen, "Future Options for NATO Nuclear Policy," *Issue Brief,* Atlantic Council of the United States, August 2011, at www.acus.org/publication/future-options-nato-nuclear-policy.

31. Kissinger, *Nuclear Weapons and Foreign Policy*, p. 144.

32. Clark, *Limited Nuclear War*, p. 12.

33. Kissinger, *Nuclear Weapons and Foreign Policy*, pp. 140–142.

34. Osgood, *Limited War Revisited*, pp. 2–3.

35. Clark, *Limited Nuclear War*, p. 4.

36. David Ochmanek and Lowell H. Schwartz, *The Challenge of Nuclear Armed Regional Adversaries* (Santa Monica, CA: RAND Corporation, April 2008).

37. See Jeffrey A. Larsen and Justin V. Anderson et al., *Qualitative Considerations of Nuclear Weapons at Lower Numbers and Implications for Arms Control,* INSS Occasional Paper 68 (Colorado Springs, CO: Air Force Institute for National Security Studies, July 2012).

38. Kissinger, *Nuclear Weapons and Foreign Policy*, p. 164.

39. Robert D. Kaplan, "Living with a Nuclear Iran," *Atlantic*, September 2010, pp. 72–73.

40. Ibid.

41. Ibid.

42. Donald M. Snow, *National Security for a New Era*, 4th ed. (Boston: Longman, 2011), p. 258.

43. Kissinger, *Nuclear Weapons and Foreign Policy*, p. 148.

2   The Origins of Limited Nuclear War Theory

Andrew L. Ross

T HE HISTORY OF US NUCLEAR POLICY, STRATEGY, AND capabilities is the history of an intellectual struggle between the proponents of a punishment-based deterrent posture and the proponents of a denial-based deterrent posture, or between a school of thought determined to achieve "total victory" in nuclear war, and a school of thought that feared "total defeat" in any nuclear conflagration.[1] The latter amounts to "deterrence plus"; that is, deterrence plus nuclear warfighting capabilities, to include the capability to fight a limited nuclear war. That ability was thought by its advocates to enhance deterrence; deterrence requires the capability to fight, survive, and win along the entire spectrum of nuclear conflict, from limited to total. Of course, advocates of a punishment-centric posture charged that a limited nuclear war capability would serve to lower the nuclear threshold—the imprudent assumption that nuclear war could be kept limited (was it less prudent to presume that it could not be?) would make it more likely that nuclear weapons would be used—and thereby erode rather than enhance deterrence.

The ascendance of a denial, warfighting emphasis, aided and abetted by the continuing development of a range of nuclear and delivery system technologies,[2] was evident in the increasing emphasis on flexibility, "nuclear options," "limited-employment options," and "limited nuclear options" (LNOs)—the selective employment of nuclear forces in ways other than the massive retaliation envisioned during the Eisenhower administration.

Concepts such as controlled, deliberate response, graduated deterrence, measured retaliation, (second-strike) counterforce, damage limitation, city avoidance, escalation management, escalation dominance (horizontal as well as vertical), active defense, and extended or protracted nuclear war were translated into Robert McNamara's flexible response, James Schlesinger's flexible or selective targeting, Harold Brown's countervailing strategy (with its preprogrammed, selective, and limited options), and Caspar Weinberger's emphasis on "prevailing."[3]

Nuclear plenty provided a de facto assured destruction, punishment capability that remained an existential, background feature of the US posture even as declaratory policy and targeting plans alike came to emphasize denial capabilities. Limited nuclear war (and related) concepts and the postures into which they were translated from the 1960s through the 1980s represented an effort to escape from the dilemmas of assured destruction gone MAD (mutual assured destruction). The attempt to escape the existential reality and logic of MAD failed. Indeed, it could not but have failed. Rather ironically perhaps, the escape attempt backfired. MAD wasn't escaped or even weakened; it was reinforced.

In short, the (perverse?) logic of limited nuclear war, whether on the strategic level or theater level, served to 1) reduce the perceived risks of nuclear use (how bad could the use of just a few, small nuclear weapons be?), 2) increase its likelihood (if it won't be so bad, why not use a few nuclear weapons?), and 3) lower the nuclear threshold (is there really that much of a difference between small nuclear weapons and advanced conventional weapons?). Limited nuclear war logic failed, however, to reduce/lower the risks or likelihood of escalation (what logic ensured that escalation would be controlled?).[4] The ever-present possibility, if not inevitability, that limited nuclear use would escalate to general nuclear war (would it be prudent to assume that such escalation was not inevitable?) ineluctably brought us back to the punishment-based logic of assured destruction. In the Cold War world of nuclear plenty, we were all MAD men (and women). The ethical dilemmas were profound;[5] the alternative, however, was worse.

Today, a decade into the twenty-first century, the scenarios that include nuclear next use no longer feature two nuclear-rich superpowers. Instead, contemporary scenarios highlight new nuclear weapons states (NWS) with more limited capabilities than those of the Cold War superpowers, and nonstate actors with nuclear ambitions but, at present, nonexistent capabilities.[6] Robert Kaplan, a member of the Defense Policy Board, recently advised that "we must be more willing, not only to accept the prospect of limited war but . . . to accept the prospect of a limited nuclear war between states."[7] The specter of limited nuclear war has reappeared.[8] That specter has been accompanied by a revival of interest in—indeed, a harkening back to—the original work on limited nuclear war and its relevance.[9] We return, therefore, to the days of yesteryear.

The Emergence of Limited Nuclear War "Theory"

Once upon a time, during the second half of the often fondly remembered but not so halcyon 1950s, limited war, including limited nuclear war, was all the rage. Air Marshal Sir John Slessor declared that "as far ahead as we need trouble to look we must be able and willing, if necessary, to fight small wars—and fight them with the right weapons."[10] A not yet eminent Henry Kissinger asserted that "the most fruitful area for current strategic thought is the conduct and efficacy of limited nuclear war."[11] These shots, drawn from pieces that appeared in 1956, were fired as the debate on limited war and its nuclear variant was heating up. Bernard Brodie, whose early work so skillfully and influentially framed nuclear policy and strategy choices, tells us that the debate emerged in 1954.[12] In his own piece that year, Brodie anticipated Kissinger's assertion by two years: "It . . . seems plain that opportunities to apply nuclear weapons usefully are much more open ended in tactical than they are in strategic use."[13]

Lawrence Freedman has pointed to Liddell Hart as the intellectual father of limited war theory.[14] In 1946, as Brodie acknowledged,[15] Liddell Hart's call for limiting war, issued when the United States possessed a nuclear monopoly, foreshadowed the debate that was to emerge in the mid-1950s: "Warfare as we have known it in the last thirty years is not compatible with the atomic age. . . . Where both sides possess atomic power, 'total warfare' makes nonsense. . . . An unlimited war waged with atomic power would make worse than nonsense; it would be suicidal. . . . It is likely that any future warfare will be less unrestrained and more subject to mutually agreed rules."[16] The efforts of the US government to assess the role that nuclear weapons might play in limited war, as Halperin has noted, began in 1948.[17]

It was in the second half of the 1950s, however, that limited nuclear war thinking and the ensuing debate hit full force. Prompted, Brodie suggested, by the advent of the hydrogen bomb, a torrent of work, much of it by those who would later be recognized as charter members of the nuclear priesthood, appeared in prominent journals and books.[18] In 1957 alone, both Henry Kissinger's *Nuclear Weapons and Foreign Policy* and Robert Osgood's *Limited War: The Challenge to American Strategy* made their appearance.[19] The turn to limited nuclear war thinking raised fundamental questions about the role of nuclear weapons, deterrence, and stability that preoccupied several generations of national security and defense analysts and planners throughout the Cold War and the post–Cold War, but still nuclear, era. This debate revealed, and was itself an indication of, the extent to which thinking about the role of nuclear weapons, whether in international affairs generally or in US policy and strategy specifically, was far from settled.

The debate emerged both against the backdrop of two episodes of major-power total war during the first half of the twentieth century and in the immediate aftermath of a distasteful, inconclusive experience with limited war in Korea. The former was regarded as suicidal in the new atomic age; the latter both as an experience not to be repeated and as a precursor of what was to come. Much like the Korean War, the limited nuclear war debate was waged in the context of a long-haul, bipolar, Cold War struggle. Aided and abetted by NSC-68 (and the Korean War), a perhaps unavoidably militarized form of containment had emerged that remained in place for the duration. Despite the Korean War, Europe, which loomed large in the limited nuclear war debate, was the de facto central front of the Cold War. No longer did America shun permanent alliances; indeed, Secretary of State John Foster Dulles was busy replicating NATO in the Middle East and Southeast Asia and entering into bilateral alliance relationships with the likes of Japan, South Korea, and Taiwan. An America that had sought to remain detached and distant, to shun foreign entanglements and military obligations, was increasingly attached and present around the world; it had become quite decidedly entangled and obligated.

The emerging limited nuclear war debate was informed and shaped too by the loss of the US nuclear monopoly, which had been unexpectedly fleeting, as well as by continued US nuclear superiority, which was feared to be fleeting. Under the "New Look" that the Eisenhower administration brought to US defense policy, however, US nuclear superiority was to compensate for the presumed conventional superiority of the Soviet Union and its Eastern bloc (and Asiatic) clients. Secretary Dulles, in a landmark January 1954 speech at the Council on Foreign Relations (CFR), called for "placing more reliance on deterrent power and less dependence on local defensive power."[20] He placed a premium, however, on achieving "a maximum deterrent at a bearable cost" (what was soon referred to as "more bang for the buck"). "Local defenses," therefore, were to "be reinforced by the further deterrent of massive retaliatory power." Dulles famously declared that the United States would "depend primarily upon a great capacity to retaliate, instantly, by means and at places of our choosing." Even though Dulles soon thereafter, in an April 1954 *Foreign Affairs* piece, acknowledged that "massive atomic and thermonuclear retaliation is not the kind of power which could most usefully be evoked under all circumstances,"[21] his own words had, to many, conveyed precisely that message. The perception stuck. Massive retaliation's consequent perceived lack of credibility, particularly under conditions of nuclear plenty, fueled the turn to limited war and the role of nuclear weapons in limited war.

In a piece that appeared the same month as Dulles's CFR speech, Brodie trenchantly anticipated the soon to be voiced objections to massive retaliation:

> The one thing which we must obviously begin to face up to in both our military and political planning is the fact that strategic bombing, in which we seem to have pretensions to monopoly privilege, is probably already a two-way capability. . . . National objectives in war cannot be consonant with national suicide. But for the future there is no use talking about an unrestricted mutual exchange of nuclear weapons as involving anything other than national suicide for both sides.[22]

Brodie was quite explicit in a subsequent piece: "At a time when the opponent will be able to do to our cities and countryside whatever we might threaten to do to his, the whole concept of 'massive retaliation' . . . will have to be openly recognized as obsolete."[23]

The response to Dulles's massive retaliation concept was provided by Brodie in a short piece that appeared in November 1954 that encapsulated much of the emerging analytical zeitgeist. For Brodie, recognition of the absurdity of total war in the nuclear age was critical: "When we are talking about an unrestricted general war we are talking about a catastrophe to which there are no predictable limits." Therefore, "the threat of unlimited war" can be used "to deter only the most outrageous kind of aggression" since "the penalties for the use of total force have become too horrible." Brodie wrote, "our present-day diplomacy based on the deterrent value of our great atomic power is in danger of being strait-jacketed by fear of the very power we hold." He acknowledged that massive retaliation "indisputably remains the only answer to a direct massive assault." Limited aggression, however, required a more limited response: "If total war is to be averted, we must be ready to fight limited wars with limited objectives—if for no other reason than that limited objectives are always better than unlimited disaster."[24]

Brodie's fear that the US nuclear deterrent would be strait-jacketed was soon echoed by Kissinger, who feared that the disproportionate risks posed by massive retaliation would paralyze the United States.[25] For him, "limited war represents the only means for preventing the Soviet bloc, at an acceptable cost, from overrunning the peripheral areas of Eurasia."[26] Liddell Hart piled on: "Would any responsible government, when it came to the point, dare to *use* the H-bomb as an answer to local and limited aggression? . . . To the extent that the H-bomb reduces the likelihood of full-scale war, it *increases* the possibilities of limited war pursued by widespread local aggression: . . . the value of strategic bombing forces has largely disappeared—except as a last resort."[27] And Slessor, while approvingly acknowledging Dulles's attempt to clarify his thoughts about massive retaliation, asserted that there is "no alternative to meeting limited aggression with limited force."[28]

It was in this context that the limited nuclear war debate emerged full force. Responses to massive retaliation voiced by the likes of Brodie, Kissinger, Liddell Hart, and Slessor prompted a critical counterstrike. The extensive literature that was generated served to reveal the considerable analytical ferment that surrounded thinking about limited war and the role of nuclear weapons in limited war. Curiously, despite the eventual reconsiderations issued by some of limited nuclear war's leading lights, it is a body of work that some have sought to resurrect, if somewhat selectively and misguidedly, of late. How we might most profitably frame this work was suggested in an insightful passage by Colin Gray: "The most influential of the limited nuclear war studies was Henry Kissinger's *Nuclear Weapons and Foreign Policy* (1957), while the most perceptive was Robert Osgood's *Limited War: The Challenge to American Strategy* (1957)."[29] Osgood's book is not only worth revisiting, it provides a framework upon which to hang other work (including Kissinger's) on limited war, whether conventional or nuclear, for or against.

Osgood on Limited War and Limited Nuclear War

Given the context of two world wars, a Cold War, and, critically, the rise of nuclear weapons, for Osgood the logic of a turn to limited war was inescapable and unassailable:

> The principal justification of limited war lies in the fact that it maximizes the opportunities for the effective use of military force as a rational instrument of national policy. . . . Limited war would be equally desirable if nuclear weapons had never been invented. However, the existence of these and other weapons of mass destruction clearly adds great urgency to limitation. . . . The stupendous destruction accompanying all-out nuclear war makes it hard to conceive of such a war serving any rational purpose. . . . Only by carefully limiting the dimensions of warfare can nations minimize the risk of war becoming an intolerable disaster.[30]

For Osgood and others, interest in avoiding a nuclear world war loomed large.[31] Brodie had juxtaposed limited war with "unlimited disaster."[32] Kissinger too highlighted the unacceptability of total war: "Never before have the consequences of all-out war been so unambiguous, never before have the gains seemed so incommensurable with the sacrifices."[33]

Brodie emphasized that the contemporary effort to limit war represented something quite new. For him, limited war

> connotes a deliberate hobbling of a tremendous power . . . for the sake only of inducing the enemy to hobble himself to a like degree. No problem like this one has ever presented itself before. The problem of modern limited war is the problem of sanctions for keeping out of action . . . precisely those instruments which from a strictly military point of view are the most efficient.[34]

In the nuclear age, particularly under the emerging if not yet extant condition of nuclear plenty, the potentially catastrophic consequences of unlimited, total war dictated the development of limited war strategy and capabilities. "As long as the necessary international political conditions for the limitation of armaments do not exist," Osgood wrote, "the best assurance that armaments will not destroy civilization lies in the limitation of their use."[35]

The recognition that the nuclear revolution had upset long-standing, traditional calculations about the ends and means of war was central to the case for limited war. That case rested in no small part on a dual reality—the impossibility of total victory and the possibility of total defeat—and represented, as well, an attempt to escape the dilemma inherent in that reality. In the nuclear age, pursuit of total victory could well result not in victory but in annihilation. This new, dual reality, particularly when paired with what was regarded as war's inevitability, counseled, indeed dictated, an unfamiliar moderation and restraint in war. Objectives and means alike must be limited. Unconditional surrender could no longer be demanded of major power adversaries. In a nuclear world, total war, if not war generally, among major powers had become absurd.

The logic of the turn to limited war was also informed by the fear that an unmatched Soviet ability to exploit the limited use of force would leave the United States in an untenable position. Osgood highlighted this fear early on in his call to (limited) arms:

> If the United States is unwilling to take the risk of total war under certain circumstances, the Communists are likely to discover it. If the United States is incapable of effective limited resistance, the Communists will probably know it. . . . The Communist threat of limited aggression, coupled with the inability of the United States to contain limited aggression by limited means, will act as a powerful form of blackmail, which will tend to dissolve the political bonds of the free world and prepare the way for bloodless conquests.[36]

For Osgood and others, the Greek Civil War, Berlin Blockade, Korean War, and Indochina War (later known as the Vietnam War) indicated that the post–World War II years were a period of limited war.[37] Osgood argued that "the world is ripe for unlimited war. . . . We cannot say that unlimited war is inevitable or that we may not actually be on the threshold of a new era of limited war."[38] The United States could ill afford to be nuclear-bound in an era of limited war that, ironically, had been ushered in by the nuclear revolution. America, Osgood urged, had to be prepared "to fight the kinds of wars most likely to occur."[39] That required "a diversified military capacity, capable of countering Communist aggression under a variety of contingencies"[40]—the capability to fight and win not only at the upper (nuclear) end of the spectrum of conflict but along the entire spectrum and across all of its dimensions (conventional as well as nuclear). Kissinger advised that "as long as we are confronted by an opponent capable of initiating nuclear war against us, we require a continuous spectrum of nuclear and nonnuclear capabilities."[41] In his view, "a strategy of limited war . . . would use our retaliatory power as a means to permit us to fight local actions on our own terms and to shift to the other side the risk of initiating all-out war."[42] The call for limited war capabilities, including limited nuclear war capabilities (later "limited nuclear options"), thus developed in tandem with the call for enhancing US and NATO conventional capabilities.

The nuclear shadow loomed large over the limited war enterprise. An emerging, and inevitable, nuclear stalemate (aka "balance of terror"), Osgood noted, yielded "a calculus of risks that leads the nuclear powers from rationally and intentionally precipitating total war."[43] The realization, shared by the United States and the Soviet Union, that the unlimited use of nuclear weapons would result in "such terrible devastation as to outweigh any conceivable advantages"[44] led Osgood to an ineluctable, and seemingly prudent, conclusion: "If we act on the assumption that a continuing limitation of war is possible, then there is some hope that war will remain limited; but if we act on the assumption that total war is either impossible or inevitable, then we shall forfeit this hope."[45]

For Osgood and his fellow travelers, limited war, including limited nuclear war, was the solution to the dilemma of the nuclear age, a dilemma captured, variously, as "all or nothing," "holocaust or humiliation," "suicide or surrender," or "sudden destruction or slow defeat."

Defining, and Parsing, "Limited"

But just what is a "limited war"? In a nuclear age, what's so limited about limited war, particularly limited nuclear war? Limited war, obviously, was something less than unlimited war. In an age when unlimited war promised total destruction, did limited war promise merely less than total destruction? If unlimited war was to be equated with unlimited disaster, was limited war merely limited disaster? Given the exponential increase in firepower that nuclear weapons bring to bear, might limited nuclear war prove to be the equivalent of unlimited conventional war?

To his credit, Osgood did not shrink from the task of specifying the meaning of "limited." Beginning on the very first page of the book, he sought to help his readers understand what was meant by "limited war":

A limited war is one in which belligerents restrict the purposes for which they fight to concrete, well-defined objectives that do not demand the utmost military effort of which the belligerents are capable and that can be accommodated in a negotiated settlement. Generally speaking, a limited war actively involves only two (or very few) major belligerents in the fighting. The battle is confined to a local geographical area and directed against selected targets. . . . It demands of participants only a fractional commitment of their human and physical resources. It permits their economic, social, and political patterns of existence to continue without serious disruption.[46]

What is limited about limited war would seem readily apparent:

- Objectives sought (or not sought)
- Number of belligerents
- Geographical scope
- Temporal scope
- Means employed (or not employed)
- Target set
- Extent of disruption:
  —Economic
  —Social
  —Political

Having, seemingly, delimited the meaning of limited war, Osgood immediately muddied the waters:

Limited war, however, is not a uniform phenomenon. Such a war can be limited in different ways; it can be limited in some respects and not in others. . . . A war can be limited in geographical scope but virtually unlimited in the weapons employed and the targets involved within the area of combat. . . . A war can range over an extensive geographical area and involve a large number of belligerents and yet . . . remain limited in the scale of its battles. . . . A war may be limited from the perspective of one belligerent, yet virtually unlimited in the eyes of another.[47]

The perhaps inevitable definitional flailing about included an attempt to define limited war by what it was not—unlimited war:

An unlimited war is fought with every means available in order to achieve ends that are without objective limits or that are limited only by the capacity of the belligerents to destroy the enemy's ability to resist. In unlimited war the belligerents either fight for no well-defined objectives at all, other than the destruction of the enemy, or else fight for objectives which threaten values so important as to be beyond compromise and which, therefore, compel the belligerents to exert their utmost military capacity toward breaking the enemy's will and securing an unconditional surrender.[48]

Osgood reserved "total war" for "that distinct twentieth century species of unlimited war in which all the human and material resources of the belligerents are mobilized and employed against the total national life of the enemy."[49]

The distinction between unlimited and limited war, Osgood conceded, was "partly a matter of degree." He insisted, however, that in practice the distinction was clear (or at least "clear enough").[50] His examples of wars that featured "extreme means and extreme ends" included the annihilation of Carthage by Rome, Europe's sixteenth- and seventeenth-century religious wars, the French Revolutionary and Napoleonic Wars, and World War I and II.[51]

The distinctions drawn between unlimited and limited war would seem to lead to the conclusion that, at bottom, limited wars entail limited objectives and means. Osgood, however, asserted that there was one distinguishing characteristic of limited war: limited objectives.[52] As long as objectives remain suitably limited, therefore, limited (nuclear) wars could involve a small number of adversaries—or not. Such wars could be geographically and temporally constrained—or not. The means employed could be limited—or not. The number of nuclear weapons employed could be limited—or not. The nuclear weapons employed could be limited to nonstrategic weapons—or not. The number of strategic nuclear weapons employed could be limited—or not. The target set could be constrained—or not. The extent of social, economic, and political disruption could be limited—or not.

Kissinger too grappled with the difficulties inherent in defining limited war. As did Osgood, he rejected conceptualizations based on military distinctions:

> There exists no way to define a limited war in purely military terms. On the contrary, wars can be limited only by political decisions, by defining objectives which do not threaten the survival of the enemy. Thus an all-out war is a war to render the enemy defenseless. A limited war is one for a specific objective which by its very existence will establish a certain commensurability between the force employed and the goal to be attained.[53]

Aside from the not altogether mundane objection that what might be limited for one belligerent might be unlimited for another, highlighting limited objectives as the distinguishing characteristic of limited war raised the disturbing and seemingly illogical possibility that unlimited means could legitimately be employed for limited objectives. That feature of the definitions advanced by Osgood and Kissinger opened the door to the employment of nuclear weapons in limited war—and to the no less dangerous notion of limited nuclear war.

Limited War Strategy

Work on limited war strategy built upon the conceptual foundation laid by Osgood and his fellow travelers. That work was highly contextual. The balance of terror, whether delicate or not, between two scorpions in a bottle focused minds powerfully.[54]

Containment was thought to require both total war and limited war capabilities. The two were viewed as symbiotic. As Osgood put it, "The capacity to wage one kind of war is insufficient without the capacity to wage the other."[55] He pointed to three central objectives served by total war capabilities: deterrence of "major aggression" against "areas essential to our security"; deterrence of actions "incompatible with limited war"; and the ability to "fight a large-scale war."[56] The ability to deter, fight, and win total wars required the ability to deter, fight, and win limited wars. As Osgood put it: "The chief function of our capacity for total war will be to keep war limited and to strengthen our diplomacy against the blackmail that a strong and unscrupulous power can wield. However, the fulfillment of this function will not be sufficient for the purposes of containment unless it is accompanied by a ready capacity to resist lesser aggressions by limited war."[57] Limited wars were not to be considered lesser-included cases. The ability to deter, fight, and win in the least likely contingencies—total wars—did not necessarily ensure the ability to deter, fight, and win in the most likely contingencies—limited wars. Success in limited conflicts required capabilities tailored to those conflicts; those capabilities were not merely a subset of the capabilities needed for total war. Required was not only strategic nuclear offensive and defensive parity but local conventional ground force superiority. A local superiority that provided the ability "to occupy and control territory," rather than simply obliterate it, was deemed to provide "a substantial advantage" in the event of total war.[58] Kissinger pointed to "the importance of creating distinct forces for both all-out and limited wars."[59] Not only, therefore, were the capabilities required for the successful prosecution of the most likely but lower-risk contingencies known as limited war not included among those required for the less likely but higher-risk contingencies known as total war, they were regarded as critical to the achievement of success in the later as well as in the former. "Preparation for limited war," Osgood argued, "is as vital to American security as preparation for total war."[60]

Limited war required that ends and means be balanced: limited ends would be matched by limited means. Challenges to the political status quo were to be foresworn: "The specific political objectives for which the United States must be prepared to fight limited wars will not entail radical changes in the status quo."[61] Osgood's emphasis on the need to limit political objectives was echoed by William Kaufmann: "Limited war cannot be a means of bringing about a radical alteration in the distribution of power; that would be a contradiction in terms."[62]

Limits on the scale of war—area, weapons, targets, manpower, number of belligerents, duration, intensity—were to be observed. The key operational limits were those on geographical scope, weapons, and targets. Wars were to be kept local. To the extent possible, multiple, simultaneous local wars were to be avoided. Flexible weapons systems, strategies, and tactics "capable of supporting limited objectives under a wide variety of conditions" were considered ideal.[63] Kissinger called for systems that were "flexible and discriminating" and units that were highly mobile and possessed substantial firepower.[64] Also desirable were capabilities that facilitated a clear distinction between strategic and tactical means and targets, such as ground forces able to respond to aggression locally.

For Osgood, the greatest challenge was to adapt nuclear weapons to limited war requirements. Tactical nuclear weapons, he argued, "carry greater promise than any other weapon of enabling us to fight limited wars on an equal basis against numerically superior forces."[65] Further, "tactical nuclear weapons, especially the low-yield battlefield weapons, can play a decisive role in supporting containment by giving the United States an adequate capacity for limited war at a tolerable cost."[66] Kissinger declared that "limited nuclear war represents our most effective strategy against nuclear powers or against a major power which is capable of substituting manpower for technology."[67] "The introduction of nuclear weapons on the battlefield," Kissinger promised, "will shake the very basis of Soviet tactical doctrine."[68] Edward Teller cited claims that "small nuclear weapons will neutralize the Russian advantages of central location, massive conventional manpower, and surprise. The great power and mobility of the new weapons can also be used to regain an equal chance in a limited conflict."[69]

Osgood cautioned against equating nuclear weapons and total war and conventional weapons and limited war; nuclear weapons are not necessarily incompatible with limited war. After all, the difference between multimegaton nuclear blockbusters and low-yield kiloton weapons is greater than that between conventional blockbusters and artillery shells.[70] Indeed, "the special technological requirements of limited war are particularly marked in the realm of mobile, airborne troops capable of employing low-yield nuclear weapons and the most advanced conventional weapons with precision against military targets."[71] Nuclear weapons' force multiplier effects were emphasized, but the limits of their military efficacy were recognized. They were not to be regarded as a panacea for limited war's challenges. While tactical nuclear weapons would "provide a given number of troops with more firepower than conventional weapons,"[72] they were not expected to reduce troop requirements. Nor were they expected to reduce defense expenditures.[73] Nuclear weapons, whether tactical or otherwise, had no utility in irregular warfare. Nuclear use, even if merely of tactical nuclear weapons, that resulted in a response in kind would not necessarily be advantageous. Hiroshima- and Nagasaki-sized weapons would have to be used selectively if a conflict were to remain limited.

If a conflict were to remain limited, horizontal and vertical nuclear escalation alike posed risks, as described by Kerry Kartchner and Michael Gerson in Chapter 7 of this volume. Osgood explicitly pointed to the need to avoid both sets of risks:

> The possibility of using tactical nuclear weapons in a manner proportionate to limited objectives would seem to depend largely upon the feasibility of two methods of limitation: (a) confining the use of these weapons to a limited geographical area and (b) using them with precision against military targets without destroying strategic targets and the large centers of population.[74]

Paul Nitze too underlined the need to observe geographical and targeting constraints:

> It is to the West's interest, if atomic war becomes unavoidable, that atomic weapons of the smallest sizes be used in the smallest area, and against the most restricted target systems possible, while still achieving for the West the

particular objective which is at issue. . . . It is to the interest of the West that the means employed in warfare and the area of engagement be restricted to the minimum level which still permits us to achieve our objectives.[75]

Neither horizontal nor vertical escalation was acceptable. Either could blow the lid off of a limited conflict.

In his discussion of the meaning of limited war, Bernard Brodie highlighted the need for deliberate restraint: "One basic restraint always has to be present if the term 'limited war' is to have any meaning at all: strategic bombing of cities with nuclear weapons must be avoided."[76] For Brodie, limited war required that any strategic bombing be avoided.[77]

Osgood emphasized both the necessity and feasibility of distinguishing between tactical and strategic uses of nuclear weapons. The necessity of the distinction must be conceded; a limited war would not long remain so in the face of the strategic employment of nuclear weaponry. Osgood maintained that,

> theoretically, the distinction is feasible on three major conditions: (a) if tactical targets can be distinguished logically and physically from strategic targets in a manner that both belligerents recognize as legitimate; (b) if nuclear weapons can be used with sufficient precision to destroy specific tactical targets and those targets only; (c) if the belligerents are willing to tolerate strikes upon occasional strategic targets as accidental or incidental to attacks upon legitimate tactical targets.[78]

While theoretically feasible, in reality Osgood's conditions seem rather fragile. The distinction between tactical and strategic, whether regarded as legitimate or not, could not but be highly context dependent. Osgood argued that "there is a good prospect that the condition of precision could be met by the smaller bombs and missiles and by further development of low-yield artillery weapons of from two to ten kilotons' power, designed for use against enemy troops on the battlefield."[79] However, any use of nuclear weapons could well have been, and now likely would be, regarded as strategic. And how in the fog of war could an adversary be confident that the occasional strike on a strategic target was accidental or incidental rather than intended?

The Challenge of Achieving Mutual Restraint

Osgood was not unaware of the fragility of the conditions upon which the maintenance of a viable distinction between tactical and strategic rested. But the manner in which he sought to shore up those conditions should not have inspired confidence. Essentially, a belligerent was expected to demonstrate limited intentions by limiting the destruction wrought in the belief that other belligerents would reciprocate. In his own words: "The limitation of war may depend upon the ability of each belligerent to establish in the mind of the others a presumption that it is conducting the war according to definite and practicable restraints that are contingent upon the adversary doing likewise."[80] While acknowledging that "the distinction between tactical and strategic nuclear weapons may be nebulous in military terms," Kissinger insisted that "every state has a powerful incentive to make some distinction, however tenuous its logic." For him, the fear of the consequences of an all-out nuclear war "should be utilized to guarantee the 'limits' of war and diplomacy."[81] For both Osgood and Kissinger, a declaratory policy of "graduated deterrence" built on the distinction between strategic and tactical was expected to enhance the likelihood that mutual restraint would be maintained.[82]

Underlying the willingness, even seeming eagerness, to integrate nuclear weapons into the strategy for fighting a limited war is the assumption that nuclear and conventional weapons are not significantly different. That assumption, of course, flew in the face of a deeply engrained impression that the nuclear revolution had introduced a capability that was indeed profoundly different; the hydrogen bomb only served to strengthen that impression. Yet, Osgood asserted, "there are no rational grounds for regarding low-yield atomic battlefield weapons as any more horrible and inhumane than napalm or, for that matter, TNT."[83] Henry Kissinger, declared that "it is far from certain that a conventional war . . . would produce less devastation than a nuclear war, and in certain circumstances it may produce more."[84] Kissinger proclaimed as well that "we cannot afford even the implication that nuclear weapons are in a special category, apart from modern weapons in general, for this undermines the psychological basis of the most effective United States strategy."[85] Osgood further argued that "in considering the role of tactical nuclear weapons in a strategy of limited war, we must reckon with the fact that before long the Communists will also acquire an arsenal of these weapons. Their achievement will probably mark the time when nuclear weapons will be considered conventional."[86] We see here, then, a relatively early instance of what has been referred to as the conventionalization, or mainstreaming, of nuclear weapons. In the future, according to Osgood, nuclear as well as conventional weapons would be used by nuclear-capable major powers.[87] Wars in which only conventional weapons would be employed were increasingly unlikely. For some, that recognition provided a great incentive to avoid wars between, or among, nuclear-capable powers. For Kissinger and Osgood, it meant that the use of not only conventional weapons but nuclear weapons must be incorporated into operational planning.[88]

As we have seen, Osgood recognized that the use of Hiroshima- and Nagasaki-sized weapons must remain quite selective if a conflict were to remain limited. He was relatively sanguine, however, about the prospects for keeping nuclear escalation in check. While acknowledging the risk of miscalculation, escalation from tactical to strategic use, he argued, should not be regarded as inevitable: "It would be a great mistake to assume that the use of tactical nuclear weapons must necessarily lead to the use of strategic city-busters and total war; it might actually provide the best chance of keeping warfare limited when a power would otherwise have to choose between defeat and strategic retaliation."[89] Air Marshal Sir John Slessor assured a worried world that the risk of nuclear escalation was "diminishing every day."[90] Kissinger advised that we not "be defeatist about the possibility of limiting nuclear war."[91] Indeed, Kissinger asserted, "there is no inevitable progression from limited nuclear war to all-out thermonuclear war."[92] Teller shared his "belief that limited nuclear war can very well stay limited. In fact, during the course of such a war danger of an all-out war will be at a minimum."[93] The postulated lack of inevitability depended on the continued ability, in the midst of hostilities that had gone nuclear, of the parties concerned to differentiate between tactical and strategic targets—between battlefield targets and population and industrial centers, for instance—and intentions.

Other analysts were far less sanguine.[94] Bernard Brodie, for instance, noted that "the problems involved in the tactical use of atomic weapons seem to have peculiarly forbidding difficulties. . . . We tend in the end to get the same result in considering unrestricted tactical war in the future that we get in unrestricted strategic war. In each case the conclusion tends toward the nihilistic."[95] In a subsequent piece Brodie noted that "the use of any kind of nuclear weapon greatly increases the difficulties in the way of maintaining limitations. . . . It is much easier . . . to distinguish between use and non-use of nuclear weapons than between the use of, say, a 10-kiloton atomic weapon and a weapon two or three times as large."[96] James King too cast doubt on the escalation optimism voiced by Osgood:

> Once nuclear power is committed, it probably cannot be effectively stalemated short of total war. . . . This . . . is the major shortcoming of nuclear limits—that they are neither identifiable nor stable. In actual nuclear conflict . . . military incentive lies with the side that is the more willing to run the risk of total nuclear war, while the tenuousness of the limits makes the risk of total war very nearly incalculable.[97]

Liddell Hart objected that "once any kind of nuclear weapon is actually used, it could all too easily spread by rapid degrees, and lead to all-out war."[98] Kaufmann proffered the rather practical objection that "since the Russians are now approaching parity with us in nuclear stockpiles . . . and in delivery systems, it would seen desirable to consider foregoing the use of atomic weapons for tactical purposes, so long as one of the objects of policy is to keep a conflict limited."[99] George Ball's assessment of the controllability of escalation, while written in the context of decisions about escalation in that limited war known as the Vietnam War, is very much on point here:

> It is the nature of escalation that each move passes the option to the other side, while at the same time the party which seems to be losing will be tempted to keep raising the ante. To the extent that the response to a move can be controlled, that move is probably ineffective. If the move is effective, it may not be possible to control—or accurately anticipate—the response. . . . Once on the tiger's back we cannot be sure of picking the place to dismount.[100]

Fortunately, or perhaps unfortunately, appeals to "evidence" at the time (or today) are to little avail.[101] There is no evidence. Atomic bombs have been employed but twice. In both instances they were employed by a fledgling nuclear power with no stockpile to speak of against a non-nuclear state. Neither party was capable of nuclear escalation. Michael Howard put it well in his defense of Brodie's emphasis on deterrence against Colin Gray's call for a theory of nuclear victory, an unapologetic call for nuclear warfighting, when he wrote that "this is all guesswork. But what is absolutely clear is that to engage in nuclear war, to attempt to use strategic nuclear weapons for 'warfighting' would be to enter the realm of the unknown and the unknowable, and what little we do know about it is appalling."[102]

Assessment

In his classic *Strategy in the Missile Age*, which first appeared in 1959, Bernard Brodie wrote: "The conclusion that nuclear weapons *must* be used in limited wars has been reached by too many people, too quickly, on the basis of too little analysis of the problem."[103] Morton Halperin's perceptive review of the limited nuclear war literature concluded on a trenchant note: "The instances in which the United States should introduce nuclear weapons in a limited war are likely to be rare, and the burden of proof should rest squarely on those advocating such first use."[104] There is little reason today to question the conclusions reached by Brodie and Halperin.

Indeed, two of the foremost champions of limited nuclear war soon came to recognize the error of their ways. In the face of penetrating, even damning, assessments such as those advanced by Brodie and Halperin, Kissinger, uncharacteristically, backpedaled. Recognizing (finally?) the obvious, Kissinger conceded, first, to "doubts as to whether we would know how to limit nuclear war": "While it is feasible to design a theoretical model for limited nuclear war, the fact remains that fifteen years after the beginning of the nuclear age no such model has ever achieved general agreement. It would be next to impossible to obtain from our military establishment a coherent description of what is understood by 'limited nuclear war.'"[105] Noting that the lack of experience with tactical nuclear weapons posed the not inconsiderable possibility of miscalculation—"both sides would be operating in the dark"—Kissinger acknowledged as well that "a nuclear war will be more difficult to limit than a conventional one."[106] Also acknowledged was a point that had been emphasized by Brodie: "The dividing line between conventional and nuclear weapons is more familiar and therefore easier to maintain . . . than any distinction within the spectrum of nuclear weapons."[107] Kissinger conceded that Soviet nuclear plenty had undermined his previous calculus of the cost and benefits of limited nuclear use. Rightly or wrongly, nuclear superiority had heightened confidence in the feasibility of limited nuclear war; parity not inconsiderably eroded that confidence. Third, it was conceded that arms control had yielded a new framework: "Nuclear weapons have been placed in a separate category and stigmatized as weapons of mass destruction without any distinction as to type or device."[108] Consequently, Kissinger now advised, "the conventional capability of the free world should be of such a size that a nuclear defense becomes the *last* and not the *only* recourse."[109]

Osgood too backed off his previous insistence on the importance of adapting nuclear weapons to limited war requirements. In a reappraisal that appeared in 1969, Osgood stood his ground on limited war but admitted that ideas about limited nuclear war had "died from indifference and incredulity."[110] Subsequently, in both of two pieces that appeared in 1979, Osgood wrote of waning confidence in tactical nuclear warfare and raised questions about the utility of limited nuclear, or strategic, war options.[111] The implications of Soviet nuclear plenty for the credibility of US limited nuclear war options had become quite evident: "The utility of limited strategic war as a means of controlling the process of escalation following the resort to nuclear weapons is undermined . . . by the growing Soviet counterforce capability."[112]

The literature on limited war and limited nuclear war is riddled with ambiguity and imprecision. Even the term "limited war" is ambiguous. It was defined as much in terms of what it is not—unlimited, or total, war—as what it is. Where is the line between limited war and unlimited war, between limited nuclear war and unlimited nuclear war?

The linkage of limited ends and means is helpful, indeed meaningful, but has its limits. As John Garnett has suggested, linking ends and means "raises questions about the relationship between the two. Do we fight with limited means because we have limited objectives, or do we settle for limited objectives because we are determined to fight with only limited means?"[113] In the nuclear age, is it not the potentially catastrophic consequences of employing particular means that has led to the embrace of limited objectives? As Brodie correctly noted, "The restraint necessary to keep wars limited is primarily a restraint on ends, not means. . . . We want to keep war limited simply because total war as it would be fought today and in the future against a well-armed enemy is simply too unthinkable, too irrational to be borne."[114] Contrary to the assertions of Kissinger and Osgood, it is the necessity of employing limited means that dictates the pursuit of limited ends, not limited objectives that dictate the employment of limited means.[115]

In the aftermath of the nuclear revolution, particularly following the advent of the hydrogen bomb, it would not have been unreasonable to equate limited war with conventional war. Centuries of experience, however, with non-nuclear warfare, including the world wars of the first half of the twentieth century, had demonstrated mankind's ability to wage total war with what during the nuclear era were regarded as the relatively limited capabilities of conventional weapons. But champions of the limited nuclear war enterprise failed to acknowledge that Hiroshima and Nagasaki had dramatically demonstrated that even the limited use of nuclear weapons could be the equivalent of unlimited conventional war.

Nor was it clear, as Freedman has pointed out, how tactical nuclear weapons were to be employed.[116] Were they merely the nuclear equivalent of conventional weapons, to be used offensively or defensively? Or were they to provide battlefield nuclear deterrence, whether based on punishment or denial?

The distinction between "tactical" and "strategic," which was central to the limited nuclear war enterprise, was notoriously imprecise. Champions of the limited nuclear war enterprise failed to specify the location of the dividing line between the two. Battlefield use of tactical nuclear weapons could perhaps qualify as purely tactical. But limited nuclear war need not be confined to a battlefield. Limited nuclear strikes against other than clearly battlefield targets, such as those located in the rear, on the territory of an ally, or, particularly, in the homeland of an opponent, could well be regarded as strategic, even if restricted to warfighting, or counterforce, targets.

In addition, the employment of tactical nuclear weapons could be regarded as the onset of a strategic attack. And "collateral damage" resulting from the use of tactical weapons could be considered strategic. Similarly, the equation of tactical with counterforce and strategic with countervalue was off target. Counterforce strikes need not be limited to the battlefield and limited counterforce strikes (on an ICBM field, for instance) outside of the battlespace could reasonably be regarded as strategic. Any counterforce strike, no matter how limited, on targets within the homeland of an opponent would be regarded as strategic.

Conclusion

Much, of course, has changed since the development of limited war and limited nuclear war thinking in the second half of the 1950s. Yet the fundamental points of contention surrounding limited nuclear war remain with us today:

- What are the implications of limited nuclear war strategies and capabilities for deterrence? Do they enhance or erode deterrence?
- Is the shift from deterrence based on punishment to deterrence based on denial that is inherent in limited nuclear war strategies and capabilities to be embraced or resisted?

- Do limited nuclear war strategies and capabilities raise or lower the nuclear threshold?
- Can a nuclear war be kept limited?

If there is to be war, today, as in the past, the most effective way to limit it in what remains a nuclear age is to refrain from the use of nuclear weapons. The distinction between nuclear use and nonuse remains "more familiar and . . . easier to maintain"[117] than any distinction that may be employed to differentiate between, for instance, "tactical" and "strategic" nuclear weapons, or between their limited and unlimited use. The firewall between conventional and nuclear is distinct; if war is to be limited, it must not be breached. Since 1945, the international community has refrained from crossing the nuclear threshold. The use of nuclear weapons has come to be regarded as taboo; their nonuse is not only the norm but a norm. Nuclear abolition remains a distant goal; the formal institutionalization of the nonuse of nuclear weapons need not be.

Notes

1. The classic works here include Glenn H. Snyder, *Deterrence and Defense: Toward a Theory of National Security* (Princeton, NJ: Princeton University Press, 1961); Robert Jervis, *The Meaning of the Nuclear Revolution: Statecraft and the Prospect of Armageddon* (Ithaca, NY: Cornell University Press, 1989); and Robert Jervis, "Why Nuclear Superiority Doesn't Matter," *Political Science Quarterly*, Vol. 94, No. 4 (Winter 1979–80), pp. 617–633.

2. An insightful overview is provided by Thomas G. Mahnken, *Technology and the American Way of War since 1945* (New York: Columbia University Press, 2008).

3. See Henry S. Rowen, "The Evolution of Strategic Nuclear Doctrine," in Laurence Martin, ed., *Strategic Thought in the Nuclear Age* (Baltimore: Johns Hopkins University Press, 1979), pp. 131–156; Aaron L. Friedberg, "The Evolution of U.S. Strategic 'Doctrine'—1945–1981," in Samuel P. Huntington, ed., *The Strategic Imperative: New Policies for American Security* (Cambridge, MA: Ballinger, 1982), pp. 53–99; and Tami Davis Biddle, "Shield and Sword: U.S. Strategic Forces and Doctrine since 1945," in Andrew J. Bacevich, ed., *The Long War: A New History of U.S. National Security Strategy since World War II* (New York: Columbia University Press, 2007), pp. 137–206.

4. Would everyone really have come to their senses in the heat of a nuclear exchange, even a "limited" nuclear exchange?

5. National Conference of Catholic Bishops, *The Challenge of Peace: God's Promise and Our Response*, a Pastoral Letter on War and Peace (Washington, DC: National Catholic Conference, 3 May 1983); Joseph S. Nye, *Nuclear Ethics* (New York: Free Press,

1986); and Bruce M. Russett, "Ethical Dilemmas of Nuclear Deterrence," *International Security*, Vol. 8, No. 4 (Spring 1984), pp. 36–54.

6. See, for instance, Paul I. Bernstein, John P. Caves, Jr., and John F. Reichart, *The Future Nuclear Landscape*, Center for the Study of Weapons of Mass Destruction, Occasional Paper No. 5 (Washington, DC: National Defense University Press, April 2007), available at www.ndu.edu/WMDCenter/docUploaded/CSWMD_OP5.pdf; National Intelligence Council, *Global Trends 2025: A Transformed World* (Washington, DC: National Intelligence Council, November 2008), available at www.dni.gov/nic/PDF_2025/2025_Global_Trends_Final_Report.pdf; George H. Quester, *Nuclear First Strike: Consequences of a Broken Taboo* (Baltimore: Johns Hopkins University Press, 2006).

7. Robert D. Kaplan, "Living With a Nuclear Iran," *Atlantic*, Vol. 306, No. 2 (September 2010), p. 73.

8. In addition to Kaplan, "Living With a Nuclear Iran," see Keir A. Leiber and Daryl G. Press, "The Nukes We Need: Preserving the American Deterrent," *Foreign Affairs*, Vol. 88, No. 6 (November/December 2009), pp. 39–51; David Ochmanek and Lowell H. Schwartz, *The Challenge of Nuclear-Armed Regional Adversaries* (Santa Monica, CA: RAND, 2008); David Isenberg, "The Return of Limited Nuclear War?" Counter-Punch.org, 2 May 2008, available at www.counterpunch.org/isenberg05022008.html; accessed 12 August 2010.

9. Kaplan's "Living With a Nuclear Iran" is a fawning return to Henry A. Kissinger's *Nuclear Weapons and Foreign Policy* (New York: Harper & Brothers, for the Council on Foreign Relations, 1957).

10. Sir John Slessor, "The Great Deterrent and Its Limitations," *Bulletin of the Atomic Scientists*, Vol. 12, No. 5 (May 1956), p. 141.

11. Henry A. Kissinger, "Force and Diplomacy in the Nuclear Age," *Foreign Affairs*, Vol. 32, No. 3 (April 1956), p. 360.

12. Bernard Brodie, "More About Limited War," *World Politics*, Vol. 10, No. 1 (October 1957), p. 116.

13. Bernard Brodie, "Nuclear Weapons: Strategic or Tactical," *Foreign Affairs*, Vol. 32, No. 2 (January 1954), p. 226. On the evolution of Brodie's views about limited nuclear war and other things nuclear, see Barry H. Steiner, *Bernard Brodie and the Foundations of American Nuclear Strategy* (Lawrence: University Press of Kansas, 1991).

14. Lawrence Freedman, *The Evolution of Nuclear Strategy*, 3rd ed. (New York: Palgrave Macmillan, 2003), p. 93

15. Brodie, "More About Limited War," p. 114.

16. B. H. Liddell Hart, *The Revolution in Warfare* (New Haven, CT: Yale University Press, 1947), pp. 98–99.

17. Morton H. Halperin, "Nuclear Weapons and Limited War," *Journal of Conflict Resolution*, Vol. 5, No. 2 (June 1961), p. 147. Unfortunately, these kinds of pieces no longer appear in the *Journal of Conflict Resolution*. See also Morton H. Halperin, *Limited War in the Nuclear Age* (New York: John Wiley & Sons, 1963).

18. Brodie, "More About Limited War," p. 113.

19. Kissinger, *Nuclear Weapons and Foreign Policy*; and Robert E. Osgood, *Limited War: The Challenge to American Strategy* (Chicago: University of Chicago Press, 1957).

20. Dulles' CFR speech is available at www.freerepublic.com/focus/f-news/1556858/posts.

21. John Foster Dulles, "Policy for Security and Peace," *Foreign Affairs*, Vol. 32, No. 3 (April 1954), p. 356.

22. Brodie, "Nuclear Weapons: Strategic or Tactical?," pp. 226–227.

23. Bernard Brodie, "Strategy Hits a Dead End," *Harper's Magazine*, October 1955, p. 37.

24. Bernard Brodie, "Unlimited Weapons and Unlimited War," *Reporter*, 18 November 1954, pp. 16, 18, and 19.

25. Kissinger, "Force and Diplomacy in the Nuclear Age," p. 350.

26. Kissinger, *Nuclear Weapons and Foreign Policy*, p. 147.

27. As quoted in Freedman, *The Evolution of Nuclear Strategy*, p. 95.

28. Slessor, "The Great Deterrent and Its Limitations," p. 145.

29. Colin Gray, "What RAND Hath Wrought," *Foreign Policy*, No. 4 (Autumn 1971), p. 114. For contemporary reviews of the Kissinger and Osgood books, see Harold Karan Jacobson, "Scholarship and Security Policy: A Review of Recent Literature," *Journal of Conflict Resolution*, Vol. 3, No. 4 (December 1959), pp. 394–400; William W. Kaufmann, "The Crisis in Military Affairs," *World Politics*, Vol. 10, No. 4 (July 1958), pp. 579–603; James E. King, Jr., "Nuclear Weapons and Foreign Policy I—Limited Defense," *New Republic*, 1 July 1957, pp. 18–21; and James E. King, Jr., "Nuclear Weapons and Foreign Policy II—Limited Annihilation?" *New Republic*, 15 July 1957, pp. 16–18.

30. Osgood, *Limited War: The Challenge to American Strategy*, p. 26.

31. Robert E. Osgood, "The Reappraisal of Limited War," in *Problems of Modern Strategy, Part I*, Adelphi Paper No. 54 (London: International Institute for Strategic Studies, 1969), p. 42.

32. Brodie, "Unlimited Weapons and Unlimited War," p. 19.

33. Kissinger, "Force and Diplomacy in the Nuclear Age," p. 359.

34. Brodie, "More About Limited War," pp. 114–115.

35. Osgood, *Limited War: The Challenge to American Strategy*, p. 27.

36. Ibid., pp. 6–7.

37. Robert E. Osgood, "The Post-War Strategy of Limited War: Before, During and After Vietnam," in Laurence Martin, ed., *Strategic Thought in the Nuclear Age* (Baltimore: Johns Hopkins University Press, 1979), pp. 93–130, returned to this theme. Seymour J. Deitchman, *Limited War and American Defense Policy* (Cambridge, MA: MIT Press, 1964), is useful on this point.

38. Osgood, *Limited War: The Challenge to American Strategy*, p. 123.

39. Ibid.

40. Ibid., p. 7.

41. Kissinger, *Nuclear Weapons and Foreign Policy*, p. 188. Kissinger called for "the development of a wide spectrum of capabilities" (p. 146).

42. Ibid., p. 149.

43. Osgood, *Limited War: The Challenge to American Strategy*, p. 126.

44. Ibid., p. 127.

45. Ibid., p. 140.

46. Ibid., pp. 1–2. A useful review of the meaning of limited war is provided by John Garnett, "Limited War," in John Baylis, Ken Booth, John Garnett, and Phil Williams, *Contemporary Strategy, Vol. 1, Theories and Concepts*, 2nd ed. (New York: Holmes and Meier, 1987), pp. 187–208. For extended discussions of the meaning of limited war that are coupled with a series of case studies, see Robert McClintok, *The Meaning of Limited War* (Boston: Houghton Mifflin, 1967), and Christopher M. Bacek, *The Logic of Force: The Dilemma of Limited War in American Foreign Policy* (New York: Columbia University Press, 1994).

47. Osgood, *Limited War: The Challenge to American Strategy*, p. 2. Oskar Morgenstern too acknowledged the imprecision of the notion of limited war: "We cannot state precisely the point in the whole gamut of different forms of violence where a war stops being limited and begins to be unrestricted." Oskar Morgenstern, *The Question of National Defense* (New York: Random House, 1959), p. 137.

48. Osgood, *Limited War: The Challenge to American Strategy*, pp. 2–3.

49. Ibid., p. 3.

50. Ibid.

51. Ibid.

52. "There is one characteristic of overriding importance in distinguishing among wars: the nature of the objectives of which the belligerents fight. The decisive limitation upon war is the limitation of the objectives of war." Osgood, *Limited War: The Challenge to American Strategy*, p. 4. See also Morgenstern, *The Question of National Defense*, p. 139.

53. Kissinger, "Force and Diplomacy in the Nuclear Age," p. 357. His extended discussion of limited war is provided in Kissinger, *Nuclear Weapons and Foreign Policy*, pp. 132–173.

54. Even mediocre minds.

55. Osgood, *Limited War: The Challenge to American Strategy*, p. 235.

56. Ibid.

57. Ibid., p. 237.

58. Ibid., p. 236.

59. Kissinger, *Nuclear Weapons and Foreign Policy*, p. 160. For his discussion of the required air, ground, and naval capabilities, see ibid., pp. 155–167.

60. Osgood, *Limited War: The Challenge to American Strategy*, p. 237.

61. Ibid., p. 238.

62. William W. Kaufmann, "Limited Warfare," in William W. Kaufmann, ed., *Military Policy and National Security* (Princeton, NJ: Princeton University Press, 1956), p. 127.

63. Osgood, *Limited War: The Challenge to American Strategy*, p. 249.

64. Kissinger, *Nuclear Weapons and Foreign Policy*, pp. 156 and 157. On these points, see also Morgenstern, *The Question of National Defense*, pp. 145–148.

65. Osgood, *Limited War: The Challenge to American Strategy*, p. 251.

66. Ibid., p. 258.

67. Kissinger, *Nuclear Weapons and Foreign Policy*, p. 199. Limited nuclear war here is akin to the limited strategic war discussed in Klaus Knorr and Thornton Read, eds., *Limited Strategic War* (New York: Frederick A. Praeger, 1962). Ian Clark, *Limited Nuclear War: Political Theory and War Conventions* (Oxford: Martin Robertson, 1982), examines limited nuclear war in the context of the historical development of thought on limited war.

68. Kissinger, "Force and Diplomacy in the Nuclear Age," p. 360. For a contemporary discussion of the role of limited war strategy in the NATO context, see Malcolm W. Hoag, "The Place of Limited War in NATO Strategy," in Klaus Knorr, ed., *NATO and American Security* (Princeton, NJ: Princeton University Press, 1959), pp. 98–126.

69. Edward Teller, "The Feasibility of Arms Control and the Principle of Openness," in Donald G. Brennan, ed., *Arms Control, Disarmament, and National Security* (New York: George Braziller, 1961, for the American Academy of Arts and Sciences), p. 133.

70. Osgood, *Limited War: The Challenge to American Strategy*, pp. 248–249.

71. Ibid., p. 249.

72. Ibid., p. 251.

73. John Slessor, *The Great Deterrent* (New York: Frederick A. Praeger, 1957), p. 266.

74. Osgood, *Limited War: The Challenge to American Strategy*, p. 253.

75. Paul H. Nitze, "Atoms, Strategy and Policy," *Foreign Affairs*, Vol. 34, No. 2 (January 1956), pp. 187–188.

76. Bernard Brodie, *Strategy in the Missile Age* (Princeton, NJ: Princeton University Press, 1959, 1965), p. 310.

77. Ibid., p. 314.

78. Osgood, *Limited War: The Challenge to American Strategy*, p. 254.

79. Ibid.

80. Ibid., p. 255.

81. Kissinger, "Force and Diplomacy in the Nuclear Age," p. 359.

82. Osgood, *Limited War: The Challenge to American Strategy*, pp. 256 and 258–259; Kissinger, "Force and Diplomacy in the Nuclear Age," p. 359. Nitze, "Atoms, Strategy and Policy," pp. 187–198, also embraced graduated deterrence. For the case for and discussions of graduated deterrence, see Anthony W. Buzzard, "Massive Retaliation and Graduated Deterrence," *World Politics*, Vol. 8, No. 2 (January 1956), pp. 228–237; Anthony W. Buzzard, John Slessor, and Richard Lowenthal, "The H-Bomb: Massive Retaliation or Graduated Deterrence?," *International Affairs*, Vol. 32, No. 2 (April 1956), pp. 146–165; and P. M. S. Blackett, *Atomic Weapons and East-West Relations* (Cambridge: Cambridge University Press, 1956).

83. Osgood, *Limited War: The Challenge to American Strategy*, p. 257.

84. Kissinger, *Nuclear Weapons and Foreign Policy*, p. 188.

85. Kissinger, "Force and Diplomacy in the Nuclear Age," p. 362.

86. Osgood, *Limited War: The Challenge to American Strategy*, p. 257.

87. Kissinger, "Force and Diplomacy in the Nuclear Age," p. 357, agreed that "any war is likely to be a nuclear war."

88. "We must count upon these [nuclear] weapons becoming an integral part of our military policies and our national strategy." Osgood, *Limited War: The Challenge to American Strategy*, p. 258.

89. Ibid., p. 136.

90. Slessor, "The Great Deterrent and Its Limitations," p. 146.

91. Kissinger, *Nuclear Weapons and Foreign Policy*, p. 188.

92. Ibid., p. 192. Morgenstern, an escalation optimist of the first order, sneeringly asserted that "the idea that any atomic weapon, any atomic explosion, is a disaster of a magnitude that the world cannot stand, that is spells the beginning of the end of the earth, that it poisons the atmosphere for future generations, is, of course, unmitigated nonsense." Morgenstern, *The Question of National Defense*, p. 153.

93. Teller, "The Feasibility of Arms Control and the Principle of Openness," p. 134. Further, on p. 133: "I can see no clear-cut reason why a limited war should necessarily grow into an all-out war. The assertion of this necessity is merely the Russians' way of advancing the threat of a massive retaliation. They know very well that the employment of tactical nuclear weapons would be to our great advantage. They try to use every possible means of dissuading us from using them. They are doing it more subtly by stating that all-out war is a necessary result of any use of nuclear weapons rather than by stating that all-out war will be started by their side as a measure of retaliation."

94. The debate between escalation optimists and pessimists was reviewed by Halperin under the heading "Stability of Limited Nuclear War." Halperin, "Nuclear Weapons and Limited War," pp. 151–153. Halperin here argued that, contrary to Kissinger, conventional limited war is more stable than limited nuclear war.

95. Brodie, "Strategy Hits a Dead End," pp. 35 and 36.

96. Brodie, "More About Limited War," p. 117.

97. James E. King, Jr., "Nuclear Plenty and Limited War," *Foreign Affairs*, Vol. 35, No. 2 (January 1957), p. 243.

98. As quoted in Freedman, *The Evolution of Nuclear Strategy*, p. 111.

99. Kaufmann, "Limited Warfare," p. 121.

100. As quoted in Leslie H. Gelb, with Richard Betts, *The Irony of Vietnam: The System Worked* (Washington, DC: Brookings Institution, 1979), p. 111. A useful review of work on escalation is provided by Lawrence Freedman, "On the Tiger's Back: The Development of the Concept of Escalation," in Roman Kolkowicz, ed., *The Logic of Nuclear Terror* (Boston: Allen & Unwin, 1987), pp. 109–152. A recent, useful return to work on escalation is Forrest E. Morgan, Karl P. Mueller, Evan S. Medeiros, Kevin L. Pollpeter, and Roger Cliff, *Dangerous Thresholds: Managing Escalation in the 21st Century* (Santa Monica, CA: RAND Corporation, 2008).

101. For operational planners, at least.

102. Michael E. Howard, "On Fighting a Nuclear War," *International Security*, Vol. 5, No. 4 (Spring 1981), p. 14.

103. Brodie, *Strategy in the Missile Age*, p. 330 (emphasis in the original).

104. Halperin, "Nuclear Weapons and Limited War," p. 165.

105. Henry A. Kissinger, "Limited War: Conventional or Nuclear? A Reappraisal," *Daedalus*, Vol. 89, No. 4 (Fall 1960), p. 806.

106. Ibid., p. 807.

107. Ibid.

108. Ibid., p. 808.

109. Ibid., p. 809 (emphasis in the original).

110. Osgood, "The Reappraisal of Limited War,", p. 45.

111. Robert E. Osgood, *Limited War Revisited* (Boulder, CO: Westview Press, 1979); and Osgood, "The Post-War Strategy of Limited War," pp. 93–130.

112. Osgood, *Limited War Revisited*, p. 58.

113. John C. Garnett, "Limited 'Conventional' War in the Nuclear Age," in Michael Howard, ed., *Restraints on War: Studies in the Limitation of Armed Conflict* (Oxford: Oxford University Press, 1979), p. 79.

114. Brodie, *Strategy in the Missile Age*, pp. 312–313.

115. Limited-war theory, as Freedman put it, "was not a theory about the primacy of political objectives over military means, but of the primacy of military realities over political objectives." Freedman, *The Evolution of Nuclear Strategy*, p. 100.

116. Ibid., p. 92.

117. Kissinger, "Limited War: Conventional or Nuclear?," p. 807.

3 The United States and Discriminate Nuclear Options in the Cold War

Elbridge A. Colby

DOES THE UNITED STATES NEED TO BE ABLE TO CONduct limited nuclear operations? As today's US policymakers wrestle with this question, they would do well to consider the US experience with this profound and vexing issue during the Cold War. The Cold War Communist Bloc presented the US-led security system that still exists and the nuclear umbrella that shelters it with its most stressing tests. Could the West rely only on massive retaliation and its conventional forces to deter the Soviet Bloc from aggression and coercion, or did it need to prepare for more limited nuclear options? Was limited nuclear war even feasible, let alone advisable? The gravity of the Communist threat and the stakes involved compelled US policymakers to struggle to find satisfactory answers to these pressing challenges.

Though the Cold War experience produced few straightforward "lessons learned" on these issues, important insights can be gleaned from it. Successful strategies can rarely be reduced to guidelines beyond the very general, in large part because they are adapted to the particularities of a given competition. What worked against the Soviet Union might not work against Iran or China or North Korea. But the scale of the challenge posed by the Communist threat forced the US government to engage in serious and clear thinking on the problem of limiting nuclear war, thinking which still obtains even in a much changed world.

Perhaps the most important theme is that the US government, once it saw that America would be vulnerable to a devastating Soviet nuclear strike, answered the basic question of this chapter by recognizing that the United States did need to develop and prepare for limited and controlled use of its nuclear forces for strategic effect.[1] While administrations differed on how best to conduct a limited nuclear conflict, they consistently sought to be able to do so from the early 1960s through the end of the Cold War (with the partial exception of the second part of the Johnson administration). Understanding why this was the case, and drawing the right conclusions from the experience, should help us to stay rooted in the basic dynamics of nuclear strategy, dynamics that, while they operate differently in today's world, remain essentially the same as when they were first uncovered and explored during the Cold War.

The Early Years: Superiority

In the early years of the Cold War there was essentially no limitation in US nuclear war plans. Rather, in this period doctrine called for using US nuclear forces, once authorized, in a single, general strike.[2] American policymakers saw this as tenable because the United States initially enjoyed a nuclear monopoly and then, after the Soviet detonation of their first atomic weapon, marked nuclear superiority. In practice this meant that, had a conflict between Washington and Moscow escalated to the general level, the United States would have been able to prevail—at least to the extent that the United States could, as James Schlesinger later put it, "essentially flatten the Soviet Union, with only the most limited Soviet ability to retaliate against the continental United States."[3] In other words, the United States could conceive of engaging in an unrestricted nuclear war with the Soviet Union for some deep interest and, while suffering gravely, in some circumstances view its victory as worth the losses. The United States did not therefore appear to need limited nuclear options.

This American escalatory advantage, well known to both Washington and Moscow, likely played a significant role in the early Cold War standoffs of the 1940s and 1950s. When Truman deployed B-29 bombers to Britain during the Berlin Crisis of 1948–49 and during the Korean War, when Eisenhower issued nuclear threats to try to end the Korean War and against Beijing over the Taiwan Strait, and even as late as the Berlin Crises and Cuban Missile Crisis of the late 1950s and early 1960s, the Americans were fortified by the knowledge (or at least belief) that, should the Communists resist and push the conflict to the nuclear level, the United States could not only win but also emerge from the conflict essentially intact, or at least as a functioning society.[4] This ability to counter Soviet pressure with the threat of nuclear escalation not only proved useful strategically but also allowed the United States and its NATO allies to minimize spending on more expensive conventional forces.

Nor were these threats to escalate to general nuclear attack mere diplomatic legerdemain—rather, US war plans closely conformed to the principle of rapid and total escalation.[5] Indeed, President Eisenhower in particular remained throughout his administration personally committed to the early and general use of nuclear weapons in response to Soviet aggression. His view was that the more the Soviets believed that aggression would lead to general war and employment of the massively superior US arsenal, the more effective deterrence would be.[6] The Eisenhower administration therefore early on embraced a policy of "massive retaliation" to deter Soviet bloc aggression based on the threat to employ nuclear weapons at the time and place of its own choosing.[7] Nuclear planning followed suit as the US military developed plans to execute a major strike against the Soviet Union in order to destroy its capability to wage war and, specifically, preempt its ability to strike at the United States. War plans throughout the 1950s emphasized delivery of a "knock-out" preemptive blow that would destroy or disable Soviet forces before they could strike.[8] In line with this approach, the first integrated nuclear war plan, SIOP-62, finalized in December 1960, was essentially a single, massive, basically inflexible strike package.[9]

As Soviet nuclear warhead and delivery system production ramped up and improved in quality over the course of the 1950s, however, many both within and outside the government began to focus on the realization that the American nuclear advantage was closing. At some point in the coming years, it was feared, the Soviets would be able to field a force that could, regardless of US actions, inflict damage upon the United States well beyond what was acceptable for anything but the most vital of interests. This prompted efforts to begin grappling with ways to maintain deterrence against Soviet aggression and coercion even in a situation in which the United States would not enjoy the ability to sufficiently limit damage to itself in a nuclear war with the USSR. Several questions dominated these efforts. What would deterrence require once the Soviets obtained a secure second strike capability? Once they did, would Moscow actually be deterred by threats to resort to general nuclear war over Soviet aggression, let alone less dramatic coercion, against Western

Europe? Would the United States, in the classic quandary, be willing to trade Boston for Bonn or Washington for Paris? If not, would the United States then need to regain nuclear superiority, even as that goal faded further from view with the Soviet Union's fielding of larger numbers of impressive new systems? Or did the United States need to conduct a limited nuclear war to try to bridge this gap between an increasingly dubious threat of massive attack and its inability to regain superiority over the USSR?[10]

Kennedy/Johnson: The Need for Options to the Fore, Then Abandoned

It was in this context that serious and sustained thinking about the possibilities of limited nuclear options took center stage. Though the Eisenhower administration had begun to explore options other than massive retaliation during its second term, such thinking came to the fore only with the Kennedy administration.[11] Kennedy's national security platform was, in fact, based in large part upon the accusation that Eisenhower's defense policy was irresponsible because of its allegedly incredible and dangerous reliance on nuclear forces to deal with contingencies beyond the existential. Even after being apprised of the massive American superiority once in office, such advantage seemed of distinctly limited value to Kennedy, who remarked during the Cuban Missile Crisis deliberations that "they've got enough to blow us up anyway."[12]

The Kennedy administration, led above all by Secretary of Defense Robert McNamara, therefore forwarded an alternative strategy of "flexible response." This strategy, though still focused on large exchanges, was designed to provide the West with plausible options for reaction to Soviet aggression or provocation short of resort to general war, options that would allow a conflict to remain limited (primarily in its quarantining of cities) and that would be roughly correlated in cost, both suffered and inflicted, to the scale of the provocation. As McNamara explained in highly influential speeches to NATO defense ministers in Athens and at the University of Michigan in 1962, the threat to resort to general nuclear war, even in the waning condition of nuclear superiority, did not solve all the potential challenges to NATO interests, nor did it necessarily allow the West sufficiently to limit damage to itself in the event of a general exchange with the Soviet Union. McNamara's deduction was twofold. First, because nuclear weapons would not likely be used except in the most pressing circumstances, the West needed to augment its non-nuclear forces to compensate for the Soviet advantage in the European conventional balance, which had become increasingly salient in light of Moscow's growing nuclear arsenal. This led to greater investment by the United States in conventional forces and urging by Washington to the allies to increase their own conventional expenditures. Second, if the West was forced to resort to nuclear weapons, there should be ways of controlling and thereby limiting the nuclear exchange, so that their use did not inexorably lead to an absolute catastrophe that could not be correlated with any plausible strategic objective.

In particular, McNamara and his confederates in the Pentagon and at institutions like the RAND Corporation touted a "no cities" approach that would focus nuclear attacks upon the forces of the opponent, withholding attacks against population centers in the interests of giving the adversary the incentive to do the same. As McNamara explained in a September 1961 memorandum to Kennedy outlining his recommended path forward for the US nuclear posture, the forces he advocated for would enable the United States to pursue a counterforce limited nuclear war by "provid[ing] major improvements to the quality of our strategic posture: in its survivability, its flexibility, and in its ability to be used in a controlled and deliberate way under a wide range of contingencies."[13] To this end, McNamara ordered a substantial revision to the SIOP, resulting in SIOP-63.[14] In contrast to SIOP-62's single option, the new plan offered five major strike options, as well as various possibilities for withholding attacks.[15] Nonetheless, SIOP-63 was still far from a truly effective limited war plan, as the options presented remained tremendously large in scale. Still, the plan did, for the first time, introduce the principle of limitation into American nuclear war planning.

Movement toward incorporating greater discrimination into US nuclear policy essentially halted there, however, as McNamara and other influential defense policymakers turned away from their earlier focus on limiting nuclear war over the course of the 1960s. This apostasy was driven by a variety of factors, primarily the conviction that it would be difficult, if not impossible, to control nuclear conflict and thus that efforts at control were better directed at minimizing the possibility that nuclear weapons were used at all rather than at what they saw as vain and dangerous attempts to rely on the threat of limited nuclear use.[16] Alongside this conviction was the belief that what McNamara saw as the insatiable budgetary demands of the military services for more spending on strategic forces and the formidable growth of Soviet strategic forces made focusing on capping the arms race—including US modernization programs—crucial for both financial and security reasons.[17] In the place of limitation, then, McNamara and the Johnson administration began to emphasize the concept of assured destruction, the notion that stability would best be guaranteed by a situation in which each side would be deterred by the knowledge that the other side could respond to a first strike with a devastating retaliatory attack. Though by no means inherently incompatible with the principle of limited nuclear use, assured destruction in McNamara's hands became a substitute rather than a complement to the development of more flexible options, and efforts to build more limitation into US nuclear war plans sagged and essentially stopped.[18] Indeed, in his rhetoric McNamara moved away from the search for any limitation of the nuclear instrument whatsoever, though he apparently believed that the United States would always in practice retain more discriminate options.[19]

As was well noted at the time, the logical implication of minimizing reliance on US nuclear forces meant that the forces for effective deterrence needed to be found elsewhere. For McNamara this replacement was to be conventional forces, and he tirelessly promoted the improvement of NATO's nonnuclear defenses, famously leading to NATO's adoption of its flexible response strategy in 1967. But the combination of the Soviet Union's rapid augmentation of its strategic and theater nuclear forces, the weakening of the American military position in Europe because of the war in Vietnam, and the persisting lack of interest on the part of European NATO members in strengthening their conventional forces meant that McNamara's theoretical solution of substituting non-nuclear for nuclear capabilities remained essentially that—theoretical. Rather, by the end of the Johnson administration NATO's conventional defenses remained inferior to those of their Warsaw Pact opponents. That said, US and NATO forces retained a very substantial arsenal of theater nuclear weapons in Europe, validated by NATO's flexible response decision in MC 14/3, which provided an intermediate deterrent capability between a conventional defense and US strategic forces. But, unsurprisingly in light of McNamara's skepticism about the controllability of nuclear conflict and the Soviets' insistence that they would respond massively to NATO nuclear use, neither the United States nor NATO found a satisfactory way to plan for the employment of these theater nuclear forces that solved the problems of escalation control that likewise afflicted the US strategic deterrent.

By the end of the Johnson administration, despite all the storm and fury over US nuclear policy in the 1960s, US nuclear war plans remained essentially unchanged in form from SIOP-63, providing some very modest degree of flexibility but essentially still structured for massive strikes designed to limit retaliatory damage.[20] The upshot of this history was that, by the end of the Johnson administration, the ability of the United States to use its strategic nuclear forces in limited and controlled ways, and thus for contingencies other than the existential, was very modest.[21]

Nixon/Ford: The Search for Limited Options Begins in Earnest

Confronting this brittle posture as it entered office in 1969, the Richard Nixon administration sought actively to develop more meaningful options for the use of nuclear forces.[22] As the administration's formal statement of foreign policy succinctly asked: "Should a president, in the event of a nuclear attack, be left with the single option of ordering the mass destruction of enemy civilians in the face of the certainty that it would be followed by the mass slaughter of Americans?" This question had become more pressing as the prospect of assured Soviet retaliation had become plainly more likely with the appearance of the first effective Soviet ballistic missile–carrying submarines, the *Yankee* class SSBN, off the East Coast in 1968.[23] The answer, to the Nixon administration, was: not if at all possible. "No President should ever be in the position where his only option in meeting such aggression is an all-out nuclear response." Instead, the administration argued, the United States must "maintain a broad choice of options" involving "greater flexibility."[24] This would take the form of introducing limited nuclear options (or, LNO) into the SIOP nuclear war plan.

Driven by the need to find options, National Security Advisor Henry Kissinger immediately began pushing for more "discriminating options" for the use of nuclear forces "under circumstances other than 'massive retaliation.'"[25] The administration was motivated not only by an abstract concern about the advisability of the existing US posture, but also by the specific concern that the later Johnson-McNamara shift away from controlled use and toward an emphasis on assured destruction had raised dangerous doubts about the credibility of the US willingness to use its strategic forces over a conflict in Europe. As James Schlesinger later put it, "In the 1960s, Secretary of

Defense McNamara's 'body language' told the Soviets that . . . theater nuclear weapons would be used to defend Western Europe but U.S. strategic systems would not. . . . LNO [the Nixon administration policy of preparing for limited nuclear conflict] was designed to blow away the idea of MAD . . . and to reestablish the linkage of the U.S. deterrent in Europe to the strategic arsenal."[26] At the same time, however, the administration's review of the US strategic posture revealed that the United States was unprepared for a controlled nuclear war, finding that the United States had "very limited capabilities for a small strategic attack."[27] Instead, the administration found that existing US nuclear weapon employment plans consisted primarily of pre-planned large-scale nuclear strikes against Soviet and Chinese military targets, with additional options for large strikes against urban/industrial areas, for a total of five options.[28] All of the options envisioned the use of hundreds or thousands of warheads. Furthermore, the capability to conduct ad hoc planning for discriminate, controlled strikes was very limited.[29] Through a combination of conscious policy on the part of the Kennedy and Johnson administrations, organizational inertia on the part of the military, and inaction in the face of the complexities and costs of developing serious discriminate nuclear employment capabilities, such a capability simply did not exist in other than inchoate form by the early 1970s.

Despite a slow beginning, over the course of the next eight years the Nixon and Gerald Ford administrations tried to rectify this. In government policy documents, formal statements, and budget submissions, the administrations of these two presidents sought to lay the conceptual groundwork for such discriminate nuclear options and, from there, to begin building a functioning capability to exercise selective nuclear use. Internally, in early 1972 the Department of Defense chartered a high-level panel chaired by Director of Defense Research and Engineering John Foster that led to National Security Study Memorandum 169 in February 1973, directing an interagency working group to develop recommendations for a new national nuclear policy.[30] In July of that year, the interagency group submitted a lengthy analysis arguing for the need for limited nuclear employment options.[31] This document, endorsed by Secretary of Defense James Schlesinger and Kissinger, formed the basis for the new nuclear policy outlined in National Security Decision Memorandum 242, of which a substantial portion was dedicated to "planning limited nuclear employment options." NSDM-242 dictated that early and acceptable war termination was to be the principal objective of US nuclear employment, and

that that objective required "planning a wide range of limited nuclear employment options which could be used in conjunction with supporting political
and military measures (including conventional forces) to control escalation.
Plans should be developed for limited employment options which enable the
United States to conduct selected nuclear operations, in concert with conventional forces, which protect vital U.S. interests and limit enemy capabilities to continue aggression."[32] This suggested the need to develop an array of
plausible options, not merely truncated versions of a general war plan, as was
effectively the case in SIOP-63. Options were also to be crafted to enable the
United States to communicate both resolve and restraint to the adversary.

The Nixon administration then began efforts to institutionalize these
broad policy goals. Within the executive branch, Schlesinger signed off on
a revised Nuclear Weapons Employment Policy (NUWEP) in April 1974 that
gave the Joint Chiefs of Staff more concrete direction for how to plan for use
of US nuclear forces.[33] The 1974 NUWEP forthrightly stated that "escalation
control" was the US objective should deterrence fail, and that such escalation control could be grasped by employing nuclear forces selectively, including through the practice of withholding strikes against leadership targets and
population centers and through the maintenance of strategic reserve forces
necessary for continued deterrence during conflict. Options were structured
into four categories: major attack options and selected attack options (meaning large-scale but, in the case of the latter, segmented strike plans), limited
nuclear options (meaning smaller-scale options "intended to observe different or more limited escalation boundaries or seek different or more limited
objectives in order to persuade an enemy to terminate hostilities without
resorting to larger nuclear exchanges"), and regional nuclear options (meaning options for responding to attacking enemy forces with US nuclear forces
already located within a given theater of operations).[34]

Schlesinger also emphasized this point to a broader public, including a Congress deeply suspicious of funding efforts that some saw as making nuclear weapons more usable. In a memorable statement, Schlesinger
argued that the United States needed "alternatives other than suicide or surrender. . . . It needed options which did not imply immediate escalation to
major nuclear war." To wit, he contended that "deterrence can fail in many
ways. What we need is a series of measured responses to aggression which
bear some relation to the provocation, have some prospect of terminating
hostilities before general nuclear war breaks out, and leave some possibility

for restoring deterrence." The hope, Schlesinger explained, was to "be able to bring all but the largest nuclear conflicts to a *rapid* conclusion before cities are struck." The posture required "the forces to execute a wide range of options in response to potential actions by an enemy, including a capability for precise attacks on both soft and hard targets, while at the same time minimizing unintended collateral damage."[35]

The sense that, if war came, the United States needed to be able to try to limit nuclear use was, without question, keenly felt and expressed at the top of the government and in some parts of the bureaucracy. Efforts to integrate the policy into actual plans, posture, and procurement were, however, slower and less complete.[36] Schlesinger himself recognized that the changes required to shift US nuclear forces toward a more selective and controlled targeting approach would take years, but believed that changing US declaratory policy was the first step in creating the conditions from which such an approach could emerge. Pushing the Joint Strategic Planning Staff (JSTPS) and the Strategic Air Command (SAC) to change their war plans and modernizing the requisite hardware to conform to the doctrine would, he believed, follow.[37]

To this end the SIOP was substantially revised, resulting in SIOP-5, issued on January 1, 1976. This SIOP was an attempt to institutionalize the Schlesinger doctrine by providing for multiple limited and selective strike options. The plan, which remained in force until 1983, eventually came to incorporate over 40,000 individual targets, and included limited, selected attack, and regional nuclear options, as well as withholds for countries and classes of targets.[38]

Meanwhile, advances in technology and weaponry offered new and superior capabilities, such as increased missile accuracy, that enabled the shift in doctrine.[39] These included development and procurement programs such as for the Trident submarine-launched ballistic missile (SLBM), which was more accurate than its Poseidon predecessor; the formidable theater-range Pershing II intermediate-range ballistic missile (IRBM); accurate and low-signature cruise missiles; and the first Defense Support Program orbital infrared detection satellites, which provided an earlier warning capability. Together these programs offered superior and new capabilities and therefore more options for employment (albeit often as a consequence of technological advance and bureaucratic inertia rather than the conscious pursuit of limited options).

By the end of the Ford administration, then, the United States had definitively adopted and begun pursuing a nuclear posture that allowed for the limited strategic use of nuclear weapons. While the full set of technical and institutional capabilities needed to make such limited options fully reliable and plausible remained elusive, the Nixon and Ford administrations had set the United States on the path toward trying to realize real limited nuclear capabilities.

Carter: Continued Pursuit of Limitation, with Different Emphasis

The Jimmy Carter administration, despite a change in rhetoric from its predecessors, continued the Nixon and Ford administrations' pursuit of plausible limited nuclear employment options. Although its focus on a "countervailing strategy" emphasized different criteria for what should be targeted and focused on denying the Soviet Union any victory even on its own terms, the Carter administration's nuclear policy, like that of its Republican predecessors, continued in earnest the search for limited options short of general release of nuclear weapons.

The centerpiece of the Carter administration's policy on limited nuclear capabilities was Presidential Directive 59 (PD-59), promulgated, after extensive internal deliberations, in July 1980. The Carter administration approach was driven in large part by a sense that the Nixon/Ford reforms had not gone far enough in developing limited and flexible nuclear capabilities. As NSC staff member William Odom put it in a memorandum to National Security Advisor Zbigniew Brzezinski, NSDM-242 had "yielded the appearances of flexibility without the substance."[40] The administration was also seized by the proposition that US nuclear capabilities needed to be more clearly capable of convincing Soviet leaders that they would not come out of a nuclear war favorably.[41] PD-59 therefore ordained that the United States needed nuclear capabilities sufficient such that "any adversary would recognize that no plausible outcome would represent a victory on any plausible definition of victory." The directive also heavily emphasized the importance of flexibility, enduring command and control, and selectivity in the application of nuclear force. It stated that "improvements should be made to our forces, their supporting C3 [command, control, and communications] and intelligence, and their employment plans and planning apparatus, to achieve a high degree of flexibility, enduring survivability, and adequate performance in the face of actions." The directive also specifically called out the importance of "an ability to design nuclear employment plans on short notice in response to the latest and changing circumstances," highlighting the value of integrating the most current intelligence in selecting targets for limited strikes.[42] These policies were then reflected in the 1980 NUWEP, promulgated by Secretary of Defense Harold Brown in October 1980. The NUWEP summarized the heart of PD-59 as "direct[ing] that U.S. targeting plans provide flexible sub-options in ways that will enable us, to the extent that the survival of C3I allows, to employ nuclear weapons consonant with our objectives and the course of the conflict."[43]

While PD-59 exhibited differences in emphasis from NSDM-242, viewed in the broader historical context of US nuclear policy its hallmark was continuity. Secretary of Defense Brown, in explaining the administration's new strategy, for instance emphasized this fundamental consistency of the effort with preceding strategies. As he explained in an influential speech to the Naval War College in August 1980, "We must have forces, contingency plans, and command and control capabilities that will convince the Soviet leadership that no war and no course of aggression by them . . . could lead to victory, however they define victory. . . . Operationally, our countervailing strategy requires that our plans and capabilities be structured to put more stress on being able to employ strategic nuclear forces selectively."[44] Brown underlined that "P.D. 59 is *not* a new strategic doctrine. . . . It *is*, in fact, a refinement, a codification of previous statements of our strategic policy. P.D. 59 takes the same essential strategic doctrine, and restates it more clearly, more cogently, in the light of current conditions."[45] The policy explicitly endorsed the ability of the United States to "attack, in a selective and measured way, a range of military, industrial, and political control targets" and called for the continued effort "to improve . . . the options necessary to protect our interests."[46]

While agreeing with the general need for options, the policy was different in some important respects from the Nixon/Ford administrations' approach. Brown's own primary claim for distinctiveness was that the Carter administration was more concretely implementing the ability to conduct limited nuclear war through developments in the flexibility of planning and the effectiveness, endurance, and survivability of command, control, and communications.[47] The administration focused especially on the salience of command, control, and communications, issuing PD-53 to ensure "connectivity between the national Command Authority and strategic and other appropriate forces to support flexible execution of retaliatory strikes."[48] The administration also claimed that the policy focused more than its predecessors on using selective strikes for broadly military purposes designed to blunt Soviet aggression rather than merely as indicators of the strength of US resolve and the gravity of the interests at stake.[49]

Another distinction between the Schlesinger doctrine and the countervailing strategy was the latter's more conscious focus on targeting what Soviet leadership valued most. Motivated by the assessment that the Soviets appeared to believe they could win a nuclear war, an assessment grounded in observation of Soviet force posture development and doctrinal writings, the countervailing strategy sought to posture US forces such that it would be clear to the Soviets that they would lose more than they would gain in any nuclear conflict. This meant that the countervailing strategy focused more on targeting potential instruments of post-exchange dominance rather than the recovery assets that had been prioritized under the Schlesinger doctrine.[50] Despite this focus and a heightened rhetorical pitch regarding the focus of the strategy on the Soviet leadership and what it valued, leadership targets were kept low on the target list to enable intra-war bargaining. These differences from the Schlesinger doctrine led the Carter administration to revise the SIOP modestly, resulting in the NUWEP of October 1980, at the very end of the administration's tenure, which in turn yielded SIOP-5F, which included a greater focus on leadership targets.[51]

The Carter administration's grappling with limited nuclear war was not confined, however, to strategic forces. The combination of increasing European skepticism about the US commitment and ability to defend its NATO allies against Soviet coercion or aggression and the impressive modernization of Soviet forces, particularly theater nuclear forces such as the highly capable SS-20 mobile IRBM, forced the Carter administration to deal with the long-neglected theater nuclear forces of NATO.[52] What would be able to deter Soviet aggression if the strategic nuclear shield of the United States was neutered by parity and the Strategic Arms Limitation Treaty (SALT)? skeptics such as German Chancellor Helmut Schmidt asked. This, he and many others argued, put the spotlight on theater nuclear and conventional forces that would enable the Alliance to conduct a limited campaign short of far less plausible general nuclear response to Soviet aggression.[53] Anxiety about the American commitment was exacerbated by a more amorphous weakening of confidence in American leadership, concern that was rubbed especially raw by the American about-face on the deployment of enhanced-radiation weapons.

The concerns about theater nuclear forces were subsets of broader issues of American credibility in a world of parity. NATO's decision in 1979 to go forward with its own program of theater nuclear force modernization, based on the deployment of highly accurate and fast-flying mobile Pershing II IRBMs and ground-launched cruise missiles (GLCMs), coupled with offers to negotiate with the Soviet Union on reductions of theater nuclear forces, was largely motivated by the perceived need to take firm action to show the Alliance's resolve and ability to meet Soviet challenges along the spectrum of potential challenges, including conflicts confined to the European theater of operations.[54] While the deployment of these systems offered new capabilities to NATO, they did not represent a break from the Carter administration's broader commitment to exploring ways to use nuclear forces selectively. The introduction of modernized theater nuclear forces into Europe was part and parcel of the general effort to make the American commitment to defend Europe more credible and capable, including through forces whose use in a limited fashion was more believable, though substantial doubt must remain that a coherent plan for how to use these theater forces in a way that would plausibly limit escalation was ever developed. Nevertheless, failure to do so would not have distinguished them from their predecessor theater nuclear capabilities.[55]

This was especially important because, by the early 1980s, the aspiration to provide an effective conventional defense of NATO Europe expressed in the Alliance's adoption of the flexible response strategy did not appear to have been achieved. As Supreme Allied Commander Europe General Bernard Rogers stated bluntly in 1982, "Alliance conventional capabilities today are clearly inadequate to meet the growing Warsaw Pact conventional threat. . . . NATO's continuing failure to fulfill its conventional needs means that we now must depend upon the use of theater nuclear weapons to accomplish our missions of deterrence *and* defense."[56] Thus the Allies' failure to meet the conventional force goals of the flexible response doctrine made the credibility of the Alliance's resorting to some kind of limited nuclear capability even more salient.

Despite its differences from the Schlesinger doctrine, the broad contours of the Carter doctrine for nuclear employment thus remained very much in tune with the Nixon/Ford policy. Administrations throughout the 1970s agreed that the United States could not be restricted to responding to Soviet bloc aggression only with massive nuclear strikes but rather needed to prepare to use nuclear forces selectively. The Carter administration's countervailing strategy offered a variation on the theme proposed by the Schlesinger doctrine, but in response to the question of whether the United States needed to be able to fight a limited nuclear war, it offered basically the same answer.

Reagan/Bush: Continuity, with Progress on Implementation

The Ronald Reagan administration entered office dedicated to redressing the perceived military imbalance created by Soviet nuclear and conventional advances and US neglect of its military forces during the preceding decade.[57] In the nuclear field, the administration redoubled efforts to deploy the MX ICBM, Trident II D5 SLBMs, submarine-launched cruise missiles, and B-2 stealthy penetrating heavy bombers; moved forward with the introduction of Pershing IIs and GLCMs into Europe; and resuscitated the B-1 heavy bomber that the Carter administration had canceled. While it agreed to honor but refused to push for the ratification of the SALT II agreement, the Reagan administration also eventually pushed forward an ambitious arms control agenda that would, toward the end of the Reagan years and into the George H.W. Bush years, yield a network of treaties with the Soviet Union.

Yet while the Reagan administration ushered in a series of new policies on nuclear weapons, such as the centrality of strategic defense, on the question of whether the United States needed to be able to fight a limited nuclear war, it too followed in the path of all preceding administrations since the late 1960s.[58] For instance, Secretary of Defense Caspar Weinberger, citing McNamara, Schlesinger, and Brown, explained in 1982:

> U.S. nuclear capabilities were increased in order to provide the President with the option of using nuclear forces both to support our general purpose forces and to respond selectively (on less than an all-out basis) to a limited Soviet nuclear attack. . . . This concept of flexible response remains as a central principle of our strategy today. . . . This means that [nuclear forces] should be capable of being used on a very limited basis as well as more massively.[59]

Moreover, while the administration emphasized the need to show greater firmness to the Communist bloc, it maintained essentially the same criteria for deterrence as had its predecessor.[60]

A main distinction of the Reagan administration's approach was its focus on being able to convince the Soviets that they could not prevail in a "protracted" nuclear conflict with the United States, a possibility which the preceding administrations had addressed but not emphasized as forthrightly. Thus Reagan's National Security Decision Directive (NSDD) 32 of May 20, 1982, ordained that "the United States will enhance its strategic nuclear deterrent by developing a capability to sustain protracted nuclear conflict."[61] Even here, however, the administration, under intense political pressure for its alleged belligerency, tacked back toward the legacy official nuclear policy and framed its emphasis on a protracted conflict within the by then well-established US effort to be able to employ nuclear weapons selectively. As Weinberger wrote in a letter to a large number of US and European newspapers, "There is nothing new about our policy. . . . We must have a *capability* for a survivable and endurable response—to demonstrate that our strategic forces *could* survive Soviet strikes over an extended period. Thus we believe we could deter any attack."[62] As with the US and NATO theater nuclear force modernization decisions of the period, the underlying point was to prevent the Soviets from believing they could escape the basic deterrent logic that they would lose more than they would gain by initiating any significant aggression.

Where there was movement during the Reagan years, however, was on actually making substantial progress in implementing the policy of limited nuclear options. As Leon Sloss, a leading figure in the development of PD-59, admitted, "PD-59 had introduced lots of options into the SIOP, but they were paper options," and the 1982 NUWEP had not focused on introducing serious limited options into war plans.[63] The Reagan administration's initiatives included dedicated and focused efforts both within the Department of Defense to ensure that US war plans actually offered plausible limited options—as opposed to, in effect, preludes to general attacks masquerading as discrete strikes—and with the Congress to obtain the legislative backing necessary to make the policy a reality.[64]

Specifically, OSD officials had found by the mid-1980s that US war plans did not present the president with credible, truly limited options; in actuality the Joint Strategic Target Planning Staff (JSTPS) and SAC's purportedly limited strikes bore little relation to the theoretical constructs advocated since the introduction of the Schlesinger doctrine. Instead, the options that had actually been developed involved numbers, trajectories, and launch points that would be unlikely to be perceived by the Soviets as limited. Starting in 1985, OSD officials, backed by Secretary Weinberger and led by Franklin Miller, succeeded in persuading the military planners in Omaha to develop credible small limited nuclear options and to include them in real plans. These new options were designed as "short, sharp spikes" in nuclear violence that would, through careful attention to their launch points, trajectories, and numbers, be perceived by the Soviets as limited in nature. The strikes would be targeted to impede Soviet military operations in order to impose delay and thus create time for deliberation and negotiation. These options were formally incorporated into the revised NUWEP of 1987 and SIOP-6E of 1988.[65]

Overall, the Reagan administration ushered in important changes on a number of fronts related to nuclear strategy, but evidenced a basic continuity on the need for limited options. This need was reflected in the continuing emphasis on the requirement for limited options in declaratory policy but also in forceful bureaucratic movements actually to ensure that the JSTPS, SAC, and other key organizational elements created and sustained the capability to conduct truly limited nuclear strikes.[66] While many of the key documents of this period pertaining to US planning for limited nuclear employment remain classified, there is little to suggest that the Reagan administration deviated from its stated policy of preparing and posturing for limited nuclear war.[67]

Entering office as the Cold War came to a close and the focus of American nuclear policy shifted from deterrence to arms control and nuclear security, the Bush administration nonetheless essentially continued wholly its predecessor's policy on limited nuclear options, retaining key personnel in responsible positions and further implementing the policy by incorporating options into US war plans that were limited and tailored to situations the president might actually face.[68]

Themes and Observations

During the Cold War the US government, once it perceived that the Soviets would eventually achieve the assured ability to inflict unacceptable damage on the US homeland, came to believe that the United States needed to be able to employ its nuclear forces in a limited manner. Preparation for controlled use was necessary to be able to retain the benefits of nuclear weapons, whose use in an unrestrained fashion was taken to be of dubious credibility and therefore of limited utility. While administrations differed about how limited nuclear use would be conducted, particularly beginning with the Nixon administration they did not differ on the basic premise that the United States did need to be able to employ nuclear weapons selectively.[69] Nor was this effort merely confined to the declaratory level. Beginning with SIOP-63, accelerating with SIOP-5 in 1976, and coming to fruition with the late SIOP-6 series of 1986 and after, US war plans included specific, concrete options for limited nuclear use. Why?

Despite the confidence that many outsiders had in the sufficiency of some combination of minimalist nuclear deterrence and conventional forces, the US government was never ready to rely on such a sanguine assessment of what deterrence against the Soviet Union required. Once the USSR was able to field a serious second-strike capability, presidents and their advisors—and their European NATO counterparts—clearly felt the need to develop options for responses to possible Soviet aggression, adventurism, or coercion that would draw strength from the US nuclear capability without having to resort to an incredible threat to launch a massive nuclear strike that would invite the annihilation of the United States. This perceived need persisted throughout the second half of the Cold War, in large part because the aspiration to reduce NATO's reliance on nuclear forces in exchange for a robust conventional shield remained, at least until the 1980s, just that—an aspiration. Throughout the Cold War, therefore, the defense of Europe was seen to rely on nuclear forces and, with the advent of parity (and even some degree of Soviet advantage), the only plausible way out of the conundrum seemed to be to find ways to use US nuclear forces in a controlled, selective fashion. In consonance with this view, after years of policy pronouncements emphasizing the need for limited nuclear options, the Department of Defense eventually did succeed in developing such options for the president.

This is not to say that the effort fully succeeded, at least with respect to creating an orderly, let alone attractive, plan for how a limited nuclear war would be conducted. While a definitive history must await the opening of the relevant archives, the judgment that the United States never fully solved the problems associated with limited nuclear employment during the Cold War seems justified. In part this was due to the habit of new administrations of shifting guidance, making consistent implementation of a given policy difficult and leaving the actual force more subject to the vagaries of other factors, such as the procurement process and bureaucratic inertia. Another important element was that actual force development, which did not always conform to the wishes of the policymakers in office, set important constraints on what could be accomplished at any given time. Most salient, however, is that constructing a plan for employing nuclear weapons during a conflict in a selective and rational fashion is exceedingly challenging, not purely because of the technical factors, though these are immensely complex themselves, but also because such an employment plan must factor in the anticipated behavior of the adversary (as well as third parties). Planning for such an eventuality requires combining assessments about phenomena that are hard to predict, such as the performance of weapons systems in nuclear conflict scenarios, with things that simply cannot be known, such as whether an opponent will observe the limits which the initiator wishes to set. These factors made planning for limited nuclear employment enormously difficult and, to a great degree, inherently speculative.

In fact, the United States had no firm idea as to whether the Soviet Union would even consent to keep a nuclear war limited. Indeed, even though Soviet doctrine through most of the Cold War reflected the strong view that nuclear war could not be limited and therefore stated that any use by the United States would result in a total response, the Soviets themselves may not have known how they would respond.[70] Though Soviet views began to shift beginning in the 1960s and eventually began to lead toward a limited war doctrine along US lines by the 1980s, the United States had no way of predicting with confidence how the Soviets would react to limited American use. Nonetheless, the United States persisted in holding to a limited nuclear options policy, principally because it saw itself as having little choice.[71]

So did planning for limited nuclear war actually work as a deterrent? Some, noting British Foreign Secretary Denis Healey's quip that 5 percent probability will do for deterrence of opponents but 95 percent is needed for reassurance of allies, would say that the effort helped calm exaggerated fears in the West of the insufficiency of NATO's defense, but was beyond what was needed to deter the Soviets. Given the nature of the question, no definitive answer can be ventured, though there can be no question that the real prospect of escalation to general nuclear war always remained the foundation of effective deterrence of Communist bloc aggression. But a fair assessment must conclude that the serious search for ways to use nuclear forces for selective, plausibly rational purposes—rather than in a mere fit of senseless destruction—helped strengthen the sense among the Soviet leadership that the United States was in earnest about actually using nuclear weapons should its vital interests be transgressed.[72] In the 1970s and early 1980s the Soviets knew that using their theater superiority in Europe and their ability to inflict unacceptable damage on the US homeland would have involved the serious risk of the conflict escalating to a general nuclear exchange, but they also knew that no one in the West wanted that to happen, at least suggesting that advantage could be sought in the seam. The US emphasis on limited nuclear options, however, showed them that the United States had choices other than suicide or surrender, and thus that Washington's posture was not so brittle. This was crucial to reinforcing to the Soviets that initiating any conflict with the West would very likely prompt the Americans to use nuclear weapons, making any plausible Soviet objective not worth the cost.[73] Indeed, the fact that the Soviets did build multiple options into their nuclear war plans suggests that they saw Washington's threat to conduct limited nuclear strikes as real enough to require that Moscow develop options of its own other than total release.

Lessons from Cold War Experience

Perhaps the most impressive theme from this history is the consistent sense in the US government, once US vulnerability was established, that limited nuclear options were needed. This sense was rooted not only in the anticipation of the annihilating Soviet retaliation that would have in all probability followed a massive American strike, but also in the recognition of the enormity of launching a large, indiscriminate strike in anything short of the most dire contingency—and perhaps even then. Given that the United States can expect to continue to want to deter aggression and coercion against itself and its allies and that the practical unattractiveness and moral repulsiveness of unconstrained use will also persist, this strongly suggests that the United States will continue to need to be prepared to employ its nuclear arsenal selectively and in a controlled manner. This need might become more acute if the United States again faces a situation in which it is extending its security umbrella to militarily vulnerable allies while its opponent enjoys both local military superiority and the ability to strike against the US homeland, a situation that may arise in East Asia. As US conventional superiority cannot be expected to endure forever everywhere, limited nuclear options may again prove the best way to extend deterrence at a tolerable cost and level of risk.

The Cold War history does not appear to offer definitive direction as to *how* to conduct limited nuclear strikes. At the conceptual level, there was broad continuity in seeing the value of limited nuclear options as lying in the use of nuclear forces to protect US interests by inflicting discrete but real costs on an adversary and demonstrating the willingness to resort to further nuclear use while showing restraint in order to limit the scope of war. This logic was generally taken to entail ruling out targeting population centers during initial phases of conflict, but consensus ended there. Should limited strikes be directed at diminishing the opponent's capacity to strike and thus at his nuclear forces, leadership facilities, and command and control facilities or, conversely, should such attacks be directed primarily at inflicting pain and imposing delay while cordoning off his strategic capabilities, at least in the early stages of escalation? The debate was never resolved, nor, since it involves contextual assessments of value and risk, can it be. Still, limited strikes seem to correlate best with the basic logic of the policy when employed against targets that are sufficiently important for their loss to cause pain for or impose constraints or delay upon the opponent but that are neither so valued as to on their account prompt larger retaliation nor vital to the victim's retaliatory capability. The suppression of an opponent's retaliatory force is an objective conceptually distinct from limited options, and indeed one that could well undermine the core goal of limiting a conflict if counterforce attacks cause the opponent to fear for the survival of his second-strike capability.[74] As Schlesinger pointed out, the quintessence of limited nuclear options is "selectivity," not counterforce.[75] Practically speaking, this suggests that limited nuclear strikes should be directed, at least in the initial stages of a conflict, against targets isolated from both the enemy's populace, leadership redoubts, strategic forces and their enabling capabilities, and targets such as general purpose forces, especially those of relevance to the conventional war that would almost certainly accompany (or whose potential would shadow) such a limited nuclear conflict.

Another theme of the Cold War history is the continued drive for flexibility and adaptivity in planning, response, and employment capabilities and for supremely effective and enduring command and control. Such qualities remain easy to identify but difficult to develop, as the long struggle to institutionalize the capabilities needed to conduct these limited options indicates. Nonetheless, the continuing push by a succession of administrations to develop such capabilities points to the inherent value of being able to control nuclear operations effectively, even in a war.

Yet an equally clear lesson of the Cold War history is the need for policymakers, if they are serious about developing and maintaining limited nuclear options, to ensure that declarations of policy are actually translated into real programming and operational guidance, and, ultimately, are reflected in war plans at US Strategic Command (STRATCOM) and the relevant regional combatant commands, as well as in procurement both of weapons systems and of supporting capabilities, such as command and control assets.[76] Cold War history clearly demonstrates that this translation of policy statement into practice cannot be taken for granted. McNamara's early drumbeat for controlled options, for instance, yielded little in the way of real changes to the nation's actual war plans by the end of his tenure, and even the more earnest Nixon-Ford efforts had only mixed success in altering the military's plans and processes, let alone its deeply embedded culture of massive strike and preemption. Thus, while STRATCOM's culture today may be more receptive to the idea of limited options, policymakers nonetheless need to be sure that there is follow through.

The interactive relationship among strategy, technological development, plans, and organizational factors such as procurement is another important theme. Over the course of the Cold War, the anticipation or realization of technological advances enabled and in some cases compelled shifts in strategy.[77] In the case of limited nuclear options, the vastly increased accuracy of US weapons allowing for precise targeting using lower-yield warheads, along with essential advances in command and control and other capabilities, enabled the Nixon administration's shift to the Schlesinger doctrine. Such a course had been far less feasible with the inaccurate and less reliable weapons and systems of the Eisenhower era. This suggests that responsible US leaders need to pay close attention to and invest in the developments of capabilities that can enable limited nuclear employment in a continually evolving technological environment.

A final theme is balance. The United States during the Cold War appears never to have fully solved the problem of how to use nuclear weapons while reliably keeping conflict limited, let alone of how to "win" a nuclear war. And yet, even though NATO's theater defenses in Europe remained inferior to the Warsaw Pact's, the Soviets never sought to capitalize fully on their apparent military advantages in the 1970s and 1980s. Does this mean that they would have been deterred from aggression even if the United States had forsworn limited nuclear employment? Perhaps, but that certainly would have been a far riskier proposition for the West. Instead, it suggests that the United States did not need to solve every problem, did not need to have a well-developed plan for besting the Soviets at every level of escalation in every contingency—as long as nuclear use remained plausible. It was enough to be serious and to be seen to be serious that, in the event the Soviet Union ventured to test Washington's resolve in defending its vital interests, the United States would have nuclear options short of massive, annihilating strikes, and that Washington was in earnest about resorting to them.

Yet it also must be remembered that too much confidence that nuclear use could and would be kept limited would have been and remains unwise. The distinct prospect that any nuclear use might well lead to cataclysm was and remains a vital component of effective deterrence. The fact that a nuclear exchange with the United States terrified Brezhnev and Kosygin and, no doubt, their predecessors and successors, assuredly helped keep the great struggle frigid rather than hot.[78] This is not to counsel complacency—the need for real plans remains—but to emphasize that the will and resolve to employ nuclear weapons are, at root, more important than precisely how they are postured and used. Artful planning and strong rhetoric are supplements to the basic reality of nuclear weapons, not substitutes for it. Nuclear weapons are, in their essence, weapons whose effectiveness stems from their immense destructiveness, a destructiveness that makes actions that prompt their use almost impossible to justify. Nuclear strategies and plans, including limited options, should reinforce this basic truth, not seek to displace it.

Notes

The author would like to thank the following for their helpful recollections and/or comments: Franklin Miller, Austin Long, Robert Jervis, Andrew Erdmann, Michael Albertson, Patrick Lobner, Roman Martinez V, Hans Kristensen, Grayson Murphy, David Yost, Paul Davis, and Vice Admiral Jerry Miller, USN (Ret.).

1. This chapter focuses on the concept of limited nuclear options, understood to mean the limited use of nuclear weapons for deliberately strategic or political effect beyond the contest between the military forces of the combatants. This encompasses the use of any nuclear weapons, including those classified as "theater" or "tactical" weapons, for strategic effect but not the use of nuclear weapons for purely military purposes designed to gain battlefield advantage, in large part because such usage is fundamentally focused on the achievement of military effects and thus presents a different set of (profound and possibly intractable) problems.

2. For histories of this nuclear war planning of this period, see Ernest May et al., *History of the Strategic Arms Competition, 1945–1972* (U.S. Department of Defense, 1981); David A. Rosenberg, "The Origins of Overkill: Nuclear Weapons and American Strategy, 1945–1960," *International Security* 7, no. 4 (Spring 1983), 3–71; and David A. Rosenberg, "Reality and Responsibility: Power and Process in the Making of United

States Nuclear Strategy, 1945–1968," *Journal of Strategic Studies* 9, no. 1 (March 1986), 35–43.

3. James R. Schlesinger, "The Postwar Era: The Eagle and the Bear," *Foreign Affairs* (Summer 1985), available at www.foreignaffairs.com/articles/39917/james-schlesinger/the-postwar-era-the-eagle-and-the-bear. This basic strategic imbalance between the United States and the USSR prevailed from the 1940s through the 1950s. Throughout this period, though the Soviets developed atomic weapons and delivery systems, the United States remained well ahead, by the 1950s deploying thousands of high-yield thermonuclear weapons upon delivery systems that could preempt the ability of the Soviet Union to deliver more than a limited number of such weapons against American targets.

4. John Gaddis estimated that, in October 1962, the US advantage in strategic weaponry was approximately 17 to 1. John L. Gaddis, *We Now Know: Rethinking Cold War History* (Oxford: Oxford University Press, 1997), 262.

5. US nuclear war plans remain almost universally classified. This chapter's analysis of the planning and operational impact of limited nuclear options therefore relies on relevant declassified and reliable secondary sources as well as the author's discussions with knowledgeable officials with access to SAC's plans.

6. As Eisenhower argued in 1956, the only prudent course would be "to get our striking force into the air immediately upon notice of hostile action by the Soviets." Massive retaliation would be the "key to survival." The president's approach was incorporated into nuclear war plans. Rosenberg, "The Origins of Overkill," 42–43. See also Marc Trachtenberg, *A Constructed Peace: The Making of the European Settlement, 1945–1963* (Princeton, NJ: Princeton University Press, 1999), 256; and David A. Rosenberg, "Nuclear War Planning," in Michael Howard et al., eds., *The Laws of War: Constraints on Warfare in the Western World* (New Haven, CT: Yale University Press, 1994), especially 170–175. Indeed, in Rosenberg's estimation, "the Eisenhower administration appears to have actively discouraged the development of constraints on nuclear war planning" (ibid., 171). For an excellent history of Eisenhower's thinking on this matter, see Evan Thomas, *Ike's Bluff: President Eisenhower's Secret Battle to Save the World* (Boston: Little, Brown, 2012).

7. See, e.g., National Security Council Document 162, "Basic National Security Policy," U.S. Department of State, *Foreign Relations of the United States, 1952–1954, National Security Affairs, Volume II, Part I* (Washington, DC: Government Printing Office, 1984), 489 et seq.

8. See, for instance, Trachtenberg, *A Constructed Peace*, 172.

9. "The only options specified in the plan pertained to varying levels of the alert force; no provisions existed for discriminating the attack either by country or by target category. Basically, the plan was intended to deliver the largest strike that available U.S. forces could marshal at the time of attack." May et al., *History of the Strategic Arms Competition*, 467–468. See U.S. Strategic Command, History and Research Division, *History of the Joint Strategic Target Planning Staff: Background and Preparation of SIOP-62*, available at National Security Archive, www.gwu.edu/nsarchiv/nukevault/

ebb285/sidebar/SIOP-62_history.pdf. SAC's history of SIOP-63 summarized, "SIOP-62 had certain, if limited, features of flexibility, but essentially the plan was tailored for reaction of the complete force and in retaliation." U.S. Strategic Command, History and Research Division, *History of the Joint Strategic Target Planning Staff: Preparation of SIOP-63*, available at National Security Archive, www.gwu.edu/nsarchiv/nukevault/ebb285/sidebar/SIOP-63_history.pdf.

10. For examples of this line of thinking, see Chapter 2, by Andrew Ross, which examines early works on limited nuclear war. See also Robert E. Osgood, *Limited War: The Challenge to American Strategy* (Chicago: University of Chicago Press, 1957); and William W. Kaufmann, "The Requirements of Deterrence," in W. W. Kaufmann, ed., *Military Policy and National Security* (Princeton, NJ: Princeton University Press, 1956).

11. For intimations of this thinking, see Eisenhower's "Basic National Security Policy" of August 1959, NSC 5906/1, available in U.S. Department of State, *Foreign Relations of the United States, 1958–1960, National Security Policy; Arms Control and Disarmament* (Washington, DC: Government Printing Office, 1996), 292 et seq. This document placed "main reliance" of US national security strategy on nuclear weapons, but recognized the need for "a flexible and selective capability including nuclear capability" to combat local aggression (295–296).

12. U.S. Department of State, *Foreign Relations of the United States: 1961–1963, Volume XI, Cuban Missile Crisis and Aftermath* (Washington, DC: Government Printing Office, 1996), Document 21, 62.

13. Draft Presidential Memorandum from Secretary of Defense McNamara to President Kennedy, September 23, 1961, available in U.S. Department of State, *Foreign Relations of the United States, 1961–1963, National Security Policy* (Washington, DC: Government Printing Office, 1996), Document 46, 143.

14. For the Kennedy administration's efforts to revise the SIOP to reflect these objectives, see May, *History of the Strategic Arms Competition*, especially 587–608.

15. *Preparation of SIOP-63*, 14 and 28.

16. See, for histories of this development, *History of the Strategic Arms Competition*, especially 510–608 and 799–805; Henry S. Rowen, "Formulating Strategic Doctrine," *Commission on the Organization of the Government for the Conduct of Foreign Policy*, Appendices, Volume 4 (Washington, DC: U.S. government Printing Office, 1975), 231–232; and Rosenberg, "Nuclear War Planning," 181–183.

17. See the interview of McNamara in Michael Charlton, *From Deterrence to Defense: The Inside Story of Strategic Policy* (Cambridge, MA: Harvard University Press, 1987), 17–18.

18. For greater detail on the definition of "assured destruction," see McNamara's Draft Presidential Memorandum to President Johnson, "Recommended FY 1966–1970 Programs for Strategic Offensive Forces, Continental Air and Missile Defense Forces, and Civil Defense," December 3, 1964, available www.gwu.edu/nsarchiv/nukevault/ebb311/doc02.pdf.

19. McNamara later claimed to have believed that, even in the absence of credible plans, the United States would still be able to conduct a limited nuclear war. He

therefore did not dedicate the effort and resources to trying to make such employment practicable. See Rosenberg, "Reality and Responsibility," 48–49. Rosenberg's skepticism of the merits of this belief is well justified.

20. Desmond Ball, "Development of the SIOP, 1960–1983," in Ball and Jeffrey Richelson, eds., *Strategic Nuclear Targeting* (Ithaca, NY: Cornell University Press, 1986), 70.

21. See *History of the Strategic Arms Competition*, 607–608; and Rowen, "Formulating Strategic Doctrine," 232.

22. For a history of the early part of this effort, see William Burr, "The Nixon Administration, the 'Horror Strategy,' and the Search for Limited Nuclear Options, 1969–1972: Prelude to the Schlesinger Doctrine," *Journal of Cold War Studies* 7, no. 3 (Summer 2005), 34–78.

23. George W. Baer, *One Hundred Years of Sea Power: The U.S. Navy, 1890–1990* (Stanford, CA: Stanford University Press, 1996), 396.

24. "First Annual Report to the Congress on U.S. Foreign Policy for the 1970s," February 18, 1970, *Public Papers of the President of the United States, Richard Nixon, Containing the Public Messages, Speeches, and Statements of the President, 1970* (Washington, DC: Government Printing Office, 1971), 173.

25. See, for instance, memorandum from Kissinger to President Nixon, "Additional Studies of the U.S. Strategic Posture," July 1, 1969, available at www.gwu.edu/nsarchiv/NSAEBB/NSAEBB173/SIOP-9a.pdf.

26. Interview of James R. Schlesinger by John G. Hines, October 29, 1991, available at www.gwu.edu/nsarchiv/nukevault/ebb285/vol%20II%20Schlesinger.PDF, 129. See also Terry Terriff, *The Nixon Administration and the Making of U.S. Nuclear Strategy* (Ithaca, NY: Cornell University Press, 1995).

27. National Security Council, Defense Program Review Committee, "U.S. Strategic Objectives and Force Posture Executive Summary," January 3, 1972, 36, available at www.gwu.edu/nsarchiv/NSAEBB/NSAEBB173/index.htm#10.

28. See the "Joint Staff Briefing of the Single Integrated Operational Plan" to President Nixon, January 27, 1969, available at www.gwu.edu/nsarchiv/NSAEBB/NSAEBB173/SIOP-1.pdf. For a description of the options, see Burr, "The Nixon Administration," 44.

29. Burr, "The Nixon Administration," 45. Needless to say, this calls into question McNamara's confidence that limited nuclear war plans could have been developed in the event of a conflict under conditions of great stress and danger.

30. National Security Study Memorandum [NSSM] 169, "U.S. Nuclear Policy," February 13, 1973, available at http://nixon.archives.gov/virtuallibrary/documents/nssm/nssm_169.pdf. For a history of the Foster Panel, see Burr, "The Nixon Administration," 69–76.

31. NSSM 169 Summary Report, June 8, 1973, available at www.gwu.edu/nsarchiv/NSAEBB/NSAEBB173/SIOP-21.pdf.

32. National Security Decision Memorandum [NSDM] 242, "Policy for Planning the Employment of Nuclear Weapons," January 17, 1974, available at http://nixon.archives.gov/virtuallibrary/documents/nsdm/nsdm_242.pdf.

33. The NUWEP, an organizational innovation, itself represented an effort to provide more flexibility and options for national leaders in the war plans. See Charles P. Hopkins, *Unclassified History of the Joint Strategic Target Planning Staff (JSTPS)* (Omaha: U.S. Strategic Command, 1990), 7.

34. Memorandum from Major General John A. Wickham, Jr., to Major General Brent Scowcroft, "Policy Guidance for the Employment of Nuclear Weapons [NUWEP]," April 3, 1974, available at www2.gwu.edu/~nsarchiv/NSAEBB/NSAEBB173/SIOP-25.pdf.

35. Secretary of Defense James R. Schlesinger, *Annual Defense Department Report for FY1975* (Washington, DC: Government Printing Office, 1974), 38 and 44.

36. William Odom, who played an intimate role in nuclear policy issues during the Carter administration, found during the beginning of that presidency that planners at SAC were still seeking "political guidance" as to how exactly to plan for limited nuclear use, resorting in its absence to smaller target sets of adversary weapons. See William E. Odom, "The Origins and Design of Presidential Decision-59: A Memoir," in Henry D. Sokolski, ed., *Getting MAD: Nuclear Mutual Assured Destruction, Its Origins and Practice* (Carlisle, PA: Strategic Studies Institute, 2004), 181. See also Henry Kissinger, *White House Years* (Boston: Little, Brown, 1979), 217–218; and Janne E. Nolan, *Guardians of the Arsenal: The Politics of Nuclear Strategy* (New York: Basic Books, 1989), 123–125.

37. Hines interview of Schlesinger.

38. Desmond Ball, "U.S. Strategic Forces: How Would They Be Used?," *International Security* 7, no. 3 (Winter 1982–1983), 35–38. Nonetheless, the doctrine of NSDM-242 was never fully implemented due to technical and political challenges. Leon Sloss and Marc Dean Millot, "U.S. Nuclear Strategy in Evolution," *Strategic Review* 12, no. 1 (Winter 1984), 23.

39. The Nixon administration noted that the incorporation of options for flexibility did not necessarily require "drastic change in our nuclear programs," in part because existing systems provided inherent promise for flexible employment. See "First Annual Report to the Congress on U.S. Foreign Policy for the 1970s." See also Rowen, "Formulating Strategic Doctrine," 227–228. Schlesinger made this point explicitly in Annual Reports. See FY1975 *DOD Annual Report*, 5, and the Secretary of Defense James R. Schlesinger, *Annual Defense Department Report for FY1976* (Washington, DC: Government Printing Office), II-5.

40. See memorandum of William E. Odom to Assistant to the President for National Security Affairs Zbigniew Brzezinski, "Draft PD on Nuclear Targeting," March 22, 1980, available at www.gwu.edu/nsarchiv/nukevault/ebb390/docs/3-22-80%20Odom%20memo.pdf. Odom argued that the Nixon/Ford administrations did not link acquisition and employment policy following NSDM-242, and thus the Defense Department did not buy systems to implement the new doctrine of flexibility.

For an earlier Carter administration view of the Nixon/Ford era efforts, see the memorandum of Zbigniew Brzezinski to President Carter, "Our Nuclear War Doctrine: Limited Nuclear Options and Regional Nuclear Options," March 31, 1977, available at www.gwu.edu/nsarchiv/nukevault/ebb390/docs/3-31-77%20ZB%20to%20Carter.pdf.

41. For an emphasis on influencing Soviet leaders' calculations about post-nuclear-war scenarios, see the November 1978 report of the influential Leon Sloss–led "Nuclear Targeting Policy Review," available at www.gwu.edu/nsarchiv/nukevault/ebb390/docs/11-1-78%20policy%20review%20summary.pdf.

42. Presidential Directive 59, "Nuclear Weapons Employment Policy," July 25, 1980, available at www.gwu.edu/nsarchiv/nukevault/ebb390/docs/7-25-80%20PD%2059.pdf.

43. U.S. Department of Defense, "Policy Guidance for the Employment of Nuclear Weapons (NUWEP)," October 1980, available at www.gwu.edu/nsarchiv/nukevault/ebb390/docs/10-24-80%20nuclear%20weapons%20employment%20policy.pdf.

44. Secretary of Defense Harold Brown, remarks delivered at the Convocation Ceremonies for the Naval War College, Newport, Rhode Island, August 20, 1980, available in Philip Bobbitt, Lawrence Freedman, and Gregory F. Treverton, eds., *U.S. Nuclear Strategy: A Reader* (New York: New York University Press, 1989). See also Secretary of Defense Harold Brown, *Department of Defense Annual Report for FY1981* (Washington, DC: Government Printing Office, 1980), 65–68. Though PD-59 was not finalized until late in the Carter administration, the administration had elevated the development of limited options from early on, including in PD-18 of August 26, 1977. Ball, "Development of the SIOP," 76.

45. See Brown, Newport speech, *U.S. Nuclear Strategy*, 410.

46. *Department of Defense Annual Report for FY1981*, 66–67.

47. See Brown, Newport speech, *U.S. Nuclear Strategy*, 413. For the actual implementing directives, see PD-59, 2. See also Sloss and Millot, "U.S. Nuclear Strategy in Evolution," 24.

48. Presidential Directive 53, "National Security Telecommunications Policy," November 15, 1979, www.jimmycarterlibrary.org/documents/pddirectives/pd53.pdf.

49. See Walter B. Slocombe, "The Countervailing Strategy," *International Security* 5, no. 4 (Spring 1981), especially 23. The Schlesinger doctrine, meanwhile, had more clearly focused on using limited nuclear options to demonstrate resolve. 1974 NUWEP, 6–7. That said, the distinction between the two approaches lay primarily in degree of emphasis.

50. Interview of Franklin Miller by the author, October 18, 2010.

51. Desmond Ball and Robert Toth, "Revising the SIOP: Taking War-Fighting to Dangerous Extremes," *International Security* 14, no. 4 (Spring 1990), 67–68.

52. For a history, see David N. Schwartz, *NATO's Nuclear Dilemmas* (Washington, DC: Brookings Institution Press, 1983), 193–253.

53. Chancellor Helmut Schmidt, 1977 Alastair Buchan Memorial Lecture, October 28, 1977, available in *Survival* 20, no. 1 (January/February 1978), 2–10. See also Henry Kissinger, "The Future of NATO," in Kenneth A. Myers, ed., *NATO—The Next Thirty*

Years: The Changing Political, Economic, and Military Setting (Boulder, CO: Westview Press, 1980), 3–14.

54. *The North Atlantic Treaty Organization: Facts and Figures* (Brussels: NATO, 1989), 218.

55. Robert McNamara in 1983 quoted a member of NATO's High Level Group stating that "NATO has not yet managed to agree on guidelines for the follow-on use of nuclear weapons if a first attempt to communicate NATO's intentions through a controlled demonstrative use did not succeed in persuading the adversary to halt hostilities." Robert S. McNamara, "The Military Role of Nuclear Weapons: Perceptions and Misperceptions," *Foreign Affairs* (Fall 1983), 69–70. From a limitation perspective, the principal distinguishing advantage of the Pershings and GLCMs was that they would operate and launch from within the theater of conflict. Why the Soviets would see the relevant criterion as where a nuclear weapons was launched *from*—as opposed to what it was targeted *against* or how big a yield it delivered—was never clear. These problems of how to limit the military or tactical use of nuclear weapons appear to have plagued NATO throughout the Cold War. See, e.g., Kissinger, "The Future of NATO," 8; Schwartz, *NATO's Nuclear Dilemmas*, 235–236; McGeorge Bundy et al., "Nuclear Weapons and the Atlantic Alliance," *Foreign Affairs* (Spring 1982), 756; and the conclusions from a classified conference held at Sandia National Laboratories in 1990 on the history of NATO's theater nuclear policy recorded in David S. Yost, "The History of NATO Theater Nuclear Force Policy: Key Findings from the Sandia Conference," *Journal of Strategic Studies* 15, no. 2 (June 1992), 248–255.

56. General Bernard W. Rogers, "The Atlantic Alliance: Prescriptions for a Difficult Decade," *Foreign Affairs* (Summer 1982), 1152. See also Secretary of Defense Caspar W. Weinberger, *Annual Report to the Congress for Fiscal Year 1984* (Washington, DC: Government Printing Office, 1983), 51.

57. See, for instance, National Security Decision Directive (NSDD) 12, "Strategic Forces Modernization Program," October 1, 1981, available at www.fas.org/irp/offdocs/nsdd/nsdd-12.pdf. This early policy directive focused on improving the effectiveness, survivability, and resiliency of strategic forces rather than on their ability to meet limited employment objectives.

58. See, e.g., Sloss and Millot, "U.S. Nuclear Strategy," 20, 25.

59. Secretary of Defense Caspar Weinberger, Testimony to the Senate Foreign Relations Committee, December 14, 1982, in Philip L. Cantelon et al., eds., *The American Atom: A Documentary History of Nuclear Policies from the Discovery of Fission to the Present* (Philadelphia: University of Pennsylvania Press, 1991), 222.

60. See, e.g., NSDD 75, "U.S. Relations with the USSR," January 17, 1983, available at www.fas.org/irp/offdocs/nsdd/23-1957t.gif, 2.

61. NSDD 32, "U.S. National Security Strategy," May 20, 1982, available at www.fas.org/irp/offdocs/nsdd/nsdd-032.htm, 5.

62. Letter of Secretary of Defense Caspar Weinberger to *New York Review of Books* et al., August 23, 1982, available at www.nybooks.com/articles/archives/1982/nov/04/secretary-of-defense-weinbergers-letter-of-august-/ (emphasis in the original).

63. Quoted in Nolan, *Guardians of the Arsenal*, 251.

64. Caspar W. Weinberger, "U.S. Defense Strategy," *Foreign Affairs* (Spring 1986), 680–682.

65. Interview of Franklin Miller by author, September 15, 2010. For a history, see Nolan, *Guardians of the Arsenal*, 251–261.

66. See, for instance, Scott Sagan, *Moving Targets: Nuclear Strategy and National Security* (Princeton, NJ: Princeton University Press, 1989), 48–57, and chap. 2; Nolan, *Guardians of the Arsenal*, 251–261.

67. NSDD 13 of October 19, 1981 on "Nuclear Weapons Employment Policy" remains classified, as does the particularly controversial Fiscal Year 1984–1988 Defense Planning Guidance. See, however, NSDD 281, "Nuclear Weapons Command and Control," August 21, 1987, available at www.fas.org/irp/offdocs/nsdd/23-3035a.gif, which continued the focus on flexible and responsive capabilities. See also Richard Halloran, "Protracted Nuclear War," *Air Force Magazine* (March 2008), 59, available at www. airforce-magazine.com/MagazineArchive/Pages/2008/March%202008/0308nuclear. aspx; and David M. Kunsman and Douglas B. Lawson, *A Primer on U.S. Strategic Nuclear Policy* (Albuquerque, NM: Sandia National Laboratories, 2001), 64.

68. Interview with Franklin Miller, February 17, 2012.

69. Indeed, David Rosenberg judged that "the history of nuclear strategy in the Nixon, Ford, Carter, and Reagan administrations centers on the search for such flexible options." Rosenberg, "Reality and Responsibility," 50.

70. See, for instance, interview of Gen.-Col. (Ret.) Andrian A. Danilevich by John G. Hines, September 21, 1992, 31–32 and 64, available at www.gwu.edu/nsarchiv/ nukevault/ebb285/vol%20iI%20Danilevich.pdf; and interview of Vitalii Leonidovich Kataev and Viktor Popov by John G. Hines, May–June 1993, 101, available at www.gwu. edu/nsarchiv/nukevault/ebb285/vol%20II%20Kataev.PDF.

71. Schlesinger, for instance, was well aware of this quandary, and had in mind limited nuclear strikes that he believed, despite Moscow's claims, would not provoke the Soviets to escalate to general nuclear war. Schlesinger explained that he "did not expect the Soviet Union to escalate from a small-scale American use of tactical nuclear weapons along the flanks ... to a global nuclear war. ... He hoped that if the U.S. reacted to a conventional Soviet attack with selective nuclear strikes, that the USSR would have refrained from escalating to global use." To Schlesinger, "the essence of LNO [Limited Nuclear Options] lay in U.S. declaratory commitments to the employment of selected nuclear strikes against a Soviet/Warsaw Pact conventional attack on Western Europe. ... Schlesinger did not care whether the Soviets believed in LNO, so long as they believed that the U.S. was convinced of the feasibility of LNO. Even if the Soviets refused to believe that a nuclear war could be limited, they would still be deterred because, in their view, a limited U.S. strike would lead to an all-out nuclear war, a very self-deterring prospect." In terms of targeting, Schlesinger envisioned "launching a small strike against real targets, such as Henhouse radars in the Soviet Arctic, avoiding cities and other targets that would produce large casualties ... and keeping the number of weapons low." See interview of Schlesinger by

Hines, 129–130. He also envisioned at least the capability to conduct limited hard-target attacks, especially if the Soviets attacked the US ICBM force first. DOD Annual Report FY1976, II-5.

72. The Soviets took the US threat to resort to limited nuclear use seriously enough to prepare responses to selective US nuclear strikes, including the possibility of employing so-called dosage strikes. See, for instance, interview of Danilevich by Hines, 58–59.

73. See, for instance, interview of Gen.-Col. Varfolomei Vladimirovich Korobushin, former Deputy Chief of the Strategic Rocket Forces, by John G. Hines, December 10, 1992, 106, available at www.gwu.edu/nsarchiv/nukevault/ebb285/vol%20 II%20Korobushin.PDF.

74. For further elaboration of the logic of this point, see Thomas Schelling, *Arms and Influence* (New Haven, CT: Yale University Press, 1966), especially chap. 5; and Charles Glaser, *Analyzing Strategic Nuclear Policy* (Princeton, NJ: Princeton University Press, 1990), 53–54.

75. Interview of Schlesinger by Hines, 129.

76. For a useful analysis of these factors in the Cold War lens, see Rosenberg, "Reality and Responsibility," 35–42.

77. On this point, see Donald MacKenzie, *Inventing Accuracy: A Historical Sociology of Nuclear Missile Guidance* (Cambridge, MA: MIT Press, 1993).

78. See, for instance, the description by Gen.-Col. Danilevich of the fearful refusal of Soviet leader Leonid Brezhnev to push the button for simulated release of Soviet nuclear forces during an exercise in 1972. As Danilevich described, Brezhnev and Kosygin were "visibly terrified" by the prospects of a serious nuclear exchange. Interview with Danilevich, September 21, 1992, 27.

4 Post–Cold War US Nuclear Strategy

Paul I. Bernstein

THIS CHAPTER TRACES THE EVOLUTION OF US NUCLEAR strategy in the post–Cold War period, continuing the narrative presented in Chapters 2 and 3. It demonstrates that the effort begun decades ago to enhance the ability of the United States to employ nuclear weapons with greater selectivity continued after the fall of the Soviet empire. Increasingly, though, innovations in nuclear employment planning and targeting have focused less on Russia and more on regional threats that became a more salient security concern for the United States beginning in the 1990s, in particular regional actors prepared to challenge the status quo and armed with weapons of mass destruction (WMD). The United States today does not proclaim a strategy of limited nuclear war, and the stated policy of the Obama administration is to narrow the circumstances under which the use of nuclear weapons would be contemplated. Still, policymakers cannot rule out the possibility that conflict with any number of actors could lead to circumstances under which the use of nuclear weapons will be among the options a president will need to consider. While this chapter does not speculate on what those circumstance might be or the specific nuclear options that might be put before a US president, it is a reasonable assumption that the employment of nuclear weapons would be viewed as a last resort and a means to achieve decisive war termination.

Beyond Russia—The Bush 41 Years

When George H. W. Bush assumed the presidency in January 1989, he did not move to replace the nuclear strategy established by President Ronald Reagan in 1981. That strategy had emphasized prevailing in a protracted nuclear war with the Soviet Union—one that might last up to 180 days.[1] The Reagan strategy—much like its predecessor in the Carter years embodied in Presidential Directive 59—sought to exploit the fears of the Soviet leadership that a prolonged nuclear conflict would undermine its political control.

The strategic objectives of the protracted war doctrine had been incorporated into the Single Integrated Operational Plan (SIOP)—the nuclear war plan developed and maintained by Strategic Air Command (SAC)—in October 1983 (SIOP-6) and subsequently into plan revisions through SIOP-6F (October 1989). Employment planning emphasized the ability to target the Soviet leadership and destroy the regime's means of political and military control.[2] An ambitious nuclear modernization program was promoted to support the strategy, including the MX intercontinental ballistic missile and the Trident D5 submarine-launched ballistic missile. At the same time, the Reagan years saw a significant reduction in the number of targets in the National Strategic Target Data Base, accomplished largely through the elimination of targets associated with missions whose relative importance had diminished.[3]

Many argued that the Reagan strategy diverged sharply from earlier strategies in its open avowal to seek victory in a nuclear war with Moscow and its perceived shift toward a warfighting doctrine. At the operational level, however, changes to target planning represented a further refinement of "flexible response" and the process begun in the early 1960s to provide the president with a greater range of more discriminate employment options, with steadily increasing emphasis on Soviet forces, war-supporting industry, and leadership, and decreased reliance on holding cities explicitly at risk. Complementing the further movement toward limited nuclear options that would be pre-planned were emerging advances in planning tools that promised more responsive targeting techniques. "Adaptive planning" as it matured allowed military planners to create options for the president not limited to pre-planned strike packages, thus further enhancing the leadership's ability to tailor—and limit—the use of nuclear weapons.

As noted in the preceding chapter, the Bush administration continued the process of integrating limited nuclear options into employment planning.

The logic of providing the president with the widest possible range of options should the use of nuclear weapons have to be contemplated remained just as powerful after the end of the Cold War. While President Bush and his advisors may not have felt a sense of urgency to revisit the protracted war strategy, witnessing the profound changes unfolding in the Soviet bloc they certainly recognized the need to adopt nuclear policies that could help promote stability and prevent dangerous nuclear crises from emerging as the Soviet empire disintegrated. A principal concern was to reduce the risks posed by the vast arsenal of nuclear weapons scattered across Soviet territory. This led to innovative policy initiatives such as the Nunn-Lugar Cooperative Threat Reduction program and the Presidential Nuclear Initiatives of 1991–92.[4]

It was also clear that political change demanded a fresh look at the nuclear planning process. In November 1989, Secretary of Defense Richard Cheney directed that a comprehensive review of the SIOP be undertaken. Completed in April 1991, this review, according to the few contemporary accounts publicly available, led Cheney and General Colin Powell, Chairman of the Joint Chiefs of Staff, to conclude that the SIOP was out of date, lacking clear objectives, and plagued by methodological problems.[5] An important result of the review was a further significant reduction of targets in Russia, former Soviet republics, and former Warsaw Pact states, leaving a SIOP target base of approximately 2,500, according to at least one public account.[6]

There was also growing concern about new types of strategic dangers. Threat assessments had already begun to highlight the proliferation of weapons of mass destruction (WMD) as an increasingly serious challenge to US interests and military dominance. Shortly before the United States invaded Iraq in 1991, the Bush administration signaled to the Iraqi leadership that it was prepared to respond with tactical nuclear weapons to Iraqi use of chemical or biological weapons and other heinous acts.[7] While Iraq did not employ these weapons against coalition forces, in the aftermath of Operation Desert Storm the possibility that the United States would confront regional adversaries capable of employing WMD became an important premise of defense planning generally and nuclear planning in particular. The Defense Department's 1992 annual report stated that "the possibility that Third World nations may acquire nuclear capabilities has led the department to make adjustments to nuclear and strategic defense forces and to the policies that guide them," and that nuclear strategy "must now also encompass potential instabilities that could arise when states or leaders perceive they have little to lose from employing weapons of mass destruction."[8]

Translating the new guidance into responsive operational plans required a new approach to employment planning. US Strategic Command (STRATCOM), established in 1992 to replace Strategic Air Command, had to reconfigure a planning methodology focused principally on the Cold War threat to one now also capable of supporting global operations against a more diverse set of adversaries in contingencies whose political-military objectives could vary widely. This involved the acceleration of adaptive planning concepts to develop what STRATCOM characterized as a "flexible, globally focused war-planning process" designed to respond to "spontaneous threats which are more likely to emerge in a new international environment unconstrained by the superpower standoff."[9] According to General Lee Butler, the first commander of STRATCOM, new adaptive planning capabilities would offer "unique solutions, tailored to generic, regional dangers involving weapons of mass destruction."[10] The SIOP approved in July 1993 became, in the language of STRATCOM planners, the "living SIOP," an operational plan based on the "continuous analysis of guidance, forces, and target changes."[11]

The First Nuclear Posture Review—The Clinton Years

Consideration of nuclear strategy during the first term of Bill Clinton was dominated by the congressionally mandated Nuclear Posture Review (NPR) completed in 1994. While the NPR provided an opportunity to consider major revisions to strategy and forces, in the end it led to only modest changes to force posture and almost none to employment doctrine. The NPR adopted a cautionary stance toward Russia, noting that the political changes set in motion in the late 1980s were hopeful but could not be considered permanent and that Russia continued to maintain a large nuclear capability that could be directed against the United States. The NPR articulated a "lead and hedge" strategy, whereby the United States would continue to press for further progress in US-Russia arms control but avoid precipitous changes in nuclear policy and posture so as to hedge against the reversal of reforms in Russia. The NPR asserted that the overall role of nuclear weapons had diminished in the post–Cold War world and that as a result the United States required a smaller arsenal. At the same time, the United States would maintain a nuclear triad as well as a significant capability to deploy a larger force if the security situation warranted.

The 1994 NPR cited growing WMD proliferation as an important feature of the new security environment and recognized that nuclear deterrence played a role in managing this strategic challenge. How much of a role was one of the more hotly contested issues in the NPR deliberations.[12] Many civilian leaders were cautious about signaling too strong a reliance on nuclear weapons to deter regional WMD threats, especially chemical and biological weapons, for two reasons. First, such a policy could work against the goal of further reducing nuclear forces. Second, perceptions that the United States was increasing the role of nuclear weapons by planning for nuclear strikes against non-nuclear states could undermine assurances Washington had provided to non-nuclear weapons states and complicate US efforts to achieve a positive outcome at the upcoming review conference of the Nuclear Nonproliferation Treaty (NPT).[13]

Other participants in the NPR process pressed for a more expansive role for nuclear weapons to both deter and provide military options against the full range of regional WMD-related targets. In the end, the rollout of the NPR presented a mixed picture. Briefings to Congress suggested a prominent role for nuclear weapons in counterproliferation.[14] The public presentation of the NPR findings was more circumspect. The adjusted nuclear posture elevated counterproliferation to a role co-equal with "direct deterrence" and several other strategic imperatives associated with the nation's nuclear forces.[15] Moreover, the NPR retained the policy by which the United States reserved the right to use nuclear weapons first in any conflict, despite efforts by some participants to promote a no-first-use doctrine. However, in discussing the capabilities required to counter WMD, the NPR placed greatest emphasis on strengthened prevention efforts, more robust conventional forces, and missile defense.

Largely out of the public eye, the operational community continued to integrate regional WMD targeting into nuclear planning. In the run-up to the NPR, the Defense Department issued a revised doctrine for joint nuclear operations. The document stated that "deterrence of the employment of enemy WMD, whether it be nuclear, biological, or chemical, requires that the enemy leadership believes the United States has both the ability and will to respond promptly and with selective responses that are credible (commensurate with the scale or scope of enemy attacks and the nature of US interests at stake) and militarily effective."[16] STRATCOM began to develop region- and country-specific nuclear operational plans, focused on WMD-related targets in so-called rogue states.

Real world events underscored the question of how nuclear weapons could be leveraged or even used to deal with regional WMD threats. In 1996, when it became publicly known that Libya was constructing a large underground chemical weapons facility in Tarhuna, Secretary of Defense William Perry issued several public warnings to the Qaddafi regime demanding that the site be abandoned. He declared that the United States would not permit the site to be completed, and reserved the right to take "drastic, preventative measures" toward this end.[17] These statements seemed to reinforce earlier remarks Perry had made in discussing US capabilities to deter chemical weapon attacks, in which he referred to both advanced conventional munitions and nuclear weapons as part of the range of effective alternatives available to the president.[18] Some Pentagon officials went further, suggesting that the United States lacked credible non-nuclear options against the Libyan facility (and others of its type) and would have to rely on a new generation of nuclear weapons capable of penetrating into underground or hardened structures in order to destroy it.[19] While the Defense Department was quick to clarify that the United States had no intention of launching a nuclear strike against the Libyan site, this episode nonetheless suggested (as had the Gulf War experience with Iraq) that at times senior officials see utility in issuing nuclear threats in the belief they are likely to have a powerful deterrent effect, even if doubts exist about the necessity of such threats or the willingness of the United States to make good on them.

After completion of the Nuclear Posture Review in 1994, three years would pass before the Clinton administration adopted a new nuclear strategy by issuing Presidential Decision Directive (PDD) 60 in November 1997. PDD 60 replaced Reagan-era guidance that for sixteen years had called for the United States to plan for protracted nuclear war with the Soviet Union and, later, Russia. According to the briefing provided by a White House official and contemporary press accounts, PDD 60 "removes from presidential guidance all previous references to being able to wage a nuclear war successfully or to prevail in a nuclear war. . . . The emphasis in this PDD is therefore on deterring nuclear wars or the use of nuclear weapons at any level, not fighting [with] them."[20] At the same time, PDD 60 retained the option to initiate nuclear use against aggressors—including non-nuclear states—that have prospective access to nuclear weapons,[21] and reportedly directed the development of nuclear options for contingencies involving WMD threats to the United States, as well as expanded limited attack options against China.[22]

The Aftermath of 9/11—The Bush 43 Years

The presidency of George W. Bush saw a more complete transition to a nuclear planning enterprise that fully integrates regional contingencies. This process took place in the shadow of the terrorist attacks of September 2001, which underscored that the United States faced radical threats against which a proactive strategy leveraging the full range of US military capabilities was required. New kinds of strategic capabilities were needed to deter, defeat, and defend against asymmetric attacks. Nuclear weapons might be less central as an element of the future US-Russia relationship—thus creating an opportunity to reduce strategic nuclear force levels—but nuclear weapons remained a vital instrument of national power and had an important role to play in preparing for possible confrontations with regional states intent on challenging the United States or its allies. While overshadowed by the ground wars in Southwest Asia initiated after 9/11, the effort during the Bush years to retool the US strategic forces posture was an important development that generated serious debate and led to notable changes in policies and plans.

While the 2001 Nuclear Posture Review was prepared before the attack on the World Trade Center and the anthrax letters that followed, its avowed goal to present a blueprint for transforming the US strategic posture dovetailed well with the post-9/11 need to convey a dynamic response to an increasingly complex and dangerous security landscape. In presenting the NPR, Defense Department officials characterized the security environment as one in which the United States faced multiple sources of potential conflict and a range of contingencies, many involving states of lesser overall power possessing or seeking WMD and ballistic missiles. There were several implications. Deterrence was more uncertain because of the nature of the regimes posing potential threats. More varied capabilities were needed to avoid over-reliance on nuclear threats. And nuclear plans needed to be more flexible given the range of contingencies.[23]

Contingencies defined by the NPR were not detailed scenarios for conflict with specific states but more a series of planning categories against which nuclear force requirements could be weighed. For immediate contingencies that were current and well understood, and for unexpected contingencies that could emerge quickly with little warning, operationally deployed nuclear forces provided for deterrence and response. Because Russia was no longer considered an immediate threat, these nuclear forces could safely be reduced, nuclear weapons could recede to the background in US-Russian relations, and the US could move away from the Cold War's threat-based approach to force planning.

However, other immediate contingencies, as well as the requirements of unexpected and potential contingencies (those that could plausibly emerge in the future), placed a limit on how far nuclear reductions could go. Moreover, existing forces would not be sufficient to address emerging challenges. New types of nuclear capabilities were needed to meet the operational requirements of regional conflict with WMD-armed adversaries. In reporting to Congress, Secretary of Defense Donald Rumsfeld and his aides noted that the NPR called for a US capability to "modify, upgrade, or replace portions of the extant nuclear force or develop concepts for follow-on nuclear weapons systems better suited to the nation's needs."[24] Specifically, it was argued, the existing nuclear stockpile featured many warheads that would deliver large yields with modest accuracy, whereas deterring and defeating new WMD-capable challengers required weapons with lower yields and greater accuracy, and an ability to defeat hardened and deeply buried structures.[25]

The effort to improve nuclear capabilities in the period after the NPR was issued was often referred to as "nuclear transformation." Broader than weapons initiatives alone, transformation also encompassed enhancing readiness to conduct underground nuclear explosive tests and modernizing the nuclear weapons production complex to ensure a more responsive infrastructure. However, it was the weapons initiatives that proved most controversial. The pursuit of weapons with low yields, tailored effects, and earth penetrating capabilities was considered important by many in the Bush administration because these systems were viewed as more likely to deter rogue states—especially those that were investing in hard and deeply buried structures to protect WMD or state leaders, and those that might believe the United States would be "self-deterred" from using nuclear weapons because of the collateral damage likely to be generated by its relatively high-yield weapons. The NPR presumed that deterrence would be enhanced by these new weapons because adversaries would view them as more likely to be used by an American president.

The rationale for expanding nuclear capabilities was less persuasive outside administration circles. There was significant resistance from members of Congress of both political parties and among elements of the strategic policy community outside of government. Some critics were not persuaded that these new nuclear weapons would provide significantly improved capabilities in relation to existing stockpile weapons. Others believed the administration needed to show a stronger commitment to arms control before asking Congress to support new stockpile capabilities. More vocal were those arguing that pursuit of these weapons undermined US leadership in nonproliferation at a time when Washington was working actively to prevent other states from acquiring nuclear weapons.

The most vigorous opposition came from those who viewed the new weapons initiatives as dangerously counterproductive precisely because they promised more usable capabilities for a limited nuclear war—that is, they were seen as lowering the threshold of nuclear use and enabling a nuclear warfighting strategy that seemed premised on the expected failure of deterrence. Especially in the context of the 2002 National Security Strategy, which outlined a doctrine of preemption to respond to gathering threats, the idea of providing the president with such capabilities struck some legislators and outside experts as unwise. Unable to overcome opposition to its efforts to develop and field these new types of nuclear weapons, the Bush administration ultimately retreated and moved on to new concepts designed to ensure the enduring reliability and effectiveness of the existing nuclear stockpile.

Initiatives to develop new nuclear capabilities may have faltered, but operational plans were being developed or adapted in response to the requirements of the NPR and other high-level guidance. New employment planning guidance was issued in June 2002 as National Security Presidential Directive (NSPD) 14, "Nuclear Weapons Planning Guidance," implementing key elements of the NPR. This document remains classified but reasonably can be assumed to have directed changes to planning with respect to Russia, China, and the WMD proliferators central to the contingencies outlined in the NPR. These changes presumably reflected a growing number of potential WMD conflict scenarios that might require nuclear responses, but also the integration of conventional strike options in keeping with the concept of the New Triad introduced in the NPR.[26]

In January 2003, STRATCOM was assigned the global strike mission in order to ensure the availability of plans for prompt, long-range strikes against regional targets using both kinetic and non-kinetic means. For more traditional war planning, requirements were becoming more complex with the need to develop options for multiple adversaries across multiple contingencies, drawing on a smaller stockpile of nuclear weapons and a limited set of non-nuclear force capabilities. The idea of the SIOP—a single operational plan dominated by nuclear strikes that historically had required months to prepare and refine—was quickly growing obsolete. In the words of STRATCOM commander Admiral James Ellis, "STRATCOM is changing the nation's nuclear war plan from a single, large, integrated plan to a family of plans applicable in a wider range of scenarios." In March 2003 the SIOP became Operations Plan (OPLAN) 8044. In 2008 this plan in turn became OPLAN 8010, "Strategic Deterrence and Global Strike." According to open source accounts that rely on declassified documents, OPLAN 8010 is indeed a "family of plans" for the use of both nuclear and non-nuclear weapons against a handful of potential adversaries. Employment plans vary in size, objectives, and degree of readiness, and include options that can be adapted quickly in response to emerging crises or rapidly changing circumstances.[27]

The deterrence plans generated by STRATCOM utilize an analytic methodology that operationalizes the principles of the Deterrence Operations Joint Operating Concept of 2006.[28] The central idea of this operating concept is that deterrence is an influence operation directed at the calculations and decisions of adversary leaders. Adversary thinking and behavior are shaped by perceptions of the benefits of a course of action, the costs of a course of action, and the consequences of restraint (i.e., of not following a course of action). The OPLAN 8010 methodology seeks to develop the means of decisive influence by first constructing a detailed adversary profile and then developing and assessing courses of action tailored to the requirements of deterring the adversary.

Paradigm Shift—The Obama Years (2009–2012)

More so than any president since Ronald Reagan, Barack Obama has sought to break with conventional wisdom on nuclear weapons. Less than three months into his presidency, speaking in Prague, Czech Republic, he articulated a vision for the "peace and security of a world without nuclear weapons" and pledged to "put an end to Cold War thinking" by reducing the role of nuclear weapons in US national security policy.[29] In what has become commonly known as the Prague Agenda, Obama outlined an ambitious program encompassing changes to US nuclear policy, additional arms control with Russia, and steps to strengthen the global fight against nuclear proliferation and terrorism. Some of the specific measures in the Prague Agenda carried forward initiatives begun in the Bush years, but some were significant departures from inherited policy, and the overall strategic mindset was dramatically different from years past.

In publicly embracing the eventual elimination of nuclear weapons, Obama was not indicating an intent to move quickly toward abolition. Rather, he was announcing a long-term aspirational goal in the hopes of catalyzing stronger near-term action on the most urgent elements of the Prague Agenda—in particular, international efforts to prevent nuclear terrorism and the further spread of nuclear weapons. In this view, the most important thing the United States can do to encourage a more robust approach to these challenges is to demonstrate a clear commitment to disarmament and restraint in its own nuclear policies. This will strengthen US moral authority in the fight against proliferation and help foster an international political climate more conducive to taking tougher steps. This approach is advanced through the rhetoric of abolition and through policies that re-engage the United States in traditional nonproliferation diplomacy and arms control, reduce the salience of nuclear weapons in security policy, and mobilize the international community to act on pressing problems.

This set of assumptions and program for action were reaffirmed and amplified in the Nuclear Posture Review issued in April 2010. Unlike the 2001 NPR, the 2010 report was prepared as a public document with a set of deliberate messages directed at both domestic and international audiences. The report is organized around five key objectives for US nuclear policies and posture:

1. Preventing nuclear proliferation and nuclear terrorism;
2. Reducing the role of US nuclear weapons in US national security strategy;
3. Maintaining strategic deterrence and stability at reduced nuclear force levels;
4. Strengthening regional deterrence and reassuring US allies and partners;
5. Sustaining a safe, secure, and effective nuclear arsenal.[30]

These prioritized objectives represent a sharp shift from previous statements of nuclear strategy, which focused principally on deterrence and associated force requirements. By highlighting as most important the prevention of nuclear proliferation and nuclear terrorism, and treating as a lesser priority traditional deterrence and capability considerations, the 2010 NPR sought to establish a clear linkage between US nonproliferation policy and nuclear weapons policy. The latter would now serve the former, a linkage that had been rejected vigorously by the Bush administration. The emphasis on proliferation and terrorism also served to downplay nuclear planning contingencies, which were an important feature of the 2001 NPR. The need to plan for possible nuclear scenarios remained, of course, but a key premise of the 2010 NPR was that state-on-state nuclear war was a considerably less urgent danger than the rising risks of proliferation and terrorism. Thus, these scenarios were not discussed in the document.[31]

With respect to the second objective, the NPR narrows the circumstances under which the United States will consider the use of nuclear weapons, in effect reducing the ambiguity long associated with US declaratory policy. The NPR states that the United States will not use or threaten to use nuclear weapons against any state in compliance with its NPT obligations, even if it uses chemical or biological weapons. The United States reserves the right to adjust this policy if warranted by the evolution of the biological weapons (BW) threat—an indication of the dynamic and uncertain nature of this threat and a recognition that a particularly damaging or heinous attack using BW could lead to consideration of a nuclear response. For nations not in compliance with their NPT obligations, "there remains a narrow range of contingencies in which US nuclear weapons may still play a role in deterring a conventional or CBW attack against the United States or its allies and partners."[32] An obvious interpretation of this last formulation is that it is intended as a warning to states like Iran and North Korea that their defiance of the international community in pursuit of nuclear weapons will continue to carry significant risk.

The NPR thus seeks to balance the need to retain nuclear options to address certain strategic challenges while emphasizing an overall policy of restraint:

> The United States is therefore not prepared at the present time to adopt a universal policy that the "sole purpose" of U.S. nuclear weapons is to deter nuclear attack on the United States and our allies and partners, but will work to establish conditions under which such a policy could be safely adopted. Yet this does not mean that our willingness to use nuclear weapons against countries not covered by the new assurance has in any way increased. Indeed,

the United States wishes to stress that it would only consider the use of nuclear weapons in extreme circumstances to defend the vital interests of the United States or its allies and partners. It is in the U.S. interest and that of all other nations that the nearly 65-year record of nuclear non-use be extended forever. As President Ronald Reagan declared, a "nuclear war cannot be won and must never be fought."[33]

The effort to convey reduced reliance on nuclear weapons was most clearly expressed in these words. Later sections of the document reinforce this emphasis by anticipating future nuclear force reductions below levels codified in the New START Treaty and stating that the United States will not develop new nuclear warheads. Thus there is no plan to expand nuclear capabilities. At the same time, the nuclear triad will be maintained, and there will be significant new investment to sustain existing stockpile capabilities and modernize delivery platforms. These investments were described in general terms in the NPR and their funding profile appeared subsequently in formal budget submissions and other reports mandated by Congress. Projected initially at nearly $200 billion over ten years, this substantial commitment to nuclear forces might have appeared to some as inconsistent with the pledge to reduce reliance on nuclear weapons. However, without this commitment US Senate ratification of the New START Treaty would not have been possible.

Having articulated a policy of reduced reliance on nuclear weapons in the NPR, the Obama administration in 2011 initiated a formal review of nuclear strategy, employment planning, and force requirements. The results of this analysis were issued in a number of classified and unclassified documents in June 2013. The classified documents reportedly include a new presidential policy directive (PDD) on nuclear weapons employment strategy and a supporting report to Congress. The accompanying unclassified reports and fact sheets itemize a number of policy measures designed to put into practice reduced reliance on nuclear weapons. These include deliberate planning for non-nuclear strike options, reducing the role of launch-under-attack in US planning, and a revised approach to nuclear stockpile planning that will allow hedging against technical and geopolitical risks to be achieved with fewer weapons. Additionally, the new policy guidance concludes that deterrence goals can be met while pursuing up to a one-third reduction in deployed nuclear weapons from the levels established in the New START Treaty—preferably through negotiations with Russia.[34]

Guidelines for employment planning are addressed in these unclassified documents only in general terms. Credible plans to use nuclear weapons are required in the event that deterrence fails. These plans should emphasize the most plausible 21st-century contingencies and largely counterforce missions against potential adversaries. Even with reduced deployed nuclear forces, the United States does not rely on "counter-value" or "minimum deterrence" strategies.[35]

Recently, there has been some debate in the US analytic community on the question of how best to deter and, if necessary, wage limited nuclear war against regional nuclear-armed adversaries, and whether the US nuclear arsenal is optimally configured to support strategic objectives in such wars. Echoing some of the ideas that animated the aforementioned "nuclear transformation" agenda associated with the 2001 Nuclear Posture Review, scholars Kier Lieber and Daryl Press have argued that to deter nuclear escalation during conventional wars against WMD-armed foes—when such states will have strong incentives to brandish or use their nuclear weapons to compel a cease-fire or gain strategic leverage—the United States should adopt a counterforce strategy designed to neutralize an adversary's ability to launch initial or follow-on nuclear strikes. Especially important for this mission are "low casualty nuclear weapons" to be delivered with high accuracy to avoid the collateral effects certain to be associated with strikes by the high-yield weapons that dominate the US nuclear arsenal.[36] Indeed, "high accuracy delivery systems with low-yield weapons should form the backbone of the US nuclear deterrent" going forward.[37] As the US contemplates further nuclear reductions, preference should be given to retaining the lowest-yield warheads and leveraging the revolution in precision to improve the accuracy with which they can be delivered.

Critiques of this argument vary. Some critics counter that the United States already possesses weapons suitable for low-yield counterforce attacks and is not, as a matter of policy, planning to reduce them in favor of retaining higher-yield warheads. Others argue that the principal counterforce challenge that would face the United States in a limited war scenario—fixing the location of mobile WMD systems—is fundamentally an intelligence problem and not a weapon effects problem requiring a nuclear solution. Still others suggest that the most effective strategy to deter nuclear escalation in a regional conflict is not to refine counterforce capabilities to achieve greater targeting confidence in limited nuclear strikes but to provide hostile regimes strong incentives for nuclear restraint, in particular by not seeking regime change. Finally, some critics argue that the safer path to stability at a time when the United States is seeking to contain regional proliferation is not to make limited nuclear war a more credible—and therefore likely—option, but to reduce the overall salience of nuclear weapons in strategy.[38]

Other analysts have argued for reviving the study of a new nuclear earth penetrating munition to strengthen deterrence of regional WMD-armed adversaries that have located strategic facilities deep underground and/or in mountains.[39] The goal is to deny adversaries the sanctuary provided by the hardest and deepest of these structures, which may be capable of withstanding the effects of even the most advanced US strike systems. As long as such a sanctuary exists, it is argued, adversaries may feel some sense of immunity from US military action, perhaps enough the tip the balance against restraint, thereby undermining the effectiveness of US deterrent threats. The 2001 NPR promoted the idea of a new nuclear earth penetrator, but the Bush administration eventually abandoned the effort in light of political opposition. Current arguments to revisit this question are motivated largely by the continued investment of states like North Korea and Iran in hardened and buried structures to protect nuclear weapons development efforts, leadership, and other strategic assets.

There continues to be significant opposition to a new nuclear earth penetrator on both political and technical grounds.[40] The 2010 NPR would seem to rule out the development of such a capability, though advocates argue that it is possible to adapt existing warheads to achieve the required attributes. An additional consideration is the fielding of a new conventional munition that reportedly is capable of holding at risk Iran's most heavily fortified underground facilities.[41] This may not fully obviate the case for investigating additional nuclear options, but overall its seems reasonable to conclude that a significant change in the threat, political, and/or technological context will be required to create the conditions under which such work could be contemplated.

Conclusion

The United States may now seek to minimize the role of nuclear weapons in its security policy and strictly limit the circumstances under which nuclear weapons would be used. However, even if this policy is sustained by future administrations, alone it cannot eliminate the possibility of nuclear conflict.

As the following chapter demonstrates, other influential states possess nuclear weapons and contemplate their use in various forms of regional or local conflict, some of which certainly would engage US interests directly or indirectly. Dangerous regional nuclear flashpoints already exist (e.g., India-Pakistan), and new ones could materialize (e.g., Israel-Iran). Moreover, new nuclear weapon states could emerge. If the bomb spreads to regions prone to instability and conflict, prospects for nuclear crisis and conflict likely will rise.

Notes

1. Because it has been declassified, National Security Decision Directive 32 of May 23, 1982 (cited in the preceding chapter) is the appropriate reference for documenting the Reagan "protracted nuclear war" strategy. It is widely assumed that the strategy was first articulated in NSDD 13, 19 October 1981. While the public literature commonly refers to NSDD 13, this document remains classified.

2. Enabling the new emphasis on "prompt counter-leadership" targeting was a 1982–83 Defense Intelligence Agency study that identified additional leadership facilities, including an extensive network of hardened and mobile sites. Other changes in employment planning resulting from NSDD 13 included greater emphasis on Soviet "strategic relocatable targets" (especially mobile missile and C3 systems), and adaptive planning capabilities to support rapid retargeting.

3. Desmond Ball and Robert C. Toth, "Revising the SIOP," *International Security*, Vol. 14, No. 4 (Spring 1990), p. 67. The National Strategic Target Data Base was reduced from roughly 50,000 to roughly 14,000 targets.

4. The Presidential Nuclear Initiatives comprised a series of unilateral but parallel political commitments undertaken by George H. W. Bush, Mikhail Gorbachev (President of the USSR), and Boris Yeltsin (President of the Russian Federation following the dissolution of the USSR) to eliminate, remove from operational status, and cancel modernization programs for a range of strategic and tactical nuclear systems. See Susan J. Koch, *The Presidential Nuclear Initiatives of 1991–1992*, Case Study 5, Center for the Study of Weapons of Mass Destruction, National Defense University (Washington, DC: National Defense University Press, September 2012).

5. Janne Nolan, *The Elusive Consensus: Nuclear Weapons and American Security after the Cold War* (Washington DC: Brookings Institution Press, 1999), pp. 29–31.

6. This is attributed to General Lee Butler, first commander of US Strategic Command, as cited in Hans Kristensen, "Targets of Opportunity," *Bulletin of the Atomic Scientists* (September/October 1997), pp. 22–23, available at www.fas.org/programs/ssp/nukes/doctrine/targeting.pdf. Other unpublished estimates put the number of residual targets in Russia at approximately 4,000.

7. Analysts continue to seek a definitive explanation for why Iraq did not use chemical or biological weapons in the first Gulf War. See Scott D. Sagan, "The

Commitment Trap: Why the United States Should Not Use Nuclear Threats to Deter Biological and Chemical Weapons Attacks," *International Security*, Vol. 24, No. 4 (Spring 2000), pp. 85–115; and Sagan, "Deterring Rogue Regimes: Rethinking Deterrence Theory and Practice," Stanford University Center for International Security and Cooperation, July 8, 2013, available at www.nps.edu/Academics/Centers/CCC/Research/PASCC.html. See also Amarzia Baram, "Deterrence Lessons from Iraq: Rationality Is Not the Only Key to Containment," *Foreign Affairs*, Volume 91, Number 4 (July–August 2012), pp. 76–90.

8. Kristensen, "Targets of Opportunity."

9. Ibid., p. 24.

10. Ibid.

11. Ibid.

12. For a detailed account, see Hans Kristensen, "Changing Targets II: A Chronology of U.S. Nuclear Policy against Weapons of Mass Destruction," April 2003, *Greenpeace*, pp. 14–17, www.nukestrat.com/pubs/ChangingTargets2.pdf

13. In 1978 the United States issued "negative security assurances," pledging not to employ nuclear weapons against non-nuclear weapon states unless they were allied with a nuclear weapons state. This was part of an effort to strengthen support for the Nuclear Nonproliferation Treaty (NPT), which had entered into force only eight years earlier.

14. Kristensen, "Changing Targets II," p. 17.

15. Other key strategic objectives associated with the nuclear posture included stability, hedge, alliance commitments, declaratory policy, stewardship, and threat reduction.

16. Cited in Nolan, *The Elusive Consensus*, pp. 67–68. The document cited is Joint Chiefs of Staff, "Doctrine for Joint Nuclear Operations," Joint Publication 3–12, 29 April 1993. Released under the Freedom of Information Act.

17. Nolan, *The Elusive Consensus*, p. 78.

18. Ibid.

19. Kristensen, "Targets of Opportunity," p. 27.

20. David M. Kunsman and Douglas B. Lawson, *A Primer on U.S. Strategic Nuclear Policy*, Sandia Report SAND2001–0053 (Sandia National Laboratories, January 2001), p. 67.

21. Nolan, *The Elusive Consensus*, p. 13.

22. Kristensen, "Changing Targets II," p. 23.

23. The 2001 Nuclear Posture Review was never released publicly in report form and remains classified. The only public presentation of the document was an unclassified briefing provided by Assistant Secretary of Defense for International Security Policy J. D. Crouch. See *Special Briefing on the Nuclear Posture Review*, January 9, 2002, available at www.defenselink.mil/transcripts/2002/t01092002_t0109npr.html. The report was leaked to a number of news organizations, and excerpts also appeared on the Internet.

24. Keith Payne, *The Great American Gamble: Deterrence Theory and Practice from the Cold War to the 21st Century* (Fairfax, VA: National Institute Press, 2008),

p. 434. Payne cites two original sources: Donald H. Rumsfeld, "Adapting U.S. Strategic Forces," *Department of Defense Annual Report to the President and the Congress, 2002*, chap. 7, p. 4, available at www.defenselink.mil/execsec//adr2002.html_files/chap7.htm; and *Statement of the Honorable Douglas Feith, Undersecretary of Defense for Policy*, Senate Armed Services Committee, *Hearing on the Nuclear Posture Review*, February 14, 2002, p. 7 (Prepared text).

25. Payne, *The Great American Gamble*, p. 434.

26. The New Triad was a central element of the 2001 NPR and signaled a transition from the Cold War–era triad of nuclear forces (intercontinental ballistic missiles, submarine-launched ballistic missiles, and strategic bombers) to a broader portfolio of strategic capabilities based on nuclear and non-nuclear strike capabilities, defenses, and responsive infrastructure. In this construct, conventional systems capable of delivering strategic effects were viewed as an important future element of war plans that historically were exclusively nuclear.

27. Hans Kristensen, "Obama and the Nuclear War Plan," *Federation of the American Scientists Issue Brief*, February 2010, www.fas.org/programs/ssp/nukes/publications1/WarPlanIssueBrief2010.pdf.

28. U.S. Department of Defense, *Deterrence Operations Joint Operating Concept*, December 2006, www.dtic.mil/futurejointwarfare/concepts/do_joc_v20.doc.

29. Office of the Press Secretary, The White House, "Remarks by President Barack Obama," April 5, 2009, www.whitehouse.gov/the_press_office/Remarks-By-President-Barack-Obama-In-Prague-As-Delivered.

30. U.S. Department of Defense, *Nuclear Posture Review Report*, April 2010, p. iii, www.defense.gov/npr/.

31. As one analyst noted in assessing the 2010 NPR, "the Pentagon is still aware that there are scenarios in which nuclear weapons might be used against the U.S. and thus must be guarded against and prepared for. But, this year's drafters saw the wisdom in not spelling these out, choosing to stress instead that all-out nuclear confrontation is, indeed, the least of our nuclear concerns in the 21st century and the least likely (although still possible) scenario." See Ralph A. Cossa, "The 2010 Nuclear Posture Review: Moving toward 'No First Use,'" *PacNet Newsletter* #17, http://csis.org/publication/pacnet-17-2010-nuclear-posture-review-moving-toward-%E2%80%98no-first-use%26quot;;%3Eread.

32. Nuclear Posture Review (2010), p. 16.

33. Ibid.

34. Office of the Press Secretary, The White House, "Fact Sheet: Nuclear Weapons Employment Strategy of the United States," June 19, 2013, www.whitehouse.gov/the-press-office/2013/06/19/fact-sheet-nuclear-weapons-employment-strategy. See also Department of Defense, "Report on Nuclear Employment Strategy of the United States Specified in Section 491 of 10 U.S.C.," June 2013, www.defense.gov/pubs/ReporttCongressonUSNuclearEmploymentStrategy_Section491.pdf.

35. Department of Defense, "Report on Nuclear Employment Strategy of the United States Specified in Section 491 of 10 U.S.C.," p. 4.

36. Kier Lieber and Daryl Press, "The Nukes We Need," *Foreign Affairs*, Vol. 88, No. 6 (November/December 2009), pp. 39–51.

37. Ibid., p. 49.

38. For a number of these critiques, see "Second Strike: Is the U.S. Nuclear Arsenal Outmoded?," *Foreign Affairs*, Vol. 89, No. 2 (March/April 2010), pp. 145–152.

39. See, for example, Elbridge A. Colby, "Why We Should Study Developing Nuclear Earth Penetrators—And Why They Are Actually Stabilizing," *Foreign Policy Research Institute E-Notes*, May 2011, www.fpri.org; and Jeffrey Lewis and Elbridge Colby, "How to Worry Kim Jong-il," *Diplomat*, September 23, 2011, http://thediploat.com/2011/09/23/how-to-worry-kom-jong-il/.

40. See David Wright, "North Korea and a New Earth Penetrator," *All Things Nuclear*, September 26, 2011, http://allthingsnuclear.org/north-korea-and-a-new-earth-penetrator/; and Robert W. Nelson, "Low Yield Earth Penetrating Nuclear Weapons," *Science and Global Security*, Vol. 10, Issue 1 (2002), pp. 1–20.

41. The 30,000-pound Massive Ordnance Penetrator (MOP) has been reported in the press to be ready for deployment since fall 2012. See Spencer Ackerman, "Air Force's Mega-Bunker-Buster Bomb Is Finally Ready," *Wired*, July 26, 2012, http://wired.com/dangerroom/2012/07/massive-ordnance-penetrator/.

II MANAGING THE RISK OF NUCLEAR WAR IN THE 21ST CENTURY

5 The Emerging Nuclear Landscape

Paul I. Bernstein

THIS CHAPTER SURVEYS THE EMERGING GLOBAL nuclear landscape and considers the prospects for limited nuclear war in light of trends in the spread of nuclear weapons and the emerging doctrine of key nuclear states. The propensity of the emerging security environment toward limited nuclear war will be shaped largely by the degree to which nuclear capabilities expand and the way nuclear-armed regional powers view the utility of nuclear weapons to wage and win wars. The chapter focuses on prospects for further nuclear proliferation, the dangers associated with a proliferated world, and developments in key regions and countries, including India, Pakistan, Russia, China, North Korea, and Iran.

The discussion of China is longer and more detailed because the rich debate about China's nuclear development, both inside China and among Western experts, continues to yield a particularly strong flow of insight with important implications for US policy in a region that is growing in geopolitical significance. This chapter provides an opportunity to capture these insights. That is not to suggest that the prospects for limited nuclear war involving the United States are greater with respect to China; rather, it simply reflects the growing importance of the US-China strategic relationship and the continuing effort of Western regional and functional specialists to understand Chinese developments at a time when Beijing remains reluctant to be more transparent. Without question, the United States has vital interests at stake in nuclear competition, crisis, and conflict that engage any of the countries addressed in this chapter.

Future Proliferation—Alternative Visions

Fifty years ago experts and national leaders expressed fears of a world with perhaps two dozen or more nuclear-armed states. That world has not materialized, as the pace of nuclear proliferation has in fact been modest in relation to those projections. In the nearly seven decades of the nuclear age, ten nuclear weapon states have emerged—roughly 1.5 per decade. These include the five legally recognized nuclear weapon states (China, France, Russia, United Kingdom, and United States), four de facto nuclear weapon states (India, Israel, North Korea, and Pakistan), and one former nuclear weapon state (South Africa) that willingly gave up its small stockpile.[1] A number of other states terminated nuclear weapon development efforts before achieving a weapons capability. As proliferation analysts have learned, motivations to "go nuclear" typically are more complex than commonly appreciated, and the technical and administrative capacities required to acquire a weapons capability are formidable. The web of external restraints that has been erected over time—the international regime of treaties, technology controls, and legal and behavioral norms—has reinforced these factors in helping to limit the spread of nuclear weapons. So, too, have direct actions by states to delay, disrupt, and even destroy key elements of nuclear weapons programs.[2]

Will this historical pace be maintained—suggesting one or two new members of the nuclear club over the next twenty years—or will the pace of nuclear proliferation accelerate? Opinions in the expert community differ on this question. Some look at the historical record and see no reason to expect a fundamental shift in proliferation dynamics leading to many more nuclear possessors or a highly proliferated world. This largely optimistic assessment is grounded to a significant degree in the view that the traditional realist or neo-realist emphasis on security drivers tends to exaggerate the propensity of states to proliferate by discounting a range of other factors, to include domestic political and economic forces that may work against a decision to pursue a nuclear option, and the technology and bureaucratic factors that constrain the ability of states to divert civil nuclear power programs to military purposes.[3] This more expansive view of motivations and capabilities yields a low expectation of further nuclear proliferation in the period ahead. Commenting on just such a finding from a comprehensive forecast of proliferation using a case study construct, proliferation experts William Potter and Gaukhar Mukhatzhanova note:

> Although surprising in terms of prevailing conventional wisdom about a pending proliferation pandemic, the results, in fact, are consistent with the historically slow pace of proliferation, and the failure of most prior forecasts of proliferation doom to materialize. They also are compatible with a number of theories of nuclear choice . . . that point to key roles played by individual leaders and/or domestic ruling coalitions and the exceptional circumstances that must pertain for states to abandon nuclear restraint. Although these theories do not exclude the possibility that a number of additional states will decide to pursue nuclear weapons in the next ten years, they highlight the risky and unusual, if not extraordinary, nature of the decision and the significant impediments to its successful implementation.[4]

For proliferation pessimists, the historical record is of little comfort, and empirical analysis of cases tends to discount the possibility of surprise and systemic factors such as the perceived weakening of the global nonproliferation regime. They point to the many ways this regime has been challenged over the last twenty years, exposing major gaps in the system of political, legal, and technology restraints intended to prevent or limit the further spread of nuclear weapons.[5] As a result, nuclear weapons programs in problem states such as North Korea and Iran have been able to advance, creating a persistent state of confrontation in the neighborhood of those states, a crisis of confidence in the NPT, and the possibility of a proliferation "cascade." The efforts of these two states, as well as Libya, were enabled in part by a sophisticated black market in nuclear technology operated by non-state actors from Pakistan that has called into question both the conventional conception of the "loose nukes" problem and the very premise of controlling technology as a supply-side solution to the proliferation challenge.

Additionally, it is increasingly clear that proliferating states have begun to collaborate in a process of mutual self-help that began with the sharing of missile technology but appears to have advanced in some cases to nuclear weapons-related technology as well.[6] In this way and others, the proliferation process itself has become more complex and opaque, harder to detect and track, and less resistant to the web of constraints constructed around the NPT regime. Further, widespread acceptance of India and Pakistan—two key states outside the treaty—as legitimate nuclear powers is seen by many as a serious compromise of the nonproliferation system that will make it more difficult to enforce universal nonproliferation standards.

The weakened state of the nonproliferation regime is seen as signaling a new phase of the nuclear era that will be characterized by growing nuclear "self-interest," the spread of fuel cycle capabilities to many more states, the erosion of the norm against nuclear acquisition, persistent regional proliferation crises, the emergence of new, hostile nuclear states, the competitive pursuit of nuclear weapons in regional arms races, and heightened escalation pressures in local conflicts. Commenting on the possibility of this type of nuclear future, scholars Steven Miller and Scott Sagan have noted:

> In the past, rapid cascades of nuclear proliferation—though sometimes predicted—have not occurred and are not certain to occur in the future. But the dynamic could well be different if the nonproliferation regime is thought to be eroding and more NNWS [non-nuclear weapons states] possess the latent capability to manufacture nuclear weapons. The reassuring record of a past era marked by few NWS [nuclear weapons states], a sturdy norm against acquisition, a reasonably sound nonproliferation regime, very infrequent spread of nuclear weapons to new states, and possession of fuel cycle capabilities by only a few states may not be a reliable guide to the future if trends slide in a negative direction.[7]

The Impact of Further Proliferation

Will a world that is more rather than less proliferated be inherently less stable and more dangerous? Here, too, there are optimists and pessimists. A number of prominent scholars have argued that the further spread of nuclear weapons may have a stabilizing effect on the international system, acting to limit local or regional conflicts to the level of conventional warfare and even helping to ameliorate regional rivalries and prevent wars from breaking out. Kenneth Waltz is perhaps most closely associated with this school of thought, arguing that the principles of rational deterrence theory will obtain across a range of regional settings because "the likelihood of war decreases as deterrent and defensive capabilities increase. Nuclear weapons make wars hard to start."[8] This is true for both large and small nuclear powers because the leaders of these states can be expected to be highly sensitive to the costs of deterrence failure and war when confronting a nuclear-armed rival. The costs of nuclear conflict are sufficiently high and transparent that even a small risk of war can produce strong deterrence. This dynamic rests importantly on a number of beliefs: that nuclear rivals will develop secure second-strike capabilities perceived as able to withstand a first strike and inflict an unacceptable level of retaliation; that small nuclear arsenals are amenable to relatively simple command and control that limit the danger of unauthorized or accidental use; and that new nuclear states will be sufficiently adept at nuclear signaling so as to minimize the risks of miscommunication, misperception, and escalation.[9]

This universal "assumption of rationality" is viewed skeptically by other scholars who anticipate profoundly destabilizing outcomes in a more proliferated world, contributing to heightened risk of regional nuclear war. A common critique of rational deterrence theory with respect to new nuclear states is that such regimes are likely to engage in risk-taking behavior, especially in the early period following the acquisition of nuclear weapons, both in conflicts with regional nuclear rivals where the risks of escalation may be discounted or downplayed, and in conflicts with more powerful states where regime survival is seen to be at stake.[10] A further critique, more rooted in psychology, holds that the leaders of new nuclear states may lack the experience and temperament required to make deterrence work. Some scholars, notably Scott Sagan, have also argued that deterrence may be prone to failure for reasons rooted in organizational theory—specifically, that the lack of "positive mechanisms of civilian control" and the prospect for unstable civil-military relations in new nuclear-armed states will lead professional military organizations to behave in ways likely to produce deterrence failures and deliberate or accidental war, and to act as poor stewards of deterrent forces.[11] Destabilizing behaviors are likely to include biases in favor of preventive war and/ or deliberate attacks against vulnerable forces, organizational resistance to developing secure second-strike forces, and a propensity to underestimate the likelihood of unauthorized or accidental use. Sagan notes, "Organizational biases could encourage worst-case assumptions about the adversary's intent and pessimistic beliefs about the prospects for successful strategic deterrence over the long term."[12]

South Asia

Thus, rather than an assumption of rationality, pessimists for a variety of reasons see an "assumption of pathology" as more likely in a proliferated world. They see some of these pathologies on display in the behavior of new nuclear weapon states, particularly in the periodic crises and clashes between India and Pakistan over the last two decades. Sagan, for instance, argues that the influence of the Indian military produced serious risks of preventive war in the 1980s, despite a sustained tradition of assertive civilian control. He questions the ability of the Pakistani and Indian militaries to maintain survivable nuclear forces, citing episodes where military actions undermined the survivability of nuclear assets and the secrecy attached to highly sensitive operations and forces. He also sees significant potential for unauthorized or accidental use.[13]

The persistence of such behaviors, he concludes, could contribute to future crises on the subcontinent with increased risks of preventive or preemptive strikes, or even the deliberate limited use of nuclear weapons on the battlefield.[14] For example, Pakistan's pattern of issuing nuclear threats and alerting its nuclear forces in crisis situations could, in a future crisis, create pressures for Indian decisionmakers fearful that nuclear attacks by Pakistan were imminent. Likewise, were India successfully to develop and field significant missile defense capabilities, pressures to consider preventive strikes against Pakistan's nuclear forces and infrastructure could result.[15]

The Kargil conflict of 1999, unfolding only one year after each nation openly demonstrated its nuclear status through a series of underground tests, is viewed by many experts as undermining the optimistic view that nuclear powers will not go to war with one another. As scholar Timothy Hoyt observes of Kargil, "the theoretically stabilizing aspects of non-deployed, opaque nuclear forces failed in practice to prevent regional aggression with a substantial potential for nuclear escalation."[16] Assessing lessons learned from Kargil (as well as subsequent crises), a group of Indian, Pakistani, and American experts concluded, pessimistically, that New Delhi and Islamabad have learned and applied a number of "wrong lessons." Most prominently, both sides seem to remain confident that a policy of brinksmanship will yield strategic benefits, and that low-level conflict can be prevented from escalating to the nuclear level.[17]

Indian strategy now seems to envisage limited conventional conflict under the nuclear umbrella and escalation dominance over Pakistan. A principal goal is to deny Pakistan any advantage from the threat of nuclear escalation.

Thus, India's so-called proactive strategy envisions rapid strikes into Pakistan to achieve quick battlefield victories and seize Pakistani territory without generating a nuclear response. Because New Delhi's objectives in executing such strikes would be limited (e.g., punishing Pakistan for acts of sponsored terrorism), and the stakes for Pakistan less than existential, Indian strategists question Pakistan's willingness to escalate.[18] However, to hedge against the possibility, India asserts that the use of nuclear weapons against Indian forces anywhere in the region of conflict will trigger a large-scale nuclear response. Forced by Kargil to consider more seriously how to operationalize its nuclear deterrent, India now seeks to "create a legitimate, usable, and survivable nuclear force that can exercise a range of possible military options in order to enhance deterrence."[19] Underwriting this shift are a new command and control system and increased capacity to deliver nuclear weapons.

Pakistani military strategists and experts counter that limited military actions by India indeed would trigger a nuclear response; credibly threatening such a response to bolster deterrence is now central to Pakistan's nuclear strategy. Post-Kargil, Pakistan has modified nuclear command and control arrangements with the goal of ensuring that nuclear weapons will be readily available to military leaders during a crisis and for early use in a conflict to counter Indian military gains. By signaling a low nuclear threshold, Pakistan seeks to heighten India's sense of nuclear risk early in a conflict and undermine its effort to control a process of escalation. Similarly, by announcing a series of nuclear "red lines" or conditions that could trigger the use of nuclear weapons, Pakistan seeks to limit India's conventional options in a limited war.[20] Pakistan's nuclear doctrine, while still officially described as "credible minimum deterrence," in fact has evolved toward one reliant on the early first use of nuclear weapons.

Vipin Narang has characterized Pakistan's nuclear doctrine as one of "asymmetric escalation"—a strategy "geared for the rapid (and asymmetric) first use of nuclear weapons against conventional attacks to deter their outbreak, operationalizing nuclear weapons as usable warfighting instruments." In Narang's formulation, this doctrine fully integrates nuclear weapons into military forces and requires "the ability to disperse and deploy assets extremely quickly and to enable their release on the battlefield through predelegative procedures to military end users in the event of a crisis; it is thus the most aggressive option available to nuclear states."[21]

In practice, Pakistan now seeks to threaten the first use of lower yield nuclear weapons in a tactical environment in order to forestall an extended conventional war in which India's significant advantages in manpower and materiel would almost certainly be decisive. Narang contends that Pakistan's reported stockpile of 70–90 weapons, in combination with a growing weapons production capacity and several short-range delivery systems, appear sufficient to underwrite the asymmetric escalation posture that envisions first use against tactical or operational targets while maintaining a reserve that can survive and thereby deter an Indian retaliatory strike.[22] Some observers have suggested that given the relatively low threshold for nuclear use, the pre-emptive employment of nuclear weapons by Pakistan cannot be ruled out, especially in response to something like India's "Brasstacks" live fire exercise of 1986–87.[23]

Among the dangers associated with a doctrine of asymmetric escalation is the great stress imposed on command and control to ensure credibility and the heightened risk of inadvertent use that results. The highly delegative structure implied by Pakistani doctrine likely encompasses the rapid assembly, movement, release, and delivery of nuclear weapons in crisis situations.[24] It is reasonable to ask whether, under stressful battlefield conditions, central control of nuclear weapons will yield to military exigencies and the decisions of operational commanders. As Narang observes,

> To make its asymmetric escalation posture credible, Pakistan seems to be augmenting positive controls over its nuclear weapons by developing weak negative controls, or removing them altogether, so that officers have the physical ability to assemble and release nuclear weapons should they deem it necessary, regardless of whether they are vested with the authority to do so. . . . Whatever negative controls exist to ensure the security and safety of Pakistan's arsenal during peacetime, they are likely circumventable, by design, for deterrence purposes in a crisis or conflict situation with India.[25]

Escalation risks are heightened by the continued deployment by each side of conventionally armed but nuclear-capable short-range ballistic missiles. These missiles are likely to be used early in a conflict, and present a number of risks. One is the possibility that their launch in conventional mode could be misinterpreted as part of a nuclear attack. Another is that their successful use against one side's nuclear forces or infrastructure could trigger a nuclear response. Many experts believe that existing bilateral crisis management arrangements are inadequate to address these risks.[26] In the future, escalation risks will grow further if, as seems plausible, the Indo-Pakistani nuclear rivalry extends to the maritime domain, and each side chooses to rely on naval platforms with dual conventional and nuclear missions.[27]

Russia

Not unlike Pakistan, Russia has openly adopted an expanded role for nuclear weapons in local or regional conflict as its conventional military power has eroded. In addition, it may be developing new nuclear capabilities tailored to limited war scenarios. Discussions about the early use of nuclear weapons appear to have begun in the early 1990s, leading over time to a steady lowering of the nuclear threshold as Russian nuclear forces were assigned the role of deterring not just strategic conflict but regional conventional conflict as well. In the regional war context, the first use of nonstrategic nuclear weapons (NSNW) has been envisioned in decreasingly extreme circumstances. Based on the statements of senior Russian national security officials in 2009, many analysts expected the military doctrine issued in 2010 to extend this to the domain of "local" wars as well, and to provide explicitly for preemptive nuclear strikes.[28]

However, the publicly issued doctrine of February 2010 offered only a brief and general statement on the circumstances of nuclear use.[29] While it provided no explicit indication of increased readiness for nuclear first use in a broader range of contingencies, observers point out that the more detailed articulation of Russia's nuclear strategy is most likely reserved for the classified document issued on the same day, "Foundations of State Policy in the Area of Nuclear Deterrence to 2020."[30]

Regardless of the precise formulation to be found in classified documents, it is clear that Russia's nuclear strategy today encompasses a concept for deterring and terminating conventional war based on the threat of limited nuclear strikes for the purposes of "demonstration" and "de-escalation." In this context, these terms refer to a "limited counter-force nuclear strike in the theater of military operations"—an action compensating for conventional force weakness intended to compel the adversary's withdrawal by signaling Russia's high stake in the conflict and its willingness to escalate the level of violence in order to prevail.[31] This approach, premised as it is on the strategy of nuclear first use against a conventionally superior adversary to alter the political dynamics of conflict, is strikingly similar to the concept of flexible response that defined NATO's strategy for many years. It also deviates sharply from decades of Soviet Cold War doctrine claiming that limited nuclear war was not a viable concept and that the process of nuclear escalation could not be controlled. However, viewed through the lens of today's "correlation of forces" as seen from Moscow, one can expect this doctrine to endure as long as Russia's conventional military power remains deficient in relation to perceived threats.

Writings by Russian specialists and military exercises indicate that NSNW are central to regional deterrence and warfighting, though it is possible that strategic nuclear forces could also play a role.[32] The effort to develop a new generation of NSNW appears to have begun in the late 1990s. According to Israeli scholar Dima Adamsky, emphasis has been on low-yield, high-precision, "clean" weapons (i.e., with limited radiation output) that can act as a "nuclear scalpel" to achieve effects in regional or local conflicts with low or limited collateral damage. Research and development along these lines is believed to have accelerated beginning in 1998, and by the mid-2000s weapon systems based on these concepts were aggressively being promoted by the design community. Exactly where this has led is unclear. Adamsky reports:

> Presumably the R&D on a new generation of nuclear weapons produced some significant scientific results. While the designers' efforts to promote a new generation of nuclear weapons are obvious, it is less clear how these ideas were accepted outside the nuclear elite, in the broader Russian strategic community. The available information is contradictory and insufficient to make a definitive determination.[33]

Thus it is conceivable that highly accurate, low-yield nuclear munitions will become an important element of Russia's nuclear arsenal. Beyond this, there are indications of increased attention being paid to research into pure fusion weapons that conceivably could lead to even more novel capabilities.[34] One concern is that possession of such capabilities will in fact enable Russia to operationalize its professed doctrine, heightening the prospect of early nuclear use in regional or local conflict where Russian conventional forces are insufficient to deter an adversary or ensure victory at acceptable cost. Another is that Russia's efforts may motivate or even enable other advanced nuclear states to develop similar capabilities, fueling "vertical proliferation" along qualitative lines. As one analyst has noted, "Russia's leadership in diversifying their nuclear arsenal to focus on low yield weapons, according to Russian sources, is paving the way for China and India to follow suit."[35]

China

China has long asserted two core functions for nuclear weapons: to deter nuclear threats and use against China, and to respond to nuclear attacks. China espouses a policy of no first use of nuclear weapons, limited development of nuclear forces, and avoidance of nuclear warfighting and nuclear arms races. The principal force requirement is an arsenal of long-range nuclear missiles capable of surviving attack and delivering unacceptable damage in response. Such an assured retaliation force has been the sine qua non of the overriding imperative to prevent nuclear coercion. Most Western analysts believe the ongoing modernization of Chinese strategic nuclear forces is consistent with these principles. The nuclear arsenal has remained modest in size even as the technical constraints on building a larger, more advanced force have eased.[36] The widely held explanation is that those making decisions about nuclear strategy—senior political, military, and scientific leaders—see nuclear weapons as possessing only limited utility for China and hold relatively simple beliefs about the role these weapons should play in China's defense. These views have persisted and prevailed for decades, ensuring that priority has remained on the requirements of assured retaliation at the strategic level.[37]

At the same time, it is clear that not all strategists and commanders in the People's Liberation Army (PLA) and its Second Artillery Force (SAF) have accepted assured retaliation as the exclusive frame for Chinese strategy.[38] And as the security environment has become more complex, as the technology available to both China and its potential adversaries has advanced, and as domestic and organizational constraints on the development of nuclear strategy have eased, Chinese doctrine indeed has evolved to encompass a broader set of deterrence and operational tasks that envision an expanded role for nuclear weapons.[39] Thus, in addition to the bedrock requirement for a credible assured retaliation capability—what many refer to as minimum deterrence—Chinese nuclear doctrine now features a more offensive and operationally oriented element widely characterized as "limited deterrence" or "limited retaliation."

This is best understood as encompassing a "nuclear counterstrike campaign" to shock the adversary and restore deterrence after China has been attacked by nuclear weapons. As one analyst has described it, "China would use a nuclear counterstrike to cripple an adversary's capabilities and to foster the maximum psychological effect in one massive counterattack in order to bring about a halt to further nuclear exchanges—or possibly even the entire military conflict."[40] To implement such a strategy, a range of countervalue, counterforce, and countermilitary targets need to be held at risk.

Close observers of Chinese strategic affairs note that this evolution of nuclear doctrine reflects more than just an effort to move from a defensive to an offensive posture. Rather, it reflects the PLA's ongoing struggle to "link conventional and nuclear weapons with the operating requirements of potential high tech local wars over resources and territory around China's periphery . . . so as to deter and, if necessary, deny an adversary victory in any conceivable conventional and nuclear conflict."[41] The goal is to broaden the utility of China's nuclear posture and enhance the credibility of deterrence in the kinds of conflicts China is likely to encounter in its own region.

Limited deterrence thus seems firmly embedded in a deterrence framework; China does not appear to be preparing to wage extended nuclear conflict through precision nuclear strikes as part of an escalation control strategy, but rather to threaten and if necessary execute nuclear strikes below the strategic level to de-escalate a conflict. Still, in embracing the idea that deterrence below the strategic level requires posing a threat that is operationally credible in the context of local conflict, the concept of a nuclear counterstrike campaign clearly extends Chinese doctrine beyond the confines of assured destruction, minimum deterrence, and countervalue targeting.

Principles articulated in Chinese defense white papers of the last decade, such as "self-defensive nuclear strategy" and "counterattack in self-defense," appear to reinforce this model of deterrence.[42] Of course, these same white papers also enshrine the principles of "limited development" of nuclear weapons, and a "lean and effective nuclear force," signaling limits on the acquisition of nuclear forces. This raises questions about what type and number of nonstrategic nuclear forces are required to underwrite credible nuclear counterstrike campaigns, and about the degree of investment that can be expected in these systems.

China does not appear to have made a major investment in nonstrategic nuclear weapons that presumably would signal preparedness to engage in limited nuclear strikes, though there is a great deal of uncertainty surrounding this question. In the mid-1990s, Alastair Iain Johnston argued that Chinese strategists began investigating the doctrinal aspects of NSNW in the 1950s, and pointed to writings in the 1980s and 1990s that expressed strong interest in NSNW as a capability required to fight "high-tech limited wars." But other than low-yield nuclear tests decades ago and some exercises in the 1980s that simulated the use of tactical nuclear weapons, this aspect of nuclear operations and weaponry does not appear to have received sustained conceptual, operational, or developmental attention.[43]

Looking to the future, in trying to determine how fully China will operationalize the concept of nuclear counterstrike campaigns, it will be important to watch whether China begins to produce nuclear-armed versions of new medium and intermediate-range ballistic missiles and land-attack and air-launched cruise missiles.[44] If nuclear-armed—and if supported by modernized early warning and command and control systems enabling quicker reaction times—these missiles would provide greater flexibility than their predecessors to execute such operations. One must also factor into this discussion China's continued adherence to its nuclear testing moratorium and the degree to which this would constrain the PLA's capability to acquire modern warheads suited to these missiles.[45]

A question that increasingly preoccupies Western analysts is whether a limited nuclear counterstrike could come in response to non-nuclear attacks that threatened China's strategic deterrent or other vital interests. In recent years this question has grown in prominence as the United States has fielded missile defenses in growing numbers and invested in the development of conventional global strike systems—capabilities that, if sufficiently robust, potentially could pose an operational threat to China's nuclear deterrent force. This possibility has triggered an internal (but increasingly visible) debate about China's policy of no first use (NFU) of nuclear weapons, a policy which dates back to 1964. The issue at the center of this debate concerns the circumstances under which China may need to resort to the use of nuclear weapons, and whether there should be a third core objective for nuclear weapons—to deter and defeat non-nuclear attacks that pose a threat to vital interests.

Western scholars largely contend that authoritative PLA writings regarding doctrine, plans, and training continue to maintain the assumption that China can and will absorb a first nuclear strike, and that nuclear counterstrikes will occur only "under nuclear conditions."[46] They see little or no development of the idea of employing nuclear weapons to compensate for conventional force deficiencies or respond to conventional aggression.[47] But they also acknowledge Chinese sources that indicate alternative views—that credible warning of a nuclear attack, or high-intensity attacks on Chinese nuclear forces or other important strategic targets, could (or should) prompt nuclear use.[48]

And it is now commonplace to hear Western experts report on remarks or statements by Chinese military figures and civilian strategists, often not for attribution, suggesting that NFU is not absolute, leaving open the possibility of nuclear use in response to non-nuclear attacks.[49] Thus, while NFU remains China's official policy, reaffirmed publicly in government pronouncements, today there clearly is a greater degree of doctrinal ambiguity than in the past as China seeks to strengthen deterrence against what is perceived as a growing non-nuclear high-tech threat. As a result, US planners and policymakers must consider that, as one analyst has noted, "no first use might not apply in certain situations that would be seen as equivalent of a 'first use,' including conventional strikes on China's nuclear forces or facilities as well as strikes on strategic targets like the Three Gorges Dam or the top Chinese leadership."[50] The Chinese debate over NFU undoubtedly will continue, and Chinese statements on this matter will remain among the most important indicators of official attitudes on the use of nuclear weapons, especially in the absence of a substantive bilateral dialogue on nuclear issues.

Some analysts have sought to view questions related to NFU, the potential for escalation to nuclear conflict, and Chinese views on the nuclear threshold more explicitly through the lens of a possible US-China confrontation over Taiwan. This is the scenario most likely in the foreseeable future, if it materializes, to reveal how doctrinal principles will be put into practice. Taiwan is a core military priority and represents a national sovereignty issue the stakes of which may be sufficiently high to compel the Chinese leadership to consider seriously the possibility of nuclear escalation should circumstances warrant.

Brad Roberts notes that neither side appears to have devoted much effort to preparing for the failure of deterrence in a Taiwan crisis and the challenges of restoring deterrence and managing processes of nuclear escalation and de-escalation. Roberts observes that many Chinese experts appear to believe that the burden of escalation in such a war will fall on the United States, that China will be able to manipulate US risk perceptions so as to secure its vital interests, and that the United States would be the party forced to concede. Not surprisingly, most American experts hold starkly opposing views. Given the uneven record of US-China crisis management, this may bode poorly for containing the risks of a high stakes confrontation in the Taiwan Strait.[51]

Some Western experts believe that if faced with a clear choice to capitulate or escalate, the Chinese leadership would choose the latter—in part because of political considerations, and in part because of core doctrinal principles that emphasize "seizing the initiative," "active defense," rapid response to enemy attacks, and early actions to create shock and shape the battlefield. Roberts notes that the principle of seizing the strategic initiative, now considered central to waging war against a superior adversary, has led to an increased emphasis on preemption in planning for conventional campaigns. A principal focus of this planning is China's growing conventional missile force, which has assumed a critical role within the Second Artillery Force and provides increasingly capable and reliable means to conduct precision strikes against land-based targets and surface ships in support of coercive diplomacy, deterrence, and military campaigns, especially in a Taiwan scenario.[52]

A second question that has begun to preoccupy Western analysts is the degree to which this growing capability could contribute to the risk of escalation to the nuclear level. Conventional ballistic and land attack cruise missiles are fully integrated into the organization and operations of the Second Artillery Force, which is responsible for "dual deterrence and dual operations."[53] There appear to be well-developed concepts for these missiles in deterrence and strike operations, but uncertain consideration of escalation risks and how they may need to be managed.[54] This is especially worrisome given doctrinal statements indicating that in a conflict with a nuclear-armed adversary, conventional strike campaigns would be carried out "under nuclear deterrence conditions." The full and precise meaning of this may be open to interpretation, but it suggests that while executing conventional missile attacks to achieve warfighting objectives the SAF may also be posturing, exercising, or even demonstrating nuclear-armed missiles to achieve deterrence goals.[55] These conventional and nuclear missiles would be co-located at SAF bases that in the past were nuclear-only, and would use the same command and control infrastructure.[56] .

If, as one assessment has noted, the "sequential and possibly combined employment of conventional and nuclear missile brigades is deemed a source of political and military strength" by the Chinese leadership, a number of concerns are raised.[57] The most obvious goes to the challenge of controlling escalation in a crisis or the early stages of a war, in particular the danger of inadvertent escalation to the nuclear level. Anticipating Chinese military operations using conventional ballistic and cruise missiles, US military and political leaders undoubtedly would consider strikes to cripple them and their supporting command and control systems. Would these attacks be interpreted in Beijing as part of conventional first strike against China's nuclear deterrent, even if that was not the intent?[58] And what if, in the course of such strikes, Chinese nuclear assets inadvertently were destroyed or damaged? Alternatively, could conventional missile launches from bases associated with nuclear missiles mistakenly be interpreted by the United States as the beginning of a nuclear attack?

China may see this approach as strengthening the survivability of its nuclear deterrent by raising the risks for Washington in contemplating conventional strikes on Chinese nuclear forces. But it also carries the potential to undermine the goal of avoiding nuclear war if the inherent escalation risks are not properly managed. To some observers, these dangers are compounded by organizational tendencies that serve to obscure how China would behave and seek to communicate under the stressful conditions of a crisis with a nuclear-armed adversary—and that therefore could be destabilizing.[59] To yet other commentators, this approach raises questions about how the PLA and SAF view the nuclear-conventional firebreak, and could even signal that they no longer see conventional and nuclear war as distinct categories of conflict.

It is also worth noting that recent assessments of China's conventional ballistic missile capabilities cite authoritative publications discussing electromagnetic pulse (EMP) warheads for short- and medium-range systems, particularly for the purpose of paralyzing the operations of carrier battle groups.[60] One recent study cites the following passage in an influential book on strategy produced by senior PLA officers, reinforcing interest in EMP weapons but attempting to define them as instruments of local war, as distinct from more traditional nuclear weapons supporting deterrence at the strategic level:

> As information technology develops and it has more influence on the function of nuclear weapons, the discharge of nuclear energy will also be included in information control and applied in the struggle over the control of information rights (such as the electromagnetic pulse weapon being developed). Nuclear weapons may walk out of deterrence and be used in actual combat. But this kind of nuclear war is the nuclear war included in hi-tech local wars, and its essence is hi-tech local war.[61]

A final question bearing on the prospects for limited nuclear war is the degree to which aspects of Chinese strategic culture may influence the risks of escalation. As Michael Swaine has observed, China historically has exhibited varying behaviors in managing crises. Chinese concepts emphasize a deliberate, incremental, and symmetric approach to crisis management and escalation, featuring pauses and diplomatic signaling, and Beijing's actions frequently have embodied this approach. At other times, China has been willing to utilize "sudden, rapid, asymmetrical escalation" to create faits accomplis and shock the adversary, especially to counter perceived threats to state survival, defend its territorial integrity, or forestall a much larger conflict.[62]

Some commentators see this tendency as characteristic of earlier, revolutionary generations of Chinese leadership, in contrast to the contemporary leadership cadre, which is cautious and risk averse, unlikely to engage in sudden, rapid escalation absent a serious provocation or threat to core interests. Others contend that "Chinese leaders throughout history have favored offensive approaches to crises and value displaying resolve and seizing initiative," and that contemporary conditions—in particular popular nationalistic sentiment—will create pressures likely to reinforce historical patterns of aggressive crisis behavior.[63]

How these tendencies play out in the future and particularly in the context of a major crisis over Taiwan cannot be predicted. Noting that both sides place great value on demonstrating resolve in a crisis and are willing to do so through sudden, dramatic actions, Swaine offers a cautionary note that bears on the possibility of nuclear escalation:

> This common emphasis on displaying resolve through decisive action is particularly dangerous in a serious Sino-U.S. crisis because it creates the belief, on both sides, that effective deterrence might require very strong threats or applications of force. The danger is compounded by offensive military doctrines at the operational, campaign, and tactical levels. Military forces might become more assertive in a crisis than civilian leaders prefer, thereby undermining coordination between diplomatic and political moves. Such an outcome is even more likely if there is poor coordination between civilian and military leaders in the overall decision-making process. Some Western observers believe the Chinese government suffers from this problem.[64]

North Korea and Iran

In the second decade of the 21st century, the long struggle to prevent North Korea and Iran from becoming nuclear-armed states increasingly is giving way to a recognition that prevention may not be a fully achievable goal and that greater attention must be paid to how each of these countries may seek to leverage its nuclear weapon capabilities. This is no small task, as these states cloak their nuclear activities in great secrecy, making them difficult intelligence targets. Their strategic intentions, decisionmaking practices, plans and capabilities may be difficult to assess and influence. Moreover, there appears to be little open writing or analysis of nuclear strategy. Thus, we may not learn more by simply looking harder; unless and until this aspect of their respective nuclear development emerges with a greater degree of clarity, efforts to anticipate how North Korea or Iran would manage a nuclear crisis, manipulate nuclear threats, or employ nuclear weapons unavoidably will be characterized by a significant degree of speculation.

At the same time, it seems likely that leaders in Pyongyang and Tehran have in mind some "theory of victory" that can be underwritten by nuclear capability. Put differently, the significant financial and political investment each regime has made over decades to acquire nuclear capability strongly suggests a belief in the utility of nuclear weapons to mitigate or even solve their most serious security dilemmas. As a general proposition, for governments of this kind the theory of victory has a strong existential element expressed in terms of regime survival. Nuclear capability is seen as the ultimate guarantor of survival against US-led military campaigns to impose regime change. Thus, at the strategic level, the possession of nuclear weapons is seen as providing the means to deter outside intervention, divide US-led alliances and coalitions and, if necessary, wreak vengeance. The strategic leverage provided by nuclear weapons, and their ability to shape the political and psychological battlefield, derive from the belief that their possession fundamentally alters the US assessment of risk in confronting regional challengers and contemplating wars to defeat them.

This calculus aligns well with the initial nuclear capabilities proliferators of this kind are likely to develop, which may present a threat to hold cities and large areas at risk but little potential for operational and tactical-level strikes requiring a greater degree of discrimination and precision. If nuclear weapons are to provide the means to shape the military battlefield as well, states like North Korea and Iran will have to consider developing different classes of capability, much like most of the world's other nuclear powers have done. The ability to deploy and deliver more diverse nuclear weapons more accurately would support strategies to delay, disrupt, and defeat military operations, for instance, by holding at risk critical military targets such as large air bases and facilities supporting the reception and staging of forces, and possibly large military formations. How deeply political and military leaders in North Korea and Iran have thought about the role of nuclear weapons in this dimension is unclear. Whether they would be prepared to make the necessary investment is yet another key question. One should not assume the answer to either of these questions. One possibility is that both regimes will think about their nuclear capability principally as a source of political influence, strategic deterrence, and regime survival, and leave to other weapons of mass destruction, such as chemical or biological weapons, or other asymmetric capabilities, the role of countering the military operations of outside powers in the event of conflict.

North Korea

While the United States and other regional powers continue to pursue the verifiable nuclear disarmament of North Korea, the country must now be considered a de facto nuclear weapon state, having successfully conducted underground nuclear tests in 2006, 2009, and 2012. The regime's public state-ments suggest an intention to remain nuclear-capable and seek international recognition of its nuclear status. It is unclear whether the North has produced deliverable nuclear warheads, or is even capable of doing so, but it is widely believed to be working intensively to manufacture a weapon that can be mated to one or more of its ballistic missile systems. Almost certainly this will remain the regime's priority in the period ahead, though as it produces more fissile material through its uranium enrichment infrastructure, it is conceiv-able that consideration will be given to producing other types of warheads as part of an operational nuclear stockpile. By some estimates, North Korea could possess nearly 50 nuclear weapons by 2016.[65]

As long as the regime possesses a basic nuclear weapons capability that cannot reliably be delivered by conventional means, it seems likely to lever-age this capability principally to support its strategy of threats and limited provocations. Some analysts speculate that Pyongyang may feel emboldened by the 2012 nuclear test to contemplate more aggressive military action in its ongoing effort to intimidate South Korea and extract political and economic concessions, believing both Seoul and Washington will be restrained from responding forcefully.[66]

More dangerous would be North Korea's adoption of an "early use" strategy, stating or signaling that it is prepared to employ nuclear weapons as early as necessary in any conflict in which it faced a decisive setback or imminent defeat. This would be intended to deter a full-scale combined forces response to an invasion of the South. It is unknown whether Pyongyang would be prepared to make good on this threat; the actual employment of one or more of its nuclear weapons would be risky, though the leadership would be weighing this risk in relation to the prospect of military defeat and regime collapse. Possible uses of nuclear weapons include a demonstration shot (for example, at sea) to signal resolve and a willingness to escalate, an EMP shot also designed to signal resolve but with potential to disrupt US and South Korean military operations, and other, more tactical applications also intended to disrupt operations. Some experts believe Pyongyang could launch nuclear-armed short- or medium-range ballistic missiles at US bases in the region or even at South Korean and Japanese cities, raising the prospect of major devastation and loss of life.[67]

Iran

It remains to be seen whether Iran will be content to stockpile fissile material that could be quickly weaponized or actually move to produce one or more nuclear devices in defiance of the international community. In the former scenario, where Iran maintains a ready capability to manufacture a weapon but also the legal patina of non-nuclear status, one would not expect there to be public discussion or statements on matters related to Iranian nuclear strategy. The latter scenario would reflect a calculation by the leadership that the strategic benefits of producing a weapon outweighed the risks and costs. This development could remain secret and unspoken, possibly signaling a posture of nuclear opacity or ambiguity—not unlike Israel's—in which case discussions of doctrine likely would also remain out of view. Alternatively, Iran could announce its nuclear weapon status through statements and/or actions, such as an underground test. If there is an open declaration or demonstration of nuclear weapon status, then the question of what to say about strategy and doctrine will at some point assume greater urgency in order to convey desired messages both internally and externally. To what degree the regime is working on this today is unknown, at least through open sources.

Speculation on nuclear strategies Iran could adopt ranges widely from the minimal and defensive to the expansive and assertive. Paul Bracken suggests a number of options: a minimal deterrent of perhaps 10–20 bombs to deter

Israeli and American attack; a defensive deterrent twice as large to provide an added measure of survivability and deter interventions aimed at achieving regime change; an offensive deterrent relying on high alert status, frequent nuclear exercises, launch-on-warning posture, and extended deterrence policies; a strategy of provocation and crisis-making; and a purely political strategy that forgoes the development of military doctrine in favor of leveraging nuclear weapon status to achieve political goals.[68] These choices may or may not encompass the full range of possibilities; as noted above, nuclear opacity may be a plausible pathway for Tehran.[69] Some analysts have argued that lacking the ability to match the sophistication of the American or Israeli nuclear force, Iran is likely to think asymmetrically in seeking to leverage its nuclear weapons, just as it has adopted asymmetric approaches in other areas of potential conflict.[70]

Questions of nuclear force readiness and launch on warning are of particular concern because they bear importantly on command and control and the prospects for escalation in crisis and conflict. As Gregory Giles has observed:

> Despite its significant strategic depth, Tehran may deem it necessary to adopt a higher degree of readiness for a nascent nuclear force, particularly since fears of a preventive attack by Israel or the United States undoubtedly will grow the closer Iran comes to possessing the bomb. This raises the possibility of a more delegative command and control system for Iranian nuclear weapons. It also raises the risk of inadvertent escalation resulting from false warnings or unauthorized action—that is, the system could "fail deadly." To mitigate this risk, Iran's clerical leadership might create a new organization for nuclear weapons, one that was more professional and reliable than either the regular military or the IRGC [Islamic Revolutionary Guard Corps]. Such bureaucratic differentiation and counterbalancing would be consistent with past Iranian behavior.[71]

Whether the leadership of a nuclear Iran will possess the wisdom to manage these risks proactively is unknown. Certainly, these risks have focused the attention of US military planners on the possible implications for stability in the region. The 2011 National Military Strategy captures this concern: "The prospect of multiple nuclear-armed regimes in the Middle East with nascent security and command and control mechanisms amplifies the threat of conflict, and significantly increases the probability of miscalculation or the loss of control of a nuclear weapon to non-state actors."[72]

Conclusion

This chapter, though far from comprehensive, nevertheless reveals a variety of doctrinal experience and evolution bearing on the possibility of limited nuclear war. This possibility is inherent in the doctrine of some states, such as Russia and Pakistan, both of which clearly see their prospects for deterring conflict as critically dependent on the threat of early nuclear use against conventionally superior adversaries. To make this threat credible, adaptations to organization, capabilities, command and control, and intelligence are required. India questions Pakistan's threat to escalate rapidly against small-scale conventional actions, but cannot rule out the possibility and thus is compelled to threaten disproportionate retaliation. While each side questions the credibility of the other's deterrent threats, both seem to be refining doctrine and forces in ways that will lead to larger arsenals, greater attention to military planning for nuclear use, and a steady lowering of the nuclear threshold. The subcontinent remains a dangerous nuclear flashpoint where deterrence could fail and nuclear escalation could unfold in a variety of ways that still may not be fully appreciated by the political and military elites on both sides.

China's nuclear policy reflects national political concerns and the long-held views of its leadership regarding the fundamentally political role of nuclear weapons and the overarching goal of preventing nuclear blackmail by maintaining an assured retaliation capability. Yet Chinese nuclear doctrine under the aegis of the PLA and SAF has evolved to encompass a broader set of tasks that attempts to link nuclear weapons with the requirements to deter or prevail in local, high-technology wars. Thus, China now plans for "nuclear counterstrike campaigns" below the level of strategic warfare. While this concept appears firmly embedded in a framework of deterrence, a number of factors could generate escalatory pressures and act to lower the threshold for nuclear use, including the fielding of US missile defense and global strike systems, and China's growing conventional missile force. The former puts pressure on China's no-first-use policy, while the latter contributes to the risk of unintended escalation to the nuclear level.

Finally, there is the question of how new or emerging nuclear weapon states will organize, plan, and behave as nuclear weapons become available to their armed forces. Will states like North Korea and Iran limit their ambitions to minimum deterrence postures based on modest nuclear holdings, or will they develop more expansive capabilities, embrace more complex operational doctrines, and adopt more uncertain command and control structures? Will their approach to nuclear weapons follow Western models at all, or will they adopt approaches tailored to their own unique circumstances—for example, coercive bargaining in the case of North Korea and nuclear opacity in the case of Iran—that challenge more conventional conceptions of nuclear doctrine? The answers to these questions will significantly shape the prospects for limited nuclear war in the decades ahead, and will have profound implications for regional and global security. Investigating them should be a priority for scholars and practitioners alike.

Notes

1. The five permanent members of the United Nations Security Council are legally recognized as nuclear weapon states by the 1968 Nuclear Nonproliferation Treaty. India, Pakistan and North Korea are self-declared nuclear powers, all of whom have openly conducted nuclear explosive tests. Israel maintains a policy of not acknowledging its nuclear weapon status, but this status is common knowledge.

2. Examples include Israel's strike against Iraq's Osirak reactor complex in 1981 and, more recently, against Syria's near-complete reactor at al-Khibar in 2007, as well as a number of alleged efforts, reported in the media, by the United States and Israel to sabotage Iran's nuclear program.

3. William C. Potter and Gaukhar Mukhatzhanova, "In Search of Proliferation Trends and Tendencies," in William C. Potter and Gaukhar Mukhatzhanova, eds., *Forecasting Nuclear Proliferation in the 21st Century, Volume 2, A Comparative Perspective* (Stanford, CA: Stanford University Press 2010), 338–341.

4. Ibid., 341.

5. A good example of an assessment lamenting the erosion of the nuclear nonproliferation regime in the post–Cold War era can be found in "Heading for a Fourth Nuclear Age" by Ariel Levite. Levite refers to the period of 1993–2010 as one of "complacency and disillusion." See www.ifri.org/files/Securite_defense/Levite_Fourth_Nuclear_Age.pdf, accessed 15 May 2013.

6. As an example of this phenomenon, the aforementioned reactor in Syria appears to have been closely modeled on North Korea's reactor at Yongbyon, and may have been financed by Iran.

7. Steven E. Miller and Scott D. Sagan, "Alternative Nuclear Futures," *Daedalus*, Vol. 139, No. 1 (Winter 2010), 135, at www.mitpressjournals.org/doi/pdf/10.1162/daed.2010.139.1.126, accessed 15 May 2013.

8. Scott D. Sagan and Kenneth N. Waltz, *The Spread of Nuclear Weapons: A Debate Renewed* (New York: W.W. Norton, 2003), 45.

9. Ibid., 20, 23–26, 49–51. See also Timothy D. Hoyt, "Kargil: The Nuclear Dimension," in Peter R. Lavoy, ed., *Asymmetric Warfare in South Asia* (Cambridge: Cambridge University Press 2009), 145.

10. Some emerging research suggests that the period following the acquisition of nuclear weapons poses significant risk of adventurism before states have the opportunity to engage in "nuclear learning." The phenomenon whereby stable nuclear deterrence permits or encourages wars at the conventional level between nuclear rivals is often referred to as the "stability/instability paradox," a term coined by Glenn Snyder. A small nuclear power engaged in conflict with a superior power may see its survival at risk and thus may believe that the threat of nuclear use will work in its favor. This phenomenon, whereby the larger power may be deterred by the smaller, is often referred to as reflecting the "balance of resolve" or the "asymmetry of stakes."

11. Sagan and Waltz, *The Spread of Nuclear Weapons*, 47–48.

12. Ibid., 49, 101.

13. Ibid., 92–95, 101–106.

14. Ibid., 98.

15. Ibid., 98–99.

16. Hoyt, "Kargil," 169.

17. Zachary Davis, "A Decade of Nuclear Learning: Ten Years after the South Asian Nuclear Tests," Center on Contemporary Conflict, US Naval Postgraduate School, March 2009, 1, at www.nps.edu/Academics/SIGS/ccc/conferences/recent/Nuclear-LearningMar09_rpt.html, accessed 15 May 2013.

18. Ibid., 2. See also Zachary Davis, "Stepping Back from the Brink: Avoiding a Nuclear March of Folly in South Asia," *Arms Control Today*, Volume 39 (January/February 2009), at www.armscontrol.org/act/2009_01-02/stepping_back_from_the_brink, accessed 15 May 2013.

19. Hoyt, "Kargil," 163, 168.

20. Ibid., 163, 166. Conditions for nuclear use, as stated in December 2001 by Pakistan Strategic Plans Division, are significant loss of territory, destruction of large parts of the army or air force, economic "strangulation" of Pakistan, and domestic destabilization. Not surprisingly, these are general and vague, allowing for wide interpretation and the maintenance of ambiguity.

21. Vipin Narang, "Posturing for Peace? Pakistan's Nuclear Postures and South Asian Stability," *International Security*, Vol. 34, No. 3 (Winter 2009/10), 44, available at www.mitpressjournals.org.

22. Ibid., 57. According to some media accounts, Pakistan is developing small, low-yield nuclear weapons (possibly of sub-kiloton yield) as well as short-range artillery rockets for their delivery. See Jeffrey Lewis, "Pakistan's Nuclear Artillery?," *Arms Control Wonk*, 12 December 2011, at http://lewis.armscontrolwonk.com/archive/4866/pakistans-nuclear-artillery, accessed 15 May 2013.

23. The Brasstacks exercise involved an estimated 250,000 Indian troops and 1,500 tanks, and led to countermoves by Pakistan, which feared the exercise could be the opening phase of a large-scale attack. Sagan and others argue that Brasstacks was in fact an effort by the Indian military to provoke Pakistan into war and thereby provide an opportunity to neutralize Pakistan's nuclear program. See Sagan and Waltz, *The Spread of Nuclear Weapons*, 93–95; and Waheguru Pal Singh, "India's Nuclear Use

Doctrine," in Peter R. Lavoy, Scott D. Sagan, and James J. Wirtz, eds., *Planning the Unthinkable: How New Powers Will Use Nuclear, Biological, and Chemical Weapons* (Ithaca, NY: Cornell University Press 2000), 135–138.

24. Narang, "Posturing for Peace?," 66. See 65–70 for a more detailed discussion of command and control considerations.

25. Ibid., 70.

26. Davis, "Stepping Back from the Brink."

27. See Iskander Rehman, "Drowning Stability: The Perils of Naval Nuclearization and Brinkmanship in the Indian Ocean," *Naval War College Review*, Vol. 65, No. 4 (Autumn 2012), 64–88.

28. See Dima Adamsky, *Russian Regional Nuclear Developments*, Long Term Strategy Group, September 2010, 11–12; and more broadly, Keir Giles, "The Military Doctrine of the Russian Federation 2010," *Research Review*, NATO Defense College, February 2010; and Stephen J. Blank, ed., *Russian Military Politics and Russia's 2010 Defense Doctrine* (Carlisle, PA: Strategic Studies Institute, March 2011). On the specific point regarding preemptive use, Giles notes that on the day following publication of the 2010 military doctrine, Nikolai Patrushev, Secretary of the Russian Security Council, appeared to be maintaining the view that preemptive strikes were possible. Patrushev is quoted as stating, "We are not going to attack anyone, but neither are we going to wait for the moment when a strike is made against us." See Giles, "The Military Doctrine of the Russian Federation 2010," 6.

29. "The Military Doctrine of the Russian Federation," text of report by Russian presidential website, 5 February 2010, at www.carnegieendowment.org/files/2010russia-military_doctrine.pdf.

30. Giles, "The Military Doctrine of the Russian Federation 2010," 2; Adamsky, *Russian Regional Nuclear Developments*, 12.

31. Adamsky, *Russian Regional Nuclear Developments*, 13.

32. For evidence from military exercises, see ibid., 27–30.

33. Ibid., 49–50.

34. Nathan Picarsic, *Russian Nuclear Developments: Workshop Report*, Long Term Strategy Group, September 2010, 5.

35. Ibid., 11.

36. David C. Gompert and Phillip C. Saunders, *The Paradox of Power: Sino-American Strategic Restraint in an Age of Vulnerability* (Washington, DC: National Defense University Press 2011), 55.

37. For a good overview of these arguments, see M. Taylor Fravel and Evan S. Medeiros, "China's Search for Assured Retaliation," *International Security*, Vol. 35, No. 2 (Fall 2010), 48–87.

38. Alastair Iain Johnston, writing in the mid-1990s, argued that PLA and SAF strategists who viewed minimum deterrence as too defensive and passive had developed comprehensive arguments for shifting to a posture that resembled the Western concept of flexible response and envisioned limited nuclear warfighting. See Alastair Iain Johnston, "China's New 'Old Thinking'—The Concept of Limited Deterrence," *International Security*, Vol. 20, No. 3 (Winter 1995/96), 5–42.

39. For a discussion of domestic and organizational constraints on the development of nuclear strategy, see Fravel and Medeiros, "China's Search for Assured Retaliation," 66–75.

40. Evan S. Medeiros, "Evolving Nuclear Doctrine," in Paul J. Bolt and Albert S. Willner, eds., *China's Nuclear Future* (Boulder, CO: Lynne Rienner, 2006), 64.

41. Johnston, "China's New 'Old Thinking,'" 42.

42. Fravel and Medeiros, "China's Search for Assured Retaliation," 76–77.

43. In the last twenty years the US intelligence community has offered differing assessments of whether China possesses tactical nuclear weapons, and contemporary DoD reports on military developments in China do not reference such weapons when discussing Chinese nuclear capabilities. A 2011 report issued by the Union of Concerned Scientists cites a number of official and unofficial US sources indicating that China possesses a stockpile of air-deliverable nuclear weapons, but that these weapons have no "primary mission." See Gregory Kulacki, "China's Nuclear Arsenal: Status and Evolution," Union of Concerned Scientists, May 2011, at www.ucsusa.org/assets/documents/nwgs/UCS-Chinese-nuclear-modernization.pdf, accessed 15 May 2013. The short-range ballistic missiles China deploys are assessed to be conventionally armed.

44. Fravel and Medeiros, "China's Search for Assured Retaliation," 85.

45. Bates Gill, James Mulvenon, and Mark Stokes, "The Chinese Second Artillery Corps: Transition to Credible Deterrence," in James Mulvenon and Andrew Yang, eds., *The People's Liberation Army as Organization, Reference Volume v1.0* (Santa Monica, CA: RAND Corporation, 2002), 559.

46. Fravel and Medeiros, "China's Search for Assured Retaliation," 79–80.

47. Brad Roberts, "The Nuclear Dimension: How Likely? How Stable?," in Michael D. Swaine, Andrew N. D. Yang, and Evan S. Medeiros, eds., *Assessing The Threat: The Chinese Military and Taiwan's Security* (Washington, DC: Carnegie Endowment for International Peace, 2007), 220.

48. Fravel and Medeiros, "China's Search for Assured Retaliation," 79–80; and Thomas J. Christensen, "The Meaning of the Nuclear Evolution: China's Strategic Modernization and US-China Security Relations," *Journal of Strategic Studies*, Vol. 35, No. 4, 447–487, at http://dx.doi.org/10.1080/01402390.2012.714710, accessed 15 May 2013. At pp. 474–481, Christensen argues that doctrinal writings of the Second Artillery Force suggest a flexible conception of NFU that would broaden the circumstances triggering nuclear use, and an operational orientation toward mixing conventional and nuclear coercive strategies and capabilities in a way that blurs the firebreak between conventional and nuclear war. He refers specifically to the book, *Science of Second Artillery Campaigns*.

49. Roberts, "The Nuclear Dimension," 223–227; and Michael Mazza and Dan Blumenthal, "China's Strategic Forces in the 21st Century: The PLA's Changing Nuclear Doctrine and Force Posture," Nonproliferation Policy Education Center, 5–7, at www.npolicy.org.

50. M. Taylor Fravel, "China Has Not (Yet) Changed Its Position on Nuclear Weapons," *Diplomat*, 22 April 2003, at http://thediplomat.com/2013/04/22/china-has-not-yet-changed-its-position-on-nuclear-weapons, accessed 15 May 2013.

51. Roberts, "The Nuclear Dimension," 229–234.

52. For a discussion of China's conventional missile efforts, see Michael S. Chase and Andrew S. Erickson, "The Conventional Missile Capabilities of China's Second Artillery Force: Cornerstone of Deterrence and Warfighting," *Asian Security*, Vol. 8, No. 2 (2012), 115–137; and John W. Lewis and Xue Litai, "Making China's Nuclear War Plan," *Bulletin of the Atomic Scientists*, Vol. 68, No. 5 (2012), 45–65, at http://bos.sage-pub.com/content/68/5/45, accessed 15 May 2013.

53. Chase and Erickson, The Conventional Missile Capabilities of China's Second Artillery Force," 116. Lewis and Xue use the formulation "double deterrence, double operations, and double command" ("Making China's Nuclear War Plan," 53).

54. Chase and Erickson, "The Conventional Missile Capabilities of China's Second Artillery Force," 122.

55. Ibid., 125.

56. Lewis and Xue, "Making China's Nuclear War Plan," 61.

57. Ibid., 60.

58. Christensen, "The Meaning of the Nuclear Evolution," 480.

59. Chase and Erickson, "The Conventional Missile Capabilities of China's Second Artillery Force," 131. The authors observe: "China experts themselves worry that China's stove-piped, hierarchical bureaucracy, with military and civilian decision-making only truly integrated by the leader at the top, is particularly unsuited to crisis management" (131).

60. Ibid., 127.

61. Barry D. Watts, "Nuclear Conventional Firebreaks and the Nuclear Taboo," Center for Strategic and Budgetary Assessments, 2013, 64–65. Watts is citing Peng Guangqian and Yao Youzhi, eds., *Science of Strategy* (Beijing: Military Sciences Press, 2001), 361. The authors are PLA generals.

62. Michael D. Swaine, "Sino-American Crisis Management and the U.S.-Japan Alliance: Challenges and Implications," in Michael M. Mochikuzi, ed., *The Japan-U.S. Alliance and China-Taiwan Relations: Implications for Okinawa* (Washington: Sigur Center for Asian Studies, 2008), 83–104. See in particular 88–89. For a comprehensive, case-study-driven analysis of Chinese crisis management and deterrence signaling, see Paul H. B. Godwin and Alice L. Miller, "China's Forbearance Has Limits: Chinese Threat and Retaliation Signaling and Its Implications for a Sino-American Military Confrontation," *China Strategic Perspectives* No. 6, Center for the Study of Chinese Military Affairs, National Defense University, April 2013.

63. Swaine, "Sino-American Crisis Management and the U.S.-Japan Alliance," 88–89.

64. Ibid., 89.

65. David Albright and Christina Walrond, "North Korea's Estimated Stocks of Plutonium and Weapon-Grade Uranium," Institute for Science and International Security, 16 August 2012, 30, 39.

66. See, for example, John Arquilla, "Rolling the Iron Dice: Can Kim Jong Un Use His Nukes and Get Away With It?," *Foreign Policy Situation Report*, 8 April 2013, at www.foreignpolicy.com/articles/2013/04/08/rolling_the_iron_dice, accessed 15 May

2013. Arquilla posits an incursion by the North of several tens of kilometers into South Korea, supported by cyberattacks designed to disrupt South Korean and US command and control.

67. Joel S. Wit and Jenny Town, "7 Reasons to Worry about North Korea's Weapons," *Atlantic*, 16 April 2013, at www.theatlantic.com/international/archive/2013/04/7-reasons-to-worry-about-north-koreas-weapons/275020/, accessed 15 May 2013. See also Joseph S. Bermudez, Jr., "The Democratic People's Republic of Korea and Unconventional Weapons, in Lavoy, Sagan, and Wirtz, eds., *Planning the Unthinkable*, 198.

68. Paul Bracken, *The Second Nuclear Age: Strategy, Danger, and the New Power Politics* (New York: Times Books, 2012), 142–151.

69. See, for example, Jean-Loup Samaan, "Israel and Iran Move Toward 'Nuclear Opacity,'" *Al-Monitor*, 24 April 2013, at www.al-monitor.com/pulse/originals/2013/04/toward-nuclear-opacity-middle-east.html?utm_source=&utm_medium=email&utm_campaign=7033, accessed 15 May 2013.

70. Ibid., 143.

71. Gregory F. Giles, "The Islamic Republic of Iran and Nuclear, Biological, and Chemical Weapons," in Lavoy, Sagan, and Wirtz, eds., *Planning the Unthinkable*, 101.

72. "The National Strategy Military Strategy of the United States of America," 3, at www.jcs.mil/content/files/2011-02/020811084800_2011_NMS_-_08_FEB_2011.pdf, accessed 15 May 2013.

6 Future Scenarios of Limited Nuclear Conflict

Thomas G. Mahnken

THERE HAS BEEN CONSIDERABLE DEBATE OVER THE past several years regarding the future of the US nuclear posture and of nuclear weapons more broadly. Discussion regarding the current and future utility of nuclear weapons has emerged in reaction to a greatly changed nuclear landscape. Whereas for decades nuclear weapons were the exclusive property of a handful of powerful, advanced states, today the ranks of the nuclear powers include the backward (North Korea) and the unstable (Pakistan). Today more than ever it is the weak rather than the strong that seek nuclear arms.

The relationship between nuclear and conventional weapons has also changed, both for the United States and for others, including potential adversaries. During the Cold War, the United States looked to nuclear weapons to offset the size and strength of the Soviet Union. Specifically, it relied upon nuclear weapons to deter a Soviet invasion of Western Europe as well as conventional attacks on other allies. Today, however, it is the United States that possesses conventional superiority over the full range of adversaries. It has demonstrated its prowess in a series of wars in Southwest and Central Asia and the Balkans. It has used its high-technology advantage to coerce others into giving up territory, as it did to Iraq in 1991 and Serbia in 1999, as well as to unseat hostile regimes, as it did in Afghanistan in 2002 and Iraq in 2003. US conventional superiority provides not only a powerful deterrent, but also a motivation for others to acquire nuclear weapons. Indeed, it is the potency of the American conventional arsenal, rather than its nuclear stockpile, that provides the greater motivation for states that are hostile to the United States to acquire nuclear weapons.

Another defining feature of the strategic context is the imbalance in political stakes between the United States and potential adversaries. During the Cold War, the Soviet Union's nuclear arsenal represented an existential threat to the United States and its allies. Today we have limited stakes in many potential conflicts. A nuclear blast in a major US city would inflict horrendous casualties; it would not destroy the United States. By contrast, future adversaries are likely to see a conflict with the United States as a threat to their survival. A war on the Korean peninsula, for example, would not put at risk the existence of the United States, even if Pyongyang were to field an ICBM; it would, however, jeopardize Kim Jong-un's regime and the North Korean state. Nor would a nuclear Iran pose an existential threat to the United States. Tehran's clerics could, however, judge that a war with the United States could lead to the end of the religious regime. America's opponents will thus have a strong motivation not to escalate future conflicts.

Technology has also changed the nuclear landscape, blurring traditional distinctions between conventional and nuclear arms. Whereas commentators on the left have for years feared that fielding more discriminate nuclear weapons would "conventionalize" them, in fact conventional arms now approach the effectiveness of nuclear weapons. Soviet military theorists writing in the late 1970s were among the first to observe that precision-guided munitions (PGMs) were being fielded that had effectiveness nearing that of tactical nuclear weapons. Conventional precision-guided munitions are today capable of destroying a wide range of targets that until recently would have required nuclear weapons. In addition, the deployment of ballistic missile defenses now offers the prospect of defending the United States, its forces, and its allies against missile attack.

The changed nuclear environment, in turn, suggests that nuclear weapons could be employed in a broader set of circumstances than in the past. First, a new nuclear power could demonstrate its weapons in an effort to enhance its credibility. Second, a nuclear power could use its weapons to launch a selective attack to achieve limited political objectives. Third, a state could employ nuclear weapons as part of an incapacitating attack in an attempt to decouple American allies from the US nuclear deterrent. Fourth, a state could cross the nuclear threshold in order to forestall a conventional military defeat. Finally, given the fact that two of today's nuclear powers—North Korea and Pakistan—are of questionable political stability, now more than in the past the world faces the possibility of the collapse of a nuclear state, with implications for the loss of control over its nuclear weapons.

This chapter outlines a set of scenarios that portray situations in which states or non-state actors could employ nuclear weapons to achieve limited political aims as well as the policy debates that may attend nuclear use. All are based on extrapolations of current trends and all could plausibly occur. However, they are heuristic rather than predictive. That is, they are meant to illustrate how nuclear weapons *might* be used and to serve as the starting point for an examination of the policy and strategy issues that might ensue from their use.[1] They also serve as a venue for exploring various theories of nuclear deterrence and warfare.

Scenario 1: A Demonstration Nuclear Attack

Since the advent of nuclear weapons, theorists have tended to be divided into those who see the only utility of nuclear weapons as purely political—that is, as a deterrent—and those who have observed that nuclear weapons are also highly effective weapons. Indeed, it is their lethality as weapons that makes them effective deterrents. The former believe that the credibility of nuclear threats is inherent in the nature of the weapons themselves; the latter argue that it requires conscious effort to maintain the credibility of a nuclear arsenal.

The need to demonstrate a nuclear arsenal is inversely proportional to its size and robustness. States that have large, institutionalized, and tested nuclear stockpiles are likely to feel less need to test their capabilities than a new nuclear power. The need to demonstrate a nuclear capability might be further intensified by attempts to disarm a new nuclear power. The scenario that follows explores this dynamic in the context of Iran's acquisition of nuclear weapons.

Although the Iranian government continues to deny seeking nuclear weapons, Iran's nuclear program continues. Tehran's quest for nuclear weapons proceeds by fits and starts, however, and the program faces occasional setbacks—including some that outside observers speculate are the result of foreign covert action. It remains difficult, however, for outsiders to judge Iranian progress toward fielding a nuclear weapon. The US intelligence community, stung by its failure to understand Iraq's nuclear, chemical, and biological weapons programs in the run-up to the 2003 Iraq War, is wary of making unequivocal predictions.

Israel continues to be extremely concerned about an Iranian nuclear capability. Having received what it considers highly credible evidence that Iran is nearing a nuclear weapon capability, the Israeli government decides to strike Iran. The Israeli government approaches the US government, as well as those of Saudi Arabia, Jordan, and Iraq, and receives quiet pledges that they will not interfere. Israel then launches an air campaign against the Iranian nuclear infrastructure. The campaign, which lasts several days, appears to have been highly effective. Defense analysts across the globe credit the Israelis with success and judge that Iran has been disarmed, at least for the time being.

In fact, the Israeli campaign heavily damaged but did not destroy Iran's nuclear program. Of greater concern, Iran was farther along in its quest for nuclear weapons than outsiders realized. Indeed, it already had several nuclear devices suitable for delivery atop a ballistic missile. However, the Israeli strike did result in a public debate within Iran over the wisdom of its nuclear weapons program, with critics of the regime arguing that its recklessness had brought needless destruction on Iran.

To demonstrate that it is a nuclear power, and retains that capability despite the Israeli strike; to retaliate against Israel; and to silence domestic critics, Iran conducts a demonstration nuclear strike by launching a nuclear-armed missile against the Israeli nuclear reactor in the Negev Desert.

An Iranian demonstration attack against Israel would set in motion a complex set of interactions. Iran's employment of a nuclear weapon would settle once and for all the question of whether Tehran possessed nuclear weapons. It is likely, however, that policymakers and experts outside of government, both in the United States and abroad, would continue to debate the size, readiness, and utility of Tehran's nuclear capability. Indeed, nuclear use is likely to spark more debates than it would settle.

It is beyond the scope of this chapter to trace out all the permutations that could arise. Rather, it seeks to sketch out some of the most significant policy choices that the governments of the United States, Israel, and other states in the region would face.

Israel would confront a series of difficult choices in the wake of an Iranian attack. Most immediately, it would face calls to retaliate against the nuclear attack on Dimona. Iran's attack would have pierced the shield of deterrence that has been fundamental to Israeli national security policy throughout the history of the state of Israel. However, in confronting Iran, Israel faces a basic geographic asymmetry: it would be much easier for Iran to annihilate Israel than vice versa. Even a symmetrical limited nuclear response, against the Iranian nuclear reactor at Bushehr, for example, could invite retaliation against Tel Aviv or Jerusalem.

Quite apart from any immediate retaliation, Israel would face great pressure to eliminate the opacity of its own nuclear arsenal, as well as to establish a formal, explicit nuclear doctrine to clarify the circumstances under which Israel might use nuclear weapons.[2]

The United States, for its part, would confront the thorny issue of how to reassure Israel in the wake of an Iranian nuclear attack, albeit one that avoided Israeli population centers. It is likely, for example, that the Israeli government would ask Washington for arms and intelligence to help Israel protect itself against further attacks, and likely also to retaliate against Iran. Indeed, Tel Aviv might seek tacit or explicit American support for an Israeli retaliatory strike. In the end, however, is unclear what, if anything, the United States could do that would actually avert Israeli retaliation in such a circumstance. A nuclear attack on Israeli territory would represent a body blow to the credibility of Israeli deterrence, and Tel Aviv would likely be compelled to respond, even if in so doing Israel incurred great cost.

The US government would also need to decide how to respond to Iran's undisputed emergence as a nuclear power. Most immediately, the president and his advisors would need to decide whether and how to punish Iran for its use of nuclear weapons. In using a nuclear weapon, Iran would have undermined a decades-long tradition of the nonuse of nuclear weapons.[3] One way to restore the norm would be to demonstrate that the use of nuclear weapons is counterproductive. The United States might, for example, consider ways to punish Iran for its nuclear use, ranging from economic sanctions to military action.

Beyond punishing Iran for its use of nuclear weapons, Washington would face the issue of how to deal with a nuclear Iran. Iran's possession of nuclear weapons could be expected to boost its confidence and make its government more resistant to outside pressure. It would also increase Iran's capacity to intimidate its neighbors and (in conjunction with Tehran's missile programs) those farther afield. The United States might be forced to acknowledge Iran's nuclear status as a fait accompli. More likely, the United States might seek to disarm Iran, either through sanctions or by trying to finish the work that the Israelis began.[4]

The advent of a nuclear Iran would pose difficult issues for Iran's Arab neighbors. Iran's overt acquisition and use of nuclear weapons would put great pressure on Gulf states to either balance against or bandwagon with Tehran—pressure that would likely be exacerbated by the existence of Shi'a minorities (or in the case of Bahrain, a Shi'a majority) across the Gulf states.

In response to Iran's nuclear attack on Israel, other states in the region might seek extended nuclear deterrence guarantees from the United States. The Gulf Cooperation Council states, for example, would be increasingly vulnerable to Iranian coercion. Iraq, an Arab state with a Shi'a majority on Iran's borders, would be particularly uncomfortable in Iran's nuclear shadow. Secretary of State Hillary Clinton already hinted at the possibility of American security guarantees to Iran's Arab neighbors.[5] However, extending nuclear deterrence to states in the region would be problematic for a host of reasons. The United States has traditionally extended nuclear deterrence guarantees to a select subset of its allies, but an alliance with some or all of the Gulf states seems unlikely at best. Moreover, the United States has traditionally underwritten its extended nuclear deterrence guarantees with forward-based forces. However, the United States has radically decreased the size of its forward-based forces since the end of the Cold War.

Given the problematic nature of extended nuclear deterrence in this case, the Gulf states may be tempted to seek nuclear weapons of their own—either by developing them indigenously, banding together to do so, or by attempting to purchase weapons from a nuclear state such as Pakistan. The Gulf states might also want to acquire long-range delivery means for their weapons.

The United States also might seek to reassure Iran's neighbors through non-nuclear means. For example, the United States might deploy additional forces to the region, to include strike systems to hold at risk targets in Iran, as well as air and missile defenses to protect friendly regimes from attack. Indeed, the United States might deploy additional forces on the territory of Iran's neighbors to both reassure and deter. Washington might also increase its sales of precision-guided munitions and ballistic missile defenses to friendly states in the region.

Scenario 2: A Selective Nuclear Attack

Underpinning much of nuclear deterrence theory is the assumption that the possession of nuclear weapons is stabilizing because it induces caution on the part of those who possess them. However, nuclear weapons can also provide a shield behind which a state can undertake risky behavior. The scenario that follows explores such a dynamic in the context of North Korea's nuclear arsenal.

Kim Jong-un's campaign to consolidate his power as leader of North Korea proceeded more slowly and fitfully than many experts predicted, and left him weak and beholden to military district commanders and Korean Workers Party leaders. He was eventually able to consolidate control after a massive crackdown and a wave of executions, but the regime that ensues is, if anything, even more isolated, roguish, and paranoid than that of Kim Jong-il. Despite Pyongyang's February 29, 2012, offer to halt nuclear and missile tests and to freeze uranium enrichment at Yongbyon, North Korea's nuclear program continues at other sites. As evidence of this, American and South Korean intelligence agencies receive credible reports that leaders of the Korean Workers Party and the armed forces are selling nuclear materials and technology to Myanmar. Under the authority of United Nations Security Council Resolution 1874, the United States, South Korea, Japan, and others launch a maritime interdiction operation against North Korean merchant ships that are believed to be carrying the materials. In one incident, a Japan Maritime Self-Defense warship fires on a merchant vessel before disabling it. An American boarding party searches the ship and discovers that it is carrying a load of centrifuges.

In retaliation against the boarding, North Korea launches a nuclear-armed Nodong medium-range ballistic missile against America's Kadena Air Base on Okinawa. The strike is meant to serve as a warning against further intervention in North Korean affairs. In striking Japan, the North Korean leadership hopes to galvanize support among Koreans both north and south of the DMZ while also driving a wedge between the United States, on the one hand, and the Republic of Korea and Japan, on the other.

A North Korean nuclear strike against Kadena would raise serious questions for the United States. First and foremost, the president would be forced to decide whether and how to retaliate. Such a decision would lay bare the dilemma that underpins extended nuclear deterrence: extending nuclear guarantees is meant to lessen the pressure on an ally to acquire nuclear weapons, but in so doing, the United States puts at risk its own security on behalf of an ally. According to the US-Japan Defense Treaty, the United States is committed to the defense of Japan; to not do so would mark the end of the US-Japan alliance. However, a strike on North Korea could invite further nuclear attacks on Japan, or possibly even attacks against South Korea or the United States.

Should the United States retaliate against North Korea, there would likely be a debate over the form of that retaliation. One group would doubtless argue in favor of a symmetrical response employing the use of nuclear weapons to disarm North Korea. Others, however, are likely to argue that the United States should eschew a nuclear response and retaliate with precision-guided munitions. The rationale, which assumes that conventional weapons are effective enough for a punitive response, would be that, in refraining from using nuclear weapons, the United States would help to delegitimize nuclear weapons. Additionally, relying on conventional weapons to retaliate would allow the United States to maintain the moral high ground.

Beyond the immediate issue of retaliation, the United States would face the question of how to treat the regime in Pyongyang. There would likely be considerable pressure—among Americans, but also Japanese and South Koreans—to overthrow the North Korean regime. However, the perceived threat to do so would invite further nuclear attacks by North Korea.

The Japanese government would also face difficult choices in this scenario. In the short term, Japan's ability to retaliate militarily against North Korea is limited; Tokyo would depend on Washington to do that. In the wake of such a scenario, however, Tokyo's vulnerability and dependence would likely lead to growing calls for Japan to acquire an offensive capability, including long-range strike systems and potentially nuclear weapons. Such calls would be even more vociferous if the United States were to be perceived to equivocate on retaliation against Pyongyang.

This scenario would be problematic for South Korea as well. Seoul would be caught between revulsion toward North Korean aggression and the sobering reality that unseating the regime in Pyongyang would represent a massive undertaking and could involve nuclear use against the south.[6]

Scenario 3: An Incapacitating Nuclear Attack

Russia remains the only country with a nuclear arsenal that is capable of destroying the United States. Moreover, Russian military doctrine has increasingly embraced nuclear weapons at the tactical level of war. As a result, in recent years Russia has thought more about nuclear warfighting than the United States and its allies. The scenario that follows explores how Russia might employ nuclear weapons to launch an incapacitating attack on US allies in NATO.

Many Russians continue to resent their nation's decline from superpower status. At the same time, the Russian government continues to hold tightly to its nuclear arsenal, both for the status it confers but also for the ability to use nuclear weapons to compensate for conventional weakness.

Through covert action, the Russian government begins to undermine the governments of the Baltic states. When ethnic Russians are assaulted in a riot in Vilnius, Russian troops rush in to protect them. The government of Lithuania calls upon NATO to come to its defense in accordance with Article V of the Atlantic Treaty. Russia responds with a concerted attack against NATO military bases and airfields in northern Europe, as well as a nuclear-powered electromagnetic pulse (EMP) attack against NATO command and control networks.

This scenario, involving as it does a nuclear conflict between Russia and NATO, would appear to be a case of "back to the future." However, such a conflict would take place is a geopolitical context that would both revive old debates as well as raise new ones.

As with North Korea's attack on Japan, described above, the United States would face the prospect of using nuclear weapons in support of a commitment to support allies who have been attacked. In this scenario, the United States and other NATO members would be bound by Article V of the Washington Treaty to defend their allies. In this case as well the United States would face the possibility of further Russian retaliation. But Russia, unlike North Korea, possesses the ability to devastate the United States with its nuclear arsenal. Indeed, Russia is the only state that is capable of annihilating the United States. As a result, debate within the United States over whether and how to retaliate would likely be sharp. On the one hand, some would argue that the United States is obliged to defend its allies, to include retaliation against Russia. They would further argue that the failure to do so would jeopardize not only NATO, but other U.S alliance commitments as well. Others would argue, echoing periodic debates within the Atlantic Alliance during the Cold War, that it would make no sense to trade Boston for Berlin, Washington for Warsaw, or Toledo for Tallinn.

Also influencing the debate over retaliation would be the fact that in this scenario NATO would have limited means to retaliate against Russia. The United States has decreased markedly the size of its theater nuclear forces since the end of the Cold War. According to the Department of Defense, the number of nonstrategic US nuclear warheads declined by approximately 90 percent from September 1991 to September 2009.[7] As a result, the United States would possess few options for escalating the conflict in intensity beyond conventional weapons and yet short of the use of strategic nuclear weapons.

This scenario would also raise the question of the role of the British and French nuclear arsenals. Discussions in London and Paris and at NATO headquarters would revolve around the loss of credibility to NATO if it failed to act as well as the risk of damage and escalation if it does.

Russia's employment of an EMP weapon would complicate the situation. The use of such a weapon could disrupt NATO intelligence, surveillance, and reconnaissance and command and control systems considerably and thus reduce the effectiveness of any NATO response. At the same time however, it is unclear whether such a nonlethal use of a nuclear weapon would provoke as sharp a response as nuclear use that inflicted a large number of casualties.

Finally, this scenario would raise questions of the role of ballistic missile defense in augmenting deterrence. On the one hand, the existence of both theater and strategic missile defenses could provide NATO some protection against Russian attack. It could also provide NATO members with greater confidence in the face of attempted Russian coercion. On the other hand, it is unlikely to be sufficient to provide a reliable defense against a concerted Russian attack.

Scenario 4: Nuclear Use to Prevent Battlefield Defeat

During the Cold War, US nuclear doctrine envisioned the use of nuclear weapons to prevent a conventional defeat at the hands of the Warsaw Pact. Now, however, the United States enjoys a much stronger military position against potential adversaries. That does not mean, however, that the prospect of nuclear escalation has gone away. The scenario that follows explores the issue of nuclear use to prevent battlefield defeat in the context of a conflict across the Taiwan Strait.

China feels the next economic downturn more deeply than the rest of the world. Rather than leading the rest of the world out of recession, as it did in 2009, this time China begins to drag other interdependent economies down. Just as Taiwan's growing interdependence with the mainland benefited it in a period of economic growth, it begins to hurt it in a period of economic decline. In response to domestic pressure, the government of Taiwan begins to cut its economic ties with the People's Republic. The increasingly embattled leadership in Beijing perceives Taipei's equivocation as a de facto declaration of independence and orders the People's Liberation Army (PLA) to launch a coercive campaign to force Taipei to reconsider.

The PLA launches a massive missile barrage against Taiwanese air bases and air defense facilities and declares a maritime exclusion zone in the waters surrounding Taiwan. Despite warnings from Beijing, the United States intervenes in the conflict in defense of Taiwan, surging air and sea power into the Western Pacific.

This scenario would raise the possibility of escalation on both the US and Chinese sides. Moreover, if history is a guide, it is likely that each side could miscalculate the other's stakes in a conflict and misperceive what actions would escalate the conflict.

The United States, for example, would face the prospect of having to strike the Chinese mainland as part of a campaign to protect Taiwan. In particular, US commanders might need to strike parts of the Chinese integrated air defense system (IADS) in order to achieve air superiority over the Taiwan Strait. In addition, commanders might want to strike the Chinese missile force and its associated command and control in order to interdict the missile barrage against Taiwan.

Depending upon China's assumptions about the character of a war with the United States, strikes against the Chinese mainland could raise the real possibility of escalation, potentially including the use of nuclear weapons. The structure of the Chinese missile force could further magnify escalatory pressures. The People's Liberation Army's Second Artillery Force controls both China's nuclear missiles and its conventional ones. Moreover, China fields nuclear and conventional variants of the same missiles, and at least parts of the support infrastructure for the Chinese conventional and nuclear missiles are intertwined. As a result, Chinese leaders could interpret attacks upon the Chinese conventional missile infrastructure as an attempt to disarm its nuclear arsenal. Conversely, it would be difficult for US leaders to determine whether the missiles raining down on Taiwan, and potentially US bases and territory, were armed with conventional or nuclear warheads until they hit their targets.

For the United States, the best outcome of this scenario would involve preventing China from coercing Taiwan by lifting the missile barrage and establishing air superiority over the Taiwan Strait. An operational victory by the United States, however, could set up a situation by which Chinese leaders might choose to escalate the conflict. Specifically, the Chinese leadership, having decided to use force against Taiwan but failing to achieve reunification, could believe that its legitimacy was at stake. In such a situation, the Chinese leadership might decide to escalate the conflict, perhaps by launching a nuclear missile strike against US bases in the Western Pacific, including Kadena Air Base as well as Andersen Air Force Base on Guam. Although Beijing has long espoused no first use of nuclear weapons, it is unclear whether that doctrine applies to "internal" conflicts, such as the way Beijing would view a war with Taiwan. It is also unclear whether Beijing would distinguish between attacks on US bases on foreign territory or those located on US territory.

China's use of nuclear weapons against US bases (e.g., Kadena) and US territory (e.g., Guam) would raise difficult issues for the United States. As with North Korea's attack on Japan and Russia's attack on Europe, the US government would face a difficult decision regarding retaliation, with some arguing for the use of nuclear weapons and others potentially calling for retaliation with precision-guided munitions. What is different in this case would be the fact that not only an ally had been struck by a nuclear weapon, but also the territory of the United States itself. This fact is likely to amplify calls for a response.

In either event, US strikes against China would raise the prospect of further escalation, potentially including a Chinese nuclear strike against the continental United States. It is unclear, for example, whether the Chinese would draw a distinction between a conventional attack on their territory and a nuclear one. In either event, the risk of escalation could be considerable, particularly if the Chinese leadership had staked its future on success in war.

Scenario 5: The Collapse of a Nuclear State

Historically, nuclear weapons have been the property of the strongest and most advanced states. Indeed, that is part of the reason they are so coveted. Today, however, two nuclear states—North Korea and Pakistan—face the prospect of unrest or collapse.[8] The scenario that follows explores some of the policy considerations that could attend the collapse of a nuclear state.

The Pakistani Taliban and Al Qaeda continue and expand their campaign against the Pakistani government. Moreover, both organizations seek to infiltrate the Pakistani military, intelligence services, and nuclear community. The two groups combine to launch a coordinated series of bomb attacks on the Pakistani leadership that kills the Pakistani president, prime minister, and several senior military leaders.

In the chaos that ensues before the Pakistani military can restore order, reports surface that officers sympathetic to Al Qaeda have seized control of a portion of the Pakistani nuclear arsenal. The US government is concerned that if a terrorist group like Al Qaeda gets its hands on a nuclear device, it will use it. The Indian government shares that concern.

The collapse of Pakistan and its loss of control over a portion of its nuclear arsenal would pose a momentous challenge for the United States, one that could eclipse ongoing military operations in Afghanistan. Most immediately, the United States would face the need to determine the location and status of Pakistan's nuclear weapons. Depending on the quality and timeliness of intelligence, the task could range from the challenging to the insoluble. Reliable, timely intelligence is the exception rather than the norm, and in this case trying to portray accurately a rapidly developing situation in a large, chaotic country half a world away is likely to be challenging to say the least. More likely, the United States would possess incomplete and inaccurate information on the status of Pakistani nuclear forces. In such a situation, the US government would face the prospect of having to gather such information by inserting Special Operations Forces deep into Pakistan, by flying reconnaissance (and potentially attack) aircraft in Pakistani airspace, or potentially both. In other words, the leadership of the United States would have to contemplate introducing US forces into, or violating the airspace of, a nuclear state with which we are not at war that is being convulsed by instability. Although the United States was able to launch the May 1, 2011, Abbottabad raid that killed Usama bin Laden, this scenario would require a much larger-scale intervention over a protracted period. Such a decision is likely to give a future president pause, with the urgent need for action competing with a natural aversion to risk.

Pakistan's loss of control over a portion of its nuclear arsenal would likely trigger an international debate. To many, the Pakistani government's loss of control over its nuclear arsenal would serve as evidence that it is unfit to possess them. It is likely that some in Washington and elsewhere would call for an effort to eliminate Pakistan's nuclear infrastructure to prevent further leakage, or at least to put it under international control so that it could be dismantled. However, the Pakistani government has traditionally viewed its nuclear program as central to Pakistani sovereignty and would be expected to resist any such efforts. Moreover, the Pakistani nuclear program is the object of considerable nationalistic sentiment. As a result, attempts to bring Pakistan's nuclear arsenal under control are likely to create further tension and conflict.

Pakistan would likely receive international support in its efforts to block outside intervention. China, Pakistan's most stalwart ally, has traditionally opposed intervention in the internal affairs of other states, and would likely use its power and influence in this case to support Islamabad. Other states, such as Iran, would likely support the Pakistanis as well.

To make matters worse, India is unlikely to sit idly on the sidelines as Pakistan descends into chaos; domestic pressure on India's leadership to take action would be strong. The Indian military might be asked to conduct reconnaissance flights over Pakistani air space to gather information on the status of the Pakistani nuclear arsenal. It might also deploy special operations forces to collect information or even larger formations to take control of Pakistan's weapons. Should it feel threatened, India might also launch air strikes to eliminate Pakistan's nuclear infrastructure. Such actions are likely to complicate what would already be a highly complex and fluid situation.

Observations

Policymakers and scholars alike have gotten out of the habit of "thinking about the unthinkable." As more states have acquired nuclear weapons, there have been fewer and fewer serious attempts to think through how nuclear weapons might actually be used. This chapter has sketched out some, though by no means all, such circumstances.

Three observations arise from this effort. First, as nuclear weapons spread, the task of reassuring US allies is likely to become increasingly difficult. Moreover, as these scenarios have shown, extended nuclear deterrence—a strategy whose efficacy many questioned even during the Cold War—may be even more open to question in the context of today's nuclear powers. It is worthwhile, then, to explore new approaches to enhance US extended nuclear deterrence guarantees to allies.

Second, precision-guided munitions are increasingly able to substitute for nuclear weapons. Similarly, missile defenses are able to complement offensive weapons as a way to reassure friends and deter adversaries. However, the relationship between these weapons deserves greater exploration than it has received.

Finally, the perceived effectiveness of nuclear weapons use will affect the utility of the weapons. If nuclear weapons are seen to have delivered tangible benefits, political or military, then the perceived benefit of possessing them is likely to increase. Conversely, if nuclear weapons are seen to be ineffective or counterproductive, then they will lose some of their appeal.

Notes

1. Some of what follows mirrors Duncan Brown and Thomas G. Mahnken, *Nuclear Futures Project* (Laurel, MD: Johns Hopkins University Applied Physics Laboratory, 2011).

2. See, for example, Avner Cohen, *The Worst-Kept Secret: Israel's Bargain with the Bomb* (New York: Columbia University Press, 2010).

3. T. V. Paul, *The Tradition of Non-Use of Nuclear Weapons* (Stanford, CA: Stanford University Press, 2009).

4. Eric S. Edelman, Andrew F. Krepinevich, and Evan Braden Montgomery, "The Dangers of a Nuclear Iran," *Foreign Affairs* (January/February 2011).

5. For an assessment, see Richard L. Kugler, *An Extended Deterrence Regime to Counter Iranian Nuclear Weapons: Issues and Options* (Washington, DC: National Defense University, 2009).

6. Bruce E. Bechtol, "Planning for the Unthinkable: Countering a North Korean Nuclear Attack and Management of Post-Attack Scenarios," *Korean Journal of Defense Analysis* 23, no. 1 (March 2011): 1–17.

7. "Fact Sheet: Increasing Transparency in the U.S. Nuclear Weapons Stockpile" (Washington, DC: Department of Defense, May 3, 2010), at www.defense.gov/npr/docs/10-05-03_fact_sheet_us_nuclear_transparency_final_w_date.pdf.

8. Steven R. David, *Catastrophic Consequences: Civil Wars and American Interests* (Baltimore: Johns Hopkins University Press, 2009), ch. 3.

7 Escalation to Limited Nuclear War in the 21st Century

Kerry M. Kartchner and Michael S. Gerson

A WISE PROFESSOR ONCE SAID, "YOU ONLY NEED TO learn strategic theory once." He was of course referring to the fact that basic principles of national security are virtually timeless. But, because circumstances change and we are sometimes confronted with seemingly unique challenges, it is not always clear how or which of those timeless principles apply in any given situation, especially if those circumstances change rapidly and veer in unexpected directions. Over the past ten to twenty years, there has been an ongoing systematic reassessment and reexamination of the dominant strategic paradigms and operating assumptions that prevailed within the field of strategic studies during the Cold War. This chapter joins the fray with an updated look at controlling escalation to limited nuclear war. The objective is not to present a new theory, because—as we argue in this chapter—the basic underlying principles remain unchanged, but rather to reassess the prevailing expectations that guided thinking about this subject during the Cold War, and to suggest how new circumstances may require new approaches, or at least altering the emphasis between two long-standing alternative approaches to the risk of escalation.[1]

There are several reasons that compel a reexamination of thinking about nuclear escalation dynamics. The circumstances that prevailed during the Cold War no longer pertain. A bipolar international system has given way to a more complex geostrategic landscape, with new players, each with their own motivations and ambitions, and their own perceptions of threat and preferred palette of responses. Weapons technology has advanced in sophistication and has proliferated widely, making tactical and strategic options available to a broader spectrum of regional actors than before. And, the role and international commitments of the United States as the sole remaining superpower have evolved, paradoxically constraining its options in some ways while expanding its responsibilities and obligations in others. Finally, as discussed in the introductory chapter to this volume, whereas the possibility of general, "all out" nuclear war has decreased with the end of the Cold War, the possibility of more limited nuclear use may be on the rise. If nuclear weapons are used in a future conflict, such use is likely to be limited in scale, at least in the opening round. As the opportunities for nuclear use multiply, so too do the challenges of being prepared to control, manage, or dominate the process of escalation. Revisiting the theory of escalation—while not necessarily *revising* it—in the context of the new and emerging conditions of the post–Cold War world is essential to improving our capacity for preventing and deterring crises, or any other circumstances that risk crossing the nuclear threshold.

The objective of this chapter is to identify and examine the range of motivations and processes that might lead to nuclear escalation. While other chapters in this book examine various situations in which the United States might find itself involved in a limited nuclear war, this chapter looks more broadly and conceptually at the mechanisms and pathways of escalation, and suggests some ways the United States can effectively deal with escalation pressures in future contingencies. The chapter will first review the literature on escalation from the Cold War, focusing on theories for why and how a conflict might escalate, and examining the possible paths to nuclear war that came to preoccupy and dominate Western thinking at that time. The chapter will then analyze escalation dynamics in the 21st century. This section will highlight what is different about escalation in the current and emerging international security environment and will suggest two additional motivations for escalation that may be more salient today. Finally, in exploring some of the implications of these new dynamics, we will reexamine the alternative approaches to controlling escalation represented by the "escalation control" and the "escalation dominance" schools of thought. We will argue that the concept of escalation dominance should be reexamined and resuscitated in light of the new strategic environment, and that in some circumstances it can play an important role in future nuclear confrontations.

Thinking about Nuclear Escalation during the Cold War

The Concept of Escalation

The concept of escalation was developed in tandem with theories of limited nuclear war. While it had long been recognized—and borne out by history—that a conflict could expand to higher and more diverse levels, it was not until the advent of nuclear weapons that escalation became a separate and distinct topic of analysis. As US and Soviet nuclear arsenals grew larger, more sophisticated, and more diverse in the late 1950s and early 1960s, it was becoming increasingly clear that a general nuclear war would serve no rational political ends. Total war, along with the concepts of total victory and unconditional surrender, made little strategic sense in an age of thermonuclear plenty.[2] As scholars and defense analysts began considering the possibility of smaller, more restricted conflicts involving the less-than-total use of nuclear weapons, many also began examining the potential for an initially limited conflict to reach higher levels of nuclear violence. If a lid might be kept on a nuclear conflict, so, too, might the lid come off as a conflict ran its course.

Escalation is defined as "an increase in the intensity or scope or conflict that crosses threshold(s) considered significant by one or more of the participants."[3] Escalation, as Richard Smoke argues, "crosses a saliency which defines the current limits of the war."[4] Based on this definition, three important points about escalation stand out. First, escalation occurs in the context of an ongoing conflict. While the initial outbreak of military hostilities can be considered an escalation (from peace to war) in the strictest sense, the theories and concepts of escalation developed during the Cold War assume that some form of military engagement is already underway. Second, the "saliency" or "threshold" that is crossed is relevant and important from the opponent's perspective. Escalation, like theories of deterrence, hinges on the adversary's perception of the situation. A state might take an action that it intends to be escalatory but does not cross a meaningful threshold for the opponent. Or, worse, a state might take an action that it does not believe is escalatory but is perceived by the opponent to be an important shift in the bounds of the conflict. Third, the consequences of an escalatory action cannot be reliably predicted. Escalation is a dynamic and interactive process—a "two-way street"—in which the initiating state cannot be confident of how the opponent will respond.[5] An escalation could result in no response from the opponent, in which case the escalating state might gain an important advantage; a reciprocal escalation by the opponent, thereby creating a new level of relatively proportionate conflict and placing the burden of further escalation back on the initiating state; or a counter-escalation, in which the adversary responds by escalating to an even higher or more expansive level of conflict.

The concept of escalation has played a key role in the logic of deterrence, particularly against limited nuclear attacks and conventional aggression. The possibility that an initially limited nuclear conflict might not stay limited, or that conventional aggression might somehow escalate to the nuclear level, provides a powerful disincentive for aggression. In both cases, *uncertainty* about escalation functions as the underlying mechanism of deterrence.[6] Deterrence is served by the fact that, despite the best-laid plans, decisionmakers cannot be confident that a conflict will not somehow expand to higher or more diverse levels of violence.[7]

Yet, despite holding a prominent position in many nuclear strategy and deterrence debates, there is not a well-developed qualitative or quantitative literature on escalation. Compared to the concept of deterrence, where there is a voluminous historical and especially theoretical literature, escalation has received comparatively scant attention. Moreover, in the scholarship that does exist, some of which has been quite influential, there is no coherent theory of escalation. Rather, analysts have developed a number of theories, concepts, and heuristics that shed light on the range of possibilities that might occur in an escalation process. However, we lack a robust and empirically grounded understanding of the specific conditions under which a state might decide to escalate, or an understanding of the conditions under which escalation would achieve the desired result. This section briefly analyzes some of the most important concepts of escalation, and identifies the potential motivations and pathways for an increase in violence.

Two Views of Escalation

In both theory and practice, escalation can be viewed either as a *phenomenon* of conflict—a process that occurs naturally during war—or as a deliberate *choice* made by one of both of the belligerents. In the former view, escalation is something that *happens* in war; it is a consequence of military engagement that is not necessarily under the belligerents' control. In the latter view, escalation is something that one *does*; it is an act deliberately undertaken for some particular reason.[8] The argument that wars will inevitably escalate—that war often has a life of its own and cannot be controlled—represents the first view, whereas the argument that wars can be managed, that signals can be sent with different kinds of attacks on different kinds of targets (or the lack thereof), and that states can choose the level of violence at which they fight, represents the second.

The idea that escalation can be a deliberate and carefully orchestrated act is best represented by the work of Herman Kahn. Perhaps more than any other concept, Kahn's notion of an "escalation ladder" has played a major role in shaping the escalation discourse. In developing a highly structured framework for thinking about all the different levels of conflict that were possible during the course of a war, Kahn posited a ladder consisting of 44 "rungs" of increasing violence. Beginning with nonviolent actions such as declarations and posturing, the rungs of the ladder steadily move up to limited and then large-scale conventional war; limited use of nuclear weapons for demonstration and signaling; the use of tactical nuclear weapons on the battlefield; limited nuclear counterforce strikes; large-scale nuclear counterforce; limited countervalue attacks; large-scale countervalue strikes; and, finally, "spasm" war.[9] At each rung of the ladder some element of calculation and control is involved—certain kinds of targets are deliberately struck and others are deliberately left untouched. As conflict moves up the ladder, Kahn also identified six important "firebreaks" or "thresholds" that, when crossed, represent important transitions in the nature of the conflict. The first use of nuclear weapons occurs at rung 15 in Kahn's ladder, thereby leaving many more ways in which nuclear weapons might be used.[10] In Kahn's view, nuclear weapons could be used in many different ways and against many different targets, and each had its own rung on the ladder.

Despite the prominence of the ladder concept in escalation debates, Kahn was actually quite critical of his own idea and well aware of its limitations. He was careful to emphasize that the ladder was simply a metaphor—a heuristic—that was useful primarily for identifying and organizing the range of possibilities. The ladder was not intended to be a coherent and predictive theory, nor was it supposed to represent all of the complexities involved in escalation. The ladder, Kahn argued, was "supposed to stretch and stir the imagination, not confine it."[11]

In the other view, which conceptualizes escalation as a consequence of war, something not necessarily under the belligerents' control, escalation occurs as states become more deeply involved in the conflict, as reputations are put on the line (or are perceived to be on the line), and as states commit more manpower and materiel to increase the chances of victory and vindicate earlier sacrifices. The increase in the level of violence is an inherent feature of armed conflict and a logical outgrowth of the basic desire to win. According to William Kaufmann, "because of its competitive character war places a heavy premium upon the attainment of an advantage, however fleeting; and this in turn invites imitation. As the belligerents strive to gain a comparative advantage, the conflict undergoes an expansion. In doing so it mixes up means and ends, brings more values into jeopardy, and changes the very character of the participating societies."[12]

The notion that an escalatory process can be precipitated even if neither side intends it has been an important restraint against military adventurism in the nuclear age. In any conflict there is a possibility that things might somehow spin out of control and reach levels of violence beyond what was originally intended and create costs that exceed the desired political objectives. For Thomas Schelling, one of the most influential theorists of deterrence and nuclear strategy, the potential for an escalatory process to take hold is something to be taken advantage of. Schelling was interested in how states could use nuclear weapons for coercive purposes when the execution of a nuclear threat risked retaliation in kind. One of the central strategic dilemmas in an age of survivable nuclear weapons is that the threat of nuclear use in response to anything but a major nuclear attack may ring hollow because significant nuclear pain can readily be inflicted back on the initiating state. Schelling was thus seeking to find an answer to the fundamental credibility problem that mutual nuclear possession had created.[13]

The answer, Schelling argued, was to engage in "threats that leave something to chance"—threats or actions that raise the shared risk of escalation to major war.[14] The central idea is that while it would likely be incredible, and probably unwise, to threaten large-scale war in response to anything but a major attack, a state can credibly threaten lower-level actions that, if executed, risk starting an uncertain process that could lead to further escalation. Uncertainty about how the conflict will play out underpins the logic of this argument. The objective is to undertake a particular action (or set of actions) that deliberately risk triggering a course of events in which the final outcome is not necessarily under control. In developing this line of argument, Schelling essentially combined the two images of escalation described above. In this context, a state deliberately threatens some lower-level action in order to create the real possibility of an unintended, and potentially uncontrolled, escalatory process. Credible deterrence and other coercive pressure, in Schelling's view, are achieved not by the threat to rationally engage in major conflict, since that would be tantamount to national suicide, but rather by the threat to engage in actions that increase the genuine risk of a conflagration.[15]

Motivations for Escalation

Why might a conflict escalate? At the most general level, escalation can either be unintentional or deliberate. Under the rubric of unintentional expansions in the level of violence, escalation can be either inadvertent or accidental. Inadvertent escalation refers to a situation in which a state's actions cross a threshold or saliency deemed important and significant to the adversary but are not initially recognized by the initiating state as being escalatory.[16] With inadvertent escalation, a state unwittingly escalates a conflict without knowing it. Miscalculation, miscommunication, and a lack of understanding of the opponent's red lines are the hallmarks of inadvertent escalation. Such situations may be especially dangerous and risk further escalation, since the recipient may believe that the escalation was deliberate and, in this belief, counter-escalate. But since the initiating state was unaware that its actions were perceived as escalatory, it might view the opponents' actions not as a counter-escalation but rather as an initial act of escalation, in which case it might choose a counter-escalation of its own. An important danger, therefore, of inadvertent escalation is that both belligerents believe that the other was the first to deliberately escalate, which might thereby create an escalatory pattern in which both sides believe they are merely responding to the aggressive actions of the other.

Whereas inadvertent escalation involves intentional actions that were unintentionally escalatory, accidental escalation occurs when a state commits an escalatory act that it did not intend to.[17] With accidental escalation, human or mechanical error results in some target being struck or some signal being sent that is perceived to be escalatory by the adversary. While unintentional escalation received a great deal of attention in the last decade of the Cold War, the discussion and debate have traditionally focused on situations in which escalation is a matter of choice. Deliberate escalation occurs when a state intentionally crosses a threshold relevant to its opponent in order to achieve some desired objective. The decision to deliberately escalate a conflict can be either for instrumental or coercive purposes. Instrumental escalation, as the name implies, involves an increase in violence that is intended to improve the initiating state's position in the war.[18] A state could, for example, escalate in order to increase its chances of winning the conflict. In this case, a state believes that some kind of increase in violence will achieve a battlefield advantage that will put it over the top for complete victory or a settlement on favorable terms. Equally important, a state might engage in instrumental escalation in order to avoid losing an ongoing conflict.[19] A state near defeat might deliberately escalate in the belief that the application of additional kinds or levels of force might favorably turn the tide of the war. For example, a state might employ new or more diverse weapons systems that increase its ability to inflict damage on the opponent, or it might open a new front to spread the adversary's forces more thinly across the battlespace. These are certainly risky options, but they may appear to be the best—or the only—options for a state seeking to avoid military defeat or surrender.

Whereas instrumental escalation seeks to affect the military situation on the battlefield, coercive escalation is intended to affect an opponent's strategic cost-benefit calculations. Coercive escalation uses a deliberate increase in the level of violence as a strategic signal. The actual damage inflicted as a result of the escalation is less important than what it communicates to the opponent about the initiator's resolve and about the risks of continued aggression. This form of escalation is "coercive" because it uses an expansion in violence to deter an opponent from taking additional actions or to compel an opponent to take particular actions, such as changing war aims, withdrawing forces, or seeking a negotiated settlement. A central feature of coercive escalation is that the increase in force raises the shared risk of a larger conflagration. What deters or compels is the potential for more, possibly unrestrained, violence to come. In this sense, coercive escalation is an important manifestation of Schelling's concept of "threats that leave something to chance."[20] By purposefully crossing a threshold, especially by introducing nuclear weapons, the initiator deliberately adds a new danger to the conflict that is intended to force the opponent to make a new set of strategic calculations.

Types of Escalation

Whether it occurs unintentionally or deliberately, escalation can take a number of different forms. In most discussions of escalation, especially discussions that employ Kahn's ladder metaphor, the most common type is vertical escalation, which refers to an increase in the intensity of violence. Such escalation is labeled "vertical" because, while the number of belligerents remains the same, the level of violence literally "goes up." In vertical escalation, there is a noticeable and significant quantitative expansion of the conflict, which may include using more weapons, introducing new types of weapons, or attacking a new set of targets within the current battlespace.[21]

The concept of vertical escalation plays an important role in many current debates about the potential for nuclear conflict, since many analysts posit that the most likely pathway to nuclear conflict is through an escalating conventional war. For some, a vertical escalation to the nuclear level would be for instrumental reasons—to add a new dimension of brute force on the battlefield to increase the chances of winning or to help avoid losing the conflict. Others, however, contend that vertical nuclear escalation would more likely be for coercive purposes, perhaps to compel the opponent to modify its war aims, seek a negotiated settlement, or quit the war altogether.[22] At the same time, however, the potential for vertical escalation can also exert strong pressures for caution and restraint, thereby contributing to deterrence. If nuclear weapons are a force for peace between nuclear-armed states, as many scholars have asserted,[23] it is in large part because the possibility of vertical escalation—from conventional to nuclear conflict, from limited to general nuclear war, from counterforce or countermilitary to countervalue targets. Thus, while in certain circumstances a state might see value in instrumental or coercive vertical escalation, the potential for an upward spiral after the nuclear threshold is crossed serves as an important deterrent to escalation in the first place.

Not only might escalation go "up," or vertically, so too might it go "out," or horizontally. Horizontal escalation refers to widening the area of conflict. In this case, the initiator engages in combat operations in a geographic area that was previously untouched by the war.[24] A state can engage in horizontal escalation by attacking a new area just outside the local area of battle, or by attacking a new set of targets far away from the original area of conflict, such as an opponent's cities in another part of the country or even the state's allies. In other words, the "width" of horizontal escalation can vary from nearby the ongoing conflict to quite far away from the original battlespace.[25]

States can engage in—or threaten—horizontal escalation for instrumental or coercive reasons (and sometimes both). As an instrumental action, horizontal escalation seeks to open up a new front in the conflict, thereby spreading the opponent's manpower, equipment, and resources more thinly.

By forcing the opponent to deploy forces to a new area, and consequently inhibiting the deployment of additional forces to the first area, the initiator intends to increase its chances of success in the original conflict.[26] This kind of a strategy factored into the Reagan administration's military strategy in the Persian Gulf during the Cold War. According to Secretary of Defense Caspar Weinberger, "our deterrent capability in the Persian Gulf is linked with our ability and willingness to shift or widen the war to other areas." In the event of a cutoff of oil from the Persian Gulf, the US military might "hit the Soviets at their remote and vulnerable outposts" in retaliation, rather than only striking targets in the Gulf.[27]

As a coercive action, horizontal escalation—especially the threat of horizontal escalation—could be used to deny an opponent regional base access and overflight rights. In this context, a state would threaten to attack the opponent's regional allies that might provide critical access and staging grounds for offensive operations with the objective of coercing them to deny support and stay out of the conflict. Such a strategy would combine elements of both deterrence and assurance, since the threatening state would have to credibly assure the regional allies that it would not attack them unless they provide support or actively participate in the conflict.

In addition, beyond efforts to hinder power projection and force sustainment, coercive horizontal escalation might also be used to directly deter or compel an opponent. A regional state with nuclear capabilities of limited range might threaten to strike an opponent's allies that are within reach of its nuclear forces in order to deter its adversary from taking particular actions, such as intervening in a regional conflict. While the threat would be directed against an ally, the real target of coercion would be the primary opponent, since the state would reason that even if it cannot directly threaten the adversary's homeland, the threat to devastate a close ally is enough to deter or compel.

For the United States, the potential for the coercive use of horizontal escalation is especially salient, since regional opponents like North Korea might threaten to attack US allies like Japan in order to coerce Tokyo to deny base access or to coerce the United States to refrain from engaging in a regional contingency. These possibilities have prompted the United States to develop new military capabilities and war supporting infrastructure, including more robust and capable missile defense architectures to protect allies from attack, as well as concepts like "sea basing," which utilizes naval assets for planning, staging, and managing military operations ashore in situations where base access is denied or contested.

The final "type" is temporal escalation, which refers to a significant increase in the tempo of military operations. Though rarely discussed in the literature, this form of escalation is an important component of the escalation toolbox. With temporal escalation, the initiator dramatically raises the pace of offensive operations, perhaps by increasing the number of airstrikes in a given time period or more rapidly moving force to the theater. The concept of "shock and awe," whereby US military forces conduct extremely rapid strike operations in order to debilitate, confuse, and overwhelm enemy forces, represents one recent form of temporal escalation. These kinds of actions can be used either to affect the course of the conflict—to increase the chancing of winning or to avoid losing—or in coercive form as a signal of the seriousness with which the initiator views the stakes of the conflict.

To be sure, while it is useful for analytical purposes to distinguish between vertical, horizontal, and temporal escalation as separate and discrete types, in practice they can combine, overlap, and mutually influence each other. It is possible, for example, for an escalation to be both vertical and horizontal. A state could open a new front in the conflict (horizontal escalation) with a more violent and intense attack than previously employed (vertical escalation), such as the use of nuclear weapons in a new region. Equally important, an escalation of one type might spark an escalatory response of a different type. A state might choose to respond to a horizontal escalation with a vertical escalation in the original arena, believing that a substantial increase in the level of violence in the primary battlespace will force the adversary to divert resources that it would have used in the new front back to the original theater, thereby decreasing the demand for substantial deployments to the new area.[28] Similarly, a temporal escalation might prompt a vertical or horizontal response (or both). A state could increase the pace of ongoing offensive operations to a point where it exhausts or overwhelms the opponent, thereby encouraging the adversary to introduce new weapons into the battle—perhaps nuclear weapons—or to widen the area of conflict to counteract the stepped up pace by opening up a new front and making the other side spread its forces more thinly across the battlespace.

Escalation in the Cold War

Throughout the Cold War, the concept of escalation was a central feature of academic and policy debates over military strategy.[29] The potential for escalation—whether gradually or rapidly; deliberately, accidentally, or inadvertently; vertically or horizontally—became one of the principal metrics for assessing the merits of a particular nuclear (or conventional) strategy, weapons system, or force posture. In the 1980s, for example, defense analysts criticized as provocatively escalatory the US Navy's Maritime Strategy, which called for using US attack submarines to destroy Soviet SSBNs at the outset of Soviet conventional aggression in Europe, because it would degrade Soviet second-strike capabilities and might thereby lead to nuclear escalation.[30] Similarly, in the debate over the MX missile, critics argued that the deployment of this system would be destabilizing and create escalatory pressures in a crisis or conflict because of its counterforce potential against Soviet ICBMs.[31]

Over time, the concept of escalation took on many different roles in the strategic discourse. Escalation was either something to be feared and avoided, thereby requiring cautious and restrained policies and military strategies; something to be controlled, requiring limited and carefully calibrated nuclear plans, strategic signaling, and withhold options for intra-war deterrence; something to be dominated, necessitating a large and diverse nuclear arsenal with significant counterforce capabilities; or something to be exploited, relying on deliberately provocative actions that raised the shared risk of a nuclear conflagration.

In practice, all of these views of escalation played an important role in the Cold War, sometimes in overlapping or even contradictory ways. At the broadest level, the possibility that some political or military conflict might somehow reach catastrophic levels of violence, whether deliberately or accidentally, exerted a powerful restraining affect on Washington and Moscow. Cold War crises, though they did occur, were relatively few for a heated military and ideological confrontation lasting over four decades, and when they did occur both Moscow and Washington were generally cautious in their approach.[32] At the same time, however, the United States and its NATO allies also sought to exploit the risk of escalation to enhance deterrence. Given the Warsaw Pact's numerical superiority in conventional forces in Europe, beginning in 1967 NATO relied on the threat of nuclear escalation to help deter a conventional assault on Europe. Under flexible response, NATO would first counter Warsaw Pact conventional aggression with reciprocal and proportionate force, but if NATO forces could not withstand the attack, it would engage in "deliberate escalation."[33] While the specific targets selected for an initial nuclear attack would likely be based on military considerations, the primary objective of the escalation would be for political and coercive purposes. Nuclear escalation was intended to signal NATO's political resolve, to forcefully demonstrate that the issue at stake was so important that it was willing to risk nuclear war. By crossing the nuclear threshold, NATO would be deliberately raising the shared risk that the course of events might spin out of control and lead to further escalation, thereby putting pressure on Moscow to reconsider its objectives and seek an agreeable end to the conflict before mutual catastrophe.[34]

Strategies of Escalation Control

Yet, if somehow a nuclear war did occur, the United States would have attempted to manage the conflict through strategies of escalation control. These strategies sought to contain and restrain escalatory incentives during a nuclear conflict. The underlying logic of escalation control originated in the Kennedy administration, when Secretary of Defense Robert McNamara shifted US nuclear war plans away from a single, all-out nuclear attack against the full range of military, economic, and civilian targets in Warsaw Pact countries, to a strategy that emphasized initial strikes only on Soviet nuclear forces. The central idea was that, rather than using its forces all at once, the United States would first execute a more limited strike and use its remaining weapons to deter Soviet escalation by threatening additional attacks. As McNamara explained in 1962, "We may seek to terminate a war on favorable terms by using our [remaining] forces as a bargaining weapon—by threatening further attack. In any case, our large reserve of protected firepower would give an enemy an incentive to avoid our cities and to stop a war."[35] The combination of smaller, controlled nuclear strikes and a large and survivable reserve force that would be used to threaten further attacks was at the heart of strategies for escalation control. Subsequent revisions to US nuclear war plans, especially in the Nixon and Carter administrations, were intended to provide increasingly limited and flexible nuclear options to enhance the credibility of deterrence and, if deterrence failed, to control escalation and terminate the war at the lowest possible level of violence.[36]

The "controllability" of nuclear war was a subject of intense debate during the Cold War and is germane to the discussion of alternative approaches to controlling escalation. If nuclear war cannot be controlled, and escalation was automatic and exhaustive, then little chance existed to manage it. If, on the other hand, some form of limitation could be introduced, then the prospects for escalation control were better. Defense analysts on both sides of the political divide criticized US plans for escalation control, albeit for different reasons and with different solutions. For some, the notion that escalation could be controlled once the nuclear threshold had been crossed was simply wishful thinking. In reality, there was no persuasive argument for how and why escalation control would work, especially in the midst of an intense crisis or conflict. Any nuclear use, they argued, carried a substantial risk of "rapid and catastrophic" escalation. This cast serious doubt on the wisdom of NATO's flexible response strategy, which relied on the threat of nuclear escalation to help deter a conventional attack. The inability to convincingly demonstrate how escalation would be controlled made this strategy either incredible to the Soviets, which might encourage military adventurism, or exceedingly dangerous because there was a real risk of an escalatory spiral if the strategy had to be executed. The solution, in their view, was to abandon a policy that relied on the threat of nuclear escalation and instead adopt a no-first-use nuclear policy and substantially increase NATO's conventional force posture in Europe.[37] If escalation could not be controlled, then NATO's security should rest on a deterrence strategy predicated on the threat to cross the nuclear threshold.

Defense hawks had a different solution. Their concern was not that escalation could not be controlled, but rather that the United States did not have the necessary capabilities and doctrine to control it. Merely possessing a range of limited nuclear options, as had been introduced in the Nixon administration, was not sufficient in an age of nuclear parity (and perhaps, in their view, coming Soviet nuclear superiority). Effective deterrence—especially extended deterrence—and escalation control required the United States to be able to credibly threaten to fight and win a nuclear war.[38] What the United States needed was escalation dominance, defined as "the ability to defeat Soviet aggression at all levels of violence, short of all-out war."[39] With escalation dominance, the United States would be able to fight harder, longer, and more effectively than the Soviets at all levels of conflict short of general nuclear war. Such a strategy required a favorable asymmetry in nuclear capabilities—in effect, it required nuclear superiority.[40] Advocates contended that a credible ability to fight and win at all levels of conflict would contribute to escalation control by eliminating any possible incentive for the Soviets to escalate. The ability to credibly and effectively control escalation, proponents argued, required escalation dominance.

Advocates of escalation dominance met fierce resistance from some elements of the defense community. Critics argued that escalation dominance—which would require meaningful nuclear superiority, as noted above—was simply impossible. The United States, they argued, could not "dominate" the escalation ladder because it could not fight and win a nuclear war. In a world in which both superpowers possessed thousands of nuclear weapons, many with destructive power orders of magnitude greater than the atomic bombs dropped on Japan, there was simply no way the United States could effectively and reliably limit damage to "acceptable" levels. As Henry Kissinger once famously quipped, "What in the name of God is strategic superiority? What is the significance of it, politically, militarily, operationally, at these levels of numbers? What do you do with it?"[41]

Two additional concerns that played an important role in the Cold War nuclear debate were the possibility of inadvertent or accidental escalation. Although the potential for these kinds of escalation was present throughout most of the Cold War, these issues did not come to light until several important works appeared on the subject beginning in the late 1970s.[42] Utilizing organizational theories, historical cases studies, and in-depth knowledge of the intricacies of military operations, these works argued that the risks of inadvertent or accidental escalation were greater than previously recognized. These risks were grounded in the vulnerability of strategic systems, particularly the command and control apparatus; the organizational practices and procedures of the institutions responsible for conducting nuclear operations; the relationship between civilian and military authorities in the control of nuclear forces; or the potential for conventional forces to come into contact with the adversary's nuclear systems during a conventional conflict.[43] The elucidation of a range of factors that increased the possibility of unwanted escalation, including the revelation of a number of "near misses" in past crises, added a new dimension to the risks involved in any US-Soviet confrontation.

Rethinking the Paths to Nuclear War in the 21st Century: The New Dynamics of Escalation

The Old Dynamics of Escalation

Based on the history of escalation in the US strategic discourse, four observations seem useful to frame the discussion of how the dynamics of escalation in the emerging nuclear environment may differ from those during the Cold War. First, the theory and plans for escalation during the Cold War were developed in the context of a bipolar framework. There were just two dominant players, and both spent considerable time and effort analyzing each other's force postures and warfighting doctrines. The superpowers dominated their respective alliance structures, thereby aligning and constraining their respective policies and stances. The bipolar nature of the Cold War lent itself to analysis through fairly simple two-player games with a constrained number of possible outcomes, each of which could be deconstructed to yield reasoned alternatives compatible with prevailing policy and doctrinal preferences adapted to the peculiar exigencies of the US-Soviet bipolar relationship.

Another consequence of the dominance of this bipolar framework was that players other than the superpowers did not factor as importantly in calculations of security threats. It was therefore not necessary to know or understand them, their languages, their cultures, their predispositions, their perceptions, or their aspirations and objectives. The end of the Cold War left the US strategic studies community completely unprepared to appreciate the nuances of dealing with non-Soviet cultures. US cultural egocentrism also contributed to a startling lack of broad multicultural understanding that persists to the present day.[44] Failure to understand one's prospective adversaries can contribute to deficiencies in adopting appropriate deterrence and escalation control strategies, and complicates implementing basic crisis management methods in the early stages of a contingency.

Second, there was a general recognition among the nuclear policy communities within the US and Soviet governments, developed over the course of several decades and multiple crises, that any overt clash of arms between the United States and the Soviet Union could escalate rapidly to all-out nuclear exchanges that would put civilization itself at risk. This lent not only a certain restraint to military adventurism, but also a sense of urgency to developing crisis management models, techniques, and policies for minimizing, controlling, and averting the risks of nuclear escalation. These shared experiences gave rise to a sense of common ground and mutual interest in avoiding nuclear war that provided the foundation for theories, policies, and doctrines of deterrence and escalation control that served to successfully prevent the outbreak of nuclear war.

Third, the possible paths to nuclear escalation were fairly well understood: a prolonged phase of conventional conflict leading to nuclear war as a means of breaking a stalemate or to forestall the collapse of one side or the other's battlefield position; a massive surprise nuclear attack whose objective would be to disarm the other side and diminish the damage from any retaliatory strike; escalation to nuclear use in the midst of an acute crisis; or escalation due to an accidental or inadvertent launch of nuclear forces. These possibilities in turn provided the impetus for establishing policies and procedures aimed at mitigating, or at least managing, the unique risks associated with each path. Knowing that a conventional war could rapidly escalate to nuclear exchanges, both the United States and the Soviet Union deliberately attempted to avoid direct engagement of US and Soviet armed forces. The fear of escalation through surprise attack led to an emphasis on deploying survivable second strike forces, the acknowledgment and codification of mutual societal vulnerability, and arms control measures to constrain and mitigate the effects of destabilizing weapon systems that could generate preemptive pressures in a crisis. Vast resources were devoted to preventing accidental escalation, including enhanced and redundant safety and force protection measures at operational bases and weapon storage areas, personnel reliability programs, and secure transportation procedures and equipment. Both countries adapted their respective force postures to more effectively manage each of these anticipated paths to nuclear escalation.

Fourth, because of the recognition of the dangers of nuclear escalation, and the assumptions about the limited universe of possible paths to nuclear war, both sides developed a range of approaches to and capabilities for crisis management, largely based on sequential elevation of nuclear force alert levels, and signaling through force posturing.[45] They established a common language for crisis management. They created channels for exchanges of information and communication—most notable the "hotline"—as well as institutionalized mechanisms for regular consultation. In addition, there was a presumption of a mutual desire to maintain intra-war deterrence through the development of limited nuclear options, which would create "pauses" in the conflict that would allow for negotiations.

This common approach to escalation control through crisis management was designed above all not to maximize the achievement of one's own national security objectives per se but to help prevent further escalation.[46] It thus subordinated all other policy considerations to the overriding goal of deterrence (whose success was broadly defined as the absence of nuclear weapons use), and prescribed the following principles or "rules of the crisis management game":[47]

- Keep communication channels open between parties at all times, before, during, and after a crisis develops;

- Maintain top-level civilian control of military operations;
- Create pauses in the tempo of military actions to encourage mutual restraint and to afford diplomatic efforts greater opportunity to prevail and succeed;
- Coordinate one's own diplomatic and military moves for maximum leverage and to avoid sending mixed or confusing signals;
- Confine military moves to those that constitute clear demonstrations of one's resolve and are appropriate to one's limited crisis objectives;
- Avoid military moves that may give the opponent the impression that one is about to resort to large-scale warfare and, therefore, force him to consider preemption;
- Choose diplomatic and military options that signal a desire to negotiate rather than to seek a military solution; and,
- Select diplomatic and military options that leave the opponent a way out of the crisis that is compatible with his fundamental interests.

If the primary objective of the above principles was indeed the avoidance of escalation to nuclear war, only two conclusions are admissible with respect to the Cold War record, and these outcomes are not necessarily mutually exclusive: either this approach succeeded, or there was a profound degree of fortune involved. As some have said more colloquially, "We were either really good, or really lucky." So these two possibilities beg the following corresponding questions: Can the success of the above crisis management approach be extended to the circumstances prevailing in the evolving post–Cold War environment, and/or can we count on extending our streak of good fortune in avoiding nuclear war into the emerging international security future by sheer good luck alone? If so, how long can our luck hold out in a rapidly evolving security environment?

The Dynamics of Escalation in the 21st Century
To begin to answer these questions, consider how profoundly the circumstances that once contributed to the alleged success of the crisis management approach have changed. As noted above, the United States is now confronted with multiple actors and geometrically more complicated crisis dynamics, with the addition of each successive player adding a new layer of motives, capabilities, propensities, and alliance predispositions. If nuclear weapons are

used in anger, they are more likely to be used in small, limited strikes, with political and symbolic objectives rather than strictly military goals. Given limited nuclear assets, players are unlikely to waste what few weapons they may have on strictly demonstrative detonations. Fewer deployed assets on a limited number of delivery platforms means fewer options for posturing and signaling. Crisis management efforts will involve players who lack institutionalized channels for communication or consultation. There may be multiple "ladders of escalation"—one for each player—with a different number of "rungs" on each respective ladder.

Four principal observations follow from these assertions. First, the different strategic landscape of the post–Cold War era does not necessarily change the fundamental logic and principles of escalation, but may render obsolete some of the key operating assumptions of past approaches to escalation control and crisis management. In fact, it may be dangerous and counterproductive to perpetuate policies and operational doctrines founded on past assumptions. For example, the traditional approach to escalation control assumed that all parties to a potential escalation dynamic shared a common interest in limiting escalation and avoiding crossing the threshold of nuclear use, and could be assumed to benefit from rational leaders acting rationally at all times who accepted these principles and restraints. There was the presumption that all parties shared a common desire to limit hostilities to the lowest possible level of damage consistent with national security objectives. It was also assumed that all parties recognized that political objectives would drive military decisions, and therefore all parties involved in a crisis would maintain reliable political control of their respective military forces and operations, through reliable and enduringly robust command and control mechanisms and procedures. Under these assumptions, all parties would respect restraint in avoiding targeting assets that were either required to negotiate war termination or cessation of hostilities (leadership) or that represented unnecessarily provocative thresholds (cultural or religious sites) that would elicit greater retaliation and thus exacerbate pressures for the crisis or escalation process to spin out of control.

To what extent can these same expectations of mutual restraint be expected to apply to future crises where escalation to nuclear use is a possibility? Given the range of adversaries the United States might confront in the future, the assumptions upon which traditional approaches to escalation control rested—shared interests in limiting conflict to the lowest possible level, clearly defined and mutually understood "red lines," political control of the armed forces, and restraint in targeting—cannot be taken for granted. Moreover, the paths to nuclear war may not be the same. Nuclear use may not necessarily be preceded by either a prolonged conventional phase or by a massive surprise attack. A future adversary may have no predisposition to engage in or respect reciprocal crisis management norms (including the presumption of standing down to avoid inadvertent crisis escalation). Future adversaries may not adhere to elaborate schemes for mutual signaling through sequential elevation of alert status or forces posturing, either because this is not incorporated into their respective military doctrines or because they wholly lack the capabilities to implement such schemes.

There may also be no expectation that intra-war deterrence through discriminate and limited retaliatory strikes, or pausing at successive steps of the traditional escalation ladder, will be a common objective among all actors in future crises. Traditional escalation control and crisis management approaches depended heavily on accurately conveying and receiving signals of intent, capabilities, and objectives. They required communicating through posturing and diplomatic engagement. But when communication channels do not exist or have not yet been fully established, how certain can one side be that its signals are even being detected, let alone properly interpreted in a timely fashion? Prospective adversaries may even be sending signals that other parties do not detect, or perhaps even worse, do not interpret correctly. Whatever escalation stability may have accrued to the US-Soviet bipolar relationship was established over a long time through sustained analysis and dialogue, institutionalization of communication channels, and a gradual learning curve associated with several serious crises over the course of several decades. Absent this kind of history with a future opponent, the challenges of controlling escalation are considerably greater.

Second, the nuclear taboo (or presumption of nonuse) may not be as strong among emerging nuclear powers, undermining traditional assumptions of restraint and posing more severe escalation risks.[48] Contemporary adversaries may see greater utility in threatening nuclear use, and perhaps threatening more expanded nuclear use once the threshold has been crossed, and therefore nuclear weapons may be seen as tools of coercion and compellence rather than as weapons of deterrence and last resort. The use of nuclear weapons by such adversaries may not necessarily be precipitated by external conflict, but rather by domestic circumstances, for example, to justify the leadership's investment in nuclear capabilities, to demonstrate strength, bold-ness, or courage to internal regime allies or rivals, or to divert the focus of internal unrest toward external threats. Such use would have little or nothing to do directly with US actions or policies and therefore may be little affected by US attempts to intervene or manage the resulting escalation dynamics.

Third, in future contingencies some adversaries may attempt different and more complex forms of escalation than the traditional vertical, horizontal, and temporal types discussed above. In particular, states might also con-sider "catalytic" or "asymmetric" escalation. To be sure, neither catalytic nor asymmetric escalation is conceptually new or without some historical prec-edent.[49] However, the point is that, while catalytic and asymmetric escalation may have been attempted—or at least threatened—in the past, current and emerging conditions may make them especially attractive to some countries.

Catalytic escalation involves the provocation of third parties, or parties not directly involved in the preexisting conflict. Though rarely discussed in the escalation literature, catalytic escalation is an important and highly con-sequential component of the spectrum of escalatory mechanisms. Conceptu-ally, there are two forms of catalytic escalation. The first is where a previously uninvolved third party interjects an escalatory catalyst into an existing state of crisis or war between two or more other states that provokes an escalation dynamic between those parties. In this situation, an outside state's actions or policies deliberately or unintentionally spark a deliberate or unintentional escalation between the primary antagonists. The second form is where a state involved in a crisis or conflict deliberately escalates—or threatens to esca-late—in order to "catalyze" a previously uninvolved party to intervene on its behalf, either to participate in the conflict as a belligerent or to help man-age the situation and reach a reasonable settlement. In this form of catalytic escalation, the primary target of the escalation is not the opponent, but rather an outside party (or parties) with significant interests in the specific state or region. As such, this kind of strategy is purely coercive, since the central objective is to compel third party intervention.[50]

Asymmetric escalation refers to an escalation that seeks to take the conflict in a new direction in which the opponent has some weakness or disadvantage and, presumably, the initiator has an advantage. With asymmetric escalation, a state uses weapons or tactics in ways not previously employed in the ongo-ing conflict, and that play to the initiator's strengths. Options for asymmet-ric escalation span the entire spectrum of violence, from the introduction of nuclear weapons to the use of terrorism and guerilla warfare. In this sense, asymmetric escalation does not necessarily require an increase in the scale of violence. A state could, for example, conduct asymmetric escalation by initiating cyber warfare. While these kinds of attacks might not increase the level or diversity of physical violence, they could significantly harm an opponent's economy (among other things), and therefore could be considered by the belligerents as an escalation of the overall war.

Conclusion: Resurrecting Escalation Dominance

The current and emerging strategic environment requires new approaches to the problem of escalation. During the Cold War, the primary focus of the US defense community was on crisis management and escalation control. Given the size and sophistication of the US and Soviet arsenals, true escalation dominance, it was believed, was simply impossible. In some future contingencies, however, the reverse may by true: whereas the United States might not have confidence in the ability to manage and control escalation, significant asymmetries in nuclear capabilities suggest that the United States can have escalation dominance against some future opponents.

Given the range of potential opponents the United States might face, each with its own strategic culture and risk-taking propensities, there is even greater uncertainty than in the Cold War about the ability to reliably and effectively control escalation through traditional crisis management tools. As noted above, successful escalation control depends on conditions that may no longer pertain to some future opponents: there may be limited or nonexistent reciprocal interest in avoiding further escalation; institutionalized channels of communication, as well as the important "back channels" to senior decisionmakers that played such a critical role in managing the Cuban Missile Crisis, may be weak or nonexistent; there may be no shared understanding of "red lines" and appropriate signals for negotiations and de-escalation; and alliance structures that provided mutual constraints in the past may not exist.

For these reasons, traditional approaches to escalation control cannot be solely relied upon to manage the risks of nuclear escalation in the 21st century. When reciprocity and shared interests are lacking, escalation dominance must come into play. Strategies of escalation dominance may be more relevant to some of today's nuclear escalation risks, since escalation dominance does not depend on shared commitment to a particular set of understandings or rules. Whereas escalation control depends upon some element of cooperation between the belligerents, escalation dominance relies purely upon superior brute force and war-winning strategies, coupled with the credible threat to employ those forces and strategies if necessary. While escalation dominance was once considered dangerous and inappropriate, the unpredictability of some future adversaries suggests it may be the strategy of choice in some future contingencies.

It is important to note, however, that a strategy and force posture designed for escalation dominance does not entail only an ability to fight and win at the highest levels of nuclear conflict. True escalation dominance requires the ability to credibly dominate a conflict at any level of violence. The ability to dominate at the higher end does not necessarily translate into the ability to credibly dominate at the lower end of the spectrum. Consequently, whereas the United States by virtue of the size and sophistication of its nuclear arsenal might enjoy escalation dominance over many states at the very highest levels of conflict, including general nuclear war, a future opponent might have the capabilities and resolve to dominate the escalation ladder at lower levels. Such a gap in the escalation dominance ladder could give the adversary a decided advantage at the lower end of the spectrum. For example, while the United States (or a US-led coalition) may have dominance at the upper levels of an escalation ladder in the context of a given regional crisis or conflict, it may be politically unwilling to cross lower thresholds or militarily unable to dominate at a given level. The regional aggressor would therefore have escalation dominance at those lower levels, and could thus exploit an asymmetry in capabilities and perceived risks and stakes to win the conflict or force a negotiated settlement on favorable terms.

To be sure, considerable research must be conducted to examine if, when, and how strategies of escalation dominance would be appropriate, and to determine how the ability to dominate the escalation ladder can be used to affect an opponent's cost/benefit calculations. In some cases escalation control or dominance may be more appropriate, and in many others some combination of the two is likely to be best. Regardless of which strategy is most relevant in any given situation, it is clear that the dynamics of escalation will remain an important component of any future military contingency.

Notes

The views and analysis in this chapter are those of the individual authors alone, and should not be construed as necessarily representing the views of Missouri State University, the US Department of State, the Center for Naval Analyses, or any other US government agency.

1. This chapter seeks to build on some earlier efforts to revisit the concept of escalation in a post–Cold War context. The Advanced Systems and Concepts Office of the Defense Threat Reduction Agency sponsored a study in 2005 by Science Applications International Corporation, led by Lewis A. Dunn, titled "Adversary Escalation to the Use of Nuclear Weapons: An Initial Exploration," with a final draft report dated March 12, 2005 (unpublished). More recently, the RAND Corporation undertook a thorough reexamination of escalation, in a study written by Forrest E. Morgan, Karl P. Mueller, Evan S. Medeiros, Kevin L. Pollpeter, and Roger Cliff, titled *Dangerous Thresholds: Managing Escalation in the 21st Century* (Santa Monica, CA: RAND Corporation, 2008). Other internal studies have been conducted throughout the US government, including a May 2007 study by the Deterrence and Escalation Subcommittee of the CNO's Executive Panel. Most of these, unfortunately, have not been released for public distribution, and therefore can make little or no contribution to the broader cumulative process of collectively rethinking escalation dynamics.

2. For an example of this view in the context of the early literature on limited war, see Robert E. Osgood, *Limited War: The Challenge to American Strategy* (Chicago.: University of Chicago Press, 1957), p. 26. See also Bernard Brodie, *Escalation and the Nuclear Option* (Princeton, NJ: Princeton University Press, 1966), p. 32.

3. Morgan et al., *Dangerous Thresholds*, p. xi.

4. Richard Smoke, *War: Controlling Escalation* (Cambridge, MA: Harvard University Press, 1977), p. 35.

5. Ibid., pp. 26–30.

6. Of course, the United States also developed a range of limited nuclear options to help deter limited nuclear attacks, and NATO maintained more than a "trip-wire" conventional presence in Europe to help deter a conventional attack. While these were certainly important in helping to deter attack by providing proportionate and credible military options for a wide range of potential scenarios, a broader component of deterrence was simply that the Soviets could not be confident that a limited conventional or nuclear conflict would not escalate.

7. See, for example, Thomas C. Schelling, *The Strategy of Conflict* (Cambridge, MA: Harvard University Press, 1960), chap. 8; Thomas C. Schelling, *Arms and Influence* (New Haven, CT: Yale University Press, 1966), chap. 3; and Robert Jervis, *The Meaning of the Nuclear Revolution: Statecraft and the Prospect of Armageddon* (Ithaca, NY: Cornell University Press, 1989), pp. 19–22. Herman Kahn also employs the logic of uncertainty in arguing that a conflict is likely to de-escalate after an initial nuclear escalation. According to Kahn, "there is a paradox that occurs in estimates of escalation and eruption. It is the fear of eruption that makes it likely that there will be little or no escalation after the first use of nuclear weapons. Both sides are likely to be so

frightened—both the attacker and the defender—that they are likely to agree to some kind of compromise and cease-fire almost immediately after such a use." See Herman Kahn, *On Escalation: Metaphors and Scenarios* (New York: Frederick A. Praeger, 1965), pp. 110–111.

8. On these images, see Smoke, *War: Controlling Escalation*, pp. 21–23.

9. Kahn, *On Escalation*, p. 39.

10. Kahn calls rung fifteen "Barely Nuclear War," which refers to the use of "one or more" nuclear weapons. Kahn says that nuclear use could occur either by accident or for political purposes. See ibid., p. 44.

11. Ibid., p. 37.

12. William W. Kaufmann, "Limited Warfare," in Kaufmann, ed., *Military Policy and National Security* (Princeton, NJ: Princeton University Press, 1956), p. 112.

13. For an excellent summary of this dilemma and a description of Schelling's answer to it, see Robert Powell, "Nuclear Deterrence Theory, Nuclear Proliferation, and National Missile Defense," *International Security*, Vol. 27, No. 4 (Spring 2003), pp. 89–91.

14. See Schelling, *The Strategy of Conflict*, chap. 8; and Schelling, *Arms and Influence*, chap. 3.

15. Schelling, *Arms and Influence*, pp. 97–98.

16. See Morgan et al., *Dangerous Thresholds*, p. 23.

17. Ibid., p. 26.

18. Ibid., p. 30.

19. Smoke, *War: Controlling Escalation*, p. 24.

20. See Schelling, *Arms and Influence*, pp. 109–116.

21. Kahn, *On Escalation*, p. 4.

22. See, for example, Keir A. Leiber and Daryl G. Press, "The Nukes We Need: Preserving the American Deterrent," *Foreign Affairs*, Vol. 88, No. 6 (November/December 2009), pp. 39–51.

23. See, for example, Kenneth N. Waltz, *The Spread of Nuclear Weapons: More May Be Better*, Adelphi Paper No. 171 (London: International Institute for Strategic Studies, 1981); John Lewis Gaddis, "The Long Peace: Elements of Stability in the Postwar International System," *International Security*, Vol. 10, No. 4 (Spring 1986), pp. 92–142; and Jervis, *The Meaning of the Nuclear Revolution*.

24. Kahn, *On Escalation*, pp. 4–5.

25. In developing this definition of horizontal escalation, we are deliberately combining Kahn's concepts of "horizontal" and "compound" escalation. Kahn defines horizontal escalation as a widening of the local area of conflict, and compound escalation as a widening of conflict "elsewhere than in the local area," including attacks on allies. They are not really different "types" of escalation, since both involve attacking areas outside of the original battlespace. Rather, the difference between them is a matter of degree. As such, the two concepts are not analytically distinct enough to warrant separate terms. Consequently, we consider both a form of horizontal escalation, recognizing—as Kahn certainly would—that there are

different degrees of horizontal escalation, and that some actions under this rubric are more escalatory than others.

26. Joshua M. Epstein, "Horizontal Escalation: Sour Notes of a Recurrent Theme," *International Security*, Vol. 8, No. 3 (Winter 1983–1984), p. 23.

27. Ibid., p. 20.

28. Or, a state might believe that vertical escalation in the original theater will increase its chances of a speedy victory, thereby obviating the need to fight in the new area.

29. For an excellent history of the concept of escalation in the Cold War, see Lawrence Freedman, "On the Tiger's Back: The Development of the Concept of Escalation," in Roman Kolkowicz, ed., *The Logic of Nuclear Terror* (Boston: Allen & Unwin, 1987), pp. 109–152.

30. John J. Mearsheimer, "A Strategic Misstep: The Maritime Strategy and Deterrence in Europe," *International Security*, Vol. 11, No. 2 (Fall 1986), pp. 3–57.

31. See, for example, Stansfield Turner, "The 'Folly' of the MX Missile," *New York Times Magazine*, 13 March 1983.

32. The classic example is the Cuban Missile Crisis. See Marc Trachtenberg, "The Influence of Nuclear Weapons in the Cuban Missile Crisis," *International Security*, Vol. 10, No. 1 (Spring 1985), pp. 137–163.

33. North Atlantic Military Committee, "MC 14/3 (Final): Overall Strategic Concept for the Defense of the North Atlantic Treaty Organization Area," January 16, 1968, in Gregory W. Pedlow, ed., *NATO Strategy Documents, 1949–1969*, www.nato.int/docu/stratdoc/eng/a680116a.pdf.

34. See, for example, J. Michael Legge, *Theater Nuclear Weapons and the NATO Strategy of Flexible Response* (Santa Monica, CA: RAND, 1983), pp. 9–10, 43–44; John J. Mearsheimer, "Nuclear Weapons and Deterrence in Europe," *International Security*, Vol. 9, No. 3 (Winter 1984–1985), pp. 20, 24; and T. C. Schelling, "Nuclear Strategy in Europe," *World Politics*, Vol. 14, No. 3 (April 1962), pp. 421–432. See also John P. Rose, *The Evolution of U.S. Army Nuclear Doctrine, 1945–1980* (Boulder, CO: Westview Press, 1980).

35. Quoted in Aaron Friedberg, "The Evolution of U.S. Strategic 'Doctrine'—1945 to 1981," in Samuel P. Huntington, ed., *The Strategic Imperative: New Policies for American Security* (Cambridge, MA: Ballinger, 1982), p. 68. On the history of counterforce and the "no cities" strategy, see, for example, Fred Kaplan, *The Wizards of Armageddon* (Stanford, CA: Stanford University Press, 1991); and Lawrence Freedman, *The Evolution of Nuclear Strategy* (New York: St. Martin's Press, 1981).

36. See, for example, Friedberg, "The Evolution of U.S. Strategic 'Doctrine,'" pp. 78–79; Desmond Ball, "The Development of the SIOP, 1961–1983," in Desmond Ball and Jeffrey Richelson, *Strategic Nuclear Targeting* (Ithaca, NY: Cornell University Press, 1986), pp. 70–73; and Janne E. Nolan, *Guardians of the Arsenal: The Politics of Nuclear Strategy* (New York: Basic Books, 1989), p. 110. For the history of the development of limited nuclear options, see Elbridge Colby's chapter in this volume.

37. McGeorge Bundy, George F. Kennan, Robert S. McNamara, and Gerard Smith, "Nuclear Weapons and the Atlantic Alliance," *Foreign Affairs*, Vol. 60, No. 4 (Spring 1982), pp. 753–768.

38. See Colin S. Gray and Keith Payne, "Victory Is Possible," *Foreign Policy*, No. 39 (Summer 1980), pp. 14–27.

39. This definition is from Robert Jervis, *The Illogic of American Nuclear Strategy* (Ithaca, NY: Cornell University Press, 1984), p. 59. Jervis provides a cogent critique of the role of escalation dominance in US nuclear strategy.

40. Freedman, *The Evolution of Nuclear Strategy*, p. 218; Gray and Payne, "Victory Is Possible," p. 19. A key component of meaningful US nuclear superiority is the ability to significantly limit damage to the US homeland, particularly through robust counterforce capabilities and missile defense.

41. Quoted in Henry Kissinger, *Years of Upheaval* (Boston: Little, Brown, 1982), p. 1175.

42. See, for example, John D. Steinbruner, "National Security and the Concept of Strategic Stability," *Journal of Conflict Resolution*, Vol. 22, No. 3 (September 1978), pp. 411–428. For an excellent review of three of the most important books in this literature, see Bradley A. Thayer, "The Risk of Nuclear Inadvertence: A Review Essay," *Security Studies*, Vol. 3, No. 3 (Spring 1994), pp. 428–493.

43. On the vulnerability of strategic systems, see Bruce G. Blair, *The Logic of Accidental Nuclear War* (Washington, DC: Brookings Institution Press, 1993); John D. Steinbruner, "Nuclear Decapitation," *Foreign Policy* (Winter 1981–1982), pp. 16–28; and Steinbruner, "National Security and the Concept of Strategic Stability." On the procedures for conducting nuclear operations, see Scott D. Sagan, *The Limits of Safety: Organizations, Accidents, and Nuclear Weapons* (Princeton, NJ: Princeton University Press, 1993). On civilian control of nuclear forces, see Peter D. Feaver, *Guarding the Guardians: Civilian Control of Nuclear Weapons in the United States* (Ithaca, NY: Cornell University Press, 1992). On how contact between conventional military operations and nuclear forces could lead to nuclear escalation, see Barry R. Posen, *Inadvertent Escalation: Conventional War and Nuclear Risks* (Ithaca, NY: Cornell University Press, 1991).

44. This American cultural myopia is explored in Juliana Geran Pilon, ed., *Cultural Intelligence for Winning the Peace* (Washington, DC: Institute of World Politics Press, 2009).

45. Scott D. Sagan, "Nuclear Alerts and Crisis Management," *International Security*, Vol. 9, No. 4 (Spring 1985), pp. 99–139.

46. The literature on crisis management is well represented by the following: Alexander L. George, ed., *Avoiding War: Problems of Crisis Management* (Boulder, CO: Westview Press, 1991); Parker T. Hart, *Two NATO Allies at the Threshold of War: Cyprus, A Firsthand Account of Crisis Management, 1965–1968* (Durham, NC: Duke University Press, 1990); Richard Ned Lebow, *Nuclear Crisis Management: A Dangerous Illusion* (Ithaca, NY: Cornell University Press, 1987); Gilbert R. Winham, ed., *New Issues in International Crisis Management* (Boulder, CO: Westview Press, 1988); Lynn Rusten and Paul C. Stern, *Crisis Management in the Nuclear Age* (Washington, DC: National Academy of Sciences Press, 1987); and Sean M. Lynn-Jones, Steven E. Miller, and Stephen Van Evera, eds., *Nuclear Diplomacy and Crisis Management* (Cambridge, MA: MIT Press, 1990).

47. These principles can be found in many sources from the Cold War era. This particular list is drawn from Gordon A. Craig and Alexander L. George, *Force and Statecraft: Diplomatic Problems of Our Time* (New York: Oxford University Press, 1983), pp. 206–207.

48. See George Quester, *Nuclear First Strike: Consequences of a Broken Taboo* (Baltimore: Johns Hopkins University Press, 2006); Nina Tannenwald, *The Nuclear Taboo: The United States and the Non-Use of Nuclear Weapons since 1945* (Cambridge: Cambridge University Press, 2007); and T. V. Paul, *The Tradition of Non-Use of Nuclear Weapons* (Stanford, CA: Stanford University Press, 2009).

49. Israel, for example, appears to have employed a catalytic strategy during the 1973 Yom Kippur War when in the early days of the conflict it undertook a series of activities with its rudimentary nuclear arsenal that were intended to be easily detected by US intelligence. The objective was apparently to compel US leaders to provide military equipment to Israel and to put pressure on Moscow to restrain Egypt and Syria, lest Israel use its nuclear weapons. Similarly, Pakistan adopted an asymmetric strategy in the 1990 crisis over Kashmir, deliberately signaling to the United States that it might use nuclear weapons, thereby prompting the United States to intervene in order to restrain India. The United States and NATO set the precedent for asymmetric escalation during the Cold War with the adoption of "flexible response," which deliberately threatened nuclear escalation if NATO conventional forces could not hold a conventional assault.

50. For an excellent analysis of this form of catalytic escalation, see Vipin Narang, "Posturing for Peace? Pakistan's Nuclear Postures and South Asian Stability," *International Security*, Vol. 34, No. 3 (Winter 2009–2010), pp. 41–42.

8   The End of the Nuclear Taboo?

George H. Quester

NUCLEAR WEAPONS HAVE NOT BEEN USED IN ANGER since the destruction of Hiroshima and Nagasaki in 1945. Given how many nuclear weapons have been produced since then by the United States and the Soviet Union (with Britain, France and China, followed by India, Pakistan, most probably Israel, and North Korea, and with Iran also now reaching for such weapons), very few strategists would have predicted that *none* of those weapons would come into use again in the ensuing seven decades.

"Taboos"

The pattern of nonuse has sometimes been described as the emergence of a "nuclear taboo," but this is a term that requires definition.[1] A "taboo" here must entail more than a general sense that mutual deterrence is at work, whereby one side's use of nuclear weapons would lead to devastating nuclear retaliation. Japan had no such weapons to strike back with in 1945, but after Stalin acquired his own nuclear weapons in 1949, the United States had to take nuclear retaliation into account.

A taboo is thus more than a mere ruling out of a policy option, or a mere social rejection of some behavior. We are all opposed to murder, and to tax evasion, but we would not say that there is a "taboo" against these offenses. Murders and tax evasions happen, and will be punished where the offenders can be identified and caught.

If one hunts for commonsense examples of a taboo, the best might be incest and cannibalism, where we are all taught from our youth that these are options never even to be considered, as they are categorically out of the question. One thus never sees a cost/benefit analysis of these options, as they are simply unthinkable.

It is possible that such a "taboo" phenomenon has now come to apply to the use of nuclear weapons, induced in part by the long period over which nuclear weapons have not been used, and then in turn reinforcing this pattern of nonuse. For president after president, we have been told that the American commander-in-chief does not even want to be briefed on the possibilities of such weapons being used. Where service with the Strategic Air Command in Omaha was once regarded as the most attractive career path in the US Air Force, it is so no longer, and US Navy officers are also not eager to be assigned to US Strategic Command or to serve on a "boomer" (a nuclear submarine capable of launching submarine-launched ballistic missiles, or SLBMs).

Mixed Impacts

A taboo against nuclear use can thus be seen as good news and bad news. On the positive side, the general aversion to even thinking about nuclear escalation may reflect and reinforce a generally lower likelihood of nuclear war. If the same psychological barrier to contemplating the use of these weapons takes hold in all or most of the countries around the world, we have a fair chance of moving toward the hundredth anniversary of Nagasaki without experiencing another such destruction of a city.

On the negative side, however, such a taboo may lead to a sloppiness in the handling of such weapons, as illustrated by some embarrassing lapses in American nuclear weapons management, and it may cause an absence of serious advance thinking about all the many contingencies that may emerge in the future.

An academic everywhere, by the very nature of his or her calling, might have to object to, and question, "taboos," because anything and everything in this world ought to be susceptible to a rational analysis of possible costs and possible benefits. In the universities of this world, an *unthinking rejection* of any option is to be avoided, as a crippling obstacle to a full-scale analysis.

To narrow this to a very practical matter, the "nuclear taboo" may reduce the likelihood that the United States or Russia will use nuclear weapons, but it may get in the way of a full and competent analysis of what either power, or any other responsible state, is to do if some other actor uses such a weapon.

Another Century

Looking ahead to the anniversary of Hiroshima and Nagasaki in 2045, there are logically two very interesting possibilities that emerge. First, if the pattern of nonuse persists, the world may be conducting a very grand celebration of a most major accomplishment, a hundred years of nonuse of the most deadly weapon.

As an alternative, we may have seen another such nuclear attack in the interim, with the rest of the world responding in a manner that effectively punishes such an attack, perhaps without a retaliatory follow-on response with nuclear weapons, but instead merely the imposition of a regime change on the perpetrator. The lesson thus established being that nuclear escalation was profitless and a bad idea. If this is the history by the year 2045, the anniversary would be sadder and quite a bit less grand, but might nonetheless represent something substantial to celebrate.

One important goal would thus be to survey the variety of ways that nuclear weapons might come into use again before 2045, or before 2099. A pessimistic view would see such use as increasingly likely, because nuclear weapons continue to spread to additional countries or because the very nature of a "taboo" might mean that it is bound to be violated sooner or later. A more optimistic view would take heart from the surprisingly long duration of the pattern of nonuse to date. Few would have dared predict this in 1946. If it turns out to be true, one will be able to conclude that the rational arguments for nonuse have indeed been more solid and substantial, such that we have more to work with than a simple refusal to think about options.

A parallel goal will be to speculate about the likely responses, and the *appropriate* responses, of the rest of the world if some state or non-state actor is the first to once again use a nuclear weapon in anger. To repeat, if the next such use of a nuclear weapon is effectively and appropriately punished, the lesson may not be that the taboo has come to an end, but rather that the arguments against further use of such weapons are even stronger. If the country using such a weapon is punished by having its nuclear arsenal taken away, and by the imposition of conventional disarmament as well, and perhaps a political regime change, the lesson might become quite clear.

Some analysts would argue thus that any new use of nuclear weapons will trigger a massive wave of additional nuclear proliferation, as the many countries around the world with a latent capability for producing such weapons will now find it imperative to do so. But the counter might indeed be that the shock and horror of such a nuclear escalation would produce a much tougher global crackdown against any further proliferation, with a substantial de-proliferation pressure being imposed now not just on the perpetrator, but on other marginal cases as well.

Growing Concerns

As we list the scenarios for a new use of nuclear weapons, highest on our list of concerns most probably will be a case where a terrorist organization gets control of such a bomb. The September 11 attacks substantially undercut any theories by which terrorist organizations might be inherently limited by their own motivational patterns in how much damage they wish to inflict.

One worries similarly about how restrained and rational the North Korean regime or the Iranian regime may be as they acquire control over nuclear warheads. In the case of Pyongyang, one has often seen behavior that makes no apparent sense in terms of any plausible North Korean goals.[2] And one has seen Iranian clergymen touting nuclear weapons as a way of "killing" Israel, an application of nuclear weapons that no other state has ever openly endorsed.[3]

The continuing confrontation of India and Pakistan poses another set of threats, given that the two South Asian regimes disagree so fundamentally about borders and political issues, and that both have now openly acquired nuclear weapons.[4] Strategic analysts in both these countries argue that they can handle mutual deterrence just as well as the United States and the Soviet Union did during the years of the Cold War, but this produces concerns about an overconfidence in their capabilities for "crisis diplomacy."

Some other plausible threats of a use of nuclear weapons emerge simply in response to the general military superiority imputed to American *conventional* forces, as adversaries around the world may see themselves "beat on the board" in any traditional war, as demonstrated in Operation Desert Storm, and may feel a need therefore to turn to nuclear threats to counterbalance this. In the days of the Cold War, the United States and its allies faced a plausible Soviet quantitative superiority in conventional forces, and continually turned to threats of nuclear escalation as a way of deterring any aggression by such forces and as a way of eliminating whatever "Finlandization" political shadow (where Western voters would be frightened into giving in to Soviet demands) was posed by the threat of these forces. At the end of the Cold War, however, the Soviets were beginning to impute a qualitative conventional superiority to the United States in the application of information technologies to the prospective battlefield, in what was described as a "revolution in military affairs." This is what was seemingly demonstrated in the actual application of the weapons capabilities of the United States and NATO against what the Soviets had supplied to Saddam Hussein in Iraq.[5]

Rather than seeing the United States and NATO relying heavily on the nuclear escalatory threats of "flexible response," we have instead seen the Russian military since the Cold War shifting away from "no first use" toward "flexible response." And one fear for the future is that such a reliance on nuclear threats, perhaps leading to an actual *execution* of such a threat, will show up around the globe in regimes fearing American conventional might.

This would be one version of what is more broadly styled an "asymmetrical response." American advantages in any future tank battles might be responded to by an adversary's shifting to guerrilla tactics, or to terrorist approaches. Or, at the other end of the spectrum, the shift might be to acquiring, and threatening the use of, nuclear weapons.

A very different scenario for the emergence of new nuclear threats would come not from American adversaries, but from American friends and allies, if such allies were to lose confidence in American extended deterrence, lose confidence in the security supplied by the support of American conventional forces, or lose confidence in the protection produced by the historic threat of an American first use of nuclear weapons.

The reasoning here is circular in some very important ways. If Americans are less and less willing to consider introducing nuclear weapons where an ally is attacked, this may be seen by some as a welcome sign of what they describe as the "nuclear taboo." But at some point this might tip an ally toward seeking nuclear weapons of its own, because it now finds more persuasive the logic put forward long ago by Pierre Gallois in defense of the French nuclear program: that states cannot count on a major ally's utilizing nuclear weapons, but have to acquire such weapons of their own.[6]

If South Korea were to acquire nuclear weapons because the United States no longer could be credibly seen as ready to use its own nuclear arsenal whenever war resumed in the Korean peninsula, the new risk would be that the next use of such weapons would come when Seoul responded to another conventional invasion from the North by nuclear escalation. The risk that South Korea would seek nuclear weapons of its own, when an American escalatory attack was being ruled out, has emerged before, during the time of the Jimmy Carter administration. Similar fears may emerge in the future for other states doubting American nuclear escalation commitments, perhaps in Japan facing North Korea and China, perhaps in Turkey facing Iran, and so on.

Yet another threat of nuclear use emerges even closer to home, in the problem of what the United States is to do if it is attacked with biological weapons, another weapon of mass destruction (WMD). The United States in the Richard Nixon administration committed itself not only to forego using biological weapons, but even to forego *possessing* them. When the question was posed at the time of what the United States would do if the Soviet Union cheated on similar pledges and employed biological weapons, the reassuring response was that the United States would retaliate with nuclear weapons.

Confronting the fact that a fair number of states around the world may have clandestinely developed and maintained biological weapons, the suggestion has been made that the United States might lump biological, chemical, and nuclear weapons together into the single category of "weapons of mass destruction," and then declare a policy of "no first use" with regard to this *entire* category.[7] There are Americans and others who have long been advocating an American policy of "no first use" for nuclear weapons. To broaden this to "no first use of WMD" might at first seem to be an even greater achievement of arms control restraint. But closer examination would show that it, of course, allows the United States to respond to a chemical or biological attack with a new use of nuclear weapons, thus substantially reducing the commitment of a *nuclear* no first use.[8]

The inherent problem remains, since the United States has no military capabilities for biological warfare, as to what to threaten as the appropriate response to an adversary using such weapons. Some advocates of "graduated deterrence" might have recommended that the United States retain a full array of chemical and biological weaponry, alongside conventional and nuclear forces, with a very measured policy of "tit for tat" retaliation, responding to each level of attack at the same level. But this is not now an option.

The current American posture about using nuclear weapons in such a scenario is less than totally clear. There have been periodic statements and renewals of "negative security assurances," by which nuclear weapons would not be used against an adversary that does not possess such weapons.[9] But during the warm-up for Desert Storm, when the prospect loomed that Iraq might use chemical or biological weapons, veiled threats were issued that the American response to this might be nuclear.

This is not the place to get into an extended analysis comparing the destructive threats of chemical, biological, and nuclear warfare as alternative weapons of mass destruction.[10] The bad news is that the deadly potential in these categories is indeed inexorably growing, if only because of the "dual-use" nature of the technologies involved—where even the most straightforward pursuit of peaceful objectives may generate military capabilities.

The grand celebration in 2045 of an entire century of nonuse of nuclear weapons might indeed not be so grand if one has in the meantime seen a major city devastated by a biological or chemical attack. Preventing the use of these *other* kinds of WMD will thus also have high priority, even if the thermonuclear threat still swamps these in potential.

All this is merely to note that the *next* use of nuclear weapons could indeed come from the United States, if some adversary were to first launch a devastating use of another form of WMD. In gauging the risks of an end to the "nuclear taboo," we must thus not limit ourselves to considering the possibility of obnoxious adversaries being the first to again employ nuclear weapons. We must also consider how the world is likely to react, and how we would ideally *want* the United States and its allies to behave, if some friendly power, or the United States itself, were to be the next user of such weapons.

Some Limited Nuclear Possibilities and Linked Confusions

Ever since the Soviets acquired their own nuclear arsenal there has been speculation about "limited" uses of nuclear weapons by the United States and its allies. If the Soviets could now destroy American cities, Americans might have to hold back on the nuclear destruction of Russian cities, if only to keep the necessary hostage alive to protect American cities.

In the NATO proclamations about "flexible response" this often led to debates about battlefield uses of "tactical nuclear weapons." In such a case nuclear weapons would allegedly be used to reverse the outcome of conventional tank battles, hopefully without too great a collateral damage to the

German battlefields, or to the Russian population centers downwind from such battlefields.[11]

Skeptics about limiting the collateral damage of any *nuclear* weapons thus to be used so "tactically" could point to the large size of warheads deployed, and the likely confusion and risks of further escalation. A cynic could have contended that all of the American talk about "limited nuclear warfare" in the Cold War years was merely designed to make an American nuclear escalation seem more credible to the Kremlin, thus to deter the Soviets from ever exploiting their advantage in numbers of troops and tanks.

If American presidents and American military commanders could *pretend* to believe that the use of nuclear weapons, in response to a Warsaw Pact attack on NATO, could be limited to the battlefield, thus avoiding the destruction of the major cities of the United States and the Soviet Union, it would be more plausible that they would escalate to the use of such weapons, whenever conventional defenses could not hold. This was the policy of "flexible response." The actual reality, as seen by the Soviets, and by many American strategic analysts outside the US government, might indeed have been that such a use of nuclear weapons could not be limited, and that a thermonuclear World War III would result. If the Soviets realized this, but could not be sure that President Eisenhower and his successors also realized this, then the Soviets might well be deterred from exploiting their advantage in conventional ground forces, for fear that the American escalatory response would plunge the world into total destruction.

A serious analytical question for this entire volume is whether "limited nuclear war" can ever indeed be "limited war." The basic concept of limited war is that something of major value (e.g., intact cities) is being left undamaged on the other side as a war is being fought, in exchange for something similarly valuable being undamaged on our side. If the mere crossing of the line between conventional and nuclear weapons is likely to cause open-ended damage and escalation to major nuclear fallout and other damage, some would have argued, at least in the days of the Cold War, that nuclear weapons use cannot be kept meaningfully "limited."

More Serious "Limited Nuclear War"

But the possibilities of "limited nuclear warfare" today include much more than the multi-kiloton artillery responses envisaged as responses to attacks against NATO or South Korea during the Cold War. Some of those possibilities, whether because of new weapons technology or because of the special nature of the combat scenarios, could be truly limited, perhaps entailing no human casualties at all (or at least no civilian casualties).

Some might applaud these developments as a sign that strategic planners are at last taking the idea of limited warfare, even when it becomes *nuclear* warfare, more seriously, rather than engaging in a sort of sham. But others might quite rightly fear that a new optimism about more careful aiming of nuclear warheads, with warheads that are smaller in explosive yield, will simply erode an important qualitative distinction that has underpinned the limitation of warfare ever since 1950: the nuclear taboo. This perspective could make nuclear warfare of all kinds and all magnitudes more likely in the new century.

For an example of a use of nuclear weapons that will kill no human beings at all, one can point to nuclear warheads for anti-ballistic missiles, which would detonate high in space to destroy an incoming warhead. If the incoming warhead were aimed at a city, the "nuclear escalation" high in space would presumably *save* a large number of lives, rather than taking any lives. For an example of nuclear escalation that would only kill military personnel on the other side, and *no* civilians, one might note the long-standing capabilities in various navies for utilizing nuclear depth-charges in anti-submarine warfare (ASW) operations. The submarine so destroyed, and its crew, would merely be the same target that was already under attack by conventional means, with the nuclear depth-charge simply being much more effective for this task. For either of these kinds of nuclear attack, it may hardly be obvious to the world that nuclear escalation had occurred, as it all took place deep in the ocean or high in space. The scientific sensors of the various powers would be able to detect such a blast, perhaps with certainty, perhaps only with high probability, with these powers perhaps being inclined to announce what they thought had been detected, or perhaps being inclined to keep the entire issue under wraps for the moment. Another kind of application would inflict much greater damage, but would still not endanger cities with a repetition of Hiroshima. These are nuclear detonations high in space intended to disable communications and other electronic functions by electromagnetic pulse (EMP) effects.

Some of the scenarios above introduce another set of possibilities for the future, where an accusation of a use of nuclear weapons might be put forward by some government, or by some press source, but where the data were far from conclusive. The United States has developed some very powerful conventional bombs for digging out an adversary's hardened targets, and this has been accompanied by plans and speculation about conventional warheads to be emplaced on some intercontinental ballistic missiles (ICBMs). When some large conventional warheads were detonated in the campaigns in Iraq and Afghanistan, seismic sensors in neighboring countries may not have been immediately certain that it was not a small nuclear warhead that had been used. In a situation of such uncertainty, there will be leaks that there might have been a nuclear attack.

The possibility of ambiguous cases as described here is indeed enhanced by the success of weapons designers in the world's nuclear weapons laboratories in developing smaller nuclear warheads.[12] Such an effort might stem from a sincere desire to be able to reduce or eliminate collateral civilian damage if nuclear warheads ever have to be used in the future, and sometimes simply from the scientific challenge posed in making smaller and more efficient nuclear warheads. If the moral motives are real here, the possibility also emerges of eroding a clearly discerned distinction of the past.

Leaving aside any ambiguity about the physical facts, if the world in the next several decades were to witness a clear use of nuclear weapons that had no civilian collateral damage, such as the anti-ballistic missile (ABM) or anti-submarine warfare (ASW) examples noted above, it might be faced with a great moral ambiguity about whether such a use was to be condemned. What is so morally wrong with intercepting an incoming missile (perhaps itself carrying a nuclear warhead, perhaps instead carrying only a conventional or biological or chemical warhead), if the net result was to save many lives in the targeted city? What would be so morally wrong in destroying a submarine that one had already been attacking with other means?

Anyone around the world seeking to erase the "nuclear taboo," seeking to legitimize the stockpiling and future use of nuclear weapons in general, might thus relish the examples of ABM and ASW as opening the door to limited nuclear use. But anyone worried more about the much deadlier and catastrophic possibilities in the nuclear category will have to be concerned that these particular escalations, if they are indeed the first use of a nuclear warhead since Nagasaki, will very much complicate the future.

One policy implication for all the responsible governments of the world will thus be that they should perhaps begin designing new firebreaks here. If *some* uses of nuclear weapons were to draw legitimization from all the publics involved, they may wish to prevent too many of such uses from gaining legitimacy. Advance planning is also in order for the cases noted above, since they will in some instances be ambiguous about the facts of whether the conventional/nuclear line had actually been crossed. Irresponsible press reports will always be possible, and will threaten to lead governments around the world to prepare to use nuclear weapons, simply because of the rumors that others had already used them. Establishing the facts in a manner that is regarded as reliable and authoritative may require some pooling of the assets for the scientific intelligence that is involved.

The net trend in the strategic forces of the United States, and in the Russian strategic forces these confront, is for the attainment of greater and greater accuracies in aiming, which might then be coupled to the use of smaller and smaller warheads. As is well understood in the basic analysis of the stability of the strategic balance, this is always a mixed blessing. On the good side, the collateral damage to civilian targets can be reduced by technological advances. On the negative side, however, the greater accuracies pose a threat to the survivability of the land-based missiles being targeted, thereby reducing the second-strike potential that might deter World War III. Even if these accuracies were never enough to threaten the second-strike forces of the major nuclear powers, the combination of greater accuracy and lower-yield weapons may embolden a strategic planner to consider breaking the nuclear taboo.

Scientific breakthroughs are threatening here, as weapons designers achieve lower yields and missile guidance-system designers attain greater accuracies. Conceptual breakthroughs are similarly threatening, if targeteers succeed in finding useful targets that do not entail massive damage to civilians.

The logic of the connections here has hardly been lost to the members of Congress and others concerned about maintaining limits on warfare, and the accomplishments of arms control logic that have applied since 1949. Even where the logic of patterns of mutual restraint has not been so fully articulated, the elementary logic has sometimes been deployed in determining how weapons are designed to be used. Heading off appropriations and preparations for such weapons is therefore a way to preclude their use. The congressional opposition to "bunker-busters" and to the robust nuclear earth penetrator (RNEP) in the George W. Bush administration may to some extent have been a simple vote of no-confidence in that administration, but it also reflected an alertness against the possibility that acquisition of more "discrete" nuclear weapons could increase the chances that nuclear weapons would once again be used.

The Growth of Latent Nuclear Weapons Potential

Some of the inherent difficulty in stopping the proliferation of nuclear weapons stems from the dual-use nature of nuclear technology, where the same reactors that are used to produce electric power will produce, as a by-product, plutonium, an element that can be used as additional reactor fuel for the future, but that can also be used to make atomic bombs. The world's reliance on nuclear power is likely to grow again, after the stops and starts caused by safety problems, because this may be the one abundant source of energy that does not threaten the ozone layer and does not produce global warming. But this may mean that many more nations will slide into the situation of Japan, which without much outside protest, has been acquiring a large stockpile of reprocessed plutonium, purportedly as a hedge of reactor fuel for the future.[13] When Iran tries to stockpile enriched uranium, purportedly as a reactor fuel for the future, it is quite naturally accused of wanting to acquire nuclear weapons. But Iranians sometimes respond that they are only doing the same thing as Japan. Japan, by some estimates, could now assemble a nuclear weapons stockpile in a matter of months, rather than years.

The fact that so many countries may thus acquire a latent ability to acquire nuclear weapons might portend great risks that nuclear weapons will actually get produced, and then will soon enough be used. Yet the hope remains that this potential can be mutually deterred, just as weapons use has been deterred in the past.

Much of the pattern of nonuse of nuclear weapons since 1949 has come in the logic of "no first use," whereby each side in a confrontation has held its nuclear weapons in reserve, a threat that will only be executed if the other side uses *its* nuclear weapons. The hope remains for the future that this logic will be maintained. There is also hope that a similar logic will emerge among pairs of latent nuclear powers, a logic of "no first acquisition," whereby various states could indeed make atomic bombs, but where each holds off in doing so until an adversary does so first. Argentina and Brazil might already be a very good illustration of this logic.

One obvious point may be that countries actively seeking to acquire nuclear weapons, in order to get past the barriers of the world's nonproliferation effort, are not likely to be under the influence of a "nuclear taboo," and not very likely to consider self-restraint in using such weapons. But they may still, in a very conscious manner, be capable of being deterred from actual use by the existing nuclear arsenals.

We noted earlier the interactions between nuclear proliferation and any use of such weapons, interactions which are quite complicated and which can cut in alternative directions. *If* the use of nuclear weapons can be avoided (and this is the big "if"), some nuclear proliferation may still occur, and a great deal of latent nuclear capability will have spread, but the chances of slowing and moderating this proliferation will still be good.

The Continuing Issue of Extended Nuclear Deterrence

As noted, for all the years of the Cold War, any kind of nuclear taboo was regarded as a burden by American military planners, because it threatened to undercut the credibility of the American readiness to escalate to the nuclear level if NATO allies or South Korea were attacked. It was hardly the case that American planners looked forward to nuclear war, but rather that the threat of nuclear escalation served to deter the Soviets from conventional aggression and reduce whatever political intimidation was derived from the mere prospect of a Soviet-bloc conventional attack. In what was labeled extended nuclear deterrence, the American nuclear arsenal could be used not only to deter a Soviet nuclear attack on the United States and its allies, but to deter a conventional attack on the most important of these allies. In the process, the risk of "Finlandization" would also be reduced.[14]

In all the many discussions of a Soviet ground attack voiced during the Cold War, the real threat may thus never so much have been the actual occurrence of such an attack, but rather the political results of the mere *fear* of such an attack. If West Germany or Belgium had to defer to Soviet wishes in the same manner as Finland, this would have seemed a great loss from a Western standpoint, and the risk of nuclear escalation to preclude such a result might then have seemed a price worth paying.

The Soviet presentation of the Rapacki Plan, various other proposals for nuclear-free zones, and more general proposals for a global policy of "no first use" were thus to be seen in the West as a scheme to "make Europe safe for conventional war" and to foster a nuclear taboo that would make Europe bow to the Warsaw Pact's conventional superiority. The Soviets, in short, were seen as fostering and welcoming a nuclear taboo.

Those in the West who welcomed the nuclear taboo of course saw the risks of an American nuclear escalation threat as being inherently too great a price to pay. Germany and Central Europe, at a minimum, would have been devastated in any use of "tactical" nuclear weapons, and escalation risked losing control, all the way to a thermonuclear world war.

The risks were run in the Cold War, seemingly at no cost, as Soviet tanks never rolled forward through the Fulda Gap. The threat of American nuclear escalation never had to be executed. NATO remained unattacked, and the Warsaw Pact eventually collapsed. Extended nuclear deterrence allowed the Western European countries to escape attack, and to escape the enormous economic and human costs of trying to maintain a conventional defense. The collapse of Communism in East Germany, and all across the Warsaw Pact, and then inside the Soviet Union itself, can be explained in part, of course, by the inherent advantages of a free market system over a command economy. But some of the success must also be attributed to nuclear weapons replacing an attempt to man a full-fledged and costly conventional defense.

One of the big questions for the coming decades is whether extended nuclear deterrence is still such an important consideration, still causing American leaders to welcome the "nuclear taboo" in some ways and to resist it in others. It can indeed be argued that threats of nuclear escalation are no longer needed for the protection of NATO against threats from the east, as the Warsaw Pact and the Soviet Union have been dissolved and as the United States now outnumbers Russia in the number of military-age males.

It might be Russia that feels itself beat on the board in terms of conventional force strength, so that it has quite logically moved away from endorsements of "no first use" toward something like its own version of flexible response. Some Americans might thus well conclude that it is time for the United States to endorse "no first use," not only to reduce the inherent risk of nuclear war, but to make American conventional military power more politically effective.

Yet, because of simple inertia or historical memory, there are Americans and Europeans who have been reluctant to endorse such a renunciation of extended nuclear deterrence. In terms of classical geopolitics, Russia still controls the central position on the Eurasian continent, able to strike in any direction, perhaps thus requiring that the defensive forces among its neighbors can never be reassuringly adequate unless they substantially outnumber the Russian total. Other confrontations may also seem to need the American nuclear option kept in play: South Korea facing North Korea, or Japan facing China, or Turkey and Saudi Arabia facing Iran.

The same delicate and seemingly contradictory wish list will thus remain in place into the future. The United States and its allies will surely welcome every year that goes by without nuclear weapons being used in anger. This may be a sort of global common sense, and it tends to reinforce the psychology of a nuclear taboo. At the same time, the United States and these allies may welcome a retention of the lingering threat that American nuclear weapons could come into use, in response to a chemical or biological attack by some adversary, or even simply in response to a conventional attack.

If this threat never has to be exercised, Washington and its allies will have the best of both worlds. Critics would see this as simply continuing to skate on thin ice. Supporters would see it instead as a very delicate exercise in nuclear diplomacy.

American Escalation

We have noted above the cases where it might seem necessary for the United States to threaten nuclear escalation, or even to use nuclear weapons. Yet some obvious opposing points need to be raised against America being the next country to again use such weapons.

The United States is the only country that has ever used nuclear weapons. As a result, one sees in American college classrooms and elsewhere a repeated accusation that this somehow reflects badly on American character; that other countries would not have done something so evil. Whatever the reasoned arguments about what Hitler or Stalin or Churchill might have done with atomic bombs if there were no prospect of matching retaliation, leftists and others intent on blaming capitalism and the United States for the world's problems return again and again to Hiroshima and Nagasaki as signs of unique American failings.

The practical point here is that this kind of criticism would only be renewed and reinforced if it were once again the United States that used such weapons. Conversely, the one bright spot for a future use of such weapons by some *other* power would of course be that this proved that Americans were not uniquely capable of inflicting nuclear destruction.

Arguments for "Nuclear Pacifism"

Today the debate centers around the appropriate American response if Iran or North Korea were to launch a nuclear attack. For a variety of reasons, the case can be made that the best response by the United States and its allies would *not* be nuclear, but conventional, in a policy that is sometimes styled "nuclear pacifism." This would bring to bear America's massive superiority in conventional weapons, and would presumably produce considerably less collateral damage to the civilian populations of all concerned (although the collateral damage of conventional attacks can also be large).[15] Above all, this would seem to teach the lesson that nuclear weapons and nuclear escalation do not offer advantages, but only serve to bring condign punishment on one's head.

But a problem with this avoidance of nuclear retaliation might be that the conventional forces of the United States and its partners may already be in use to the maximum of their capabilities. If North Korea or Iran invades a neighbor, and this has to be met by a maximum-effort conventional response, what *additional* punishment can be posed to deter Pyongyang or Tehran from introducing nuclear weapons?

The end of the Cold War, and the quick success of Desert Storm, had the world marveling at the power of America's conventional forces. But the experience thereafter of the American invasions of Iraq and Afghanistan has seemingly resulted in this power being over-stretched.

One might see an important difference in how Americans and others would view the moral appropriateness of nuclear retaliation after Iran or North Korea used nuclear weapons. In the North Korean case, common sense would lead one to assume that the ordinary people living in North Korea's cities were in no way to blame for what the leadership had done, since they are so totally isolated from the world. Any "mass demonstrations" endorsing Pyongyang's nuclear escalation would look as orchestrated and unreflective of real popular feeling as all the other North Korean demonstrations.

Until the 2009 Iranian elections, and the post-election protests in the streets of Tehran, there might have been a very different commonsense impression of the Iranians, as they seemed so genuinely intent on denouncing the United States and denouncing Israel. If Iran had launched a nuclear attack out of "Islamic fervor," this might have seemed much more broad-based and genuine than the rationale offered by the stilted Marxism of North Korea.

Americans and others might thus have felt much more anger against the Iranian *people*, rather than just against the regime of the Ayatollahs.

The massive conventional bombings of Germany in World War II, followed by the similar bombings of Japanese cities, culminating in the nuclear attacks on Hiroshima and Nagasaki, were morally and psychologically justified by the American and British publics by a rough-and-ready conclusion that the Germans in general had become Nazis, with a genuine support for the Fuhrer, and that the Japanese had similarly all been enthusiastic supporters of Japan's aggressions around the Far East.

Some of the aversion to another use of nuclear weapons against cities thus stems not simply from a mindless "taboo," but from a moral concern that most of the civilians hurt in such an attack today would be innocent. This was already a serious problem with the reliance on mutual assured destruction (MAD) during the Cold War, when one tended to assume that most of the Russians and almost all the East Europeans were not supporters of their Communist regimes, nor of whatever nuclear or conventional aggressions those regimes had launched. Threatening to punish the innocent so as to deter the guilty Kremlin insiders was the essence of MAD. It was always prone to moral criticisms, its best defense being that it worked, that it never had to be implemented.

The Viability of Taboos

If nuclear weapons get used again, does this eliminate the taboo? If the shock of the outrage is great enough, and the punishment is substantial enough, the answer is no. To return to some of our earlier analogies, in ordinary life we do indeed sometimes encounter cases of incest and cases of cannibalism. When these surface, society tries to punish the perpetrators, and the rest of us feel a shiver of horror. But the few instances that occur hardly lead everyone else to reexamine the costs and benefits of such behavior, or to conclude that such behavior is now generally thinkable.

One could even make a case that whatever taboo exists would not be as strong if it were not for the sacrifice of the victims at Hiroshima and Nagasaki. At the rational level, the photos of victims have made us all conclude that our own cities would be very vulnerable to nuclear retaliation. At the metarational level of a "taboo," this experience has led us all a little more to regard nuclear warfare as unthinkable.

Pessimism or Optimism?

In light of some of the points noted above, it may be premature to conclude that we cannot make it to 2045—or indeed, to 2099—without experiencing another use of nuclear weapons.

Nuclear proliferation is not totally contained, but it is not out of control by any means. The various predictions advanced for the rate of proliferation have time and time again been proved to be too pessimistic. One does not want to bet very heavily on the argument that such proliferation will simply lead to round after round of effective mutual deterrence. But even if the number of countries possessing nuclear arsenals were to double in this century, it is far from certain that deterrence would fail.

The depiction of such nonuse as a "taboo" has analytical pluses and minuses. If the aversion to nuclear use is to be analogous to our feelings about incest or cannibalism, this is politically important, and is not something to be ignored or discarded. But portraying this pattern as a taboo may underrate the strength of the explicit arguments for restraint in use here. To allow our decision processes to linger at the level of an unthinking "taboo" may lead to our forgetting the real logic of mutual deterrence. Such lazy thinking may also result in sloppiness in handling vital nuclear retaliatory forces, and may cause too little advance attention to be paid to all the possible future contingencies.

Notes

1. For references to a "taboo," see Richard Price and Nina Tannenwald, "Norms and Deterrence: The Nuclear and Chemical Weapons Taboos," in Peter Katzenstein, ed., *The Culture of National Security: Norms and Identity in World Politics* (New York: Columbia University Press, 1996), pp. 114–152; and T. V. Paul, "Nuclear Taboo and War," *Journal of Conflict Resolution*, Vol. 39, No. 4 (December 1995), pp. 696–717.

2. For a very useful analysis of North Korean behavior, see Michael Mazaar, *North Korea and the Bomb* (New York: Macmillan, 1995).

3. Such Iranian statements are noted in George Perkovich, *Dealing With Iran's Nuclear Challenge* (Washington: Carnegie Endowment for International Peace, 2003).

4. On the India-Pakistan nuclear confrontation, see Ashok Kapur, *Pakistan's Nuclear Development* (New York: Croom Helm, 1987).

5. Such an interpretation of the post-1990 conventional confrontation is outlined by Jack Mendelsohn, "NATO's Nuclear Weapons: The Rationale for 'No First Use,'" *Arms Control Today*, Vol. 29, No. 5 (July–August 1999), pp. 3–8.

6. Pierre Gallois, *The Balance of Terror* (Boston: Houghton Mifflin, 1961).

7. See, for example, Dean Wilkening and Ken Watman, *Nuclear Deterrence in a Regional Context* (Santa Monica, CA: RAND Corporation, 1995).

8. On this point, see Scott Sagan, "The Commitment Trap: Why the United States Should Not Use Nuclear Threats to Deter Biological and Chemical Weapons Attacks," *International Security*, Vol. 24, No. 4 (Spring 2000), pp. 85–115.

9. On this pattern, see Barry Posen, "U.S. Security Policy in a Nuclear Armed World," in Victor Utgoff, ed., *The Coming Crisis: Nuclear Proliferation, U.S. Interests, and World Order* (Cambridge, MA: MIT Press, 2000), pp. 157–190.

10. See Jonathan Tucker, "Preventing the Misuse of Pathogens," *Arms Control Today*, Vol. 33, No. 5 (June 2003), pp. 3–10, for some very pessimistic projections here.

11. On the logic and illogic of "flexible response," see Ivo Daalder, *The Nature and Practice of Flexible Response* (New York: Columbia University Press, 1991).

12. The possibilities of very-low-yield nuclear weapons are discussed in William Arkin, "Those Lovable Little Bombs," *Bulletin of the Atomic Scientists*, Vol. 49, No. 6 (July–August 1993), pp. 22–27.

13. On Japan's policies, see Shawn Burnie and Aileen Mioko Smith, "Japan's Nuclear Twilight Zone," *Bulletin of the Atomic Scientists*, Vol. 57, No. 2 (May–June, 2001), pp. 58–62.

14. On this concept, see Walter Laquere, *The Political Psychology of Appeasement: Finlandization and Other Unpopular Essays* (New Brunswick, NJ: Transaction Books, 1980).

15. For arguments supporting an all-conventional response, see Robert S. McNamara, "The Military Role of Nuclear Weapons," *Foreign Affairs*, Vol. 62, No. 1 (Fall 1983), pp. 59–80.

9 Deterrence, Crisis Management, and Nuclear War Termination

Schuyler Foerster

I N 1946—A YEAR FOLLOWING THE ONLY TIME THAT AN atomic bomb has been detonated as an instrument of warfare—Bernard Brodie wrote his oft-cited maxim: "Thus far, the chief purpose of our military establishment has been to *win* wars. From now on, its chief purpose must be to *avert* them. It can have almost no other useful purpose."[1] Since then, the world has survived almost a half-century of Cold War, with a residual strategic "rivalry" between the United States and Russia, while seven other countries—four of them not party to the Nuclear Nonproliferation Treaty (NPT)—have also acquired nuclear weapons.[2] Arguably, the Cold War remained "cold" precisely because of the role that nuclear weapons played in constraining both the United States and the Soviet Union from starting the third global conflict involving major powers in the 20th century.

Today, the picture looks less clear. Despite repeated calls for the elimination of nuclear weapons,[3] the world will likely still have to manage the proliferation of nuclear weapons, not only among states but also potentially among non-state actors. Although cataclysmic consequences cannot be discounted, they are not necessarily inevitable. China has been a nuclear weapons state since 1964 and has tended to view them as essentially a deterrent to attack and, at most, a weapon of denial.[4] Israel is reputed to have had a nuclear weapons capability since the late 1960s, but its policy of deliberate ambiguity about even possessing such weapons—along with the strategic realities of its relationship with the United States plus its own geopolitical vulnerability—suggests these, too, are principally for use as a deterrent, or as retaliatory weapons of last resort. For their part, India and Pakistan each flirted with the rhetoric of nuclear confrontation during the 1999 Kargil conflict, but have since—with considerable encouragement and assistance from the United States—taken some measures to improve their crisis management and weapons safety procedures.

These examples suggest that major powers with nuclear weapons have tended to act rationally. Each seems to understand the risks involved with nuclear weapons, emphasizes their deterrent role in the face of other nuclear weapons states or adversaries posing significant conventional military threats, and relies principally on conventional military capabilities as instruments of warfighting. Less clear is the attitude of North Korea, although arguably its limited nuclear capability is also principally for deterrent—and political posturing—purposes; North Korea's sizeable conventional military capability and substantial artillery targeted on Seoul from the mountains of the Demilitarized Zone suggest that nuclear weapons are not necessary to intimidate Seoul or to deter an invasion from the South.

The prospect of nuclear weapons use in the 21st century remains low, but in some respects its likelihood is actually higher than during the Cold War.[5] It is not just that there are more nuclear actors, but that there are even more states that aspire to follow, which could easily generate a dynamic of proliferation and conflict with which the Cold War antagonists never had to deal. Moreover, the chances of nuclear weapons material moving into the hands of other states or terrorist organizations increase, either because of deliberate policies of proliferation or simply the absence in weak states of sufficient controls over their own programs and infrastructure. As the National Intelligence Council framed it in its *Global Trends 2025* report:

> It is not certain that the type of stable deterrent relationship that existed for most of the Cold War would emerge naturally in the Middle East with multiple nuclear-weapons capable states. Rather than episodes of suppressing or shortening low-intensity conflicts and terrorism, the possession of nuclear weapons may be perceived as making it "safe" to engage in such activities, or even larger conventional attacks, provided that certain red-lines are not crossed. Each such incident between nuclear-armed states, however, would hold the potential for nuclear escalation.
>
> The continued spread of nuclear capabilities in the greater Middle East, where several states will be facing succession challenges over the next 20 years,

also will raise new concerns over the capacity of weak states to maintain control over their nuclear technologies and arsenals. If the number of nuclear-capable states increases, so will the number of countries potentially willing to provide nuclear assistance to other countries or to terrorists. The potential for theft or diversion of nuclear weapons, materials, and technology—and the potential for unauthorized nuclear use—also would rise. Finally, enough countries might decide to seek nuclear weapons capabilities in reaction to an Iranian capability that countries beyond the region would begin pursuing their own nuclear weapons programs.[6]

Given this somewhat increased prospect that nuclear weapons might be used in a conflict, this chapter seeks to reexamine the role of deterrence, crisis management, and war termination in the context of limited nuclear war, and to consider whether there are new issues that go beyond the traditional Cold War paradigms. In this respect, the assumption in this discussion is that any use of nuclear weapons would be "limited"—which is to say, employed to achieve discrete political ends well short of total annihilation of an adversary—and that the objective of the antagonists would be to avoid uncontrolled escalation and total annihilation.

Deterrence

Deterrence is about shaping another's perception of costs and benefits to dissuade threatening behavior.[7] "Deterrence" and "terror" share the same Latin root; to "deter" is to suggest terrifying consequences if something is done. One's ability to deter ultimately depends not only on one's *capability* to carry through with the deterrent threat, but on how the one being deterred *perceives* both the *consequences* of action and the *credibility* of that deterrent threat. Do the prospective costs of the deterrent response outweigh the prospective benefits of carrying through with one's threatening behavior?

Deterrence in the Cold War was based on the retaliatory threat of "assured destruction"—incalculable damage to both the one who is attacked and, inevitably, the attacker. The inescapable dilemma of nuclear deterrence was that the more terrifying the prospect, the less credible the deterrent threat, such that deterrence was arguably weakened. Employing nuclear weapons to demonstrate one's will to use them was not an option. Conversely, as one made the deterrent threat more credible by making the consequences less "terrible"—and relieving the political pressure on decisionmakers—the more tenuous the deterrent effect became. Fortunately, the Cold War ended before this dilemma ever had to play itself out.[8]

Deterrence is contextual. "To deter" is a transitive verb. Deterrence involves a relationship with a potential adversary, so it is essential to specify whom one wants to deter. In addition, deterrence depends on others' perception, so clearly communicating one's deterrent threat enhances its effectiveness. In that respect, one needs to know not only *whom* one is seeking to deter, but *from what* (what behavior is to be avoided), *on behalf of whom* (oneself, or others), and *with what* (the consequences if deterrence fails).

In the Cold War, these questions were relatively easy to answer. There were essentially two actors, each of whom understood the language of nuclear deterrence and the consequences of miscalculation. Even though the United States cultivated a variety of flexible options, the underlying premise was that the United States would continue to escalate in its response until the conflict was either terminated on acceptable terms—however defined—or had culminated in nuclear destruction. Of course, these "relatively easy" answers concealed enormous political difficulties, especially as the United States sought to manage Alliance relationships, in which "reassuring allies" was at least as difficult—and no less important—than deterring adversaries.[9]

Thus, for those schooled in the paradigms of the Cold War, the issue seems relatively straightforward: one seeks to deter war, which one assumes would ultimately be total war; one tries to manage the crisis to keep the war limited; and one tries to end the war before it becomes total. Even in the current context, in which the United States is more likely to face an adversary that does not possess equal or comparable conventional and nuclear military capability, nuclear use by a power weaker than the Soviet Union in the Cold War against the US or its allies engages a similar logic to that of the Cold War: the overwhelming US advantage in its own nuclear arsenal, as well as potent nonnuclear military capabilities, poses the prospect of retaliatory and punitive "assured destruction" that should be at least as credible as any such threats in the more balanced military equation of the Cold War.

With the end of the Cold War, the deterrence problem lost its almost singular focus in the nuclear standoff between the superpowers. In this "Second Nuclear Age,"[10] it is not just a question of deterring nuclear attack on the United States, although that remains a fundamental concern of US defense policy; it is also a question of managing the prospect of nuclear use in a variety of regional scenarios. This goes beyond the Cold War concept of extending deterrence to formal allies such as NATO, Japan, or the Republic of Korea. The most likely scenarios also often involve states that do not enjoy a formal security guarantee from the United States but which, nonetheless, are key to US interests in the region and globally.

What makes this 21st-century context fundamentally different, however, is that the issue goes beyond the more familiar problems of protecting US soil or its regional allies and friends against nuclear attack. Given the proliferation challenges, the United States arguably has a transcendent interest in deterring *any* nuclear use in *any* regional conflict scenario in which nuclear weapons are present, even if specific security assurances are not invoked. It is one thing for a state to deter nuclear attack against itself; it proved difficult to sustain a credible *extended deterrent* on behalf of allies; it is even more problematic to consider what might be called a *"systemic deterrent"*—dissuading another actor from breaking the de facto "taboo" against nuclear use that has existed since 1945.

US policy has not explicitly embraced this "systemic deterrent" purpose, although it is integral to the "positive security assurances" contained in UN Security Council Resolution 255 (1968). Approved as an incentive for states to become parties to the Nuclear Nonproliferation Treaty, UNSCR 255 declares that "any aggression accompanied by the use of nuclear weapons would endanger the peace and security of all states," and recognizes "that aggression with nuclear weapons or the threat of such aggression against a non-nuclear weapon State would create a situation in which the Security Council, and above all its nuclear weapons State permanent members, would have to act immediately in accordance with their obligations under the United Nations Charter."[11] This acknowledgment of a broader deterrent focus is also implicit in Washington's consistent stance since the end of the Cold War that maintaining a robust nuclear capability remains essential to assuring others who might—in the absence of that US assurance—pursue nuclear weapons themselves. In the words of the 2010 Nuclear Posture Review:

> The United States is fully committed to strengthening bilateral and regional security ties and working with allies and partners to adapt these relationships to 21st century challenges. Such security relationships are critical in deterring potential threats, and can also serve our nonproliferation goals—*by demonstrating to neighboring states that their pursuit of nuclear weapons will only undermine their goal of achieving military or political advantages, and by*

reassuring non-nuclear U.S. allies and partners that their security interests can be protected without their own nuclear deterrent capabilities.[12]

We can see a glimpse of this policy in the significant diplomatic efforts undertaken by the United States in the 1991 Iraq War ("Desert Storm") to convince Israel not to retaliate—with either conventional or nuclear weapons—to Iraqi SCUD missile attacks, while Israel repeatedly argued that it could not stand idle if it were attacked with chemical or other weapons of mass destruction, as was feared possible.[13] Clearly, any Israeli military intervention would not only have been politically inflammatory but would also have significantly complicated US political and military options. Nonetheless, it fell to the United States to provide both assurances and direct defensive assistance as the price of the Israeli government's restraint.

Admittedly, this example does not establish a more generally applicable policy to intervene in the interests of preventing nuclear use anywhere by a third party. Israel is easily a sui generis case; most other cases would likely involve South Korea, Japan, or NATO, all US allies in which an extended nuclear deterrent assurance already exists. Another prospective scenario is India and Pakistan, a case in which the United States would likely *not* threaten the use of force as a way of deterring nuclear use. Yet, active US diplomacy and assurances to both New Delhi and Islamabad were critical in containing and then ending the 1999 Kargil conflict, followed by extensive US efforts to persuade both capitals to establish mechanisms for crisis management to prevent escalation to nuclear war.[14] Since the United States played little or no role in earlier Indian-Pakistani conflicts—and there were certainly no alliance assurances involved—one presumes that this heightened US engagement stemmed in large measure from the fact that both antagonists had recently tested nuclear weapons and were flirting with the rhetoric of nuclear escalation.

In summary, the problem of deterring nuclear attacks in the world of the 21st century retains many of the same challenges that afflicted us in the Cold War—largely the credibility of a nuclear retaliatory threat when the consequences of escalation might be suicidal—although, at least for the United States, there appear to be more effective—and more credible—non-nuclear military options that could threaten damage to an aggressor. No longer is nuclear deterrence a problem involving only the United States and its allies. The number of nuclear actors is increasing (with North Korea, India, and

Pakistan) and likely to increase further (with Iran and whoever else in the Arab world might decide to respond to a nuclear Iran).

Earlier, this chapter posed four questions for a deterrence relationship: 1) who is being deterred, 2) from what, 3) on behalf of whom, and 4) with what. Now, two additional questions take on special salience: first, *who is going to do the deterring*, and, second, will the rest of the international community—most particularly the United States—*be content to rely on others* to mobilize an effective deterrent when the stakes of nuclear use go well beyond the boundaries of a particular conflict? It is unlikely these questions will be answered clearly in a period of peacetime; rather, they will emerge in a crisis, informed by the exigencies of that scenario but perhaps not answered in a systematic fashion. It is to the question of crisis management, therefore, that this discussion now turns.

Crisis Management

There is a certain hubris in discussing with any degree of confidence the problem of crisis management—or, for that matter, actual warfighting—when it comes to nuclear weapons. That hubris is compounded by the notion of a "limited" nuclear war, since the premise behind such a construct is that there are political objectives that merit not only the use of nuclear weapons but also the risk that such use will not rebound to the detriment, if not annihilation, of the user. Notwithstanding this caveat, this reality only heightens the problem of crisis management, since the stakes in any conflict threatening to escalate to nuclear weapons use take on a special significance that transcends the boundaries of the conflict itself.

The distinction used here between "deterrence" and "crisis management" is principally one of urgency. Deterrence is a posture—both with weapons and with rhetoric—that exists before the beginning of a conflict. If deterrence is successful, then conflict is avoided, and the question of actual use of nuclear weapons remains theoretical. In a crisis, however, political tensions are building to a conflict, or perhaps conflict has already begun, but the potential exists for further escalation of violence. Such escalation can take the form of increased lethality in the choice of weapons, to include the prospect of nuclear weapons use (what might be called "vertical" escalation), or the conflict might be expanded in scope or territory, potentially including additional actors (what might be called "horizontal" escalation). Although the essential purpose is the same for both deterrence and crisis management—the avoidance of conflict or its escalation—the context is fundamentally different. Decisions take on greater urgency; stakes are higher, or at least are perceived to be higher; time is compressed; deliberations often become focused, but not always clearly on the right issues or variables; rationality may be compromised.

The critical calculation in a crisis management context is whether deterrence—either of conflict or of unwanted escalation—is going to fail, because the actions one takes may potentially exacerbate the crisis and perhaps make war more likely. There is nothing new in this problem, nor is it unique to the nuclear age. World War I remains the classic example of how steps to mobilize for war—on the assumption that war could not be avoided—contributed to the dynamic toward war and perhaps made a broader war encompassing all the world's major powers inevitable.[15] Nuclear weapons would heighten the intensity and lethality if war were to erupt. In the most famous Cold War examples—May 1960 (Berlin Crisis), October 1962 (Cuban Missile Crisis), and October 1973 (Arab-Israeli War)—placing US nuclear forces on alert was, in retrospect, an effective way of communicating to the Soviet Union in a crisis that the United States would not be intimidated by Soviet threats.[16] Going on strategic alert not only placed the United States in a warfighting posture (including making weapons more survivable) but also contributed to deterrence; at the time, however, the former was predictable, but the latter could not be.

In the end, the United States did "prevail" in these three crises. In each, the United States postured to demonstrate its willingness to use nuclear weapons to protect its vital interests, and effectively communicated to the Soviet leadership what those vital interests were. Significantly, however, the Soviet Union could also claim to have prevailed: in 1960, Khrushchev asserted his position in Berlin, at least within his political constituencies; in 1962, Khrushchev could also point to an American commitment not to invade Cuba, as well as US withdrawal of medium-range ballistic missiles stationed in Italy and Turkey; and, in 1973, the Soviet Union succeeded in getting the United States to persuade Israel to spare the surrounded Egyptian Third Army, which was Moscow's principal motive for threatening direct Soviet military intervention.

These three crises highlight, of course, an essential element of effective crisis management: one is more likely to succeed if each side is able to claim that it accomplished its objectives without actually escalating the violence. As in any negotiation, one is more likely to achieve a mutually agreed outcome if all parties are able to point to gains that outweigh the costs and risks of continuing the conflict.

In the 21st century—for reasons elaborated earlier—the crisis management problem is much more complicated, but it also bears significant similarities to the Cold War. The traditional challenges of crisis management would still apply, for example, when the United States is dealing with a nuclear-armed adversary such as Russia or China. In March 1996, China conducted missile tests near Taiwan alongside a live-ammunition military exercise and an amphibious landing exercise, all to demonstrate its displeasure with growing political rhetoric in Taiwan calling for separation of Taiwan from the mainland. The United States responded by sending two carrier battle groups into the vicinity of the Taiwan Strait, and a Chinese official— perhaps amateurishly—quipped about whether the United States would be willing to "trade Los Angeles for Taiwan."[17] China warned the United States not to bring its carrier battle groups into the Taiwan Strait. (For operational reasons, the United States was not inclined to enter the strait in any event.) Ultimately the crisis subsided. Neither side seemed inclined to do more than reaffirm its established positions regarding Taiwan's relation to China. Again, the United States could say that it prevailed, but Washington has repeatedly demonstrated its willingness to counsel restraint in its dealings with Taiwan's political leadership. In short, crisis management is relatively simple when both sides share at least *some* common interest in keeping a political crisis from slipping into a military abyss. In this instance, the United States and China—much like the United States and the USSR in earlier crises—shared an abiding vulnerability to conflict. Each acknowledged that the other had vital interests at stake, about which they were clearly unwilling to negotiate. Escalation would have accomplished nothing and would have been acutely counterproductive.

As mentioned, the more troubling 21st-century issues are those that do not involve the United States directly or that involve the defense of non-nuclear allies. Israel has nuclear weapons and a doctrine of retaliation, and it has no formal security treaty or defense commitment from the United States. Yet, in both Iraq Wars (1991 and 2003), the United States prevailed upon Israel to refrain from military involvement, to defer to the United States as it pursued its political and military objectives, and to rely on the United States to take full account of Israeli security. Quite simply, it was easier if the United States were to do all the "defending" of interests—American and others'—rather than try to coordinate with an "ally" with its own nuclear weapons and agenda. Again, the distinction might be overdrawn—Israel does enjoy a strong US verbal commitment to Israeli security repeated by every US president since Truman. It is a unique variant of traditional extended deterrence on behalf of a non-nuclear ally; yet, here there is no formal alliance, and the "ally" is armed with nuclear weapons. The stakes are higher: not only does the United States want to fulfill its security assurances made to Israel, but it wants to avoid even a limited nuclear war by a nuclear-armed country fearing for its survival.

More recently, this issue has returned to center stage with respect to Iran's nuclear program and pressures from the Israeli government and within sectors of the American body politic for the United States to attack Iran's nuclear capabilities. The issue goes beyond the continuing debate as to whether Iran has decided to build nuclear weapons, or whether any military action by Israel or the United States would do more than set Iran's program back by a few years.[18] In the case of Iran, the fear is that Tehran would develop a nuclear capability that—unlike other nuclear states—it might actually employ as an instrument of policy, not so much as a threat to the US homeland but as a threat to Israel and indeed others in the region. In this regard, the consequences of an Iranian nuclear capability involve a threat that nuclear weapons might be used, quite apart from whether the target of such use is a formal US ally, a country like Israel to which the United States has extended long-standing verbal commitments, or even Arab countries for which the United States has extended no explicit security commitments.

In a crisis management context, the United States finds itself as concerned with managing Israel's desire to attack Iran as it is in seeking to tighten diplomatic pressure and economic sanctions on Iran to cease its nuclear program. To be sure, this case does not necessarily involve nuclear use, but one can argue that an attack at this juncture to cripple Iran's program would ultimately solidify Iran's determination to develop a nuclear weapon, raising at least the probability of nuclear use down the road.

As with the challenge of deterrence, the most likely—and most demanding—question is whether the United States will find itself needing to define and defend more systemic interests in a crisis. As a crisis builds, and the prospect of nuclear weapons use looms as a possibility, is there an incentive for the United States—or possibly others in the international community—to intervene even if the crisis does not otherwise involve US allies or vital interests? Is prevention of nuclear use within the international system an important enough interest in itself to warrant intervention? What form would that intervention take? Would it involve—as in the 1999 Kargil conflict between India and Pakistan—intense US diplomatic activity, attempting to shape the interest calculations of the parties involved? Would it entail—as in the Iraq Wars—a de facto defense of a nuclear-armed state to ensure that this same state did not opt to defend itself with the use of nuclear weapons? In 2012, if sanctions and diplomatic pressure were to prove insufficient in compelling Iran to terminate its program, would the United States conclude that military force to prevent Iran from becoming a nuclear weapons state was the least undesirable option; and would it ultimately justify its action not in terms of defense of allies but in terms of preventing the emergence of a nuclear weapons capability that was likely to be used, regardless of the target?

Ultimately, crisis management is about communication among antagonists when at least one party seeks to avoid escalation of the crisis to the actual use of force. It is a form of deterrence, applied in the dynamic and volatile transition between peace and war, as tensions build. As in a deterrent situation, this is a difficult enough proposition when two antagonists have only to communicate with each other. The new element occasioned by the prospect of nuclear use is whether the crisis—localized or regionalized among 21st-century antagonists—becomes a broader, global crisis in which the use of nuclear weapons, even more than the details of the dispute, is an issue. The potential for complication is significant as the number of parties and interests multiplies in the crisis.

The operational question, however, is whether there are any usable tools with which one can seek to manage a crisis of such complexity. In the Cold War, of course, the superpowers employed hotlines, confidence-building measures, arms control, and substantial interaction at multiple diplomatic, scientific, and, at times, even military levels. These tools did not emerge overnight, however, and required a substantial amount of mutual confidence that, at a minimum, each had an abiding interest to avoid miscalculation and unintended escalation in a crisis. With respect to India and Pakistan, as noted earlier, the United States has been actively engaged in promoting some of the less ambitious mechanisms—hotlines and confidence-building measures—to make it less likely that nuclear weapons would be used.

In the cases of Iran and North Korea, however, the principal antagonists do not have the kind of deep and multidimensional interaction that was normal for the superpowers in the Cold War. The absence of direct and regular diplomatic interaction and a legitimate presence in each other's capital tends to make the disputes more absolute, more existential. Effective communication across cultures and unrelated languages is difficult enough in normal interaction; it is substantially more difficult in a crisis; and it is arguably inconceivable in a crisis in which there is no extant foundation that might serve as a basis for mutual understanding.

The problem of crisis management in limited nuclear war ultimately relies on the ability of adversaries in such a conflict to communicate effectively with each other under the most strained of circumstances. In India and Pakistan's case, the United States only began to promote establishment of such crisis management channels, such as a hotline, *after* India and Pakistan had conducted nuclear tests. Before then, Indian and Pakistani nuclear programs were treated as "proliferation" problems, in which the United States was unwilling to take any step that would be seen as validating their emerging nuclear capability. Once the tests were conducted, however, then—and only then—the policy could shift from one of preaching "abstinence" to one that advocated safer "management" of the nuclear enterprise. Similarly, it is difficult to imagine conversations with Iran or North Korea about how they might develop a safer and more secure nuclear capability, or mechanisms to promote communication in a crisis, when the emphasis is on preaching—or perhaps compelling—abstinence.

Even in the best of circumstances, there is no guarantee that a crisis might not still escalate to war, including the use of nuclear weapons. In that case, the question shifts from crisis management in the interest of averting nuclear war to one of war termination at the earliest possible moment.

War Termination

In the discussion of deterrence and crisis management, the issue has been the *prospect* of a conflict involving the use of nuclear weapons. This discussion has moved up the escalatory ladder to the *actual* use of force, including nuclear weapons, but in a limited war context. The premises underlying theories of limited nuclear war include, first, that nuclear weapons can be used to achieve political objectives in war; second, that this use of nuclear weapons can be controlled; and, third, that the conflict can be brought to an end—with or without achievement of political goals—without inevitably escalating to mutual annihilation.[19] The discussions of deterrence and crisis management are embedded in this construct—one is still seeking to deter further escalation and manage a crisis that could potentially escalate out of control, even amidst the actual use of nuclear weapons.

As with deterrence and crisis management, one can presume that the dynamics of war termination strategies that characterized thinking in the Cold War would remain essentially unchanged in the context of a 21st-century conflict between the United States and Russia. The theories that evolved around this Cold War relationship emphasized strategies of war termination that fit with the operational realities of each side's nuclear arsenals. It was possible, for instance, for each side to refrain from hitting certain key high-value targets in the hope that reciprocity would be respected. It was also hoped that a shared interest in war termination would mean that neither side would target critical high-level command and control infrastructure. After all, war termination strategies can hardly succeed if there is no ability to communicate with the opposing leadership or for that leadership to be unable to communicate an order to terminate operations.

Moving to a case such as China, however, introduces important differences from the Russian case. Neither the size nor the capability of China's nuclear arsenal are on a par with that of the United States, so one cannot assume that there is a basis for mutual restraint in targeting high-value assets. One can presume that China's survival instincts would remain just as high, but it is not clear that these instincts would play out in a way comparable to those of the United States.

The novel dimension of war termination in a 21st-century limited nuclear war scenario is—as with deterrence and crisis management—the introduction of numerous other nuclear weapons states that may look to nuclear weapons to accomplish disparate political objectives. In these cases, the arsenals are more embryonic than fully developed, and the capacity to "fine tune" one's nuclear operations to fit the mandates of crisis management and war termination is likely not developed at all.

Traditional crisis management scenarios emphasized nuances in force posturing and targeting as a way of signaling one's willingness to limit a conflict or to bring a conflict to an end. Both we and the Soviet Union, for example, understood quite well in the 1973 Arab-Israeli War the significance of each other's force posturing; the result was the survival of the Egyptian Third Army as well as the end of the war on Israel's terms.[20]

The specter of limited nuclear war involving either Iran or North Korea, however, is especially troubling in part because there is much less confidence that, in a war, it could be managed effectively. While the United States or other major powers might avoid striking an adversary's high-value command and control targets as a sign of restraint, would Tehran or Pyongyang recognize such targeting actions as a deliberate signal of restraint? How would such a signal be communicated, and how might it be received?

Moreover, given the nature of the conflicts in which newer nuclear states might engage, will the concept of "limited" nuclear war even have a meaning? States that look to nuclear weapons as essentially a deterrent rather than a warfighting instrument tend to assume that the use of nuclear weapons in a conflict will eventually result not in a limited nuclear war but uncontrolled escalation. However, for states seeking to maximize the deterrent value of their few weapons, even contemplating the usability of nuclear weapons in a limited and controlled context may be seen as undermining their deterrent posture. Although one cannot divine the intentions of governments that have more recently come into possession of nuclear weapons, it is likely that the decision to employ nuclear weapons would be, in fact, a decision to deliver an annihilating blow to an adversary—hardly a "limited" political objective—while recognizing the associated risks to oneself.

Alternatively, an attacker might hope that the international community will seek to restrain the victim of attack and impose an end to the conflict before retaliation is possible. In the case of limited nuclear war in which the major powers are not directly involved, it may be that the most likely scenario for war termination will be when major powers themselves intervene to stop a conflict, with one party already having been on the receiving end of an attack and the other quite happy to terminate the conflict before retaliation brings annihilation.

Conclusion

The question posed in this chapter is whether traditional concepts of deterrence, crisis management, and war termination in limited nuclear war need to be reexamined in light of the changing global security environment of the 21st century. The answer is clearly yes, owing largely to the growing number of state and non-state actors that seek a nuclear capability for their own political purposes and that are not necessarily attuned to the cultural mores that dominated the small world of nuclear powers in the Cold War.

Although much of the logic that dominated the Cold War still applies, especially to the major powers that shaped that logic, the scope of these questions extends beyond the traditional issues involving two nuclear-armed superpowers and their respective allies, each of which emphasized the importance of deterring war on the assumption that—once war began—it would not easily remain limited, notwithstanding all the theoretical work that went into suggesting how it could be limited and terminated before mutual annihilation.

The 21st century has brought us, however, scenarios in which newer nuclear weapons states might view nuclear weapons as more than just a deterrent to attack by major powers, and actually as an employable means to achieve certain political ends. In that respect, it is appropriate to ask whether those states would even view nuclear war as possibly "limited." In that case, the onus for "limiting" the war—including intervention for crisis management and war termination—would more likely fall on major powers (notably the United States) that are not otherwise party to the conflict, much as anticipated by UN Security Council Resolution 255. This, of course, is in stark contrast with the Cold War, in which the only powers capable of intervening to stop a conflict were those engaged in it; the superpowers could only rely on themselves to stop short of the abyss of mutual annihilation.

We are left, therefore, with the question whether there is a transcendent interest within the United States and the international community to prevent nuclear use by any third party, regardless of scenario, so as to preserve a "taboo" against nuclear use that has, de facto, existed since 1945. If true, then the questions posed earlier about deterrence—1) who is being deterred, 2) from what, 3) on behalf of whom, and 4) with what—need to be reframed as a "systemic deterrent" against nuclear use, raising the additional questions of 5) who is going to do the deterring, and 6) will others be content to rely on someone else to mobilize an effective deterrent when the stakes of nuclear use are global.

Beyond the issue of deterrence, such a transcendent interest in preventing any nuclear use would pose an additional requirement to establish crisis management mechanisms to compensate for the absence or, at best, inadequacy of communication channels between prospective adversaries. Third-party diplomacy before a conflict in which nuclear weapons might be involved will be necessary, but there is no existing international arrangement to which one could reliably look to pose a credible intervention.

If, then, the "taboo" is ultimately broken—with unforeseeable consequences—and nuclear weapons are used in a regional context, one presumes that much of the international community will share an intense interest in containing the conflict. If diplomacy is not enough, however, would major powers be willing to intervene militarily in a conflict in which they are not party?

These questions will ultimately be answered as cases emerge, and not with a general principle. Typically, the tasks of deterrence, crisis management, and war termination fall to the antagonists in a conflict. With the prospect of limited nuclear war in the 21st century, it may be that major nuclear weapons states not party to a conflict may choose to intervene themselves to prevent, limit, or terminate a conflict before it can escalate to nuclear war. While 20th-century nuclear powers have had decades to consider these questions—all of which, fortunately, remain hypothetical—it is not at all clear that those who more recently acquired or who are seeking to acquire nuclear weapons will be in a position to address those same questions with any degree of predictability.

This is a central challenge of dealing with nuclear proliferation: if one cannot prevent a state from becoming a nuclear power, at what point does one tacitly accept it and focus on the tasks of managing it, and will the new nuclear state be willing to cooperate? India and Pakistan found, in their mutual conflict, some utility in trying to minimize miscalculation and unwanted escalation. It remains to be seen whether this logic has any resonance with other new nuclear powers and whether, in the years ahead, the imperative of a "systemic deterrent" becomes more evident.

Notes

The views expressed in this chapter are those of the author and do not necessarily reflect the official views of the Department of Defense, the U.S. Air Force, the USAF Academy, or the USAFA Department of Political Science.

1. Bernard Brodie et al., eds., *The Absolute Weapon* (New York: Harcourt, Brace, 1946), p. 76.

2. China, France, and the United Kingdom join the United States and Russia as nuclear weapons states recognized under the NPT; Israel, India, and Pakistan are not signatories of the NPT; North Korea withdrew from the NPT, has tested nuclear weapons, and is assumed to possess a rudimentary nuclear weapons

capability. This number of seven nuclear weapons states does not include countries that used to but no longer possess nuclear weapons (South Africa, plus the former Soviet states of Belarus, Kazakhstan, and Ukraine). For purposes of this discussion, it is assumed that Iran is actively seeking—but does not yet have—a nuclear weapons capability.

3. Most famously, in George P. Shultz, William J. Perry, Henry A. Kissinger, and Sam Nunn, "A World Free of Nuclear Weapons," *Wall Street Journal*, 4 January 2007.

4. Concerns about China's military modernization focus principally on the search for usable military instruments to counter what—in China's eyes—is largely a maritime threat, dealing only in part with Taiwan. See Jonathan Holslag, *Trapped Giant: China's Military Rise* (London: International Institute for Strategic Studies, 2010).

5. For an excellent and recent summary of this prospect, see Graham Allison, "Nuclear Disorder: Surveying Atomic Threats," *Foreign Affairs*, Vol. 89, No. 1 (January/February 2010), pp. 74–85. Allison cites, in particular, challenges from North Korea, Pakistan, and Iran; Al Qaeda's continuing interest in nuclear weapons; "cynicism" about the NPT; growing interest in nuclear energy; and contemporary lessons about the continued utility of nuclear weapons.

6. U.S. National Intelligence Council, *Global Trends 2025: A Transformed World*, December 2008, pp. 62–63.

7. For a fuller discussion of traditional deterrence theory in the Cold War, see, for example, this author's "Theoretical Foundations: Deterrence in the Nuclear Age," in Schuyler Foerster and Edward Wright, eds., *American Defense Policy*, 6th ed. (Baltimore: Johns Hopkins University Press, 1990), pp. 42–54.

8. On US and allied nuclear policy throughout the Cold War in an effort to manage this dilemma, see, in particular, Lawrence Freedman, *The Evolution of Nuclear Strategy*, 3rd ed. (London: Palgrave Macmillan, 2003).

9. See Michael Howard, "Reassurance and Deterrence: Western Defense in the 1980s," *Foreign Affairs*, Vol. 61, No. 2 (Winter 1982/1983).

10. See Keith B. Payne, *Deterrence in the Second Nuclear Age* (Lexington: University Press of Kentucky, 1996); and Paul Bracken, "The Second Nuclear Age," *Foreign Affairs*, Vol. 79, No. 1 (Jan–Feb 2000).

11. "Questions Related to Measures to Safeguard Non-Nuclear Weapon States Party to the Treaty on the Non-Proliferation of Nuclear Weapons," UN Security Council Resolution 255, 19 June 1968. The resolution was adopted by 10 votes to none; Algeria, Brazil, France, India, and Pakistan all abstained.

12. U.S. Department of Defense, *Nuclear Posture Review Report*, April 2010, p. xii (emphasis added).

13. For a discussion of Prime Minister Yitzhak Shamir's 1991 decision to suspend Israel's traditional doctrine of retaliation, see Scott Lasensky, "Restraint in the Face of Iraq Attack Is in Israel's Interest," *Council on Foreign Relations Online*, 1 November 2002, at www.cfr.org/iraq/restraint-face-iraq-attack-israels-interest/p5141.

14. See John Gill, "Dissuasion and Confrontation: U.S. Policy in Indo-Pakistani Crises," *Strategic Insights*, Vol. 3, No. 10 (October 2004), at www.nps.edu/Academics/centers/ccc/publications/OnlineJournal/2004/oct/gillOct04.html.

15. See Miles Kahler, "Rumors of War: The 1914 Analogy," *Foreign Affairs*, Vol. 58, No. 2 (Winter 1979), pp. 374–396; also Barbara Tuchman's classic, *The Guns of August* (New York: Macmillan, 1962).

16. See Scott Sagan, "Nuclear Alerts and Crisis Management," *International Security*, Vol. 9, No. 4 (Spring 1985), pp. 99–139. Also, Sean M. Lynn-Jones, Steven E. Miller, and Stephen Van Evera, eds., *Nuclear Diplomacy and Crisis Management* (Cambridge, MA: MIT Press, 1990).

17. Chen Qimao, "The Taiwan Strait Crisis: Its Crux and Solutions," *Asian Survey*, Vol. 36, No. 11 (November 1996), pp. 1055–1066.

18. See Mark Landler, "U.S. Backers of Israel Pressure Obama over Policy on Iran," *New York Times*, 3 March 2012; and Helen Cooper, "'Loose Talk of War' Only Helps Iran, President Says," *New York Times*, 4 March 2012.

19. Most of the literature on limited war, including limited nuclear war, spans the 1960s, 1970s, and 1980s, as was highlighted in the first section of this volume. With the end of the Cold War, the literature on these and other subjects has been sparse. For part of that "classic" literature on limited war, see Paul Bracken, "War Termination," in Ashton B. Carter, John D. Steinbrunner, and Charles A. Zraker, eds., *Managing Nuclear Operations* (Washington, DC: Brookings Institution, 1987), pp. 197–214.

20. See William Burr, ed., "The October War and U.S. Policy," George Washington University National Security Archive, at www.gwu.edu/nsarchiv/NSAEBB/NSAEBB98/index.htm#VIII.

III CONFRONTING THE CHALLENGES OF NUCLEAR WAR IN THE 21ST CENTURY

10 On US Preparedness for Limited Nuclear War

Bruce W. Bennett

I N THE FUTURE, THE UNITED STATES MAY BE FACED with limited nuclear war. What can the United States do to deter limited nuclear attacks by adversaries? If deterrence fails, what kinds of limited nuclear missions and objectives might it need to consider? What kinds of nuclear capabilities would be required? Most importantly, how do current US nuclear forces measure up to those hypothetical capabilities, given the existing characteristics of legacy Cold War–era weapons? This chapter lays out the basis for some initial conclusions regarding these questions.

Since the dawn of the nuclear age in 1945, the total number of US nuclear weapons has dwarfed the numbers of any state other than the Soviet Union/ Russia. In addition, US advances in nuclear weapon explosive power and delivery accuracy have generally been pace setting. During the Cold War, the United States also had a well-developed strategic nuclear doctrine and strategy, maintained high weapon alert rates even in peacetime, and was prepared to employ its forces within minutes of warning.

Today, a comparison of current US nuclear force capabilities with likely limited nuclear war requirements suggests that the United States could be better prepared. The United States and the Russian Federation still have many more nuclear weapons than any other nuclear weapon state, and even limited attacks with nuclear weapons could cause devastating damage to adversaries. But with current capabilities, a limited US nuclear attack may not be as prompt, responsive, effective, or even limited as a US president and his military personnel might want, and thereby may be inadequate to deter adversary nuclear weapon threats.[1] Some of the challenges facing US nuclear forces are common with the challenges facing all US military forces (e.g., locating an adversary's hidden nuclear weapons), while others are unique to the nuclear forces or components thereof (e.g., ballistic missile overflight). Many of these concerns could be resolved or significantly mitigated by appropriate US military investments of money and intellectual capital.

This chapter begins by discussing the challenges the United States may face that would lead to a requirement for it to threaten or conduct a limited nuclear attack. It concludes by assessing the US ability to use limited nuclear attacks in responding to adversary threats, and how those capabilities could be strengthened.

US declaratory nuclear policy envisions a narrow range of circumstances under which the United States would actually use nuclear weapons. The 2013 "Report on Nuclear Employment Strategy of the United States" says that

> The fundamental role of U.S. nuclear weapons remains to deter nuclear attack on the United States and its Allies and partners. . . . The United States will maintain a credible nuclear deterrent capable of convincing any potential adversary that the adverse consequences of attacking the United States or our Allies and partners far outweigh any potential benefit they may seek to gain from such an attack.[2]

This statement mirrors the 2010 *Nuclear Posture Review Report*,[3] which indicates that US nuclear attacks would primarily occur in response to an adversary nuclear attack on the United States or an ally. But it also allows for the possibility of US nuclear weapon use in response to "a conventional or CBW attack against the United States or its allies and partners." Still, "the United States wishes to stress that it would only consider the use of nuclear weapons in extreme circumstances to defend the vital interests of the United States or its allies and partners. It is in the U.S. interest and that of all other nations that the nearly 65-year record of nuclear non-use be extended forever."[4] This policy is intended to deter adversaries with nuclear capabilities from ever using them against US interests.

Hopefully, no country or terrorist group will ever force the United States to use nuclear weapons. But the United States must nevertheless be prepared to deal with adversary threats. In order to assess current US capabilities for limited nuclear warfare, this chapter examines the US ability to execute

TABLE 10.1. US Nuclear Forces, 2013 Vs. New START

Weapon Type	Warhead Type	Yield (Kt)	Number 2013 Del. Veh.	2013 Whds.	"Deployed"/Total New START Del. Veh.	New START Warheads
ICBM						
Minuteman III	W-78/87	335/300	450	500	400/420	400/420
SLBM						
Trident D5	W-76	100	288	768	240/280	660/760
	W-88	475		384		300/360
Bomber						
B-2	B83/B61	≤ 1,200	16	100	16/20	16/100
B-52	W-80	150	44	200	44/50	44/216
Strategic total			798	1,952	700/770	1,420/1,856
Tactical bombs	B-61	≤ 170	—	200	—	—/200
Totals				2,152		1,420/2,056

SOURCES: Hans M. KristensenandRobert S. Norris, "U.S. Nuclear Forces, 2013," Vol. 69, No. 2 (March/April 2013), p. 78; Tom Z. Collina, "U.S. Strategic Nuclear Forces under New START," Arms Control Association, at www.armscontrol.org/factsheets/USStratNukeForceNewSTART#1; "U.S. Nuclear Weapon Enduring Stockpile," August 31, 2007, at http://nuclearweaponarchive.org/Usa/Weapons/Wpngall.html.

limited nuclear attacks against a number of countries that have nuclear weapons or could in the future pose nuclear threats. The use of these countries as nominal cases is not intended to predict them attacking the United States or its allies, but rather to serve as a baseline for evaluating US nuclear weapon capabilities and deterrence potential.

Existing and Projected US Nuclear Forces

A key aspect of the US preparedness for limited nuclear war is its nuclear arsenal. Table 10.1 summarizes the forces available as of 2013 and what will likely be available in 2017 under the New START agreement. US intercontinental ballistic missiles (ICBMs) are missiles based in the continental United States that have ranges in excess of 5,500 kilometers. The US Minuteman III has a much longer range (13,000 kilometers), allowing it to cover much of the Eurasian land mass.[5] US submarine-launched ballistic missiles (SLBMs) are based on ballistic missile submarines (SSBNs); the Trident D5 missile has a range of 12,000 kilometers (with a minimum range of 2,000 to 2,500 kilometers),[6] allowing it to also cover most of Eurasia. US bombers consist of the

TABLE 10.2. Characteristics of US Strategic Forces

Weapon Type	Warhead Type	Yield (Kt)	Accuracy (CEP, m)	Delivery Probability*	Availability (Day/War)
ICBM					
Minuteman III	W-78	335	183	85%	95%
	W-87	300	183	85%	99%
SLBM					
Trident D5	W-76	100	130–183	85%	50%/78%
	W-88	475	130–183	85%	50%/78%
Bomber					
B-2	B-83	≤ 1,200	Small	85%	0%/90%
B-52	W-80	150	Small	80%	0%/90%

* This is the combined delivery vehicle and warhead reliability, plus the ability of the delivery vehicle to penetrate any defenses.

SOURCE: National Resources Defense Council, "The NRDC Nuclear War Simulation Model," 2001, at www.nrdc.org/nuclear/warplan/warplan_ch3.pdf.

NOTE: The author estimated the delivery probabilities assuming very high reliability of the missiles, bombers, and warheads, and very little ability of adversary defenses to stop nuclear weapon delivery.

B-2 (with a range of 11,000 kilometers without refueling) and the B-52 (with a range of 14,500 kilometers, which is extended by the air-launched cruise missile [ALCM] range of about 2,500 kilometers).[7] So-called tactical nuclear weapons are shown at the bottom of Table 10.1. Tactical bombs could be delivered by US fighter aircraft that are prepared for such a role.

The New START agreement defines delivery vehicles and warheads as either deployed or non-deployed, the non-deployed systems being ICBMs and bombers offline for maintenance and SLBMs on SSBNs undergoing overhaul. In addition to the non-deployed warheads, more warheads are potentially available as a reserve force. In 2013, some 2,650 warheads were held in reserve, yielding a nuclear force total of about 4,800,[8] but the reserves will likely be reduced in future years. The total warheads in 2013 or under the New START Treaty are shown in Table 10.1 and are more than the New START warhead limits (1,550) but less than the total that could be available and used over time if reserve weapons were loaded on delivery vehicles.

Table 10.2 summarizes the qualitative characteristics of US strategic forces. With the indicated missile accuracies, the weapons would be effective (greater than a 90 percent probability of destruction for arriving warheads) against point targets hardened to 200 psi or more. The bomb and cruise missile accuracies (circular error probable, or CEP) could be as small as 5 to 10 meters if these nuclear weapons are designed consistent with other modern precision bombs and cruise missiles guided by the Global Positioning System (GPS).[9] The delivery probabilities shown appear high, but would still require the use of two weapons from independent launchers to achieve as high as a 95 percent probability of destroying any given target. The weapon availability numbers for bombers on a daily basis are so low because the bombers no longer stand ground alert in peacetime. And while only some SLBMs are available in peacetime, the percentage grows after an alert is declared.

There is, however, one caution on the small CEPs based on GPS-guided delivery. Over the last several years, North Korea has periodically disrupted GPS signals within a 50 or 100 kilometer radius of the jamming devices, including along the South Korean coastlines.[10] The degree of GPS degradation was not revealed, but if it was serious, and if US bomber operations were diminished in a manner affecting accuracy, it could render bomber strikes insufficient to hold some hardened targets at risk.

Potential US Objectives in Limited Nuclear Conflict

The next step in evaluating US capabilities for limited nuclear war is to define the kinds of limited nuclear missions that the United States might consider. There is no clear agreement in the national security community on how US nuclear weapons should be used; in practice, the US decision on using nuclear weapons would need to be taken by whoever is president at the time. And presidents could clearly vary in their approach to a history-making event like the use of nuclear weapons. In a highly classified document, each president directs the military to plan nuclear options for specific types of contingencies. This document is not available for public review and discussion. Presidents are free to change their guidance as circumstances develop. Hence our ability to identify likely limited nuclear missions is conjectural.

The intent here is to describe the potential nuclear missions that US forces may be tasked to execute rather than considering only missions that any given president would employ in various circumstances, as the latter are inherently unknowable. Moreover, some possible missions may be beyond current or projected US military capabilities, and would thus likely be rejected when considered.

Adversary Threats That Could Require
a Nuclear Weapon Response

The list of threats described here is not intended to predict when the United States would use nuclear weapons, but only that it could. See Chapter 6 by Tom Mahnken in this volume for scenarios in which this may occur, and Chapter 7 by Kerry Kartchner and Michael Gerson for an explanation of the escalation dynamics that would be at play.

Two kinds of adversary threats may require a US nuclear weapon use: adversary use of or threats to use nuclear weapons or perhaps other WMD, and adversary attacks that threaten military failure when the United States may not have the conventional military capabilities to stop the failure (e.g., the Soviet threat to invade Western Europe early in the Cold War). US nuclear weapons might be used in response to threats against the United States or its allies and partners. The US "nuclear umbrella" is extended to protect US allies and partners, threatening a US nuclear weapon response to adversary use of nuclear weapons or other serious attacks against that ally. Such a nuclear umbrella is designed to assure the ally that it need not develop its own nuclear weapons.

The conditions potentially leading to limited US nuclear weapon use may include:

1. *An Adversary Demonstration Nuclear Attack.* An adversary uses one or a small number of nuclear weapons to demonstrate nuclear capability while causing minimal prompt effects damage. The adversary's primary objective would be to signal his capability and will to use nuclear weapons, thereby hoping to establish some level of deterrence against actions being considered by the United States and its allies. The adversary attack might be a pure demonstration (causing little real damage), an electromagnetic pulse (EMP) attack, or a very selective attack against US or allied military targets such as air bases or ports.

2. *An Adversary Non-Nuclear Battlefield Breakthrough.* Traditionally, the US "nuclear umbrella" in Europe and Northeast Asia was intended to stop an adversary's conventional invasion when the US and its regional allies anticipated suffering breakthroughs because they had conventional force inferiority. Now that the United States would likely have conventional force superiority in most scenarios, US analysts typically dismiss the need for a nuclear guarantee against a non-nuclear breakthrough. Still, various situations (such as adversary use of

chemical and/or biological weapons) might still require a US nuclear response.

3. *An Adversary Selective Nuclear Attack.* This category would involve the adversary's use of a small number of nuclear weapons (possibly one or two), but in this case against a city or military target, causing enough direct damage that there would tend to be stronger US incentives to respond with a nuclear weapon.

4. *An Adversary Incapacitating Nuclear Attack.* This category would involve larger adversary nuclear attacks intended to incapacitate key US or allied military or leadership capabilities. For example, an adversary could try to decapitate the US/allied political and/or military leadership (in an expanded 9/11–type nuclear scenario), try to destroy US or allied air operations by targeting combat air bases in a theater, or try to stop US force flow into a theater by targeting key airlift air bases. An adversary may also execute part of this kind of attack and threaten further attacks (for example, it might attack two out of five key airlift air bases and threaten the other three).

5. *The Collapse of a Nuclear State and/or Loss of Control of Its Nuclear Weapons.* The United States may conclude that control of adversary nuclear weapons has been jeopardized or lost. Even if nuclear weapons have not been used, the United States may decide that US nuclear weapon use is required to destroy adversary nuclear weapons that may otherwise pose a risk to a US ally or the United States.

Across these conditions, several issues would affect the likelihood and scale of a US nuclear response, such as:

- What did the adversary target (e.g., a military force or political leaders)?
- Has serious civilian damage been done in the United States or in an allied country? If so, even if a military or leadership target was the focus of the attack, the likelihood of a US nuclear response is much higher, consistent with the seriousness of the US response to the 9/11 attack.
- Is the United States or an ally in serious military jeopardy (e.g., having suffered a ground force breakthrough)? The more serious the jeopardy, the more likely is a nuclear response, especially if the situation is rapidly deteriorating.

- Was the attack against the United States or an ally or partner? The United States is more likely to respond with nuclear weapons against an attack on the US homeland, though its nuclear umbrella commitments are very important. It is less clear how the United States would act if an adversary seriously threatens a US ally and the US ally has nuclear weapons and uses them in response.

- Was the adversary a state or a non-state actor? If the adversary is a state, identifying potential targets for nuclear weapon use is feasible. But if an adversary is a non-state actor, it may be difficult to identify targets for nuclear weapon attack, or such targets may be inappropriate because of the damage that would be done to an innocent host country.

- What action did the adversary threaten if the United States employs nuclear weapons? Adversaries that are prepared to use nuclear weapons may employ threats of further nuclear weapon use to achieve escalation control against the United States. The United States would need to decide whether it can prevent such adversary escalation or cope with its effects in deciding how to act. (The concept of escalation is covered in more detail in Chapter 7 by Kartchner and Gerson.)

Facing threats like those described above, the United States might consider the use of nuclear weapons to achieve conflict termination on favorable terms (a strategic goal) or to manage any military challenges (an operational goal, including preventing or deterring further adversary nuclear attacks). However, in practice, nuclear weapons by themselves are unlikely to achieve a favorable conflict outcome. Even if nuclear weapons were used to destroy most adversary military forces, US and allied conventional forces would still need to secure the victory and stabilize the defeated country, among other tasks. Nuclear weapons would thus primarily serve in a supporting role to broader US military objectives in war.

Whether pursuing a strategic or operational goal, the United States could use nuclear weapons to defeat any military challenges, to deter further adversary attacks (especially adversary nuclear weapon attacks), and to punish the adversary for any damage done. These actions tie together the "defeat" and "deter" elements of US military strategy, employing the ability to deny adversary success in its attacks along with punishing the adversary for its actions. Denial and punishment both serve as means of achieving deterrence.[11]

The United States could seek to deny adversary success by stopping any developing military failure (US and/or allied), preventing any further catastrophic attacks (especially nuclear) by the adversary, and setting the conditions for military victory. For example, if an adversary had achieved a breakthrough against US or allied ground forces (whether using conventional forces or nuclear weapons), a denial strategy would require that the United States prevent the adversary from exploiting the breakthrough and stop the adversary for sufficient time to reestablish a coherent defense. If the adversary had used nuclear weapons, the United States might also want to neutralize the remaining adversary nuclear forces to prevent adversary follow-on nuclear attacks.

In most circumstances, US nuclear attacks meant to deny an adversary the achievement of his objectives would also represent substantial punishment. For example, the United States sought to deny Al Qaeda a safe haven for planning and training by taking the Afghan government away from the Taliban, a substantial punishment. But there may also be cases in which the United States directly punishes its adversary, with the intention of coercing or deterring the adversary but not directly denying adversary military capabilities. For example, immediately after World War II, the United States feared that the Soviets would exploit their conventional force superiority to invade Western Europe. Lacking an adequate conventional response option, the United States postulated a largely punishment-oriented nuclear response: "The atomic bomb, in the foreseeable future, will be primarily a strategic weapon of destruction against concentrated industrial areas vital to the war effort of an enemy nation. In addition, it may be employed against centers of population with a view to forcing an enemy state to yield through terror and disintegration of national morale."[12]

In the aftermath of an adversary use of nuclear weapons, the United States would potentially face a global loss of credibility in US nuclear guarantees. A nuclear umbrella had obviously failed to deter adversary use of nuclear weapons as intended. The United States would need to take serious action to reestablish the credibility of its nuclear umbrellas, probably by severely punishing the offending state or non-state actor. Some in the United States have argued that a US conventional response could do as much damage as a nuclear response against adversary nuclear weapon use, but that is not the promise of a nuclear umbrella.[13] A US failure to respond with nuclear weapons today would likely convince some allies and partners supported by a US nuclear umbrella that they either need to pursue their own nuclear weapons or face reduced regional influence and an impaired ability to deter adversaries in the future.

If an adversary only threatens the use of nuclear weapons or other major military attacks, the United States would normally seek to strengthen its deterrence. But in some cases—such as adversary preparation for nuclear attack or adversary loss of nuclear weapon control—the United States might execute a preventive attack that could even employ US nuclear weapons.

Finally, the United States would also seek to avoid a variety of negative effects of nuclear weapon use. For example, it would try to minimize the chances that a US nuclear weapon is accidentally delivered to the territory of a country other than the intended adversary (e.g., through a missile failure). The United States would try to avoid having third countries perceive that they are also under nuclear attack, and need to respond against the United States and its allies. The United States would also try to minimize the damage done to innocent parties in adversary countries or elsewhere in the battle region (so-called collateral damage), and would try to appear globally to have been proportionate and reasonable in its nuclear weapon responses. And the United States would seek to avoid the use of nuclear weapons on or near allied territory, or the contamination of allied territory by fallout radiation effects.

US Nuclear Attack Options to Achieve US Objectives

As defined earlier in this volume, nuclear war can be considered limited in terms of the objectives of the conflict and/or the means used. While the US objectives in a war may be unlimited (e.g., the call for unconventional surrender in World War II), the US use of nuclear weapons is more likely to be limited in terms of the number and types of nuclear weapons used. Thus, the US use of nuclear weapons in World War II supported unlimited warfare objectives, but the United States was unwilling and unable to use nuclear weapons to cause the total destruction of Japan. Instead, it used its entire stockpile—two nuclear weapons—coupled with its extensive use of conventional forces throughout the theater, to achieve the unlimited objectives of the war.

Others believe that nuclear weapon effects cover such a large area that even a US attack with a few nuclear weapons would cause substantial devastation. Interestingly, North Korean leader Kim Il-sung apparently held such a view in his later years; he reportedly said: "The DPRK does not intend to attack South Korea, nor could it. More than 1,000 US nuclear warheads are stored in South Korea, ostensibly for defense, and it would take *only two of them to destroy the DPRK.*"[14]

In practice, nuclear weapon effects are not as unlimited as is frequently assumed. Even the use of 50 US nuclear weapons against a small state like North Korea would likely put only three percent or less of its territory within the lethal radii of blast effects (and the percentage would be well less than one percent for larger countries like Iran, China, or Russia).[15] Thus nuclear campaigns limited to tens of nuclear weapons would have limited physical effects, though it is not clear that the adversary would perceive such attacks as limited, especially in psychological terms.

The author believes that conducting a limited nuclear war is indeed possible. It would involve using nuclear weapons with constraints on the number of weapons employed and the objectives of the US attacks. Specifically, the number of nuclear weapons used in any given attack would be *at most a few dozen* and quite possibly only one or two. And the US limited nuclear attacks would not seek civilian damage, rejecting the notions of assured destruction attacks that would maximize damage to the adversary's cities as well as massive retaliation attacks that would seek to devastate the adversary's society. Indeed, the new "Nuclear Employment Strategy" mentioned above says "The United States will not intentionally target civilian populations or civilian objects."[16]

Figure 10.1 suggests the author's view of the types of US nuclear attack options that might be appropriate to achieve the objectives described above in response to the varying conditions that could develop. The US options pictured are purely nuclear response options. In some cases, a US president may actually prefer a conventional response to an adversary nuclear attack or other serious attack, but those options are not pictured here. And US forces would likely deliver a large number of conventional munitions in combination with a nuclear attack, as will be discussed later.

The new "Nuclear Employment Strategy" formalizes the long-held expectation that US presidents would prefer a proportional response to adversary use of nuclear weapons;[17] it could be proportional in terms of the number of weapons used, the nature or targets of the attack, and/or the nature or severity of the effects of the attack. For example, if an adversary used two nuclear weapons for a nuclear demonstration, an EMP attack, or a nuclear attack on US or allied ground forces, many expect that a US president would be naturally inclined to respond using about two nuclear weapons against similar adversary targets.[18] And if an adversary attempts an incapacitating nuclear attack, a US nuclear counterforce attack of roughly similar size may be selected.

But a numerically proportional response may fail to achieve US objectives. For example, if an adversary destroys a US military air base with a single nuclear weapon, a single US nuclear weapon fired at an adversary air base would be a numerically proportional response. But such a response would not meet the likely public demands to neutralize the threat, and would also leave the United States at a disadvantage because US military air bases are far more critical to US military operations than are adversary air bases to their military operations. After all, the US destruction of any single North Korean air base would never compensate for North Korean destruction of a US air base like Kadena, Japan, which houses fighter aircraft, tankers, surveillance and command/control aircraft, and many other functions. Thus in Figure 10.1, a nuclear response in kind to adversary attacks on other military forces and facilities (e.g., air bases, ports, and naval task forces at sea) is shown to be not very appropriate. The United States may need to destroy the ballistic missiles at several adversary missile bases (requiring perhaps ten or more US nuclear weapons) to achieve a proportional effect.

More generally, the magnitude of damage expected from any nuclear attack other than a pure demonstration would almost certainly lead to calls for a US conventional, and probably nuclear, counterforce response to prevent the adversary from being able to launch any more nuclear weapons.[19] And to reduce the risk of subsequent adversary nuclear attacks, the United States might also target adversary leadership, trying to decapitate the military command system. This would be particularly true if the adversary used nuclear weapons to cause major damage to US and/or partner cities or leadership. For example, if an adversary killed 100,000 people in Seattle with a nuclear weapon, some would argue that a proportional US nuclear response against an adversary city would be both inappropriate and not enough. Instead, they would support a counterforce attack to destroy the adversary's nuclear weapon capabilities, especially against an adversary with a small nuclear force, trying to prevent further nuclear attacks that could cause damage to other US cities.

A US nuclear response against adversary ground forces is shown in Figure 10.1 as being appropriate in dealing with: 1) selective nuclear attacks on US

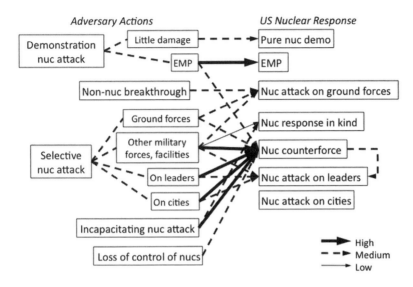

FIGURE 10.1. The Appropriateness of US Nuclear Responses to Adversary Actions

or allied ground forces, 2) selective nuclear attacks on other military forces or facilities, and 3) non-nuclear cases where an adversary achieves a break-through (e.g., the traditional Soviet threat against Western Europe). Thus, an adversary's nuclear attack on a US air base may be responded to by a US nuclear attack to break the cohesion of adversary ground forces.

Note that a US nuclear attack against adversary cities does not fit the definition of limited nuclear war suggested above, and is against the recent "Nuclear Employment Strategy."

If an adversary government collapses or otherwise loses control of its nuclear forces, those forces could be used against the United States or its partners or could be given to states or organizations that would do so. To prevent this from happening, the United States may need to launch a preemptive counterforce campaign, including some use of nuclear weapons to more quickly and completely remove the threat. Some US presidents might balk at such a "first use" of US nuclear weapons, but others may perceive the threat as sufficiently serious to justify such attacks.

In the end, the US nuclear responses in Figure 10.1 become key focal points for the net assessment of US limited nuclear war capabilities. While this section has argued for the relative appropriateness of some of these responses

TABLE 10.3   Matching US Nuclear Forces to Response Options

	Number of Nuclear Weapons*		
Response Option	Vs. Rogue	Vs. Russia	Why Nuclear Weapons?
Demonstration	1–2	1–2	Escalation control, psychological effects
EMP	1	1–3	Only option for wide effects
Strike ground forces	1–20	1–50	Faster/more destruction, psychological effects
Strike other military targets	1–5	1–50	Faster/more destruction, psychological effects
Counterforce	20–50	100s	Higher probability of damage
Strike leadership	1–5	1–30	Faster/more destruction, psychological effects

*These are the author's estimates based on the likely number of targets.

versus others, in the end the key point is that each of these kinds of nuclear attacks (other than directly against adversary civilian populations) is possible; a US president would want all of them available as possible response options from which he could pick. Indeed, a president should have available a sequence of limited nuclear attack options, allowing him a nuclear response to the initial threat posed by an adversary, but also nuclear attack options to deter or respond to an adversary's subsequent nuclear escalation. Any of the options identified in Figure 10.1 may be needed at some point in a limited nuclear war campaign;[20] any of these for which the United States lacks adequate capability would constrain a president and perhaps leave him without a desired or meaningful nuclear employment option.

A Net Assessment of US Limited Nuclear War Capabilities

This section assesses US limited nuclear war capabilities against the nuclear response options described on the right side of Figure 10.1. It does so in terms of three criteria: 1) can the United States deliver a devastating attack; 2) can the United States avoid international accidents and horizontal escalation; and 3) can a US nuclear attack achieve limited, distinct, and precision effects? These criteria are divided into key components, yielding an assessment of the ability of US ICBMs, SLBMs, and bombers to carry out limited nuclear attacks.

It is generally assumed that deterrence against adversary use of nuclear weapons or other high-end threats would be more effective if the United States can credibly threaten and deliver a devastating nuclear attack. Such an attack would require enough US nuclear weapons, though the number of nuclear weapons minimized by sufficient warhead yield, accuracy, and delivery probability. It would also require adequate range and penetration of the delivery platforms, and (for EMP attacks) platforms that can deliver nuclear warheads to a high enough altitude for detonation. Some additional considerations follow.

Number, Yield, and Accuracy

The basic requirements to accomplish nuclear attack objectives are calculated in terms of the rough number and characteristics of warheads necessary to accomplish a specific level and pattern of damage. Table 10.3 estimates the number of nuclear warheads that might be used for each US option depending upon whether the targeted country is one of the smaller rogue states (e.g. North Korea, Iran, or Syria) or Russia, a large state with substantial nuclear forces. Each of these options could be considered "limited" based upon the criteria specified above except for a counterforce attack against Russia and perhaps some of the other larger weapon uses against Russia. The United States has quite adequate nuclear forces to launch many of these attacks. And it would almost always combine these limited nuclear attacks with attacks using even larger numbers of conventional weapons.

Table 10.3 also addresses the question of why nuclear weapons would need to be used in these response options. A nuclear demonstration, for example, uses a nuclear response to demonstrate US nuclear capability and intent, hoping to control escalation (e.g., to discourage further adversary use of nuclear weapons) and cause a psychological effect on the adversary to moderate its behavior. An EMP attack may be the only way to achieve very wide area damage effects—potentially out hundreds of kilometers, with some uncertainty—against an adversary, likely in response to an adversary EMP attack. For other response options, nuclear weapons provide large amounts of physical and psychological damage in a prompt manner, and could achieve a high probability of damage against many potential targets.

For example, against countries with even modest nuclear force capabilities, a counterforce attack could require up to about 50 nuclear weapons divided between different targets, and hundreds of conventional force sorties.

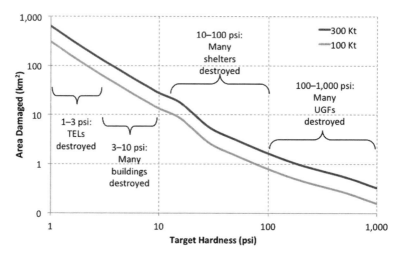

FIGURE 10.2. Geographic Areas Covered by Blast Effects at Varying Hardness
SOURCE: Samuel Glasstone and Philip J. Dolan, (U.S. Department of Defense and U.S. Department of Energy, 1977).
NOTE: Based on the optimal height of burst for each level of target hardness.

And some interesting attack synergies may be exploited. These could include nuclear weapons being used to blow down forests and other cover in potential dispersal areas, making it easier to detect surviving mobile missiles and blocking their movement so they can be targeted with conventional munitions. Or conventional sorties might be used to mine entrance roads to underground facilities to prevent the escape of adversary nuclear forces, and then the underground facilities (UGFs) hit with a nuclear weapon to assure their destruction.

Figure 10.2 shows the geographic areas that would be damaged by two typical US weapon sizes against targets of varying hardness. The "hardness" measures the level of susceptibility of assets to blast effects, with overlays on the figure indicating the kinds of targets that fall in specified hardness ranges. For example, when going after adversary ballistic missiles deployed on transporter erector launchers (TELs, damaged at perhaps one to three psi), US nuclear weapons would cover many tens of square kilometers to several hundred square kilometers, likely overturning the launchers and damaging the missiles they carry. Thus, if only one TEL or support vehicle of a dispersed Scud missile battalion (often 3 TELs) has been located, a single nuclear weapon targeted at that TEL could potentially cover enough area with lethal effects to damage the entire battalion of TELs and all supporting vehicles. In comparison, conventional weapons might require finding and attacking each vehicle separately.

Nuclear weapons are also very effective in destroying hardened targets, including UGFs and silos that tend to be important in counterforce attacks. With the weapon accuracies cited in Table 10.2, US ICBMs and SLBMs should have a high probability (90 percent or more) of damage against point targets hardened to 200 psi or so. Nuclear bombs and cruise missiles, because of their greater accuracy, should be able to achieve high damage probabilities against even much harder targets. Thus the hardest targets (especially UGFs) may best be attacked using bombers, assuming no accuracy degradation from GPS jamming or adversary launch on warning as bombers try to penetrate adversary territory to reach the hard target location.

Delivery Probability

The delivery probabilities of US nuclear weapons in Table 10.2 are high, but they may not be high enough for achieving the desired damage with only a single warhead per target. It is important to remember that in the Cuban Missile Crisis, President Kennedy asked the US Air Force for its assessment of the likely success of a preventive attack on the Russian nuclear missile facilities in Cuba and was told that there was a 90 percent probability of successfully carrying out such an attack. President Kennedy concluded that 90 percent was not good enough, and pursued other options.[21]

This concern about attack effectiveness would be particularly true with counterforce attacks. Consider a case where the adversary has five nuclear weapon storage facilities each containing four nuclear weapons. If the United States sends one nuclear weapon against each, and the US weapons have an 85 percent delivery probability and a 90 percent probability of destruction if the warhead arrives, then the expected number of surviving adversary warheads would be 4.7, enough for a fairly devastating adversary response. Even if two US warheads were assigned to each target, 1.1 adversary warheads would be expected to survive (just less than 95 percent destruction), which may still be inadequate. And this assumes that each warhead is delivered from a different missile or aircraft, so that the arrival of the two warheads is independent. The higher the target kill probability achieved from good yield, accuracy, and delivery probability, the fewer weapons that would be required to achieve any given aggregate level of damage. Still, the United States should have more than sufficient nuclear weapons to make such attacks against rogue states.

Range and Penetration

The United States must be able to deliver nuclear weapons to targets. The delivery systems must have sufficient range to reach targets and be able to penetrate adversary defenses.

US ICBMs, SLBMs, and bombers have the range to reach most countries that the United States might target. US fighter aircraft would have difficulty reaching many targets in Russia and China, and perhaps some in Iran (depending upon the bases made available for US nuclear operations). And without basing near the targeted country, fighters might also have difficulty reaching targets in other smaller countries.

Adversary air and missile defenses would seek to prevent the penetration of US nuclear forces. Any prospective adversary will have air defenses to oppose US bombers and fighters, though most adversaries will not do so very effectively. The exceptions would be Russia and perhaps China, which might seriously challenge US aircraft. US ICBMs and SLBMs would face less of a penetration challenge, though Russian defenses could in the future become a concern at least in some target areas such as Moscow.

Altitude or Height of Burst

To create significant EMP effects, a nuclear explosion needs to occur at 25 kilometers or so altitude (about 82,000 feet). That is possible with US ICBMs and SLBMs, but not with bombers or fighters, which usually operate at half that height or less.

Attribution

The United States will want its nuclear attacks to clearly target the proper countries. It will therefore want to know which country or group has attacked the United States in any given situation. And it will not want its warheads or delivery means to strike third parties or be perceived as being used carelessly. A problem in these areas could lead to an international incident and perhaps to nuclear escalation against the United States by third parties not previously involved in the conflict (so-called horizontal escalation).

The United States is most likely to use a nuclear weapon in response to an adversary attack, and especially an adversary use of nuclear weapons. But before the United States uses its nuclear weapons, it will want to be fairly certain of which state or non-state group was responsible for the adversary attack. This determination of responsibility is called attribution.

In some circumstances, attribution will be easy. For example, this would be the case if an adversary launches short-range ballistic missiles at a neighbor, because satellites and other means would identify the area from which the missiles were launched. In other cases, attribution will not be easy. This would be true, for example, if an organization smuggles a nuclear weapon into another country and covertly detonates it. And even the missile example could be problematic: the state from which the missiles were launched could claim that a rogue officer was responsible for the launches.

A thorough treatment of attribution is beyond the scope of this chapter.[22] Nevertheless, attribution could be a challenge for the United States. Consider, for example, the sinking of the ROK warship *Cheonan* in March 2010; the inability to promptly and conclusively attribute North Korea as being responsible prevented a significant ROK/US military response to the sinking. And such a military response would be a small matter compared to the level of confidence required for US use of nuclear weapons.

Overflight, Launch Location, and Booster Impacts

To reach their targets, ballistic missiles follow primarily "ballistic" trajectories. These trajectories often require overflight of other countries, and overflight can involve three problems: 1) having boosters fall on the country overflown, 2) potentially misleading overflown countries into believing that they are under nuclear attack (this could happen especially with Russia), and 3) risking a missile failure that accidentally allows parts of the missile—including the warhead(s)—to fall on an unintended country (especially one overflown). Any of these conditions could become unacceptable national or international "accidents" and also lead to horizontal escalation.

These problems affect the US ICBMs most seriously. Overflight would be a clear problem for targets in countries other than Russia because the US ICBM bases in the north-central United States were chosen for flights against Russia. Most ICBM launches would overfly Russia to get to other targeted countries. And all ICBM launches out of operational silos would be a problem because the early stages of the ICBMs would land in the United States and/or Canada.[23]

Overflight would also be a problem for US SLBMs against most countries unless SSBN launch locations have been adjusted. US SSBNs historically operated in the North Atlantic and the North Pacific. From these locations, their SLBMs would overfly various countries in trying to reach potentially targeted countries. Adjusting the operating areas for the SSBNs could help solve this problem. Map 10.1 demonstrates the launch locations for SLBMs that might have to be employed to attack targets in just the five countries (China, Iran,

North Korea, Russia, and Syria) with *relatively* acceptable overflights, assuming a Trident D-5 has a minimum range of 2,000 kilometers. Even from these locations, it is impossible to reach all locations in the targeted countries without some overflight problems.

For example, to attack Iran with SLBMs and avoid overflight, an SSBN would need to be put on station in the Indian Ocean. And to reach targets in Syria, a US SSBN would have to be put on station in the Mediterranean Sea, and even then would likely overfly Cyprus and/or Lebanon. In East Asia, to reach various target locations in China or North Korea, a US SSBN would need to be put on station in the Philippine Sea, and even then could have overflight concerns relative to Taiwan, the Ryukyu Islands, South Korea, and/or the Philippines.

Keeping an SSBN available in each of these launch locations would become difficult with the small number of SSBNs in the future US forces. That is, seven or fewer of the twelve operational SSBNs will likely be at sea during any given time. Keeping five SSBNs in these locations would be challenging because some are far forward from the SSBN bases, requiring long transit times when SSBNs would be at sea but not in their preferred launch locations.

Bombers or fighters would have fewer overflight problems because they are not limited to ballistic trajectories. Still, the potential for bomber or fighter difficulties near bases in friendly countries was illustrated by the 1966 accident that dropped four US nuclear weapons near Palomares, Spain.

Can a US Nuclear Attack Achieve Limited, Precision Effects?

Nuclear attacks of any kind would cause immense damage. Many people therefore consider the concept of a limited nuclear attack to be an oxymoron. Nevertheless, with good intelligence, strong command and control, and other factors, the United States might use, for example, four or five nuclear weapons of low yield to achieve the same or better impact against an adversary than it could achieve with ten or more high-yield nuclear weapons that lack good intelligence and other support. The smaller number of weapons would be less escalatory and potentially more effective in dealing with the military problem that nuclear weapons are being used to address. The factors that would matter in achieving relative limited, precision effects with nuclear weapons include the following.

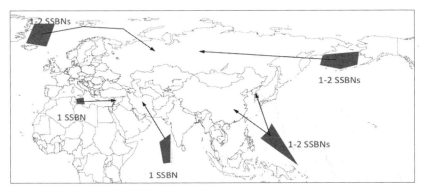

MAP 10.1. Potential SSBN Patrol Areas to Minimize Overflight Concerns
NOTE: The trajectory shown from the Greenland Sea is curved because the Great Circle route from that location would not go over Scandinavia, as a straight line would suggest.

Intelligence[24]

Some of the US nuclear attack options do not require any real target intelligence (a pure demo or an EMP attack), or the targets are readily known (e.g., air bases and ports included in "other military targets"). Other options have many targets that might not be known, such as the location of adversary nuclear weapons (for counterforce) or leaders. Both of these options and the strike on ground forces or other military targets options would also be complicated by the assets at the targets being moveable, allowing the adversary to disperse them when preparing for war. The United States would require real-time reconnaissance and target adjustment options to damage the adversary's dispersed assets. The United States has dealt with similar problems in its counterinsurgency efforts in Iraq and Afghanistan, and achieved only partial successes.

Doctrine, Strategy, and Command and Control

For decades, the United States has developed doctrine and strategy for nuclear weapon use, and prepared war plans as a basis for that use. During the Cold War, the United States used targeting concepts such as theater nuclear attacks, "massive retaliation," and "assured destruction" to characterize its planned uses of nuclear weapons, while not publicly revealing the details of its plans. Still, over time, a fair amount of information accumulated in the public literature especially regarding options that the United States considered. For example, the United States was prepared to use nuclear weapons against a Soviet conventional ground force breakthrough in Western Europe, potentially coupled with attacks on other Soviet targets in Europe, seeking to prevent a Soviet conquest of Europe. If the Soviets escalated, the United States was prepared to employ attacks of various magnitudes against the Soviet Union, eventually including attacks consistent with assured destruction.

The United States has revealed much less of its nuclear doctrine and strategy in the post–Cold War era beyond the general terms discussed at the beginning of this chapter. Still, this doctrine and strategy has to date deterred adversaries from using nuclear weapons or taking other actions that would force the United States to use nuclear weapons. But the lack of specific information on doctrine and strategy makes it impossible to evaluate their role in current US nuclear capabilities. It is only possible to speculate that if the United States is challenged by a risk-taking adversary, the lack of a more concrete (as opposed to ambiguous) US nuclear declaratory policy could negatively impact US deterrence.

To be effective, a nuclear strategy must be executed by a well-prepared command/control system. This means that the key decisionmakers surrounding the president need to understand how a nuclear war could be fought and should have developed concepts for appropriate US nuclear responses. They would need to know, for example, how various kinds and sizes of US nuclear attacks would likely affect adversary military capability, how the adversary might respond, and what the United States could do to affect that response for adversaries of different cultures, interests, and military capabilities. Little information on US efforts in this area is publicly available, forcing the exclusion of this area from the net assessment.

Timing and Simultaneity

With any type of target (e.g., a nuclear weapon storage facility) containing movable assets (e.g., nuclear weapons), nuclear and other attacks need to be promptly executed to avoid adversary dispersal of the assets before the attack. Simultaneity is also important because any attack on adversary forces, especially with nuclear weapons, could prompt an adversary to disperse assets from other targets. And adversary perception that the United States is preparing or executing counterforce attacks could lead the adversary to a "use them or lose them" strategy, where the adversary launches surviving nuclear weapons to avoid their destruction.

The US ability to promptly launch nuclear attacks is heavily a function of the command and control system. Given the US policy to "only consider the use of nuclear weapons in extreme circumstances,"[25] it is unlikely that the United States would employ a preemptive nuclear attack, and it may take hours or days in a conventional conflict before the US president concludes that the circumstances are indeed extreme. Many experts expect that, even in the aftermath of an adversary nuclear attack in a combat theater, it will take at least many hours to prepare a nuclear response package, evaluate it, make sure it meets all established requirements, get it approved by senior Defense Department leaders and then the president, transmit the package to the forces that would perform the nuclear attacks, and then execute those attacks. Attacks could be further delayed if ally approval is sought, which may be important if the attacks occur on or could damage allied territory (e.g., in the case of Korea, South Korea would view all of North Korea as territory it will inherit at the end of a war). During this preparation period, the adversary would likely be dispersing his assets from the intended US targets, significantly reducing the impact of even nuclear attacks. If different parts of the nuclear forces (e.g., bombers and SLBMs) execute the attack, it may also be difficult to achieve simultaneity given the different times involved in communicating to, preparing, executing, and delivering the different parts of the US nuclear forces.

Warhead Packaging

As Table 10.1 indicates, most of the SLBMs will be designed to carry four warheads.[26] This packaging of multiple warheads on a single missile, while providing some efficiency, also introduces a number of complications. For example, if three warheads from the same missile attack a target, then the kill probability against that target is about 85 percent (the probability that the three warheads arrive), whereas if three warheads each come from different missiles, then the kill probability is almost 99 percent. To achieve a 99 percent probability of damage against each of four targets, three missiles would need to be launched and one warhead from each allocated to each of the targets. But this would only work if the footprint of the warheads from a single missile is large enough to cover all four targets.

Multiple warhead missiles also complicate attacks that require only one or two warheads. To perform these, some missiles on each submarine might have to be loaded with only one or two warheads, reducing the number of operationally deployed US nuclear weapons. Alternatively, a four-warhead missile could be used, with all four warheads used against the intended target, though the use of extra warheads would raise the risks that the attack could be misperceived or that accidents could occur.

In practice, counterforce (or counter-leadership) targeting may never be as simple as attacking just a few confirmed targets. Nuclear weapons and leaders can be moved and dispersed, and their actual location may not be known. The adversary's delivery systems may thus also have to be targeted, and they too can be dispersed. And because of the dispersal, a series of attacks may have to be executed to eliminate all of the threat.

Collateral Damage and Fallout

Nuclear weapons used for pure demonstrations or for EMP attacks should cause very little collateral prompt effects damage or fallout. But for the other options, most US nuclear weapons could do considerable collateral damage. Figure 10.2 shows that around an airburst detonation, tens of square kilometers to over 100 square kilometers would suffer serious blast damage for people and buildings. While nuclear weapons used on ground forces or as part of counterforce attacks may detonate in rural areas, there would still likely be some collateral civilian damage. For weapons used on air bases, or ports, or against the leaders of a country, the collateral damage would likely be much higher, and potentially affect tens to hundreds of thousands of people.

Fallout is a different matter. Fallout is created mainly when the fireball of a nuclear explosion touches the ground and vaporizes stone, soil, and other materials. This vapor is carried into the fallout cloud. As the vapor cools, the radioactive material that is also in the fallout cloud forms with the particles that solidify, and these particles are carried by the wind, falling from the sky at rates dependent upon their size and shape.

With 100- to 300-Kt weapons, sufficient radioactivity can be deposited to cause casualties to unshielded people 50 or so kilometers downwind, but measurable amounts of radiation can be deposited hundreds of kilometers downwind, and will not be welcome. Thus, an attack in unpopulated areas may still hurt people downwind.

For example, depending upon the time of year and weather conditions, one or more nuclear detonations on North Korea might carry measurable fallout into South Korea, Japan, and even China or Russia. Such would not be a desired result. And the level of radiation increases as fallout clouds from multiple nuclear detonations overlap. But much of the fallout can be avoided by detonating nuclear weapons at a height of burst of several hundred meters, high enough to avoid much fireball contact on the earth's surface. Against many targets, such a height of burst (or higher) is actually desired to maximize blast effects. But a lower height of burst is required against the hardened underground facilities that would likely be hit as part of counterforce and counter-leadership targeting, making fallout a potential problem.

The Triad Reconsidered in the Light of Limited Nuclear War Requirements

The purpose of this net assessment is to determine the US capabilities to carry out limited nuclear war against various possible adversaries and in various situations. This section first examines overall US capabilities. It then examines the ability of the three major weapon types (ICBMs, SLBMs, and bombers) to meet the requirements of limited nuclear warfare.

Overall US Capabilities

The United States clearly has sufficient high-quality nuclear weapons to cause devastating damage to any adversary, using multiple limited attacks if necessary. But US forces face some challenges with overflights and achieving attribution of adversary attacks. And the United States appears to face a number of challenges in delivering limited, precise nuclear attacks. Some of these challenges are associated with nuclear attack criteria that do not vary across the nuclear force types, including intelligence and major elements of simultaneity and timing. Simultaneity and timing appear to be significant constraints on the efficiency of any US response other than demonstrations and EMP attacks.

Assessment of ICBMs

ICBMs were a great Cold War weapon, offering good capabilities to destroy identified targets with significant warhead yields, high accuracy, and high delivery probability. But US ICBM use in limited nuclear war would be more challenging, as suggested in Table 10.4. ICBM boosters would tend to land in Canada or the United States, a problematic result in a limited war. And ICBMs would overfly Russia when headed toward most potential targets, possibly causing the Russians to believe that they are being attacked with nuclear weapons. So while ICBMs would have a number of advantages over other delivery means, these problems are serious enough to suggest that ICBMs should not normally be used in truly limited nuclear war.

SLBMs

SLBMs can also cause devastating damage to adversaries. And SLBMs can avoid some of the problems that tend to disqualify ICBMs from limited

TABLE 10.4 US ICBM Capability to Execute Limited Nuclear Attack Options Today

Criteria	Pure Demo	EMP	Response Option Ground Forces	Other Mil Targets	Counterforce	Strike Leaders
Devastating attacks						
Yield, accuracy	Good	Good	Good	Good	Good	Good
Delivery prob.	Good	Good	Good	Good	Good	Good
Range, penetration	Good	Good	Good	Good	Good	Good
Altitude	—	Good	—	—	—	—
Net capability	Good	Good	Good	Good	Good	Good
Avoid accidents, horizontal escalation						
Attribution	Good?	Good?	Fair	Fair?	Fair	Fair
Overflight, location	Poor	Poor	Poor	Poor	Poor	Poor
Net capability	Poor	Poor	Poor	Poor	Poor	Poor
Limited, precise effects ➜						
Intelligence	Good	Good	F Good	F ➜ Good	Poor?	Poor?
Doctrine/C²	?	?	?	?	?	?
Simultaneity, timing	Good	Good	Poor	P ➜ Fair	Poor	Poor
Packaging	Good	Good	Good	Good	Good	Good
Collateral damage	Good	Good	Fair	P ➜ Fair	Fair	P ➜ Fair
Fallout	Good	Good	Fair	Fair	Poor	Poor
Net capability	Good?	Good?	Fair?	Fair?	Poor	Poor

nuclear operations. Still, they face some significant challenges in achieving limited and precise effects, as suggested in Table 10.5. SLBMs may have particular timing and simultaneity problems in receiving nuclear attack orders. For single targets such as pure demonstrations and EMP attacks, most SLBMs would suffer from having four warheads per missile, though this problem could be solved by a US decision to place only one or two warheads on a few SLBMs on each submarine. Unless new SSBN stationing locations have been developed, SLBMs may also face overflight problems in striking targets in several countries; if new on-station locations are adopted, the ratings for avoiding accidents and horizontal escalation would generally improve to "fair to good." And SLBM warheads have large enough yields that they could cause some serious collateral damage and fallout problems.

Bombers

As shown in Table 10.6, bombers provide good options for delivering devastating attacks, and face far less concern with overflight issues. But they still face a number of challenges in achieving limited, precise attacks. For example, the long flight times of bombers would add to the timing problems of the current US command/control system, unless at least some bombers are loaded with nuclear weapons on warning of conflict and kept on airborne alert near the theater of conflict. Bombers have the flexibility to allow for changing targets in flight, which gives them a significant advantage over ballistic missiles, especially in dynamic limited attack situations. In most other areas, bombers have good or fair evaluations, though bombers would not be appropriate for EMP attacks because they fly well below the altitude at which EMP attacks need to detonate. Bombers also have more favorable ratings for collateral damage and fallout because they allow for weapons with lower yields to be used, weapons which could be delivered very accurately (assuming no effective GPS jamming).

Fighter Aircraft

Fighter aircraft share in common many of the characteristics of bombers. However, they face range limitations in getting to some targets in Russia and China. And they may face problems with acquiring basing or staging locations. It is also not clear how much training fighter crews are given in nuclear weapon delivery, and thus whether they can perform nuclear missions promptly and with the desired precision. But fighters have the advantage of potential accuracy and the availability of small-yield weapons with which to strike hard targets with less collateral damage or fallout.

US Ability to Assure Its Allies/Partners

The US 2010 *Nuclear Posture Review Report* and the "Nuclear Employment Strategy," discussed above, may not adequately assure many US allies/partners, as suggested by the low-level, ongoing discussions on developing nuclear weapon capabilities in the literature of a number of US allies and partners. The United States needs to pursue a healthy dialogue with its allies/partners in appropriate environments, trying to be clearer on the nature of the US commitment and sensitive to the desires of US allies/partners.

The United States has pursued exactly such an effort with South Korea. The two countries agreed to set up an Extended Deterrence Policy Committee (EDPC) in 2010, and in late 2013 signed a tailored deterrence plan that "establishes a 'strategic framework' within the two countries' military alliance for dealing with 'key North Korean nuclear threat scenarios' both now and in the event of war, according to a joint statement."[27] The EDPC is giving the United States and South Korea the opportunity to plan against North Korea, which is likely the most serious nuclear weapon threat in the world today. It is also

TABLE 10.5. US SLBM Capability to Execute Limited Nuclear Attack Options Today

	Response Option					
Criteria	Pure Demo	EMP	Ground Forces	Other Mil Targets	Counterforce	Strike Leaders
Devastating attacks						
Yield, accuracy	Good	Good	Good	Good	Good	Good
Delivery prob.	Good	Good	Good	Good	Good	Good
Range, penetration	Good	Good	Good	Good	Good	Good
Altitude	—	Good	—	—	—	—
Net capability	Good	Good	Good	Good	Good	Good
Avoid accidents, horizontal escalation						
Attribution	Good?	Good?	Fair	Fair?	Fair	Fair
Overflight, location[a]	P➤Good	P➤Good	P➤Good	P➤Good	P➤Good	P➤Good
Net capability[b]	P➤Good	P➤Good	P➤Fair	P➤Fair	P➤Fair	P➤Fair
Limited, precise effects						
Intelligence	Good	Good	F➤Good	F➤Good	Poor?	Poor?
Doctrine/C^2	?	?	?	?	?	?
Simultaneity, timing	Good	Good	Poor	P®Fair	Poor	Poor
Packaging	P➤Good	P➤Good	Fair	Fair	Fair	P➤Good
Collateral dam.	Good	Good	Fair	P➤Fair	Fair	P➤Fair
Fallout	Good	Good	Fair	Fair	Poor	Poor
Net capability	F➤Good	F➤Good	Fair?	Fair?	Poor	Poor

[a]The apparent lack of an appropriate SSBN on-station location for attacks against Syria or Iran, combined with overflight problems reaching North Korea and potentially China, can cause this rating to be poor. These problems are not serious when targeting Russia. Moving to new launch locations as shown in Map 10.1 would change these ratings to fair or good.

[b]As noted in the above note, SLBMs currently have significant overflight concerns but these can be relatively easily resolved by adopting new on-station locations.

important because the United States plans to transfer control of most theater operations to a South Korean commander. That commander will need to know how his objectives will be met if the conflict crosses a nuclear threshold, allowing him to plan conventional operations that avoid collateral damage to his forces from US nuclear weapon attacks.

Conclusion: What US Capabilities Are Needed for Limited Nuclear War?

If the United States wants to develop better capabilities for limited nuclear war, it needs to pursue six kinds of improvements.

TABLE 10.6 US Bomber Capability to Execute Limited Nuclear Attack Options Today

	Response Option					
Criteria	Pure Demo	EMP	Ground Forces	Other Mil Targets	Counterforce	Strike Leaders
Devastating attacks						
Yield, accuracy	Good	Good	Good	Good	Good	Good
Delivery prob.	Good	Good	Good	Good	Good	Good
Range, penetration	Good	Good	Good	Good	Good	Good
Altitude	—	Poor	—	—	—	—
Net capability	Good	Poor	Good	Good	Good	Good
Avoid accidents, horizontal escalation						
Attribution	Good?	Good?	Fair	Fair?	Fair	Fair
Overflight, location	Good	Good	Good	Good	Good	Good
Net capability	Good	—	Fair	Fair?	Fair	Fair
Limited, precise effects						
Intelligence	Good	Good	F➤Good	F➤Good	Poor?	Poor?
Doctrine/C²	?	?	?	?	?	?
Simultaneity, timing	Good	Good	Poor	P➤Fair	Poor	Poor
Packaging	Good	Good	Good	Good	Good	Good
Collateral dam.	Good	Good	Fair	Fair	Fair	Fair?
Fallout	Good	Good	Fair	Fair	Fair?	Fair?
Net capability	Good?	—	Fair?	Fair?	P➤Fair?	P➤Fair?

- *Intelligence.* The United States needs to work closely with its allies to improve its intelligence on adversary nuclear weapon programs and other potential concealed targets. Because of adversary information security efforts, the United States likely needs to secure multiple adversary defectors (or other human intelligence sources) with current and timely knowledge of potential targets.

- *Timing and Execution.* The United States needs to develop nuclear employment plans for the various options discussed above that can be prepared and made ready to execute with little delay (especially when dealing with time-urgent targets). Such efforts will likely require extensive gaming to understand how to achieve the desired precision and the limits of nuclear weapon use. For example, these efforts will likely suggest that many of the timing problems mentioned herein could be resolved if the president approved some nuclear attacks in general terms (e.g., "The theater commander is authorized to use up to 20 nuclear weapons against adversary nuclear weapons and related delivery vehicles"), allowing the theater commander to authorize the tactical details of use (e.g., one bomber nuclear weapon being dropped at a specific latitude and longitude and at a specific time). These plans should be reviewed with senior US leaders, including (if possible) the president, to avoid a situation where the senior leaders must start from first principles to understand the proposed nuclear weapon employment, and thus take too long to approve nuclear attacks. Theater commanders and key staff would also need to be trained in nuclear weapon attacks.

- *Attribution.* While the details of attributing adversary nuclear attacks are beyond the scope of this chapter, this is an area that requires further effort.

- *On-station/Basing Locations and Overflight.* The United States needs to specify rules for overflight and discuss them with the countries that could be affected. If countries are unwilling to discuss overflight or unwilling to provide contingent release of overflight, then basing/on-station locations and flight paths need to be identified from which nuclear attacks can be promptly executed. Map 10.1 shows areas where SLBMs would need to establish on-station locations. The United States should also consider whether some new US ICBM silos ought to be located along the US west coast (e.g., at Vandenberg Air Force Base) where they could be used without dropping boosters on the United States and Canada, and with much lower overflight concerns.

- *Packaging.* The packaging of warheads on SLBMs needs to ensure that appropriate warhead mixes are available. The combination of packaging and new on-station locations may require the SSBNs to be loaded for specific assignments (e.g., an Iran package or a North Korean package) rather than having general purpose loadings.

- *Collateral Damage and Fallout.* Considerable thought needs to be given to the collateral damage and fallout that US ICBM and SLBM nuclear warheads could cause in limited nuclear war. Using lower-yield strategic or tactical bombs may be preferred in many cases, but this subject needs further study to develop tradeoffs in different targeted countries.

In addition, while many of the details of US nuclear doctrine and strategy are not publicly available, these are areas that may warrant further development. In particular, it may be important to enhance the specifics of the US nuclear declaratory policy. The theory associated with cognitive deterrence (prospect theory) suggests that some adversaries may approach nuclear weapon use as risk takers. If so, ambiguous threats of US nuclear attacks, which tended to be quite effective during the Cold War, may be inadequate to deter adversary escalation to nuclear weapon use.

Operating without constraints in limited nuclear war, the US nuclear forces could cause devastating damage to any adversary. But US nuclear forces will almost certainly face some constraints, and US presidents will need to decide what are reasonable uses of those forces. With its current capabilities, the United States may not be able to achieve the precision and limitations of nuclear weapon use that it would prefer. And some efforts may be needed to avoid complications with attributing adversary nuclear attacks and flying missiles with nuclear weapons over countries other than the country being targeted. The United States should regularly review its nuclear weapon and related capabilities and decide how to modernize, adapt, and update these capabilities for applicability to limited nuclear war requirements.

Notes

This chapter represents the views of the author and does not necessarily reflect the opinions or policies of the RAND Corporation or its research sponsors.

1. Nuclear deterrence does not occur because the US has nuclear weapons; it occurs (in part) because of what the US can threaten to do with its nuclear weapons. Failures in any of these areas may lead to a deterrence failure even if the United States eventually does use nuclear weapons in some sub-optimal manner.

2. Department of Defense, "Report on Nuclear Employment Strategy of the United States Specified in Section 491 of 10 U.S.C.," June 12, 2013, p. 4.

3. Department of Defense, *Nuclear Posture Review Report*, April 2010, at www.defense.gov/npr/.

4. Ibid., pp. viii–ix.

5. See "LGM-30G Minuteman III," *Jane's Strategic Weapon Systems*, September 13, 2010.

6. See "UGM-133 Trident D-5," *Jane's Strategic Weapon Systems*, September 13, 2010.

7. See "B-2 Spirit" at www.globalsecurity.org/wmd/systems/b-2.htm; "B-52 Stratofortress" at www.globalsecurity.org/wmd/systems/b-52.htm; and "AGM-86 ALCM/CALCM," *Jane's Strategic Weapon Systems*, September 13, 2010.

8. Hans M. Kristensen and Robert S. Norris, "U.S. Nuclear Forces, 2013," *Bulletin of the Atomic Scientists,* Vol. 69, No. 2 (March/April 2013), p. 78.

9. "Smart Weapons," GlobalSecurity.org, at www.globalsecurity.org/military/systems/munitions/smart.htm. The CEP is the distance from the target within which half of the weapons would be expected to fall.

10. John Sheridan, "South Korea To Install eLoran to Counter North Korean GPS Jamming," *Aviation International News,* August 2, 2013, at www.ainonline.com/aviation-news/aviation-international-news/2013-08-02/south-korea-install-eloran-counter-north-korean-gps-jamming; Steve Herman, "North Korea Appears Capable of Jamming GPS Receivers," *VOA News,* October 7, 2010, at www.voanews.com/english/news/North-Korea-Appears-Capable-of-Jamming-GPS-Receivers-104481239.html; "N. Korea Jamming GPS from Kaesong," *Chosun Ilbo,* October 5, 2010, at http://english.chosun.com/site/data/html_dir/2010/10/06/2010100600997.html.

11. These are two of the four elements of US national strategy that were defined under "How We Accomplish Our Objectives" in U.S. Department of Defense, *The National Defense Strategy of the United States of America*, Washington, DC, March 2005, p. i, at http://purl.access.gpo.gov/GPO/LPS59037.

12. Nuclear weapon attacks against the Soviet industrial complexes would have done little to deny a Soviet conquest of Western Europe. But against a "status quo"–oriented power like the Soviet Union, the punishment threat of city destruction was a serious deterrent. See U.S. Joint Chiefs of Staff, "Over-All Effect of Atomic Bomb on Warfare and Military Organization," J.C.S. 1477/1 (declassified, from the U.S. National Archives), October 30, 1945.

13. The argument about conventional strike effectiveness also neglects the psychological impact of a US nuclear weapon attack, something that appears to apply significant deterrence leverage against most prospective US adversaries.

14. The italics are mine. Balazs Szalontai and Sergey Radchenko, "North Korea's Efforts to Acquire Nuclear Technology and Nuclear Weapons: Evidence from Russian and Hungarian Archives," Woodrow Wilson International Center for Scholars, Cold War International History Project, Working Paper #53, August 2006, Document No. 52 (dated October 1986), p. 74. Earlier, the North Korean leadership apparently had a different perspective. A Hungarian deputy ambassador reported a conversation with a North Korean political officer in Pyongyang: "When I remarked that two or three hydrogen bombs would be sufficient to destroy an area the size of the DPRK, the officer became embarrassed, and declared, *"Comrade Kim Il Sung told us that we won the first war by means of our rock-caverns, and we would also win the second one with their help!"* See ibid., Document No. 8 (May 27, 1963), p. 37.

15. Calculations based on Samuel Glasstone and Philip J. Dolan, *The Effects of Nuclear Weapons*, U.S. Department of Defense and U.S. Department of Energy, 1977.

16. Department of Defense, "Report on Nuclear Employment Strategy of the United States," p. 4.

17. "The new guidance makes clear that all plans must also be consistent with the fundamental principles of the Law of Armed Conflict. Accordingly, plans will,

for example, apply the principles of distinction and proportionality." Ibid., p. 18. A US EMP response may initially appear to be an ideal response to an adversary EMP attack: it would cause few direct casualties, appear proportional in weapon usage and targeting, and provide perhaps the only way to shut down adversary ballistic missiles for some time over a wide area. But a US EMP attack could also damage US intelligence and aircraft assets within hundreds of kilometers of the attack, an undesired outcome. To avoid this, the United States would need to move these intelligence systems and aircraft beyond the range of an EMP attack, which would leave a gap of potentially many hours in US intelligence coverage and various aircraft missions.

19. This kind of response would be similar to the US responses to the 9/11 attacks, which involved taking actions to topple the government of Afghanistan, trying to deny Al Qaeda the territory where it was able to prepare attacks against the United States.

20. A president should also want defensive capabilities such as air and missile defense, but these are beyond the scope of this chapter.

21. "The Commander of the Tactical Air Command replied that the air strike would certainly destroy 90 percent of the missiles but that it was not possible to guarantee 100 percent effectiveness. According to Sorensen's record, 'Even then, admitted the Air Force—and this in particular influenced the President—there could be no assurance that all the missiles would have been removed or that some of them would not fire first.'" Graham T. Allison, *Essence of Decision: Explaining the Cuban Missile Crisis* (Boston: Little, Brown, 1971), pp. 123–126, 209–210.

22. For a more complete discussion, see Debra K. Decker, "Before the First Bomb Goes Off: Developing Nuclear Attribution Standards and Policies," *Discussion Paper 2011–03*, Belfer Center for Science and International Affairs, Harvard Kennedy School, April 2011, available at http://belfercenter.hks.harvard.edu/publication/20942/before_the_first_bomb_goes_off.html, accessed May 22, 2013.

23. In a major nuclear war where millions of Americans and allies would be killed, the damages caused by ICBM boosters might be considered a minor issue. But in a limited nuclear war where no nuclear weapons detonate in the United States, the impacts of ICBM boosters may significantly change in especially political importance.

24. Some of the intelligence difficulties are discussed in the Commission on the Intelligence Capabilities of the United States Regarding Weapons of Mass Destruction, "Report to the President of the United States," March 31, 2005, at www.gpoaccess.gov/wmd/index.html.

25. Department of Defense, *Nuclear Posture Review Report*, April 2010, pp. viii–ix.

26. In Table 10.1, ICBMs are planned to each have only a single warhead. And while bombers might carry multiple bombs or cruise missiles, those weapons not used by a bomber can be carried back for use later.

27. Agence France-Presse in Seoul, "South Korea and US Sign Pact to Deter North Korea Nuclear Strike," *South China Morning Post*, October 2, 2013, at www.scmp.com/news/asia/article/1322823/south-korea-and-us-sign-pact-deter-north-korea-nuclear-strike.

11 Limited Nuclear Conflict
and the American Way of War

James M. Smith

W ELL OVER A DECADE AGO CARL BUILDER WROTE that "strategic thinking by the American military appears to have gone into hiding. Planning on the tactical and operational levels flourishes, but the strategic level is largely discussed in historical terms rather than as current art."[1] Those words remain relevant today. One might even argue that the strategic level is seldom discussed even in historical terms. Builder's argument was that the national interest is best served by a military that emphasizes strategic options and capabilities that offer opportunities to succeed without combat—those presenting military power in such a way as to attain the nation's priority objectives without having to actually defeat adversary forces—as superior to ones that involve fighting and winning wars.

And Builder was not just lamenting the bygone era of nuclear centrism. He was prescient in anticipating the complex and dangerous world of today. To Builder, this was the strategic imperative for the twenty-first century: applying strategic vision so as to allow the United States to attain its security objectives in a highly insecure world without having to rely first and foremost on the application of military force. To Builder, the imperative to the "warfighter" was to use strategic vision and wisdom to avoid having to fight wars.

Further, the symptoms cited for the US military are at least as prevalent in the broader national security community: senior decisionmakers directing military employment, government offices where specific security policy focus resides and that provide the pool of experience and expertise to advise senior leadership in those areas, and down into the academic community which provides the intellectual foundations and vision of the next generations of security leadership for the nation. The imperatives of more than a decade of fighting global extremism and other imperatives of insurgency, civil war, and issues at the lower end of the traditional spectrum of conflict form the new experience base of the security community and dominate in the halls of academia, yet few programs provide focus on issues of strategic—and specifically nuclear—policy, strategy, or the operational considerations of limited nuclear warfare. The population base from which military personnel are drawn, and which also provides civilian analysts and security specialists, also risks losing its "strategic flame."

The argument of this chapter is that Builder was correct in his 1996 assessment that the "strategic flame" was in danger of being extinguished. That was over half of a "military generation" ago, so today virtually all of the personnel who had been exposed to Builder's "strategic flame" in practice before it "dimmed" have left or are now leaving active military service, and others are significantly "graying" or leaving civilian government service. Further, without strategic vision within our military force and security specialists, the United States will lack the necessary doctrinal basis and agility to confront challenges across the entire security spectrum, including the challenges of conflict involving the use of limited numbers of nuclear weapons. Operational preeminence and tactical expertise and experience with other types of conflict may not be enough to ensure national security in the face of the emerging threat environment.

This chapter develops these arguments by first providing a summary of traditional American strategic culture and the perspective and traditions that this implies for national security decisionmakers. The strategic focus here is primarily centered on issues related to nuclear weapons, nuclear policy and posture, and nuclear strategy. That summary of strategic culture is extended to the American way of war and the traditional and modern practice of the military art. Here the examination finds a "way of war" in transition, with that transition creating at least a temporary disconnect between strategic requirements and military practice (and increasingly capabilities). Second, the chapter illustrates these issues and their consequences with a brief case study of the United States Air Force, one of the two "strategic" services, one that has always been divided between the tactical and strategic worlds, and one that is today fragmented from the breadth and complexity of its wide and diverse range of mission sets. The increasing emphasis on and experience with tactical and operational missions has accelerated the extinguishing of the "strategic flame" for this, the service that should be its home and protector within the US military. Finally, the chapter summarizes the net effects of these discussions for American strategic capability and intent, and their implications for American strategic security. A few modest prescriptions are offered to arrest dangerous trends and reinforce positive practices toward rekindling and sustaining the strategic flame.

Context: Nuclear War and American Strategic Culture

Strategic culture is a useful concept in the practice of security policy observation and analysis. It is basically the expression of the realization that "different security communities think and behave somewhat differently about strategic matters. Those differences stem from communities' distinctive histories and geographies."[2] National strategic decisionmakers operate from the departure point of unique national characteristics, beliefs, and experiences that form distinct worldviews, value sets, and interests in the world. This cultural foundation need not be deterministic or permanent. It forms a departure point—an initial reaction to world events—that provides a broad perceptive frame for the initial search for additional information, and it may also frame an initial set of response options. It "informs our vision, which inspires our policy."[3]

Some of the central dimensions of the unique American strategic culture include its continental anchor, its foundations in abundance, and its belief in American exceptionalism.[4] The United States devoted the first century of its existence to securing control of the North American continent from the Atlantic to the Pacific. It secured and maintained that control, and it then enjoyed a secure homeland with no truly threatening borders or challenges to the homeland. With internal peace, it considered conflict an anomaly, and it saw only challenges deriving from its far-flung commerce and the expanding set of interests it derived from transoceanic engagement. War was to be fought only when strongly provoked; it was to be fought "over there"; and it was to be decisively concluded to return quickly to the desired normal state of peace.

This secure continental anchor with conflict sited on other continents gave rise to a perceived need to immediately and decisively respond to any homeland challenge that might arise, a belief in total victory, and a singular reliance on American power and military superiority. The United States developed the world's most sophisticated concepts and systems for logistics to take it to and sustain it in the fight, capabilities and concepts of command of the commons that were central to deployment and operations, and a fundamental belief in and reliance on technology and technical solutions to problems of time, distance, and advanced military capacity.

American strategic culture also embraced acceptance of abundance as a normal and expected state. The United States was resource rich, and that allowed industrial answers to many questions of capability and power. It could design and build whatever might be required for the fight. This contributed to a quantitative view of power and a belief in the inevitable superiority of American capacity.

This is but one aspect of the spirit of exceptionalism that underlies the American approach to the world. If the United States were sufficiently provoked to engage in trans-continental conflict (or if it were unthinkably attacked at home), Americans did not just fight with and for abundance and total victory, but for a higher purpose than solely the commercial and political interests that created the conditions of conflict. The United States fought to better the world, to remove evil, to create conditions from which this could be the "war to end all wars." Thus, from a morally superior position, the United States placed the full might of its industrial capacity behind a military/logistical and technologically superior force that could fight and be sustained across the globe for total victory.

How does nuclear war fit into this construct? The American nuclear program was born in the conditions of war that followed a direct attack on the homeland. The United States was engaged in total war, and it was believed that it was in a race with its primary adversary for the development of atomic weapons. This was a race that had to be won. The United States placed the might of its scientific and industrial systems behind the effort, succeeding in developing a revolutionary new technology in a remarkably short time. The United States employed the weapon against the nation that had attacked its homeland in a way that ended that part of the war and saved countless lives on both sides. After the war, when faced with social and economic imperatives to recover and reconstitute its domestic systems, the US government saw the atomic weapon as a technical (and cost effective) answer to our security requirements against an emerging and not yet understood threat. The bomb reflected US technical superiority, possession of which provided security for the homeland. The United States could—and did—build a system to deliver it to targets anywhere on the globe, and threatening its use reflected the values behind the concept of American exceptionalism. This role for the bomb was highly consistent with American strategic culture.

The United States initially saw the bomb as a war-winning, war-ending weapon with high military utility. As it was joined in the "atomic club" by the Soviet Union, leaders began to question the utility of nuclear conflict. They sought alternative military capabilities to all-out use of strategic nuclear weapons. This included smaller, theater-based nuclear weapons and delivery systems that were considered useable in "limited" conflicts (limited in scale and in geographic focus away from the homeland). So it wasn't the nature of the weapon that was being held at bay in the postwar strategic culture; it was the threat of nuclear employment on the homeland. Thus, strategic weapons became weapons to deter others from strategic attack on the United States (and a few close allies that the United States accepted under its "nuclear umbrella" of extended deterrence), and tactical weapons were weapons to be considered for use in regional conflicts to manage and limit any possible escalation toward strategic conflict.

Since its peak early in the Cold War, the scope of global conflict has contracted. This change in the nature of conflict has been facilitated by rapid advances in communication and transportation technologies, and the development of a global economy. As a result of these trends, the nature of conflict has changed from total wars to smaller-scale conflicts characterized by primarily political objectives and limited military engagement. Strategic nuclear weapons are seen in American culture as exceptional, with a deterrence role and with otherwise very limited to no military utility. The American politico-military elite are divided on tactical nuclear weapons: some see specific, often niche, military utility (against a regional adversary's hardened and deeply buried targets, for example), while others see no utility for these weapons at all. Nuclear weapons are still mainstays of American security, but their positions and roles are more complex.

So to summarize the contribution of strategic culture, "a unique geography, fuelling a unique history, gives rise to a distinctive way of looking at the world."[5] That vision then translates into a distinct approach to strategy and conflict in that world, and ultimately into unique operational character and characteristics.

The American Way of War

Some authors equate strategic culture and way of war, basically arguing that the distinct factors that were earlier cited as contributing to a unique cultural prism and set of strategic preferences also translate into distinct characteristics of combat.[6] Others draw distinctions between the concepts, some citing their different disciplinary origins (strategic culture from the field of political science, and way of war from military history).[7] However, all seem to agree that the concepts are closely related, with strategic culture pertaining to the national level of culture and grand strategic policy decisions, and way of war pertaining to the military level of culture and to the actual conduct of war. As Colin Gray puts it, way of war is "culture made manifest in style of warfare."[8]

This view of the two integrally related concepts as forming a "policy/practice" level of analysis hierarchy is reinforced by a key principle of the American way of war: a distinct civil-military separation and clear civilian control of the military arm. Issues of politics and policy are in the domain of the civilian leadership, leaving the soldier to focus solely on the military issues. The American military, then, is seen as apolitical, putting its focus solely on attaining the short-range victory with little focus on securing the peace that follows.[9] This has also allowed the American military to develop a warrior culture centered on tactics and operations. As Gray writes,

> Other generally accepted elements of an American way of war are that warfare should be waged on a large scale in pursuit of decisive victory; warfare should be regular in character; logistical excellence is key; military style should be aggressive, offensive, and highly mobile-maneuvrist; victory should be sought swiftly; technology provides the combat edge, and more; firepower is trumps; airpower is highly favored and is a compound expression of technology and firepower; and American casualties must be minimal.[10]

This listing offers several areas of interesting discussion of the compatibility of these elements with the American experience in the last decade of the twentieth century and the first decade of the twenty-first century; however, we confine ourselves here to an examination of where nuclear weapons fit into this picture.

Strategic nuclear weapons fit this mold well as they were first developed and were deployed as the centerpiece of American policy and strategy. They embodied decisive, large-scale warfare fought on the offensive for swift, decisive victory. They embodied technology, firepower, and airpower, and they promised positive outcomes while minimizing American casualties. However, as strategic nuclear weapons became almost exclusively deterrence weapons, their fit changed. Deterrence lives in the realm of policy, and the weapons were seen as now having primarily political roles. In the divided "policy/practice" construct, this moves strategic nuclear warfare into the civilian policy and politics sector, and away from the warrior culture of the operational way of war. As will be discussed below, these weapons and the strategic nuclear mission were segregated into a separate organizational structure within the American military, which left most of the warriors to deal with the tasks of warfighting.

Tactical nuclear weapons designed for regional, theater conflict remained as warfighting tools, and they were organizationally and operationally part of the warfighting realm. They offered the same contributions originally found in strategic nuclear weapons (swift, decisive applications of offensive technology via airpower) only as adjunct weapons to the non-nuclear battlefield. As discussed elsewhere in this volume, they were seen as useful not only for providing a route to final dominance and victory, but also for managed escalation to limit conflict to the theater and prevent escalation to broader, all-out strategic warfare. So tactical nuclear weapons were placed organizationally within the warfighting force, and they remained a central operational player for major theaters embodying vital US interests across the Cold War. As the threat environment has changed, these weapons have become more political than military in their purposes and roles, and today they too have been largely pushed away to the policy realm by the warfighters, with deleterious effects on the ability to manage limited nuclear war.

The discussion so far has described American strategic culture and the American way of war as constituting two levels of analysis—one level focusing on policy and politics among civilian strategic policymakers, and the other focusing on combat operations and being at home among military warriors. Nuclear weapons, depending on the military utility of their mission in a changing security and strategy environment, once spanned these levels. However, in today's world they have become political weapons within American culture and practice, with diminishing relevance to the warrior realm.

Military and Organizational Culture:
The Case of the US Air Force

The US Air Force was the initial and the primary organizational home of America's strategic capabilities. The problems presented by the issues above have implications for today's American way of war, as can be illustrated with a brief case study of the Air Force. It exemplified the strategic role in both its doctrine and organization. It stood as the bastion of strategic power, and it gave credible reality to the nation's strategic policy. As Gray reminds us, "in airpower the American way of war has found its perfect instrument."[11] However, that vision of a singularly strategic force was always pushed and pulled by competing visions of the role of airpower within the American way of war.

The Air and Space Battlespace

The basic duality underlying the development of American airpower was established almost from the first employment of aircraft technology in military operations. As early as World War I, Major William "Billy" Mitchell called for both "strategical" operations (independent air units carrying the war into the enemy homeland) and "tactical" operations (traditional support operations on behalf of surface combat forces).[12] He later expanded those two spheres, forming the philosophical foundation upon which the Army Air Corps (AAC) was built.[13] Mitchell's ideas took life primarily through the influence of a cadre of early airman airpower advocates, many of whom shaped the AAC through their positions on the faculty of the influential Air Corps Tactical School where they developed, refined, institutionalized, and spread the "strategic gospel" as it evolved from Mitchell.

The product of this intellectual development across the interwar period found its highest expression in the concepts of the "industrial web" strategic bombing theory that held that advanced industrialized nations presented infrastructure within which a manageable number of "strategic nodes" could be identified as forming the backbone of their industrial system. Destroying these nodes by aerial bombardment could, then, cripple the production of defense materials and weapons, and could bring economic ruin and plummeting societal morale that would force an adversary to abandon its military efforts. The strategic bombing campaign of World War II was an application of these ideas. Thus, an entire generation of future AAC and USAF leaders—the generation that fought World War II and founded the United States Air

Force as a separate service—was shaped by this World War II practice of strategic bombardment.[14]

One of Mitchell's disciples, Hap Arnold, went on to head the AAC and become the "father of the USAF." He refined Mitchell's dual concept of air-power operations, calling for air forces to conduct both "independent" air operations and "cooperative" air-ground, air-sea operations. To Arnold, a major fight would most likely start with an air phase consisting of independent air operations designed to destroy the enemy air force and significantly degrade the enemy's ability (and will) to wage war. Then, if peace had not already been gained, the ground war and cooperative airpower would enter alongside continuing independent air operations.[15] These ideas were eventually tested and applied by the US military under the rubric of "joint" operations.

While Mitchell and Arnold provided the philosophical underpinnings of the nascent Air Force, national tasking to the new service was consistent with the foundation they had built. Executive Order 9877 and the accompanying National Security Act of 1947, which established the USAF and provided its original charter, specified that it prepare forces for a mix of independent and cooperative functions. Significantly, this initial tasking added the requirement to "support national interests."[16] This would become a centerpiece of USAF doctrine and operational perspective, the source of much of the complexity of American air and space power, and of continuing tension with the warrior core of the American way of war.

As "national interests" have expanded and grown more complex, so has the mission set and task environment of the Air Force. The tasking of a mix of strategic/independent and tactical/cooperative functions was changed very little in 1948 following the summit that delineated service missions held in Key West, Florida, and when codified into DOD Directive 5100.1, which laid out those service responsibilities, in 1954 (and revised in 1958). That tasking would not change until very late in the Cold War when the 1987 edition confirmed the earlier listing of tasked functions, although with the important additions of in-flight refueling (initially with primarily strategic applications), special operations (tactical), and space operations (including the strategic functions of air and missile defenses and space control).[17] More recent editions of this core document basically repeat and reconfirm this broad task set.[18]

USAF doctrine repeated this same complex tasking, but with a strategic, independent flavor. Air Force Manual (AFM) 1–2, *United States Air Force Basic Doctrine*, the first published document on Air Force basic doctrine, came out in

1953. It defined military force as an instrument of national policy whose role is to deter first, and failing that, to repel, protect, and preserve national integrity and values. Victory was defined as attaining specific national objectives. Air's role was seen by airman as primarily to support national interests, with deterrence as a clear priority. AFM 1–2 also demonstrated a clear preference for the independent, strategic set of taskings. The doctrine saw the "greatest opportunities for decisive actions in dealing immediately and directly with the enemy's warmaking capacity—both in being and potential." This was Arnold's initial air campaign codified (with a heavy dose of the Air Corps Tactical School's "industrial web" targeting strategy thrown in as well). Finally, again borrowing from Arnold and Mitchell using only slightly different terms, the doctrine distinguished between "heartland" or strategic air operations, and "peripheral" or tactical air operations.[19] Subsequent editions generally made only insignificant changes, though one of substance in the 1959 edition added the concept of "aerospace"—defined as the "operationally indivisible medium consisting of the total expanse beyond the earth's surface"—which heralded the eventual addition of intercontinental ballistic missiles (ICBMs) to the Air Force arsenal.[20] The Air Force was reaching ever higher, and its conception of the battlespace was now extending upward toward infinity.

The USAF force structure reflected these priorities and tasks. The service was divided between two primary military commands. Strategic Air Command (SAC) was home to the bomber force (and later the ICBMs) and the strategic nuclear mission. The Tactical Air Command (TAC) was home to the fighter force and the cooperative, tactical missions (including tactical nuclear weapons employment). Airlift and homeland air defense had smaller commands within the USAF, but the core of the service was SAC and TAC. SAC was the early leader in any contests for supremacy within the USAF. The strategic nuclear mission was central, and SAC embraced that mission. As deterrence rose to national prominence as one of those "national interest" taskings, SAC served as its champion and practitioner. SAC enjoyed first place within the USAF, with SAC generals running the service for forty years.

Limited Nuclear War and
the Operationalization of the Air Force
Beginning in 1964 USAF doctrine reflected the flexible response era and its spectrum from general war through tactical nuclear operations to conventional war, and reaching down to counterinsurgency operations in Vietnam.[21]

254 Confronting the Challenges of Nuclear War in the 21st Century

The clear USAF emphasis, however, remained at the top two rungs of that spectrum, and this emphasis continued into 1979 when space and special operations were formally added to the list of USAF functions. The special operations entry reflected the legacy of Vietnam, and the addition of space reflected the realities of the time, as well as national tasking that came as early as the National Aeronautics and Space Act of 1958, assigning the USAF a range of military space responsibilities.[22] The 1984 doctrine continued the focus on airpower as an instrument of national policy by stating "the attainment of stated objectives, limited or total, defines victory." But the word "limited" indicates the shift to incorporate the broader operational spectrum below general nuclear war.[23] USAF doctrine was broadening across the entire operational realm.

Another important legacy of Vietnam and the USAF conceptual shift toward operations was the use of strategic systems in conventional and "theater strategic" but non-nuclear roles. B-52 bombers were employed in conventional roles in major air campaigns over North Vietnam. While this was a throwback strategic bombing role (in the World War II tradition), it was a marked departure from the B-52's primary nuclear deterrence role. In addition, the B-52 was also employed in tactical, carpet-bombing roles within South Vietnam, which was an even bigger departure from its strategic mission. The fact that strategic systems were used in tactical and conventional roles is not in and of itself a major issue; however, it set the precedent for such diversions that would be employed with increasing regularity in the future.

In the wake of Vietnam and against late Cold War tasking, the Air Force began a transition toward a much more operational focus to respond to growing regional imperatives. The initial product was a vision statement, *Global Reach—Global Power*, in 1990. It noted the continuing relevance of nuclear deterrence as the heart of the USAF mission, but it also noted the reality of the shift from a global nuclear emphasis to limited operational requirements in the world's regions. The new emphasis on theater, operational warfare found an Air Force particularly well suited to carry out the new national direction. The Air Force brought its unmatched perspective, speed, range, flexibility, precision, and lethality to fit the demands of regional conflict.[24] The Gulf War that directly followed the issuance of *Global Reach—Global Power* provided the Air Force a showcase for this operational capability. Note that the initial bombing campaign that formed the heart of the conflict reflected Arnold's strategic bombing prequel with John Warden's operational adaptation of industrial web nodes—even the tactical Air Force had not broken completely with its strategic roots.[25] The Gulf War experience and the *Global Reach—Global Power* vision placed the USAF firmly in the world of military operations—they centered on the operational level of war and the operational art. This resulted in a USAF emphasis on theater campaign planning and the refinement of a command and control system designed to implement the theater air campaign.

Another important factor in this period was the increasing influence of the 1986 Goldwater-Nichols Act, which mandated "jointness" for the military services.[26] The overall impact of Goldwater-Nichols has been very positive, with much improved interoperability in the field and visibly less dysfunctional rivalry in the halls of the Pentagon, but there have been a few negative implications that have flowed from the act and its implementation. One is that for the USAF it initially produced an emphasis on developing "airmindedness" or the conceptual air warrior to attempt to articulate a sense of the airman's perspective on warfare at the joint table.[27] The air warrior would be integrating operationally into the new ground-sea-air team, so the focus was overwhelmingly operational. Second, where the new mandate was almost exclusively on regional challenges and operational warfare, the strategic mission—a national tasking, but one that with the end of the Cold War again fell wholly into the realm of politics, policy, and national interest—was not seen as a part of the emerging warrior culture. This experience marked the early development of the current cadre of senior USAF leadership.

This conceptual evolution has continued across the transition following the end of the Cold War. This period has not added new roles, but it has allowed operational refinement of mission sets to flesh out the air and space arsenal to fit the new global challenges. Air-centric operations were the choice in the Balkans and for a decade between active conflicts in the Persian Gulf. This experience allowed sophisticated refinement of the air and space expeditionary campaign construct and its intricate command and control structures, as well as refined stealth and precision in air and space platforms. To this set of "independent" but operational air and space refinements was added the expansion of "cooperative" conventional airpower even in support of subconventional and special operations in Afghanistan, and of the well-orchestrated inclusion of strategic and conventional, manned and unmanned, air and space platforms into the combined arms experiences in Iraq and continuing operations in Afghanistan.

In practical terms, this period since the first Gulf War and the end of the Cold War to today has been a period of deployment and reorganization for the expeditionary Air Force. The fabled Strategic Air Command was transitioned to the United States Strategic Command in 1992, now with an expanded mix of nuclear and non-nuclear missions and a major non-USAF presence. The USAF simultaneously transitioned its Tactical Air Command into an expanded Air Combat Command (ACC) in 1992 (note the operational emphasis even in the name), now serving as home to fighters, bombers, and ICBMs. The bombers retained their nuclear mission, but they also participated increasingly in conventional roles in the succession of operations in the Balkans, the Middle East, and Southwest Asia. And the tactical nuclear mission was cut significantly in size, isolated to a single significant theater, and increasingly marginalized as a warfighting tool across this period. The focus of the USAF became centered on operational deployments and operations, its mission and vision now stated as "The mission of the United States Air Force is to fly, fight, and win ... in air, space and cyberspace" (a mantra that paralleled the traditional Army mission of "to fight and win the nation's wars"). The nuclear mission focus naturally declined in this operational environment.[28]

The ICBM force did not fit well into ACC, and the ICBMs were transferred to Air Force Space Command in 1993. Young officers in the "space and missile" career field might spend their first USAF tour in ICBMs and with the strategic nuclear mission, but the career incentive was to then move to satellite systems and the "space" side of the spectrum for the main part of their careers. The strategic nuclear mission became a sidebar in both the bomber and missile worlds of the USAF, and the tactical nuclear mission withered toward extinction, along with US capacity for conducting limited nuclear war.

The implications of these trends were certainly predictable, even if those predictions did not trigger preventative action of sufficient scope and timing. For example, a survey of Department of Defense staff nuclear expertise requirements and officer capabilities led by a retired strategic general officer in 2001 found that while current expertise was deemed sufficient for staff needs, the pool of replacement officers was declining in numbers and experience, that the United States strategic nuclear community was "living off the fat of the land," and that a "cliff" was looming over the 5–7 year horizon.[29] What was predicted for the staff was certainly true for the force in the field, and the Air Force "fell over the cliff" in the predicted timeframe, with the result being embarrassing mistakes involving nuclear weapons systems/components in 2006–7.

It should be noted that the Air Force has taken positive steps to redress these declines.[30] It has given greatly increased attention to nuclear safety, surety, and security procedures, training, practice, and assessment. It has instituted training and education toward establishing a small but sufficient "bench" of expertise for command and staff supervision and planning. Perhaps most significantly, it established Global Strike Command in 2009 as the single organizational home of USAF bombers, ICBMs, and the USAF nuclear enterprise, and it returned missile officers to a dedicated ICBM career path. It will take time to restore full confidence in the Air Force's oversight of the nuclear missions under its purview. Full success is not guaranteed and the scope of the mission set and command is likely to continue to shrink, with reduced numbers and salience of strategic nuclear weapons over time.

Implications and Conclusions

This chapter paints a fairly dark picture of American nuclear experience and expertise, and of the declining position of all things nuclear in American strategic culture, the American way of war, and American military service culture. This bodes ill for the United States' ability to think about, plan for, and acquire the operational capacity to conduct limited nuclear war, if that contingency is forced upon it. But does it matter? In early 2009 President Obama called for the eventual elimination of all nuclear weapons and for a decrease in their salience in American policy and strategy in the interim. Some observers assume a continuing and accelerated nuclear drawdown as a foregone reality. But they overlook the president's condition for movement to zero: "Make no mistake: As long as these weapons exist, the United States will maintain a safe, secure and effective arsenal to deter any adversary, and guarantee that defense to our allies."[31] The president echoed these positions in Berlin in 2013. The objective reality is that nuclear weapons will likely continue at the center of United States policy and strategy for some significant time to come. Nuclear-capable adversaries will continue to challenge the United States and its allies, and nuclear deterrence will continue as a center-point of the US approach to the world.

Deterrence is fundamentally a psychological instrument, creating the clear perception in a potential adversary's mind that it cannot win, or that it will suffer overwhelmingly unacceptable consequences, or combinations of the two, if it uses nuclear weapons against the United States or its designated vital centers (deployed American troops or critical allies, for example). As such, it hinges on the US ability to project unambiguous signals of capability and credibility, especially at the level of limited nuclear operations. Today, however, both capability and credibility are coming into question.

Capability has not been a focus here; however, the United States is the only nuclear-capable state that is not building, replacing, and undertaking significant weapons modernization. Any perception of a "crack" in the US arsenal, if not addressed forcefully, could certainly negatively impact others' perceptions of America's capability and also of its deterrence credibility. The United States has recently committed a large amount of funding and has given policy priority to modernizing its nuclear infrastructure and its weapons surety complex, plus it has committed to major life-extension programs on select nuclear weapons types to ensure continuing capability. The bottom line, however, is that if there are any questions about US capability, it is even more important to ensure the unquestioned credibility of the US deterrent.

Credibility is the bedrock of deterrence, and there are several issues raised in this chapter that have implications here. Given the rising generation of civilian leadership that has just reached the top rungs of power in this country and its almost total lack of experience or expertise in nuclear matters, there is a need to address that gap and provide tailored experiences and some meaningful tutoring while such expertise still resides in a few pockets of government and society. But there is also a deep and wide deficit in nuclear experience and expertise among the uniformed military leadership. It is this senior military cadre that the civilian leaders rely on for expert advice on such technical matters, and the numbers who can in fact deliver such advice in the nuclear arena are few, and getting fewer. As for the military force that must deliver the deterrence signals and that would be called upon to respond to an adversary's use of a nuclear weapon, those with the requisite knowledge, focus, and competence are either growing old or are very young (such as those newly assigned to Global Strike Command), and those in the latter category have a supervisory level that is capable but thin. To echo a contractor study from 2001, "we have been living off the fat of the land, and we have found mostly lean in the end."[32]

Allies openly question America's assurance when the United States does stupid things that cause them to question its commitment and credibility;

potential adversaries may also begin to question American resolve in deterrence and strategic crisis situations, leading the president to have to remind them that the United States is serious and underscore that commitment. Credibility must have a continued, permanent focus at the heart of US strategic policy and posture.

It is a gross overstatement to say that American deterrence posture and effective signaling have today failed; however, some mending and signal enhancement are indicated. At the level of military strategic forces, there must be a continued demand for excellence as the only possible level of performance. Training, education, exercises, and assessment are vital components across all areas of nuclear safety, surety, security, and operations. Second best can never be accepted. But the military also must provide meaningful, fully successful, and rewarding career patterns and expectations to attract and sustain the high-quality force that is required. As numbers decline and salience of the mission appears to be on the wane, this human management issue will become central, and may require some innovative career design decisions for US strategic forces.

The other critical area is limited nuclear warfighting. As the United States has lost much of its base at the strategic deterrence end of the spectrum, it has also lost almost its entire base for managing a limited nuclear war. Tactical nuclear weapons have been withdrawn to storage and dismantlement depots in the United States except for a small number that remain forward deployed in Europe in support of NATO. Only a small number of NATO-based aircraft and aircrews maintain mission proficiency in their employment. As the Alliance has declared that these are solely political weapons, the morale and incentives to study for and prepare for their possible use have disappeared. Nuclear targeting is a dying art, and only a handful of planners retain interest and expertise in limited nuclear warfighting.

At the very time when potential regional adversaries are developing nuclear weapons and the United States could find itself in a conflict that might involve threats or even employment of a limited number of nuclear weapons, the United States is less prepared to manage and respond in that environment. It needs to maintain the capability to plan for, exercise for, and if necessary fight in such a conflict, and that too will take deliberate decisions and deliberate steps to sustain (or re-create) the capability. This area, perhaps above all of the many areas and issues of nuclear revitalization, demands immediate attention.

This chapter has focused on the nuclear dimension of strategic leadership and nuclear strategic challenges. It is absolutely critical that the US military does the nuclear piece perfectly. No one wants to confront the catastrophe of deterrence failure or of the challenges of the detonation of even one nuclear weapon anywhere in the world. The United States needs to know how to achieve national success without war.

Notes

The views expressed in this chapter are those of the author and do not necessarily reflect the official policy or position of the United States Air Force, the Department of Defense, or the United States government.

1. Carl H. Builder, "Keeping the Strategic Flame," *Joint Force Quarterly* 14 (Winter 1996–1997): 76.

2. Colin S. Gray, "Out of the Wilderness: Prime Time for Strategic Culture," in Jeannie L. Johnson, Kerry M. Kartchner, and Jeffrey A. Larsen, eds., *Strategic Culture and Weapons of Mass Destruction: Culturally Based Insights into Comparative National Security Policymaking* (New York: Palgrave Macmillan, 2009), 226.

3. Colin S. Gray, "British and American Strategic Cultures," paper prepared for the Jamestown Symposium, "Democracies in Partnership: 400 Years of Transatlantic Engagement," March 2007, 14.

4. See ibid., 36–45. This discussion builds on Gray's points, although they are somewhat reordered and redefined here.

5. Ibid., 13–14.

6. For example, see Thomas G. Mahnken, "U.S. Strategic and Organizational Sub-Cultures," chap. 5 in Johnson, Kartchner, and Larsen, *Strategic Culture and Weapons of Mass Destruction*.

7. See, for example, Lawrence Sondhaus, *Strategic Culture and Ways of War* (New York: Routledge, 2006).

8. Gray, "British and American Strategic Cultures," 46.

9. See Antulio J. Echevarria II, *Toward an American Way of War* (Carlisle, PA: Strategic Studies Institute, March 2004). Echevarria argues that because of this trait, what we call the American way of war is basically a way of battle, not a way of war.

10. Gray, "British and American Strategic Cultures," 46. See also Colin S. Gray, "The American Way of War: Critique and Implications," in Anthony D. McIvor, ed., *Rethinking the Principles of War* (Annapolis, MD: Naval Institute Press, 2005), where he lists 12 characteristics of the American way of war: apolitical; astrategic; ahistorical; problem-solving, optimistic; culturally ignorant; technologically dependent; firepower focused; large-scale; profoundly regular; impatient; logistically excellent; sensitivity to casualties.

11. Gray, "British and American Strategic Cultures," 49.

12. Major W. Mitchell, memorandum to chief of staff, AEF, 13 June 1917, cited in I. B. Holley, *Ideas and Weapons* (New Haven, CT: Yale University Press, 1953), 47.

13. See, for example, William Mitchell, *Winged Defense* (New York: Putnam's Sons, 1925), 163–171.

14. See Thomas H. Greer, *The Development of Air Doctrine in the Army Air Arm, 1917–1941* (Washington, DC: Office of Air Force History, 1985), chap. 3, for a discussion of Mitchell's influence on and through the Air Corps Tactical School faculty.

15. Major General H. H. Arnold and Colonel Ira C. Eaker, *Winged Warfare* (New York: Harper and Brothers, 1941), 110–139.

16. Harry S. Truman, "Executive Order 9877: Functions of the Armed Forces," 26 July 1947, reprinted in Richard I. Wolf, ed., *The United States Air Force: Basic Documents on Roles and Missions* (Washington, DC: Office of Air Force History, 1987), 87–90.

17. Harry S. Truman, "Functions of the Armed Forces and the Joint Chiefs of Staff" (approval of Key West Agreement, James Forrestal, Secretary of Defense), Washington, DC, 21 April 1948, reprinted in Wolf, *The United States Air Force*, 154–169; DOD Directive 5100.1, "Functions of the Armed Forces and the Joint Chiefs of Staff," 16 March 1954, reprinted in Wolf, *The United States Air Force*, 253–273; DOD Directive 5100.1, "Functions of the Department of Defense and Its Major Components," 31 December 1958, reprinted in Wolf, *The United States Air Force*, 341–353; and DOD Directive 5100.1, "Functions of the Department of Defense and Its Major Components," 25 September 1987, reprinted in W. Michael Dunaway, ed., *Basic Documents in National Security* (Monterey, CA: Naval Postgraduate School, 1996), Enclosure 1, 1–22.

18. For example, DOD Directive 5100.1, *Functions of the Department of Defense and Its Major Components* (Washington, DC: Department of Defense, 1 August 2002).

19. Air Force Manual 1–2, *United States Air Force Basic Doctrine* (Washington, DC: Department of the Air Force, March 1953).

20. Air Force Manual 1–2, *United States Air Force Basic Doctrine* (Washington, DC: Department of the Air Force, 1 December 1959), 6.

21. Air Force Manual 1–1, *United States Air Force Basic Doctrine* (Washington, DC: Department of the Air Force, 14 August 1964).

22. Air Force Manual 1–1, *Functions and Basic Doctrine of the United States Air Force* (Washington, DC: Department of the Air Force, 14 February 1979). Chapter 2 covers USAF functions and missions.

23. Air Force Manual 1–1, *Functions and Basic Doctrine of the United States Air Force* (Washington, DC: Department of the Air Force, 16 March 1984), 1–1.

24. United States Air Force, *Global Reach—Global Power* (Washington, DC: Secretary of the Air Force/Public Affairs, 1990).

25. See John A. Warden, *The Air Campaign: Planning for Combat* (Washington DC: Pergamon-Brassey, 1989).

26. Formally The Goldwater-Nichols Department of Defense Reorganization Act of 1986.

27. See Air Force Manual 1–1, *Basic Aerospace Doctrine of the United States Air Force* (Washington, DC: Department of the Air Force, March 1992), Volume I; Air Force Doctrine Document 1 (AFDD 1), *Air Force Basic Doctrine* (Maxwell AFB, AL: Air Force Doctrine Center, September 1997 and 17 November 2003 editions).

28. See www.airforce.com.

29. Thomas Neary, John Preisinger, Lisa Ludka, and Joseph Sutter, *Nuclear Deterrence Issues and Options Study: A Baseline Assessment of DoD Staff Nuclear Expertise,* Defense Threat Reduction Agency Advanced Systems and Concepts Office Report, 21 December 2001, 23.

30. See James Schlesinger, *Report of the Secretary of Defense Task Force on DoD Nuclear Materials Management, Phase I: Review of the Air Force Nuclear Mission* (Washington, DC: Department of Defense, September 2008); and James Schlesinger, *Report of the Secretary of Defense Task Force on DoD Nuclear Materials Management, Phase II: Review of the DoD Nuclear Mission* (Washington, DC: Department of Defense, December 2008).

31. Barack Obama, "Remarks by President Barack Obama, Hradcany Square, Prague, Czech Republic," 5 April 2009, at www.whitehouse.gov/the-press-office/Remarks-By-President-Barack-Obama-In-Prague-As-Delivered.

32. The words are those of this author, paraphrasing a statement from Neary et al., *Nuclear Deterrence Issues and Options Study,* 23.

12 Limited Nuclear War Reconsidered

James J. Wirtz

F OR NEWCOMERS TO THE LITERATURE ON NUCLEAR deterrence or the history of the Cold War, the foregoing chapters will come as a harsh introduction to one of the more esoteric and macabre varieties of 20th-century strategic thought—the intellectual debate surrounding the theory and doctrine of limited nuclear war. Our current interest in limited nuclear war, however, differs from the Cold War theorists who saw the concept both as a means to obtain some political or strategic value from the threat of use or actual use of nuclear weapons in war or as a way to devise strategies to end a nuclear exchange before it ended in Armageddon. Instead, as Jeffrey Larsen observed in the introduction to the volume, we believe that a future nuclear war will in fact be limited in terms of the number of weapons used, the geographic scope of the conflict, the goals in dispute and most importantly, by the overriding objective of terminating nuclear hostilities as quickly as possible. In that sense, we do not advocate the first use or "conventionalization" of nuclear weapons by treating them as just another military instrument to be used on the battlefield to achieve some tactical or strategic objective. Instead, we believe that it behooves policymakers and scholars alike to consider ex ante what can be done to limit nuclear war once a nuclear weapon has actually been used in combat. We want to think about how to end a nuclear war in the aftermath of a single nuclear explosion. We especially want to avoid the occurrence of a desultory nuclear exchange involving a few score, or a hundred, nuclear detonations.

Mercifully, we only have a brief history of limited nuclear war, but that history does exist. The US use of nuclear weapons at the end of World War II was "limited" to the employment of only two, relatively low-yield nuclear weapons, which in fact prompted a quick termination of hostilities and led to efforts to reign in the proliferation of nuclear weapons and their further integration into national arsenals. Indeed, several observers have noted that a future incident involving the detonation of a single nuclear weapon might be viewed as such a horrendous event that it would again result in the immediate cessation of hostilities, leading to strenuous and effective efforts to halt further nuclear proliferation, while providing an opportunity to enhance global nuclear disarmament initiatives.[1] Nevertheless, the fact that the United States ceased nuclear hostilities only after it exhausted its arsenal over the skies of Japan and that the postwar effort at nuclear disarmament terminated in the Cold War arms race does not produce optimism about the course or consequences of a future limited nuclear war.

Denial as the Preferred Strategy

If states are not willing to allow a nuclear war to "run its course," efforts to limit a nuclear exchange must focus either on deterrence of war or on war termination. This simple observation, however, is complicated immediately by the fact that the strategy and politics of limited nuclear war appear to be highly scenario specific. The degree to which a nuclear war actually appears "limited," for instance, will vary depending upon whether it involves a direct attack against the United States, US allies, or is confined to third parties that are only remotely linked to US interests. Several of our contributors also noted that for small states, any use of nuclear weapons will appear decidedly unlimited by posing an immediate threat to national survival. It also is unclear if the United States or other nuclear-armed nations would be capable or willing to make credible nuclear or even conventional threats to deter a nuclear war in a situation where their immediate interests were not threatened. It also appears unlikely that third parties would become involved in a nuclear conflict for straightforward purposes of war termination due to the risk of themselves becoming a nuclear target. International criticism of states engaged in a limited nuclear exchange will be shrill and diplomatic demands for a cease-fire will be virtually universal, but all this will be drowned out by the chaos and carnage of nuclear war. In some scenarios, it is hard to escape the conclusion that the scope and destruction produced by future nuclear belligerents might only be limited by the number, yield, and range of the weapons in their arsenals.

For both theoretical and practical reasons, therefore, most of our contributors gravitate toward considering the strategic, doctrinal, and operational implications of the prospect of limited nuclear war involving the United States. To deter a conflict with an opponent that possesses a small nuclear arsenal, there is a clear preference for the adoption of denial strategies that involve significant counterforce capabilities and hold out the prospect of damage limitation and escalation dominance. Several authors note that a mix of conventional precision-strike capabilities, ballistic missile defense, and low-yield nuclear weapons would constitute a credible deterrent because opponents might actually believe that US policymakers would use this arsenal in extremis to undertake a first strike or in a disarming second strike following an opponent's first use of nuclear weapons. It is not obvious how potential opponents might view US incentives in a limited nuclear war scenario, but given the asymmetry in interests likely to be involved, most of our contributors believe that a US retaliatory position based on the massive use of nuclear weapons is unlikely to appear credible ex ante. Precise targeting, taking steps to strictly limit collateral damage, and a robust mix of offensive conventional and nuclear options combined with effective defenses seem to be crucial when it comes to making credible threats to deter limited nuclear war.

In the event of a failure of deterrence—if nuclear first use by an opponent appears imminent or has already occurred—the need for war termination on grounds favorable to US interests will become painfully apparent to US policymakers. Under these circumstances, the goal of disarming the opponent using minimal amounts of nuclear firepower in an effort to limit collateral damage will appear as a desirable strategy. In other words, a denial strategy that relies on a mix of conventional precision-strike weapons, missile defenses, and low-yield nuclear weapons should appear even more credible to an opponent during a crisis or the early stages of a nuclear war, as circumstances increase the incentives for US policymakers to actually execute deterrent threats. At the same time, the ability of the United States to inflict catastrophic levels of death and destruction in a massive nuclear attack creates a further incentive for an opponent to terminate a nuclear conflict quickly rather than suffer existential retaliation. US escalation dominance creates an incentive for the opponent not to unleash its remaining weapons in some spasmodic attack, while conventional and possibly nuclear counterforce attacks quickly degrade its remaining capabilities.

The ability of the United States to orchestrate such a finely tuned deterrent and warfighting strategy, however, is largely notional. As Bruce Bennett notes in his contribution to our volume, "a comparison of current US nuclear force capabilities with likely limited war requirements suggests that the United States could be better prepared. . . . With current capabilities, a limited US nuclear attack may not be as prompt, responsive, effective, or even limited as a US president and his military personnel might want." The United States has largely abandoned its theater capability to promptly deliver low-yield nuclear weapons in regional contingencies. Instead, the bulk of its arsenal consists of relatively large-yield nuclear weapons deployed on strategic nuclear delivery systems that were designed to meet Cold War contingencies. It also is unclear if global precision-strike capabilities, missile defense, and nuclear options, to say nothing about cyber defenses, space defenses, intelligence functions, and passive security systems, have been integrated to achieve deterrent and warfighting capabilities in potential limited nuclear war scenarios. That there has been virtually no political support for a fundamental restructuring of the US nuclear enterprise to meet limited war contingencies suggests that for the time being little progress will be made in the effort to devise new denial strategies or develop integrated conventional and nuclear offensive and defensive capabilities to deter or terminate a limited nuclear war.

The Need for Crisis Management

Given this lack of political support for developing a robust capability to deter and fight a limited nuclear war, it is not surprising that several of our contributors suggest that crisis management and an acute awareness of escalation dynamics should rise to the top of the global policy agenda. The prospect of a proliferation of small nuclear arsenals to new state and non-state actors raises fundamental questions about how the utility of nuclear threats or even the use of nuclear weapons is viewed globally and the steps that might be taken to prevent crises before they escalate to open hostilities. This concern is central to Thomas Mahnken's survey of hypothetical escalation scenarios: vertical or horizontal escalation becomes a key option that is used by militarily weaker parties to exploit the asymmetrical interests that exist between them and the United States. Once nuclear weapons are used in these scenarios, however, US policymakers are faced with a stark choice: continue the process of escalation or suffer a serious setback to US interests. The limited use of nuclear weapons seems to serve as a great equalizer between weak and strong actors. It thus behooves the United States and its allies to do everything in their power to reduce the possibility that nuclear weapons will be introduced into nascent conflicts or unfolding crises.

Three factors seem to conspire against emphasizing in diplomatic practice the need for nuclear crisis management and preventive diplomacy. First, the increased attention given to nuclear disarmament and nonproliferation tends to label states that appear to have a keen interest in acquiring nuclear weapons and integrating them into their national strategies as aberrations. In other words, realistic assessments of the growing possibility that nuclear weapons might be used in some regional conflict are viewed as counterproductive because they seem to undermine the belief that the nuclear taboo is not as widespread or as powerful as some would like to believe. As George Quester notes in his contribution to this volume, "the 'nuclear taboo' may reduce the likelihood that the United States or Russia will use nuclear weapons, but it may get in the way of a full and competent analysis of what either power, or any other responsible state, is to do if some other actor uses such a weapon." Treating nuclear weapons as an ongoing threat to international security and the concomitant need to reduce simmering regional conflicts that might lead to nuclear use are seen as a throwback to a darker age because they reintroduce the shadow of nuclear holocaust into international diplomacy. Nevertheless, as Mahnken's scenarios illustrate, it is preferable to engage in preventive diplomacy or crisis management rather than deal with the escalation dynamics that would be unleashed by the use of nuclear weapons.

Second, there is a possibility that even governments that embrace the nuclear taboo or that tend to treat nuclear weapons as lacking in utility sometimes strain international decorum by acting in ways that place undue stress on the status quo. The second Gulf War of 2003, the Russian attack on Georgia in 2008, ongoing skirmishes over insignificant islets in the South China Sea, domestic unrest in the Middle East, or various diplomatic insults create a setting in which miscalculation, inadvertent escalation, or even more deliberate military action might occur. The fact that asymmetric interests might lead some parties to believe that nuclear threats or even a limited use of nuclear weapons might shift the outcome of a crisis in their favor suggests that any display of force or use of force bears significant risks when nuclear-armed actors are involved. Once again, however, the nuclear taboo and the belief in the non-utility of nuclear weapons can make actors risk-acceptant, a behavioral characteristic that can prove self-defeating if they miscalculate the restraint or interest of other actors. The tendency to "free ride" on the restraint of nuclear actors also diminishes interest in vigorously undertaking crisis management or preventive diplomacy. As a result, the great powers that might be expected to take the lead in preventive diplomacy and crisis management continue to be willing to engage in modest forms of "brinkmanship" when it suits their interest.

Third, as the authors of this volume consistently note, limited nuclear war will be characterized by asymmetrical interests when it comes to both belligerents and third parties. Nevertheless, there also appears to be a consistent pattern of asymmetry between the incentives among nuclear-armed states when it comes to engaging in nuclear diplomacy or the actual use of nuclear weapons. The United States, for instance, is intent on reducing the role of nuclear weapons in its defense planning and in fostering efforts to slow proliferation and to reduce nuclear arsenals through arms control and disarmament. From Washington's perspective, its robust conventional force projection capabilities and its emerging long-range precision-strike capabilities offer it an alternative way of accomplishing missions that once included nuclear weapons. By contrast, states that lack robust conventional alternatives continue to see utility in nuclear threats and actual use as a way to equalize the playing field when they face opponents with superior conventional capabilities. American analysts, planners, and policymakers, however, tend to project their own estimates of the utility of nuclear use and the likelihood of nuclear war based on their own judgments about the limited desirability of introducing nuclear weapons into a conflict. Additionally, because US officials are armed with the knowledge that they have no intention to introduce nuclear weapons into a conflict, they appear to fail to understand how the prospects of US nuclear use are perceived by potential opponents and influence the scope and nature of international crises or the actual course of a conflict. As several authors suggest, there are several plausible scenarios in which US officials could realistically contemplate the first use of nuclear weapons—for example, after suffering a massive chemical or biological attack or to defend large expeditionary operations that are about to suffer a catastrophic defeat. Yet, planners and analysts rarely seem to consider the conditions under which the United States might introduce nuclear weapons into a conflict. All of this combines to create a situation in which US opponents might be more sensitive to the nuclear dimension of conflict than are US officers and officials as they plan or actually undertake some military operation.

Toward the Future

For nearly twenty-five years, two trends have come to characterize the apparent role of nuclear weapons in foreign and defense policies and the impact nuclear weapons have on world politics. Among the established nuclear powers, the nuclear enterprise is no longer a growth industry. Although nuclear deterrence remains a component of their military strategy, nuclear modernization programs are modest or nonexistent, numbers of deployed nuclear weapons are either stable or in decline, and a de facto comprehensive nuclear test ban has either slowed or stopped exploration of new weapons designs and the development of new types of nuclear warheads. The fear of a massive nuclear exchange is no longer center stage in great power politics and there are few if any issues on the strategic horizon that seem to threaten a renewal of the Cold War nuclear arms race. That this trend is both enduring and to a certain extent institutionalized in formal diplomacy (arms control) and international norms (disarmament and the nuclear taboo) would suggest that, subject to the law of diminishing returns, several nuclear arsenals will continue to shrink and atrophy in the coming decades. For many of the long-standing nuclear states, nuclear weapons are considered to be a waning asset when it comes to actual military planning and operations; nuclear arsenals provide some residual deterrent value, but they are increasingly viewed as largely irrelevant in addressing today's security threats.

States that have more recently acquired or are attempting to acquire nuclear weapons, however, are not following in the footsteps of the great powers. India, North Korea, Pakistan, and possibly Iran are hard at work developing and expanding their nuclear enterprise and the associated effort to develop modern delivery systems. In these states, nuclear programs are a growth industry. New types of nuclear weapons are apparently being deployed and incremental improvements in weapons production capacity are commonplace. Some of these actors are also placing nuclear weapons into conventional combat units. Others are developing and refining employment doctrines, which include complex strategies that integrate conventional maneuvers, nuclear threats, or actual nuclear use to present or deny opponents a fait accompli. States that have newly acquired a nuclear arsenal apparently view their weapons as having much political, strategic, operational, and tactical utility when it comes to responding to their most pressing security challenges.

The issue of limited nuclear war thus stands at the nexus between these two trends. On the one hand, the established nuclear powers tend to give short shrift to nuclear issues, while projecting their beliefs about the limited utility of nuclear weapons onto others. On the other hand, emerging nuclear powers exhibit clear indications that they do in fact see great utility in nuclear deterrence to include interest in the strategic and tactical use of their nuclear arsenals to achieve their security objectives. The confluence of these trends creates the basis of instability in world politics as states with asymmetric interests, beliefs, and capabilities deliberately or inadvertently find themselves in a nascent international crisis. Under these circumstances, the most dangerous and tragic threat that emerges is that the parties involved fail to share similar assessments of the risk of nuclear war. They also have different perspectives on how the limited use of nuclear weapons might affect the prospects of achieving their objectives. At times, a similar situation existed during the Cold War. Nevertheless, as the superpower confrontation continued, both Washington and Moscow developed a shared perception of the consequences of nuclear war and a growing aversion to direct confrontations that might prompt a nuclear exchange. Among nuclear-armed states today, this sort of convergence in beliefs about the utility of nuclear use and the risk of nuclear war is not occurring. This situation is recognized, but there is a global tendency to ignore the consequences of this divergence in attitudes and perceptions of utility out of a fear of derailing the trend toward disarmament—and to holding on to the hope that it will go away. As Jeffrey Larsen points out in his introduction to this volume, this implies that the risk of nuclear war is not zero; in fact, the possibility of such a conflict may actually be increasing. Were a nuclear conflict to break out, it is likely to be limited in nature. Accordingly, the United States may one day find itself in such a conflict, and one for which it is not well prepared.

Policymakers, however, would be well advised to pay attention to the concept and prospect of limited nuclear war. Although they may believe that trends toward nuclear nonuse, nuclear disarmament, and nuclear nonproliferation generally are on the side of the angels, they must understand that the spread of capabilities to conduct a limited nuclear war is a trend that suggests that not all nuclear enterprises are slowly winding down. They also must understand that differing conceptions of the utility of using nuclear weapons set the stage for crisis instability because actors embrace different perceptions of risk and opportunity. Most importantly, they must temper the tendency to believe that normatively desirable policies (i.e., reduction in the presence of and reliance on nuclear weapons in national strategies) will inevitably and invariably produce desirable consequences. The fact that good outcomes do not necessarily follow from good intentions suggests that even when trends are positive, policymakers must always be on guard for the emergence of negative externalities and risks. Policymakers must continue to treat nuclear war as a serious threat even as they take increasingly significant efforts to reduce their nuclear arsenals. As our authors suggest, they must guard against conditions that foster nuclear use, which for the immediate future is best embodied by the term "limited nuclear war."

Note

1. Lewis A. Dunn, "Leveraging Proliferation Shocks," in James J. Wirtz and Peter R. Lavoy, eds., *Over the Horizon Proliferation Threats* (Stanford, CA: Stanford University Press, 2012), pp. 205–220.

Index

accidental escalation, 150–51, 158
adaptive planning, 81, 83, 95n2
Afghanistan and Afghanistan War, 129, 141, 243n19, 255
Air Combat Command (ACC), US, 256
Air Force, US, case study of, 251–57
Al Qaeda, 141, 207n5, 243n19
allies' confidence in US nuclear abilities, 134, 135–36, 143, 184–86, 194, 196, 237–38, 258–59
ambiguous attacks, 181–82, 228–29
American exceptionalism, 247
American way of war, xxiv–xxv, 244–60; civilian-military divide in, 249–50; concept of strategic culture, 246; concept of way of war, 249; deterrence and, 257–59; implications of, 257–60; military and organizational culture (Air Force case study), 251–57; problems with current strategic culture, 244–45; traditional American strategic culture, 246–48
Anderson Air Force Base, Guam, 140
Arab-Israeli War (1973), 198, 203–4
Arnold, Hap, 252, 253, 254

assured destruction, 10, 11, 22, 54, 55, 112, 193, 194, 221, 231–32
asymmetric escalation, 107–8, 164–65, 171n49, 176
asymmetrical interests, 268
attribution of nuclear attacks, 181–82, 228–29, 240

battlefield nuclear weapons. See tactical nuclear weapons
Bennett, Bruce W., xv, xxiv, 211, 266
Berlin Blockade (1948-1949), 28, 50
Berlin Crisis (May 1960), 50, 198
Bernstein, Paul I., xv, xxiii, 80, 101
biological and chemical weapons, 82, 84, 85, 91, 95–96n7, 119, 132, 177–78, 181, 186, 196, 217, 268
black market in nuclear technology, 103, 123n6
boosters and booster impacts, 229, 243n23
Bracken, Paul, 120–21
Brodie, Bernard, xxiii, 5, 9, 10, 23, 25–27, 35, 37–40, 43n13, 191
Brown, Harold, 22, 60, 63
Builder, Carl, 244–45

burst, altitude or height of, 228, 234–35
Bush, George H. W., 63, 65, 81–83, 95n4
Bush, George W., xxiii, 86–89, 90, 91, 94, 182
Butler, Lee, 83, 95n6

Carter, Jimmy, 59–63, 75n36, 76n40, 76n44, 78n69, 81, 156, 177
catalytic escalation, 164, 171n49
chemical and biological weapons, 82, 84, 85, 91, 95–96n7, 119, 132, 177–78, 181, 186, 196, 217, 268
Cheonan warship, sinking of (2010), 229
China, 111–17; Cold War and, 56; crisis management approach and, 199; cultural issues in, 117, 127n59; current nuclear strategy of, 111–17, 122, 191; law yield weapons in, 110; as legally recognized nuclear weapon state, 102, 206n2; likelihood of limited nuclear war and, 17; military modernization of, 207n4; nuclear taboo and, 177, 186; PLA (People's Liberation Army), 111–13, 116, 122, 125n38, 139; post-Cold War US nuclear strategy and, 88; preparedness of US for limited nuclear war and, 221, 228, 229, 230, 234, 237; rich debate about nuclear development in and about, 101–2; SAF (Second Artillery Force), 111, 115–16, 122, 125n38, 126n48, 139; scenarios for limited nuclear conflict and, 139–40, 142; South China Sea islets, skirmishes over, 267; tactical nuclear weapons and, 112–13, 126n43; termination strategies, 203
circular error probable (CEP), 214, 215
Clark, Ian, 6, 7–8, 14–15, 46n67
Clinton, William J., xxiii, 83–86
coercive escalation, 151, 152, 153
cognitive deterrence (prospect theory), 241

Colby, Elbridge A., xv–xvi, xxiii, 49
Cold War, xxiii, 49–71; all-out nuclear scenario originally presumed in, xix, xx, 21; bipolar framework during, 159–61, 163, 193–94; under Carter, 59–63; continuing themes, drawbacks, and effectiveness of, 65–71; crisis management in, 198, 201; current strategic context compared, 129, 130, 134, 138, 143; deterrence in, 3–4, 21, 61, 67–68, 175–76, 193–94, 205; doctrine and strategy of US during, 231–32; escalation dynamics during, 144, 146, 150, 153, 155–61, 165; extended nuclear deterrence in, 184; flexible response doctrines and, 52–53, 54, 75n39; under Ford and Nixon, 55–59; under Kennedy and Johnson, 52–55; lessons from, 68–71; MAD/massive retaliation, 10–11, 12, 21–22, 25–26, 29, 51, 54, 56; nuclear superiority, plans based on, 50–52, 72n3; preparedness of US for war and, 211; under Reagan and George H. W. Bush, 63–65; SIOP, xxiii, 13, 51, 53, 55, 57–58, 61, 64, –66, 72–73n9, 81–83, 89; strategic imbalance between US and Soviets, 50–52, 72n3; tactical nuclear weapons in, 13, 20n28, 33–34, 41, 61–62, 178–79, 250; termination strategies in, 203; theories of limited nuclear war during, 10–13. See also origins of limited nuclear war theory
collapse of nuclear state, 141–42, 217, 223
collateral damage, 41, 58, 97, 110, 178–79, 181–82, 197, 220, 234–38, 236, 238, 239, 240, 265
command and control, 232, 237
compound escalation, 168–69n25
counter-leadership targeting, 95n2, 234, 235, 236, 238, 239
counterforce and countervalue, 16, 22,

40, 41, 53, 69, 93, 109, 112, 148, 152, 155, 170n40, 222, 223, 224, 225, 227, 232, 234–35, 236, 238, 239, 265–66

counterinsurgency operations, 231, 253

counterproliferation/counter-escalation, xx, 84, 150

counterstrike campaigns, 26, 111–13, 122

credibility of US nuclear threat, 134, 135–36, 143, 184–86, 194, 196, 237–38, 258–59

crisis management approach, 160–263, 165, 197–202, 203, 266–69

Cuban Missile Crisis (October 1962), 50, 52, 165, 169n32, 198, 227, 243n21

cultural issues: in China, 117, 127n59; US cultural egocentrism, 159. See also American way of war

demonstration nuclear attack scenario, 1–9, 120, 131–34, 148, 216, 221, 222, 225, 234, 235, 236

denial strategies, 264–66

deterrence, xxiv, 193–97; American way of war and, 257–59; cognitive deterrence (prospect theory), 241; in Cold War, 3–4, 21, 61, 67–68, 175–76, 193–94, 205; crisis management distinguished, 197–98; current strategic context and, 143, 191–93; denial of military and strategic objectives, deterrence by, 3–4, 21, 61, 175–76; denial strategies, 264–66; emerging global nuclear landscape and, 104–5; escalation concept and, 147, 167n6; extended nuclear deterrence, 134, 135–36, 143, 184–86, 194, 196, 237–38, 258–59; need to reexamine strategies for, 204–6; NPR on, 84; in post-Cold War US, 89, 93–94; as psychological concept, 257–58; punishment deterrence, 3–4, 21, 242n12; systemic, 195

Deterrence Operations Joint Operating Concept of 2006, 89

"deterrence plus," 21

dosage strikes, 79n72

dual-use nuclear technology, 183–84

Dulles, John Foster, 11, 24–25, 26

Eisenhower, Dwight D., 11, 21, 24, 50–52, 70, 72n6, 73n11, 170

electromagnetic pulse (EMP) attacks, 116, 120, 137, 138, 221, 225, 228, 231, 234, 236–37, 243n18

emerging global nuclear landscape, xxiii–xxiv, 101–23; black market in nuclear technology and, 103, 123n6; historical background to limited nuclear war and, 4, 12, 17–18; nuclear nonproliferation regime affected by, 103–5; origins of limited nuclear war theory and, 22–23; pace of nuclear proliferation and, 102–3; stability/instability paradox, 124n10; US Cold War and post-Cold war strategies regarding, 80, 82–83, 84–85, 93–94. See also specific countries

escalation, xxiv, 144–66; accidental, 150–51, 158; in Cold War, 144, 146, 150, 153, 155–61, 165; concept of, 146–47; counterproliferation/counter-escalation, xx, 84, 150; crisis management approach to, 160–61, 162, 163, 165; de-escalation following, 167–68n7; deterrence and, 147, 167n6; ladder metaphor for, 148, 151–52, 202; motivation for, 150–51; nuclear taboo and, 163–64, 186; as phenomenon or choice, 147–50; reasons for rethinking, 144–45; recent studies of, 167n1; in 21st century, 161–65; types of, 150–54, 164 (See also specific types)

escalation control, 16, 145, 156–58

escalation dominance, 16, 145, 157, 165–66, 265

Extended Deterrence Policy Committee
(EDPC), 237–38
extended nuclear deterrence, 134, 135–36,
143, 184–86, 194, 196, 237–38, 258–59

fallout, 179, 220, 234–35, 236, 237, 238, 239,
240
first use strategies, 39, 107–8, 109, 114, 120,
125n28, 148, 167–68n7, 176, 181, 223,
263, 265, 268
flexible response doctrines, 3, 13, 21–22,
52–53, 54, 75n39, 81, 110, 176, 178–79,
185
Foerster, Schuyler, xvi, xxiv, 191
Ford, Gerald, 56, 58–59, 60, 62, 70,
75–76n40, 78n69
France, 102, 138, 176, 207n2
Freedman, Lawrence, 10, 23, 41, 48n115,
134, 170n40

Gerson, Michael S., xvi, xxiv, 34, 144,
216, 218
Gray, Colin, 249, 260n10
Gulf states, 132, 134, 153, 186
Gulf War (Operation Desert Storm;
1991), 8, 82, 85, 95–96n7, 175, 178, 187,
196, 199, 201, 254–55

Halperin, Morton H., 23, 39, 47n94
Hiroshima, 34, 37, 41, 158, 172, 174, 180,
186, 188, 264
historical background of limited nuclear
war, xxi–xxiii. *See also* Cold War;
origins of limited nuclear war
theory; post-Cold War US nuclear
strategy
horizontal escalation, 152–53, 154, 164,
168–69n25, 197, 228

inadvertent escalation, 150, 158
incapacitating nuclear attack, 137–38, 217
India: "Brasstacks" live fire exercise
(1987-87), 108, 124–25n23; crisis

management and, 201, 202; current
nuclear strategy of, 106–7, 122, 192; as
de facto nuclear weapon state, 102,
103–4, 123n1, 196, 207n2; deterrence
strategies and, 196; Kargil conflict
(1999), 106, 107, 192, 196; Kashmir
crisis (1990), 171; law yield weapons
in, 110; nuclear programs as growth
industry in, 269–70; Pakistan,
ongoing tensions with, xx, 95, 106–9,
175; scenarios for limited nuclear
conflict and, 142
instrumental escalation, 151, 152
intelligence issues, 231, 239
international conventions and
covenants limiting war, 6, 8
Iran: adversarial behavior towards West,
xxiii; Cold War lessons regarding, 49;
concerns over nuclear development
in, xx, 118–19; crisis management
and, 200, 201, 202; current nuclear
strategy in, 120–21, 122–23; efforts to
sabotage nuclear program of, 123n2;
Israel and, 120–21, 123n2, 132–34, 175,
187; likelihood of limited nuclear
war and, 17–18; nuclear programs as
growth industry in, 269–70; nuclear
scenarios involving, 17–18; nuclear
taboo and, 175, 177, 186, 187–88;
post-Cold War US strategy and, 91,
94; preparedness of US for limited
nuclear war and, 221, 225, 229, 230;
pursuit of nuclear weapon options by,
xx, 103, 197, 207n2, 207n5; scenarios
for future limited nuclear conflict
and, 17–18, 129, 130, 132–33; Syrian
reactor possibly financed by, 123n6;
termination strategies, 204
Iraq: deterrence and crisis management,
196, 199, 201; Gulf War (Operation
Desert Storm; 1991), 8, 82, 85,
95–96n7, 175, 178, 187, 196, 199, 201,
254–55; Iranian nuclear power,

discomfort with, 134; Iraq War (2003-), 8, 129, 132, 199, 201, 255, 267; Israel and, 132, 196, 199–200; nuclear taboo and, 176, 178, 181, 187; Osirak reactor, Israeli strike against, 123n2; preparedness of US for limited nuclear war and, 231

Israel: Arab-Israeli War (1973), 198, 203–4; catalytic escalation in, 171n49; as de facto nuclear weapon state, 102, 123n1, 207n2; Iran and, 120–21, 123n2, 132–34, 175, 187; Iraq and, 132, 196, 199–200; nuclear opacity or ambiguity posture of, 120, 191–92; scenarios for limited nuclear conflict involving, 132–34; strikes against Middle Eastern nuclear programs, 123n2; Yom Kippur War, 171n49

Japan: deterrence and, 195, 196; escalation dynamics and, 153, 158, 172; Hiroshima and Nagasaki, 34, 37, 41, 158, 172, 174, 180, 186, 188, 264; Kadena Air Base, Okinawa, 135, 140, 222; North Korean threat to, 120; nuclear taboo and, 177, 183, 186, 188; preparedness of US for limited nuclear war and, 220, 222, 234; scenarios for future limited nuclear conflict and, 135–37, 140; South China Sea islets, skirmishes over, 267; US alliance with, 24

Johnson, Lyndon B., 13, 50, 54–55, 56

Johnston, Alastair, Iain, 112–13, 125n38

Joint Strategic Planning Staff (JSTPS), US, 58, 64, 65

jus ad bello and *jus in bellum,* 7

Kadena Air Base, Okinawa, 135, 140, 222

Kahn, Hermann, 148, 151, 167–68n7, 168–69n25, 168n10

Kaplan, Robert D., 17–18, 22–23, 43n9

Kartchner, Kerry M., xvi, xxiv, xxv, 34, 144, 216, 218

Kaufmann, William, 5, 12, 33, 38, 149

Kennedy, John F., 12–13, 52–53, 56, 156, 227

Kim Il-sung, 221–22

Kissinger, Henry, xxiii, 5, 9–14, 17–18, 23–24, 26–28, 31–33, 36–37, 39–40, 44n29, 44n41, 47n87, 47n94, 55, 56, 158

Korean War, 8, 24, 28, 50

Kosygin, Alexei, 71, 79n78

Larsen, Jeffrey A., xvi–xvii, xxii, xxv, 3, 263, 270

latent nuclear weapons potential, 183–84

Levite, Ariel, 123n5

Libya, 85, 103

Liddell Hart, Basil, 9, 23, 26, 38

limited nuclear options (LNO), 21, 55–56, 71n78

limited nuclear war, xix–xxv, 263–71; continuing relevance of concept of, 4; crisis management approach to, 160–263, 165, 197–202, 203, 266–69; defining, xi–xii, 5–6, 9, 29–32, 71n1; denial strategies, 264–66; desirability of, xi, 7–8, 21; future trends affecting, 269–71; historical background, assessing, xxi–xxiii; in international conventions and covenants, 6, 8; likelihood of, 17–19; literature of, 4–5, 24, 26; meaningfulness of concept, 179, 274–75; means of limiting war, 8–10; negotiations regarding, xii–xiii; non-nuclear limited war, 3, 6–8; terminating, xxiv, 202–4, 265–66; threshold theory, 15–16, 16. *See also* American way of war; Cold War; deterrence; emerging global nuclear landscape; escalation; nuclear taboo; origins of limited nuclear war theory; post-Cold War US nuclear strategy; preparedness of US for limited

nuclear war; scenarios for limited
nuclear conflict

Mahnken, Thomas G., xvii, xxiii–xxiv,
129, 216, 266, 267
massive retaliation, 3, 11, 12, 16, 21–22,
25–26, 47n93, 49, 51, 52, 55, 72n6, 221,
231
McNamara, Robert S., 22, 52–56, 63, 70,
73–74n19, 74n29, 77n55, 156
military utility of nuclear weapons, 131,
143
missile defenses, 143, 180, 181
missile launch locations and
trajectories, 229–30, 231, 240
Mitchell, William "Billy," 251–52
mutual assured destruction (MAD),
10–11, 12, 22, 56, 188
mutual restraint, 35, 36–38, 159–60, 162,
175, 205

Nagasaki, 34, 37, 41, 158, 172, 174, 186, 188,
264
Narang, Vipin, 107–8
National Intelligence Council, Global
Trends 2025 report, 192–93
National Military Strategy (2011), US, 121
National Security Decision Directives
(NSDDs): 12, 77n57; 13, 78n67; 95n1–2;
32, 64; 75, 77n60; 281, 78n67
National Security Decision
Memorandum 242 (NSDM-242), US,
56–57, 60, 75n38
National Security Presidential Directive
(NSPD) 14, US, 88
National Security Strategy (2002), US, 88
National Strategic Target Data Base,
US, 81
New Triad, 88, 97n26
Nitze, Paul, 34–35
Nixon, Richard M., 55–57, 59, 60, 62, 65,
70, 75–76n39–40, 78n69, 156, 157, 177
no first use (NFU) policies, 84, 111,

113–14, 122, 140, 157, 176, 177, 183–85.
See also nuclear taboo
nonstrategic nuclear weapons (NSNW).
See tactical nuclear weapons
nonuse, presumption/pattern of. See
nuclear taboo
North American Treaty Organization
(NATO): Cold War US operational
concepts of limited nuclear war
and, 51, 52, 54, 61–62, 64, 66–67,
70, 77n55; deterrence and, 195,
196; escalation dynamics and,
155–57, 167n6, 171n49; historical
background of limited nuclear
war and, 11, 13, 17, 20n28, 20n30;
nuclear taboo and, 176, 179, 180,
184, 185; origins of limited nuclear
war theory and, 24, 29; Russian
current nuclear strategy and, 109;
scenarios for future limited nuclear
conflict and, 137–38; tactical nuclear
weapons deployed by, 259
North Korea: adversarial behavior
towards West, xxiii; Cheonan
warship, sinking of (2010), 229; Cold
War lessons regarding, 49; concerns
over nuclear development in, xx,
118–19, 207n5; crisis management
and, 202; current nuclear strategy
in, 119–20, 122–23, 192; as de facto
nuclear weapon state, 102, 123n1,
196, 207–8n2; escalation dynamics
and, 153; nuclear programs as
growth industry in, 269–70;
nuclear taboo and, 175, 177, 186, 187;
nuclear testing and development
in, xx, 103, 119; post-Cold War US
strategy and, 91, 94; preparedness
of US for limited nuclear war and,
220–21, 222, 225, 230, 233, 234, 237–38,
242n14; scenarios for future limited
nuclear conflict and, 129, 130, 131,
135–36, 141; Syrian reactor modeled

on Yongbyon reactor, 123n6; termination strategies, 204

"Nuclear Employment Strategy" (2013), 212, 221, 223, 237

nuclear nonproliferation: emerging global nuclear landscape affecting, 103–5; Obama's call for, 257; policy initiatives to stabilize and reduce nuclear arsenal in post-*Glasnost* Russia, 82, 95n4; Prague Agenda and, 90; SALT treaties, 61, 63; START agreements, 92, *213*, 214; states giving up nuclear weapons or nuclear development, 102, 207n2; threshold for limited nuclear war and, 15–16, *16*

Nuclear Nonproliferation Treaty (NPT), 84, 91, 96n13, 103, 191, 206–7n2, 207n5

nuclear pacifism, 187–88

Nuclear Posture Reviews (NPRs), 83–84, 86–88, 90–91, 90–94, 93, 94, 96n15, 96n23, 97n26, 97n31, 195–96, 212, 237

nuclear proliferation, xix–xx; asymmetric, 107–8; conventional superiority of US, effects of, 129–30; dual-use nuclear technology, 183–84; global pace of, 102–3, 269; optimists and pessimists regarding, xx, 47n92, 47n94, 102–6, 174, 189

nuclear taboo, xxiv, 172–89; "acceptable" uses of nuclear weapons and, 179–83; biological/chemical warfare and, 86, 177–78, 181; concept of limited nuclear war and, 178–83; containment strategies and end of, 206; defined, 172–73; dual-use nuclear technology, 183–84; effectiveness of, 267; escalation dynamics and, 163–64, 186; extended nuclear deterrence, 184–86; growing concerns over potential end of, 175–78; mixed impacts of, 173–74; NFU policies, 84, 111, 113–14, 122, 140,

157, 176, 177, 183–85; nuclear pacifism and, 187–88; punishment of future aggressor as reinforcement of, 174–75; tactical nuclear weapons and, 178–79; viability of, 188

nuclear transformation, 87, 93

Nuclear Weapons Employment Policy (NUWEP), 57, 60, 61, 64, 65, 75n33

Nunn-Lugar Cooperative Threat Reduction program, 82

Obama, Barack, xxiii, xxv*m*, 80, 89–94, 257

Odom, William, 59, 75n36, 75n40

Okinawa (Kadena Air Base), 135, 140, 222

Operation Desert Storm (Gulf War; 1991), 8, 82, 85, 95–96n7, 175, 178, 187, 196, 199, 201, 254–55

Operations Plan (OPLAN) 8044 and 8010, 89

origins of limited nuclear war theory, xxiii, 21–42; assured destruction, 10, 11, 22, 54, 55, 112; caveats introduced into, 39–41; changes in nuclear scenarios and, 21–23; defining limited war for purposes of, 29–32; emergence of, 23–26; first published works, 24, 26–29; flexible response doctrines, 3, 13, 21–22; hydrogen bomb, advent of, 23, 36, 40; Kissinger and, 23–24, 26–28, 31–33, 36–37, 39–40, 44n29, 44n41, 47n87, 47n94; MAD, 10–11, 12, 22, 56; massive retaliation, 3, 11, 12, 16, 21–22, 25–26, 47n93, 49, 51, 52, 55, 72n6; mutual restraint, 35, 36–38; strategy for limited war, 32–35

Osgood, Robert, xxiii, 5, 6, 12, 14, 19, 24, 26–38, 40, 44n29, 45n52, 47n88

overflight, 229–30, *231*, 240

Pakistan: asymmetric escalation in, 171n49; black market in

nuclear technology and, 103; crisis management and, 201, 202; current nuclear strategy of, 107–8, 122, 124n20, 192, 207n5; as de facto nuclear weapon state, 102, 103–4, 123n1, 197, 207n2; deterrence strategies and, 196; India, ongoing tensions with, xx, 95, 106–9, 175; Kargil conflict (1999), 106, 107, 192, 196; Kashmir crisis (1990), 171; nuclear programs as growth industry in, 269–70; scenarios for future limited nuclear conflict and, 129, 131, 141–42; tactical nuclear weapons development by, 124n22

political utility of nuclear weapons, 131, 143, 250

post-Cold War US nuclear strategy, xxiii, 13–15, 80–95; under Bush, George H. W., 81–83; under Bush, George W., 86–89; under Clinton, 83–86; under Obama, 89–94

Prague Agenda, 89–90

precision effects, ability to achieve, 230–35, 239–40

precision-guided munitions, 143, 215

preparedness of US for limited nuclear war, xxiv, 211–41; adversary threats possibly requiring nuclear response, 216–20; assessment of capabilities, 224–30, 235–38, 236, 238, 239; declaratory US nuclear policy, 212, 231–32; delivery probabilities, 227; existing and projected US nuclear forces, 213, 213–15, 214; improving capabilities, 238–41; limited precision effects, ability to achieve, 230–35, 239; options for achieving objectives, 218–24, 223, 224; potential objectives, 215

Presidential Decision Directive (PDD) 60, 85–86

Presidential Directive 59 (PD-59), 59–61, 64, 76n44, 81

Presidential Nuclear Initiatives of 1991-92, 82, 95n4

prospect theory (cognitive deterrence), 241

punishment deterrence, 3–4, 21, 242n12

Quester, George H., xvii, xxiv, 172, 267

RAND Corporation, 16, 53, 167, 167n1

Rapacki Plan, 185

Reagan, Ronald, 63–65, 78n69, 81, 85, 89, 92, 95n1, 153

regional nuclear powers. See emerging global nuclear landscape

retaliatory use of nuclear weapons: as deterrent, 193–94; massive retaliation strategy, 3, 11, 12, 16, 21–22, 25–26, 47n93, 49, 51, 52, 55, 72n6, 221, 231; scenarios for future limited nuclear conflict and, 137–38

Ross, Andrew L., xvii, xxiii, 21

Russia: collapse of Soviet Union, 185; crisis management approach and, 199; current nuclear capabilities of, 211; current nuclear strategy of, 109–10, 122, 176; extended nuclear deterrence and, 186; first use or preemptive strategies, 109, 125n28; Georgia, attack on (2008), 267; as legally recognized nuclear weapon state, 102, 207n2; likelihood of limited nuclear war and, 17; NPR stance towards, 83; policy initiatives to stabilize and reduce nuclear arsenal in, 82; post-Cold War US nuclear strategy and, 88, 90, 92; preparedness of US for limited nuclear war and, 221, 225, 228, 229, 230, 234, 237; scenarios for future limited nuclear conflict and, 137–38; tactical nuclear weapons strategy,

109–10, 137; termination strategies, 203; threshold for limited nuclear war and, 15–16, *16*

Sagan, Scott, 104, 105, 106
Saudi Arabia, 132, 186
scenarios for limited nuclear conflict, xxiii–xxiv, 129–43; battlefield defeat, nuclear use to prevent, 138–40, 216–17; collapse of nuclear state, 141–42, 217, 223; demonstration nuclear attack, 1–9, 120, 131–34, 148, 216, 221, 222, 225, 234, 235, 236; incapacitating nuclear attack, 137–38, 217; preparedness of US for limited nuclear war and, 216–20; selective nuclear attack, 135–36, 217; strategic and existential context for, 129–31
Schelling, Thomas C., xi–xiii, xvii–xviii, 149–50, 151, 168n13
Schlesinger, James R., and Schlesinger doctrine, xxiii, 13, 22, 50, 55–58, 61–64, 69–70, 75n39, 76n49, 78–79n71
selective nuclear attack, 135–36, 217
September 11, 2001, 86, 175, 243n19
simultaneity issues, 232–33
Single Integrated Operational Plan (SIOP), xxiii, 13, 51, 53, 55, 57–58, 61, 64, –66, 72–73n9, 81–83, 89
Slessor, Sir John, 23, 26, 37
Smith, James M., xviii, xxiv–xxv, 244
South Africa, 102, 207n2
South Korea: *Cheonan* warship, sinking of (2010), 229; deterrence and, 195, 196; North Korean threat to, 119, 120, 128n66, 192; nuclear taboo and, 176–77, 180, 184, 186; preparedness of US for limited nuclear war and, 221, 230, 233, 234, 237–38; scenarios for future limited nuclear conflict and, 135–36; US alliance with, 24
Soviet Union. *See* Cold War; Russia
space, nuclear detonations in, 180

stability/instability paradox, 124n10
Strategic Air Command (SAC), US, 58, 64, 65, 72n5, 75n36, 81, 173, 253, 256
Strategic Arms Limitation Treaties (SALT), 61, 63
Strategic Arms Reduction Treaties (START), 92, *213*, 214
Strategic Command (STRATCOM), US, 70, 83, 85, 88–89, 173, 253
Syria, 123n2, 123n6, 171n49, 225, 230, 238na
systemic deterrence, 195

taboo, nuclear. *See* nuclear taboo
Tactical Air Command (TAC), 243n21, 253, 256
tactical nuclear weapons: American way of war and, 250; battlefield defeat, nuclear use to prevent, 138–40, 216–17; in China's current nuclear strategy, 112–13, 126n43; in Cold War, 13, 20n28, 33–34, 41, 61–62, 178–79, 250; current deployment of, 259; nuclear earth penetrator munition, 94, 98n41; nuclear taboo and, 178–79; in Pakistani current nuclear strategy, 124n22; preparedness of US for war and, *213*, 214; in Russian current nuclear strategy, 109–10, 137
Taiwan, 139–40, 199, 207n4
Teller, Edward, 33–34, 37, 47n93
temporal escalation, 154, 164
terminating limited nuclear wars, xxiv, 202–4, 265–66
terrorist organizations and nuclear weapons, 141, 175, 207n5
theater nuclear forces. *See* tactical nuclear weapons
threshold for limited nuclear war, 15–16, *16*
timing of nuclear attacks, 232–33, 239–40
Truman, Harry S., 50, 200, 261n16–17
Turkey, 177, 186, 198

United Kingdom, 102, 138, 207n2

United Nations Security Council
Resolutions: 255, 195, 205, 207n11;
1874, 135

United States: Chinese nuclear attack on
Taiwan, possible responses to, 139–
40; coercive horizontal escalation,
potential for, 153–54; conventional
superiority, effects of, 129–30; crisis
management approach, 197–202;
cultural egocentrism of, 159; current
strategic and existential context of,
129–31; deterrence strategies, 193–97;
as first and only country to use
nuclear weapons, 186; Israel, possible
responses to Iranian nuclear attack
on, 133–34; as legally recognized
nuclear weapon state, 102, 207n2;
limited wars engaged in by, 8; North
Korean selective nuclear attack,
possible responses to, 135–36; nuclear
monopoly/superiority, 24–25, 50–52;
nuclear taboo and, 175–78; Pakistani
collapse, possible responses to,
141–42; permanent alliances, post-
World War II commitment to, 24;
Russian incapacitating nuclear
attack, possible responses to, 137–38;
terminating limited nuclear war,
xxiv, 202–4; threshold for limited
nuclear war and, 15–16, 16. See also
American way of war; Cold War;
post-Cold War US nuclear strategy;
preparedness of US for limited
nuclear war

utility of nuclear weapons, opposing
views on, 131, 143, 248

vertical escalation, 152, 154, 164, 169n28,
197

Vietnam War, 8, 28, 38, 54, 253–54

Warden, John, 254–55

warheads: conventional non-nuclear,
180; number, yield, and accuracy of,
225–27, 226; packaging of, 233–34,
240; range and penetration of, 228

Warsaw Pact, 54, 62, 70, 78n71, 82, 138, 155,
156, 179, 185

Washington Treaty, 137

Weinberger, Caspar, 22, 63, 64, 153

Wirtz, James J., xviii, xxv, 263

Yom Kippur War, 171n49